# Now you can customize the cost data in this book using your own labor rates ...

### and generate a Adobe Acrobat® PDF version you can print and distribute (*you can even include it with your contract documents to show the basis for your pricing*)

Imagine... every cost item in this entire book, completely re-calculated to reflect your labor rates and your markup. And then imagine generating a perfectly formatted PDF version of the book displaying the adjusted costs!

**Well stop imagining and go to www.dcrbooks.com.**

There you'll find a ready-to-use interactive demo of the easy-to-use online version of the *2012 Guide to Construction Costs*. Give it a test drive! The demo version gives you full access to the entire Concrete section of the Guide. You can enter your own labor rates for 13 separate labor classifications and re-calculate every single item in the book. You can try it as many times as you wish.

And once you pay for your print copy of the 2012 Guide, you'll have full, unlimited access to the complete online version.

You're sure to find dozens of ways to use it. Print a copy for every member of your management team. Attach a copy to your contract documents. Calculate the overall cost impact of using different subcontractors. And much more.

If you have any questions regarding this new online feature, please don't hesitate to give us a call at 1-800-334-7510 (Mon-Fri 6am to 5pm Pacific Time). We'd be delighted to talk with you.

The output file will be a perfectly formatted PDF document that you can copy, share and print! Every cost item in the entire book will be automatically re-calculated to reflect your labor rates and your markup.

**DESIGN & CONSTRUCTION RESOURCES**
PO Box 2380
Vista, CA 92085-2380

www.dcrbooks.com
1-800-334-7510

**Design & Construction Resources**

ARCHITECTS CONTRACTORS ENGINEERS
# Guide To Construction COSTS

2012 Vol. XLIII

# INTRODUCTION

Architects Contractors Engineers Guide to Construction Costs 2012, Volume 43.

ISBN 978-1-58855-130-6

Copyright © 2011 by Design and Construction Resources. All rights reserved. Printed in the United States of America. Except as permitted under the United States Copyright Act of 1976, no part of this publication may be reproduced or distributed in any form or by any means, or stored in a data base or retrieval system, without the prior written permission of the publisher.

While diligent effort is made to provide reliable, accurate and up-to-date information, neither Design and Construction Resources, nor its authors or editors, can place a guarantee on the correctness of the data or information contained in this book. Design and Construction Resources, and its authors and editors, do hereby disclaim any responsibility or liability in connection with the use of this book or of any data or other information contained therein.

## EDITOR'S NOTE 2012

This annually published book is designed to give a uniform estimating and cost control system to the General Building Contractor. It contains a complete system to be used with or without computers. It also contains Quick Estimating sections for preliminary conceptual budget estimates by Architects, Engineers and Contractors. Square Foot Estimating is also included for preliminary estimates.

The Metropolitan Area concept is also used and gives the cost modifiers to use for the variations between Metropolitan Areas. This encompasses over 80% of the industry. This book is published annually to be historically accurate with the traditional May-July wage contract settlements and to be a true construction year estimating and cost guide.

**The Rate of Inflation** in the Construction Industry in 2011 was *3%*. Labor contributed a *3%* increase and materials rose *3%*.

**The Wage Rate** for Skilled Trades increased an average of *3%* in 2011. Wage rates will probably increase at a *3%* average next year.

**The Material Rate** increased *3%* in 2011. There were several increases in 2011. Price increases are back for some materials such as steel and copper, while lumber and wood products remain flat.

**Construction Volume** should be down for 2012. Housing, Industrial and Commercial Construction will be down to flat. Highway and Heavy Construction should rise slightly with the stimulus monies working but not as dramatically as expected.

**The Construction Industry** has low to moderate inflation. Some materials should inflate at a slower pace, and some should be watched carefully in 2012.

We are recommending using a *3%* increase in your estimates for work beyond July 1, 2011.

# INTRODUCTION

## CONTENTS

| | | | |
|---|---|---|---|
| DIVISION | 01 | GENERAL | 01-1 |
| DIVISION | 02 | SITE WORK | 02-1 |
| DIVISION | 03 | CONCRETE | 03-1 |
| DIVISION | 04 | MASONRY | 04-1 |
| DIVISION | 05 | METALS | 05-1 |
| DIVISION | 06 | WOOD & PLASTICS | 06-1 |
| DIVISION | 07 | THERMAL & MOISTURE | 07-1 |
| DIVISION | 08 | DOORS AND WINDOWS | 08-1 |
| DIVISION | 09 | FINISHES | 09-1 |
| DIVISION | 10 | SPECIALTIES | 10-1 |
| DIVISION | 11 | EQUIPMENT | 11-1 |
| DIVISION | 12 | FURNISHINGS | 12-1 |
| DIVISION | 13 | SPECIAL CONSTRUCTION | 13-1 |
| DIVISION | 14 | CONVEYING SYSTEMS | 14-1 |
| DIVISION | 15 | MECHANICAL | 15-1 |
| DIVISION | 16 | ELECTRICAL | 16-1 |
| SQUARE FOOT COSTS | | | SF-1 |
| AC&E ANNUAL COST INDEX | | | MM-1 |
| INDEX | | | A1-1 |

## *Metropolitan Cost Index*

The costs as presented in this book attempt to represent national averages. Costs, however, vary among regions, states and even between adjacent localities.

In order to more closely approximate the probable costs for specific locations throughout the U.S., this table of Metropolitan Cost Modifiers is provided in the following few pages. These adjustment factors are used to modify costs obtained from this book to help account for regional variations of construction costs and to provide a more accurate estimate for specific areas. The factors are formulated by comparing costs in a specific area to the costs as presented in the Costbook pages. An example of how to use these factors is shown below. Whenever local current costs are known, whether material prices or labor rates, they should be used when more accuracy is required.

**Cost Obtained from Costbook Pages**  X  **Metroploitan Cost Multiplier Divided by 100**  =  **Adjusted Cost**

For example, a project estimated to cost $125,000 using the Costbook pages can be adjusted to more closely approximate the cost in Los Angeles:

$$\$125{,}000 \quad \times \quad \frac{119}{100} \quad = \quad \$148{,}750$$

# INTRODUCTION

| State | Metropolitan Area | Multiplier |
|---|---|---|
| AK | ANCHORAGE | 132 |
| AL | ANNISTON | 81 |
|  | AUBURN | 82 |
|  | BIRMINGHAM | 82 |
|  | DECATUR | 84 |
|  | DOTHAN | 83 |
|  | FLORENCE | 84 |
|  | GADSDEN | 82 |
|  | HUNTSVILLE | 84 |
|  | MOBILE | 86 |
|  | MONTGOMERY | 81 |
|  | OPELIKA | 82 |
|  | TUSCALOOSA | 81 |
| AR | FAYETTEVILLE | 79 |
|  | FORT SMITH | 79 |
|  | JONESBORO | 78 |
|  | LITTLE ROCK | 82 |
|  | NORTH LITTLE ROCK | 82 |
|  | PINE BLUFF | 80 |
|  | ROGERS | 79 |
|  | SPRINGDALE | 79 |
|  | TEXARKANA | 79 |
| AZ | FLAGSTAFF | 94 |
|  | MESA | 94 |
|  | PHOENIX | 95 |
|  | TUCSON | 93 |
|  | YUMA | 94 |
| CA | BAKERSFIELD | 116 |
|  | CHICO | 118 |
|  | FAIRFIELD | 120 |
|  | FRESNO | 118 |
|  | LODI | 117 |
|  | LONG BEACH | 119 |
|  | LOS ANGELES | 119 |
|  | MERCED | 118 |
|  | MODESTO | 114 |
|  | NAPA | 120 |
|  | OAKLAND | 124 |
|  | ORANGE COUNTY | 118 |
|  | PARADISE | 114 |
|  | PORTERVILLE | 116 |
|  | REDDING | 114 |
|  | RIVERSIDE | 116 |
|  | SACRAMENTO | 118 |
|  | SALINAS | 120 |
|  | SAN BERNARDINO | 116 |
|  | SAN DIEGO | 117 |
|  | SAN FRANCISCO | 129 |
|  | SAN JOSE | 126 |
|  | SAN LUIS OBISPO | 113 |
|  | SANTA BARBARA | 116 |
|  | SANTA CRUZ | 120 |
|  | SANTA ROSA | 121 |
|  | STOCKTON | 117 |
|  | TULARE | 118 |
|  | VALLEJO | 120 |
|  | VENTURA | 116 |
|  | VISALIA | 118 |
|  | WATSONVILLE | 118 |
|  | YOLO | 118 |
|  | YUBA CITY | 118 |
| CO | BOULDER | 103 |
|  | COLORADO SPRINGS | 100 |
|  | DENVER | 101 |
|  | FORT COLLINS | 110 |
|  | GRAND JUNCTION | 99 |
|  | GREELEY | 108 |
|  | LONGMONT | 103 |
|  | LOVELAND | 110 |
|  | PUEBLO | 105 |
| CT | BRIDGEPORT | 113 |
|  | DANBURY | 113 |
|  | HARTFORD | 112 |
|  | MERIDEN | 113 |
|  | NEW HAVEN | 113 |
|  | NEW LONDON | 110 |
|  | NORWALK | 117 |

| State | Metropolitan Area | Multiplier |
|---|---|---|
| CT | NORWICH | 110 |
|  | STAMFORD | 117 |
|  | WATERBURY | 112 |
| DC | WASHINGTON | 105 |
| DE | DOVER | 105 |
|  | NEWARK | 106 |
|  | WILMINGTON | 106 |
| FL | BOCA RATON | 80 |
|  | BRADENTON | 80 |
|  | CAPE CORAL | 78 |
|  | CLEARWATER | 81 |
|  | DAYTONA BEACH | 75 |
|  | FORT LAUDERDALE | 83 |
|  | FORT MYERS | 78 |
|  | FORT PIERCE | 81 |
|  | FORT WALTON BEACH | 76 |
|  | GAINESVILLE | 80 |
|  | JACKSONVILLE | 78 |
|  | LAKELAND | 78 |
|  | MELBOURNE | 75 |
|  | MIAMI | 81 |
|  | NAPLES | 79 |
|  | OCALA | 79 |
|  | ORLANDO | 77 |
|  | PALM BAY | 75 |
|  | PANAMA CITY | 77 |
|  | PENSACOLA | 76 |
|  | PORT ST. LUCIE | 81 |
|  | PUNTA GORDA | 78 |
|  | SARASOTA | 80 |
|  | ST. PETERSBURG | 80 |
|  | TALLAHASSEE | 75 |
|  | TAMPA | 80 |
|  | TITUSVILLE | 75 |
|  | WEST PALM BEACH | 80 |
|  | WINTER HAVEN | 78 |
| GA | ALBANY | 86 |
|  | ATHENS | 89 |
|  | ATLANTA | 92 |
|  | AUGUSTA | 86 |
|  | COLUMBUS | 79 |
|  | MACON | 83 |
|  | SAVANNAH | 87 |
| HI | HONOLULU | 138 |
| IA | CEDAR FALLS | 91 |
|  | CEDAR RAPIDS | 102 |
|  | DAVENPORT | 106 |
|  | DES MOINES | 104 |
|  | DUBUQUE | 95 |
|  | IOWA CITY | 97 |
|  | SIOUX CITY | 91 |
|  | WATERLOO | 91 |
| ID | BOISE CITY | 102 |
|  | POCATELLO | 102 |
| IL | BLOOMINGTON | 113 |
|  | CHAMPAIGN | 109 |
|  | CHICAGO | 125 |
|  | DECATUR | 107 |
|  | KANKAKEE | 113 |
|  | NORMAL | 113 |
|  | PEKIN | 111 |
|  | PEORIA | 111 |
|  | ROCKFORD | 113 |
|  | SPRINGFIELD | 108 |
|  | URBANA | 109 |
| IN | BLOOMINGTON | 102 |
|  | ELKHART | 96 |
|  | EVANSVILLE | 99 |
|  | FORT WAYNE | 100 |
|  | GARY | 107 |
|  | GOSHEN | 96 |
|  | INDIANAPOLIS | 103 |
|  | KOKOMO | 101 |
|  | LAFAYETTE | 101 |
|  | MUNCIE | 101 |
|  | SOUTH BEND | 102 |
|  | TERRE HAUTE | 100 |

# INTRODUCTION

| State | Metropolitan Area | Multiplier |
|---|---|---|
| KS | KANSAS CITY | 120 |
|  | LAWRENCE | 109 |
|  | TOPEKA | 96 |
|  | WICHITA | 87 |
| KY | LEXINGTON | 91 |
|  | LOUISVILLE | 102 |
|  | OWENSBORO | 101 |
| LA | ALEXANDRIA | 89 |
|  | BATON ROUGE | 93 |
|  | BOSSIER CITY | 90 |
|  | HOUMA | 93 |
|  | LAFAYETTE | 91 |
|  | LAKE CHARLES | 93 |
|  | MONROE | 89 |
|  | NEW ORLEANS | 95 |
|  | SHREVEPORT | 90 |
| MA | BARNSTABLE | 124 |
|  | BOSTON | 128 |
|  | BROCKTON | 118 |
|  | FITCHBURG | 120 |
|  | LAWRENCE | 121 |
|  | LEOMINSTER | 120 |
|  | LOWELL | 124 |
|  | NEW BEDFORD | 118 |
|  | PITTSFIELD | 118 |
|  | SPRINGFIELD | 119 |
|  | WORCESTER | 120 |
|  | YARMOUTH | 124 |
| MD | BALTIMORE | 95 |
|  | CUMBERLAND | 98 |
|  | HAGERSTOWN | 90 |
| ME | AUBURN | 87 |
|  | BANGOR | 87 |
|  | LEWISTON | 87 |
|  | PORTLAND | 88 |
| MI | ANN ARBOR | 119 |
|  | BATTLE CREEK | 111 |
|  | BAY CITY | 116 |
|  | BENTON HARBOR | 111 |
|  | DETROIT | 120 |
|  | EAST LANSING | 117 |
|  | FLINT | 116 |
|  | GRAND RAPIDS | 112 |
|  | HOLLAND | 112 |
|  | JACKSON | 107 |
|  | KALAMAZOO | 111 |
|  | LANSING | 117 |
|  | MIDLAND | 115 |
|  | MUSKEGON | 112 |
|  | SAGINAW | 116 |
| MN | DULUTH | 107 |
|  | MINNEAPOLIS | 112 |
|  | ROCHESTER | 107 |
|  | ST. CLOUD | 105 |
|  | ST. PAUL | 112 |
| MO | COLUMBIA | 114 |
|  | JOPLIN | 103 |
|  | KANSAS CITY | 118 |
|  | SPRINGFIELD | 96 |
|  | ST. JOSEPH | 117 |
|  | ST. LOUIS | 115 |
| MS | BILOXI | 79 |
|  | GULFPORT | 79 |
|  | HATTIESBURG | 79 |
|  | JACKSON | 79 |
|  | PASCAGOULA | 79 |
| MT | BILLINGS | 96 |
|  | GREAT FALLS | 90 |
|  | MISSOULA | 91 |
| NC | ASHEVILLE | 73 |
|  | CHAPEL HILL | 79 |
|  | CHARLOTTE | 82 |
|  | DURHAM | 81 |
|  | FAYETTEVILLE | 75 |
|  | GOLDSBORO | 80 |
|  | GREENSBORO | 81 |
|  | GREENVILLE | 79 |

| State | Metropolitan Area | Multiplier |
|---|---|---|
| NC | HICKORY | 72 |
|  | HIGH POINT | 81 |
|  | JACKSONVILLE | 72 |
|  | LENOIR | 72 |
|  | MORGANTON | 72 |
|  | RALEIGH | 80 |
|  | ROCKY MOUNT | 72 |
|  | WILMINGTON | 72 |
|  | WINSTON SALEM | 77 |
| ND | BISMARCK | 84 |
|  | FARGO | 98 |
|  | GRAND FORKS | 81 |
| NE | LINCOLN | 84 |
|  | OMAHA | 91 |
| NH | MANCHESTER | 106 |
|  | NASHUA | 106 |
|  | PORTSMOUTH | 111 |
| NJ | ATLANTIC CITY | 126 |
|  | BERGEN | 129 |
|  | BRIDGETON | 125 |
|  | CAPE MAY | 125 |
|  | HUNTERDON | 128 |
|  | JERSEY CITY | 130 |
|  | MIDDLESEX | 129 |
|  | MILLVILLE | 125 |
|  | MONMOUTH | 129 |
|  | NEWARK | 129 |
|  | OCEAN | 130 |
|  | PASSAIC | 130 |
|  | SOMERSET | 128 |
|  | TRENTON | 128 |
|  | VINELAND | 125 |
| NM | ALBUQUERQUE | 91 |
|  | LAS CRUCES | 91 |
|  | SANTA FE | 91 |
| NV | LAS VEGAS | 109 |
|  | RENO | 97 |
| NY | ALBANY | 119 |
|  | BINGHAMTON | 116 |
|  | BUFFALO | 118 |
|  | DUTCHESS COUNTY | 119 |
|  | ELMIRA | 118 |
|  | GLENS FALLS | 120 |
|  | JAMESTOWN | 112 |
|  | NASSAU | 137 |
|  | NEW YORK | 148 |
|  | NEWBURGH | 119 |
|  | NIAGARA FALLS | 121 |
|  | ROCHESTER | 118 |
|  | ROME | 109 |
|  | SCHENECTADY | 119 |
|  | SUFFOLK | 137 |
|  | SYRACUSE | 118 |
|  | TROY | 119 |
|  | UTICA | 109 |
| OH | AKRON | 112 |
|  | CANTON | 107 |
|  | CINCINNATI | 105 |
|  | CLEVELAND | 114 |
|  | COLUMBUS | 115 |
|  | DAYTON | 115 |
|  | ELYRIA | 114 |
|  | HAMILTON | 105 |
|  | LIMA | 115 |
|  | LORAIN | 114 |
|  | MANSFIELD | 115 |
|  | MASSILLON | 107 |
|  | MIDDLETOWN | 115 |
|  | SPRINGFIELD | 109 |
|  | STEUBENVILLE | 115 |
|  | TOLEDO | 109 |
|  | WARREN | 111 |
|  | YOUNGSTOWN | 111 |
| OK | ENID | 86 |
|  | LAWTON | 86 |
|  | OKLAHOMA CITY | 85 |
|  | TULSA | 80 |

# INTRODUCTION

| State | Metropolitan Area | Multiplier |
|---|---|---|
| OR | ASHLAND | 109 |
|  | CORVALLIS | 112 |
|  | EUGENE | 112 |
|  | MEDFORD | 109 |
|  | PORTLAND | 114 |
|  | SALEM | 112 |
|  | SPRINGFIELD | 112 |
| PA | ALLENTOWN | 118 |
|  | ALTOONA | 110 |
|  | BETHLEHEM | 118 |
|  | CARLISLE | 113 |
|  | EASTON | 118 |
|  | ERIE | 112 |
|  | HARRISBURG | 113 |
|  | HAZLETON | 118 |
|  | JOHNSTOWN | 104 |
|  | LANCASTER | 93 |
|  | LEBANON | 115 |
|  | PHILADELPHIA | 134 |
|  | PITTSBURGH | 116 |
|  | READING | 119 |
|  | SCRANTON | 116 |
|  | SHARON | 112 |
|  | STATE COLLEGE | 98 |
|  | WILKES BARRE | 116 |
|  | WILLIAMSPORT | 97 |
|  | YORK | 113 |
| PR | MAYAGUEZ | 73 |
|  | PONCE | 74 |
|  | SAN JUAN | 75 |
| RI | PROVIDENCE | 122 |
| SC | AIKEN | 89 |
|  | ANDERSON | 71 |
|  | CHARLESTON | 76 |
|  | COLUMBIA | 76 |
|  | FLORENCE | 73 |
|  | GREENVILLE | 76 |
|  | MYRTLE BEACH | 73 |
|  | NORTH CHARLESTON | 81 |
|  | SPARTANBURG | 73 |
|  | SUMTER | 76 |
| SD | RAPID CITY | 81 |
|  | SIOUX FALLS | 85 |
| TN | CHATTANOOGA | 84 |
|  | CLARKSVILLE | 83 |
|  | JACKSON | 83 |
|  | JOHNSON CITY | 83 |
|  | KNOXVILLE | 80 |
|  | MEMPHIS | 84 |
|  | NASHVILLE | 83 |
| TX | ABILENE | 88 |
|  | AMARILLO | 92 |
|  | ARLINGTON | 87 |
|  | AUSTIN | 89 |
|  | BEAUMONT | 88 |
|  | BRAZORIA | 88 |
|  | BROWNSVILLE | 73 |
|  | BRYAN | 86 |
|  | COLLEGE STATION | 86 |
|  | CORPUS CHRISTI | 84 |
|  | DALLAS | 89 |
|  | DENISON | 87 |
|  | EDINBURG | 73 |
|  | EL PASO | 81 |
|  | FORT WORTH | 87 |
|  | GALVESTON | 93 |
|  | HARLINGEN | 73 |
|  | HOUSTON | 88 |

| State | Metropolitan Area | Multiplier |
|---|---|---|
| TX | KILLEEN | 77 |
|  | LAREDO | 78 |
|  | LONGVIEW | 78 |
|  | LUBBOCK | 91 |
|  | MARSHALL | 87 |
|  | MCALLEN | 73 |
|  | MIDLAND | 87 |
|  | MISSION | 73 |
|  | ODESSA | 87 |
|  | PORT ARTHUR | 88 |
|  | SAN ANGELO | 87 |
|  | SAN ANTONIO | 90 |
|  | SAN BENITO | 73 |
|  | SAN MARCOS | 89 |
|  | SHERMAN | 87 |
|  | TEMPLE | 77 |
|  | TEXARKANA | 79 |
|  | TEXAS CITY | 93 |
|  | TYLER | 84 |
|  | VICTORIA | 74 |
|  | WACO | 77 |
|  | WICHITA FALLS | 87 |
| UT | OGDEN | 95 |
|  | OREM | 93 |
|  | PROVO | 93 |
|  | SALT LAKE CITY | 92 |
| VA | CHARLOTTESVILLE | 86 |
|  | LYNCHBURG | 83 |
|  | NEWPORT NEWS | 88 |
|  | NORFOLK | 91 |
|  | PETERSBURG | 78 |
|  | RICHMOND | 90 |
|  | ROANOKE | 76 |
|  | VIRGINIA BEACH | 91 |
| VT | BURLINGTON | 97 |
| WA | BELLEVUE | 119 |
|  | BELLINGHAM | 111 |
|  | BREMERTON | 113 |
|  | EVERETT | 117 |
|  | KENNEWICK | 101 |
|  | OLYMPIA | 113 |
|  | PASCO | 100 |
|  | RICHLAND | 101 |
|  | SEATTLE | 119 |
|  | SPOKANE | 98 |
|  | TACOMA | 116 |
|  | YAKIMA | 104 |
| WI | APPLETON | 113 |
|  | BELOIT | 117 |
|  | EAU CLAIRE | 113 |
|  | GREEN BAY | 112 |
|  | JANESVILLE | 117 |
|  | KENOSHA | 118 |
|  | LA CROSSE | 114 |
|  | MADISON | 116 |
|  | MILWAUKEE | 118 |
|  | NEENAH | 113 |
|  | OSHKOSH | 113 |
|  | RACINE | 118 |
|  | SHEBOYGAN | 112 |
|  | WAUKESHA | 118 |
|  | WAUSAU | 113 |
| WV | CHARLESTON | 113 |
|  | HUNTINGTON | 113 |
|  | PARKERSBURG | 113 |
|  | WHEELING | 113 |
| WY | CASPER | 85 |
|  | CHEYENNE | 85 |

# DIVISION # 01 GENERAL

## TABLE OF CONTENTS

| | PAGE |
|---|---|
| 01020.10 - ALLOWANCES | **01-2** |
| 01050.10 - FIELD STAFF | **01-2** |
| 01310.10 - SCHEDULING | **01-3** |
| 01410.10 - TESTING | **01-3** |
| 01500.10 - TEMPORARY FACILITIES | **01-3** |
| 01505.10 - MOBILIZATION | **01-3** |
| 01525.10 - CONSTRUCTION AIDS | **01-4** |
| 01525.20 - TEMPORARY CONST. SHELTERS | **01-4** |
| 01570.10 - SIGNS | **01-4** |
| 01600.10 - EQUIPMENT | **01-4** |
| 01740.10 - BONDS | **01-6** |

# HOW TO USE THIS BOOK

**Labor Columns**

- ➢ Units *include* Workers Comp., Unemployment, and FICA on labor (approx. 35%).
- ➢ Units *do not include* general conditions and equipment (approx. 10%).
- ➢ Units *do not include* contractors' overhead and profit (approx. 10%).
- ➢ Units are Government Prevailing wages.

**Material Columns**

- ➢ Units *do not include* general conditions and equipment (approx. 10%).
- ➢ Units *do not include* sales or use taxes (approx. 5%) of material cost.
- ➢ Units *do not include* contractors' overhead and profit (approx. 10%) and are FOB job site.

**Total Columns (Subcontractors)**

- ➢ Units *do not include* general contractors' overhead or profit (approx. 10%).

**Quick Estimating Sections** - For Preliminary and Conceptual Estimating

- ➢ Includes all labor, material, general conditions, equipment, taxes.

© *2011 By Design & Construction Resources*

## DIVISION # 01 GENERAL

| | | | UNIT | LABOR | MAT. | TOTAL |
|---|---|---|---|---|---|---|
| **01020.10** | **ALLOWANCES** | | | | | |
| 0090 | Overhead | | | | | |
| 1000 | | $20,000 project | | | | |
| 1040 | | Average | PCT. | | | 20.00 |
| 1080 | | $100,000 project | | | | |
| 1120 | | Average | PCT. | | | 15.00 |
| 1160 | | $500,000 project | | | | |
| 1180 | | Average | PCT. | | | 12.00 |
| 1220 | | $1,000,000 project | | | | |
| 1260 | | Average | PCT. | | | 10.00 |
| 1480 | Profit | | | | | |
| 1500 | | $20,000 project | | | | |
| 1540 | | Average | PCT. | | | 15.00 |
| 1580 | | $100,000 project | | | | |
| 1620 | | Average | PCT. | | | 12.00 |
| 1660 | | $500,000 project | | | | |
| 1700 | | Average | PCT. | | | 10.00 |
| 1740 | | $1,000,000 project | | | | |
| 1780 | | Average | PCT. | | | 8.00 |
| 2000 | Professional fees | | | | | |
| 2100 | | Architectural | | | | |
| 2120 | | $100,000 project | | | | |
| 2160 | | Average | PCT. | | | 10.00 |
| 2200 | | $500,000 project | | | | |
| 2240 | | Average | PCT. | | | 8.00 |
| 2280 | | $1,000,000 project | | | | |
| 2320 | | Average | PCT. | | | 7.00 |
| 4080 | Taxes | | | | | |
| 5000 | | Sales tax | | | | |
| 5040 | | Average | PCT. | | | 5.00 |
| 5080 | | Unemployment | | | | |
| 5120 | | Average | PCT. | | | 6.50 |
| 5200 | | Social security (FICA) | " | | | 7.85 |
| **01050.10** | **FIELD STAFF** | | | | | |
| 1000 | Superintendent | | | | | |
| 1020 | | Minimum | YEAR | | | 82,555 |
| 1040 | | Average | " | | | 120,393 |
| 1060 | | Maximum | " | | | 171,990 |
| 1080 | Field engineer | | | | | |
| 1100 | | Minimum | YEAR | | | 63,063 |
| 1120 | | Average | " | | | 97,461 |
| 1140 | | Maximum | " | | | 143,325 |
| 1160 | Foreman | | | | | |
| 1180 | | Minimum | YEAR | | | 45,864 |
| 1200 | | Average | " | | | 74,529 |
| 1220 | | Maximum | " | | | 108,927 |
| 1240 | Bookkeeper/timekeeper | | | | | |
| 1260 | | Minimum | YEAR | | | 26,371 |
| 1280 | | Average | " | | | 34,398 |
| 1300 | | Maximum | " | | | 57,330 |
| 1320 | Watchman | | | | | |
| 1340 | | Minimum | YEAR | | | 18,345 |

## DIVISION # 01  GENERAL

| | | UNIT | LABOR | MAT. | TOTAL |
|---|---|---|---|---|---|
| **01050.10** | **FIELD STAFF, Cont'd...** | | | | |
| 1360 | Average | YEAR | | | 22,932 |
| 1380 | Maximum | " | | | 36,691 |
| **01310.10** | **SCHEDULING** | | | | |
| 0090 | Scheduling for | | | | |
| 1000 | $100,000 project | | | | |
| 1040 | Average | PCT. | | | 2.00 |
| 1080 | $500,000 project | | | | |
| 1120 | Average | PCT. | | | 1.00 |
| 1160 | $1,000,000 project | | | | |
| 1200 | Average | PCT. | | | 0.75 |
| 4000 | Scheduling software | | | | |
| 4020 | Minimum | EA. | | | 440 |
| 4040 | Average | " | | | 2,520 |
| 4060 | Maximum | " | | | 50,450 |
| **01410.10** | **TESTING** | | | | |
| 1080 | Testing concrete, per test | | | | |
| 1100 | Minimum | EA. | | | 20.00 |
| 1120 | Average | " | | | 33.50 |
| 1140 | Maximum | " | | | 67.00 |
| 1160 | Soil, per test | | | | |
| 1180 | Minimum | EA. | | | 40.00 |
| 1200 | Average | " | | | 100 |
| 1220 | Maximum | " | | | 270 |
| **01500.10** | **TEMPORARY FACILITIES** | | | | |
| 1000 | Barricades, temporary | | | | |
| 1010 | Highway | | | | |
| 1020 | Concrete | L.F. | 4.18 | 11.75 | 15.93 |
| 1040 | Wood | " | 1.67 | 3.85 | 5.52 |
| 1060 | Steel | " | 1.39 | 4.12 | 5.51 |
| 1080 | Pedestrian barricades | | | | |
| 1100 | Plywood | S.F. | 1.39 | 2.75 | 4.14 |
| 1120 | Chain link fence | " | 1.39 | 3.10 | 4.49 |
| 2000 | Trailers, general office type, per month | | | | |
| 2020 | Minimum | EA. | | | 210 |
| 2040 | Average | " | | | 340 |
| 2060 | Maximum | " | | | 690 |
| 2080 | Crew change trailers, per month | | | | |
| 2100 | Minimum | EA. | | | 120 |
| 2120 | Average | " | | | 140 |
| 2140 | Maximum | " | | | 210 |
| **01505.10** | **MOBILIZATION** | | | | |
| 1000 | Equipment mobilization | | | | |
| 1020 | Bulldozer | | | | |
| 1040 | Minimum | EA. | | | 200 |
| 1060 | Average | " | | | 410 |
| 1080 | Maximum | " | | | 680 |
| 1100 | Backhoe/front-end loader | | | | |
| 1120 | Minimum | EA. | | | 120 |
| 1140 | Average | " | | | 200 |
| 1160 | Maximum | " | | | 450 |
| 1180 | Crane, crawler type | | | | |

© 2011 By Design & Construction Resources

# DIVISION # 01  GENERAL

| | | UNIT | LABOR | MAT. | TOTAL |
|---|---|---|---|---|---|
| **01505.10** | **MOBILIZATION, Cont'd...** | | | | |
| 1200 | Minimum | EA. | | | 2,150 |
| 1220 | Average | " | | | 5,280 |
| 1240 | Maximum | " | | | 11,330 |
| 1260 | Truck crane | | | | |
| 1280 | Minimum | EA. | | | 490 |
| 1300 | Average | " | | | 760 |
| 1320 | Maximum | " | | | 1,310 |
| 1340 | Pile driving rig | | | | |
| 1360 | Minimum | EA. | | | 9,770 |
| 1380 | Average | " | | | 19,540 |
| 1400 | Maximum | " | | | 35,180 |
| **01525.10** | **CONSTRUCTION AIDS** | | | | |
| 1000 | Scaffolding/staging, rent per month | | | | |
| 1020 | Measured by lineal feet of base | | | | |
| 1040 | 10' high | L.F. | | | 12.50 |
| 1060 | 20' high | " | | | 22.50 |
| 1080 | 30' high | " | | | 31.50 |
| 1100 | 40' high | " | | | 36.25 |
| 1120 | 50' high | " | | | 43.25 |
| 1140 | Measured by square foot of surface | | | | |
| 1160 | Minimum | S.F. | | | 0.55 |
| 1180 | Average | " | | | 0.94 |
| 1200 | Maximum | " | | | 1.69 |
| 1220 | Safety nets, heavy duty, per job | | | | |
| 1240 | Minimum | S.F. | | | 0.36 |
| 1260 | Average | " | | | 0.44 |
| 1280 | Maximum | " | | | 0.95 |
| 1300 | Tarpaulins, fabric, per job | | | | |
| 1320 | Minimum | S.F. | | | 0.25 |
| 1340 | Average | " | | | 0.42 |
| 1360 | Maximum | " | | | 1.11 |
| **01525.20** | **TEMPORARY CONST. SHELTERS** | | | | |
| 0010 | Standard, alum. with fabric, 12'x20'x15' Ht. | S.F. | | | 16.75 |
| 0020 | 12'x20'x20' Ht. | " | | | 19.25 |
| **01570.10** | **SIGNS** | | | | |
| 0080 | Construction signs, temporary | | | | |
| 1000 | Signs, 2' x 4' | | | | |
| 1020 | Minimum | EA. | | | 35.75 |
| 1040 | Average | " | | | 86.00 |
| 1060 | Maximum | " | | | 300 |
| 1160 | Signs, 8' x 8' | | | | |
| 1180 | Minimum | EA. | | | 97.00 |
| 1200 | Average | " | | | 300 |
| 1220 | Maximum | " | | | 3,050 |
| **01600.10** | **EQUIPMENT** | | | | |
| 0080 | Air compressor | | | | |
| 1000 | 60 cfm | | | | |
| 1020 | By day | EA. | | | 95.00 |
| 1030 | By week | " | | | 280 |
| 1040 | By month | " | | | 860 |
| 1200 | 600 cfm | | | | |

## DIVISION # 01 GENERAL

| 01600.10 | EQUIPMENT, Cont'd... | UNIT | LABOR | MAT. | TOTAL |
|---|---|---|---|---|---|
| 1210 | By day | EA. | | | 550 |
| 1220 | By week | " | | | 1,640 |
| 1230 | By month | " | | | 4,930 |
| 1300 | Air tools, per compressor, per day | | | | |
| 1310 | Minimum | EA. | | | 36.50 |
| 1320 | Average | " | | | 45.75 |
| 1330 | Maximum | " | | | 64.00 |
| 1400 | Generators, 5 kw | | | | |
| 1410 | By day | EA. | | | 91.00 |
| 1420 | By week | " | | | 270 |
| 1430 | By month | " | | | 840 |
| 1500 | Heaters, salamander type, per week | | | | |
| 1510 | Minimum | EA. | | | 110 |
| 1520 | Average | " | | | 160 |
| 1530 | Maximum | " | | | 330 |
| 1600 | Pumps, submersible | | | | |
| 1605 | 50 gpm | | | | |
| 1610 | By day | EA. | | | 73.00 |
| 1620 | By week | " | | | 220 |
| 1630 | By month | " | | | 660 |
| 1675 | 500 gpm | | | | |
| 1680 | By day | EA. | | | 150 |
| 1690 | By week | " | | | 440 |
| 1700 | By month | " | | | 1,310 |
| 1900 | Diaphragm pump, by week | | | | |
| 1920 | Minimum | EA. | | | 130 |
| 1930 | Average | " | | | 220 |
| 1940 | Maximum | " | | | 450 |
| 2000 | Pickup truck | | | | |
| 2020 | By day | EA. | | | 140 |
| 2030 | By week | " | | | 400 |
| 2040 | By month | " | | | 1,240 |
| 2080 | Dump truck | | | | |
| 2100 | 6 cy truck | | | | |
| 2120 | By day | EA. | | | 360 |
| 2130 | By week | " | | | 1,090 |
| 2140 | By month | " | | | 3,290 |
| 2300 | 16 cy truck | | | | |
| 2310 | By day | EA. | | | 730 |
| 2320 | By week | " | | | 2,190 |
| 2340 | By month | " | | | 6,580 |
| 2400 | Backhoe, track mounted | | | | |
| 2420 | 1/2 cy capacity | | | | |
| 2430 | By day | EA. | | | 750 |
| 2440 | By week | " | | | 2,280 |
| 2450 | By month | " | | | 6,760 |
| 2500 | 1 cy capacity | | | | |
| 2510 | By day | EA. | | | 1,190 |
| 2520 | By week | " | | | 3,560 |
| 2530 | By month | " | | | 10,690 |
| 2600 | 3 cy capacity | | | | |
| 2620 | By day | EA. | | | 3,840 |

© 2011 By Design & Construction Resources

# DIVISION # 01  GENERAL

|  |  |  | UNIT | LABOR | MAT. | TOTAL |
|---|---|---|---|---|---|---|
| **01600.10** | **EQUIPMENT, Cont'd...** | | | | | |
| 2640 | By week | | EA. | | | 11,510 |
| 2680 | By month | | " | | | 34,540 |
| 3000 | Backhoe/loader, rubber tired | | | | | |
| 3005 | 1/2 cy capacity | | | | | |
| 3010 | By day | | EA. | | | 450 |
| 3020 | By week | | " | | | 1,370 |
| 3030 | By month | | " | | | 4,110 |
| 3035 | 3/4 cy capacity | | | | | |
| 3040 | By day | | EA. | | | 550 |
| 3050 | By week | | " | | | 1,640 |
| 3060 | By month | | " | | | 4,930 |
| 3200 | Bulldozer | | | | | |
| 3205 | 75 hp | | | | | |
| 3210 | By day | | EA. | | | 640 |
| 3220 | By week | | " | | | 1,920 |
| 3230 | By month | | " | | | 5,760 |
| 4000 | Cranes, crawler type | | | | | |
| 4005 | 15 ton capacity | | | | | |
| 4010 | By day | | EA. | | | 820 |
| 4020 | By week | | " | | | 2,470 |
| 4030 | By month | | " | | | 7,400 |
| 4070 | 50 ton capacity | | | | | |
| 4080 | By day | | EA. | | | 1,830 |
| 4090 | By week | | " | | | 5,480 |
| 4100 | By month | | " | | | 16,450 |
| 4145 | Truck mounted, hydraulic | | | | | |
| 4150 | 15 ton capacity | | | | | |
| 4160 | By day | | EA. | | | 770 |
| 4170 | By week | | " | | | 2,330 |
| 4180 | By month | | " | | | 6,720 |
| 5380 | Loader, rubber tired | | | | | |
| 5385 | 1 cy capacity | | | | | |
| 5390 | By day | | EA. | | | 550 |
| 5400 | By week | | " | | | 1,640 |
| 5410 | By month | | " | | | 4,930 |
| 7000 | Scraper | | | | | |
| 7010 | Elevated scraper, not including bulldozer, 12 c.y. | | | | | |
| 7020 | By day | | EA. | | | 1,250 |
| 7030 | By week | | " | | | 3,750 |
| 7040 | By month | | " | | | 10,620 |
| 7100 | Self-propelled scraper, 14 c.y. | | | | | |
| 7110 | By day | | EA. | | | 2,500 |
| 7120 | By week | | " | | | 7,490 |
| 7130 | By month | | " | | | 21,240 |
| **01740.10** | **BONDS** | | | | | |
| 1000 | Performance bonds | | | | | |
| 1020 | Minimum | | PCT. | | | 0.64 |
| 1040 | Average | | " | | | 2.00 |
| 1060 | Maximum | | " | | | 3.18 |

© 2011 By Design & Construction Resources

# DIVISION # 02  SITE CONSTRUCTION

## TABLE OF CONTENTS | PAGE

| | |
|---|---|
| 02210.10 - SOIL BORING | 02-2 |
| 02220.10 - COMPLETE BUILDING DEMOLITION | 02-2 |
| 02220.15 - SELECTIVE BUILDING DEMOLITION | 02-2 |
| 02225.20 - FENCE DEMOLITION | 02-4 |
| 02225.50 - SAW CUTTING PAVEMENT | 02-4 |
| 02225.60 - TORCH CUTTING | 02-5 |
| 02230.50 - TREE CUTTING & CLEARING | 02-5 |
| 02315.10 - BASE COURSE | 02-5 |
| 02315.20 - BORROW | 02-5 |
| 02315.30 - BULK EXCAVATION | 02-5 |
| 02315.40 - BUILDING EXCAVATION | 02-7 |
| 02315.45 - HAND EXCAVATION | 02-7 |
| 02315.50 - ROADWAY EXCAVATION | 02-7 |
| 02315.60 - TRENCHING | 02-7 |
| 02315.70 - UTILITY EXCAVATION | 02-8 |
| 02315.80 - HAULING MATERIAL | 02-8 |
| 02340.05 - SOIL STABILIZATION | 02-9 |
| 02360.20 - SOIL TREATMENT | 02-9 |
| 02370.40 - RIPRAP | 02-9 |
| 02455.60 - STEEL PILES | 02-9 |
| 02455.65 - STEEL PIPE PILES | 02-9 |
| 02455.80 - WOOD AND TIMBER PILES | 02-9 |
| 02465.50 - PRESTRESSED PILING | 02-10 |
| 02510.10 - WELLS | 02-10 |
| 02510.40 - DUCTILE IRON PIPE | 02-10 |
| 02510.60 - PLASTIC PIPE | 02-10 |
| 02530.20 - VITRIFIED CLAY PIPE | 02-11 |
| 02530.30 - MANHOLES | 02-11 |
| 02530.40 - SANITARY SEWERS | 02-11 |
| 02540.10 - DRAINAGE FIELDS | 02-11 |
| 02540.50 - SEPTIC TANKS | 02-12 |
| 02630.70 - UNDERDRAIN | 02-12 |
| 02740.20 - ASPHALT SURFACES | 02-12 |
| 02750.10 - CONCRETE PAVING | 02-12 |
| 02810.40 - LAWN IRRIGATION | 02-13 |
| 02820.10 - CHAIN LINK FENCE | 02-13 |
| 02820.20 - WOOD FENCE | 02-13 |
| 02840.40 - PARKING BARRIERS | 02-13 |
| 02880.70 - RECREATIONAL COURTS | 02-13 |
| 02910.10 - TOPSOIL | 02-14 |
| 02920.10 - FERTILIZING | 02-14 |
| 02920.30 - SEEDING | 02-14 |
| 02935.10 - SHRUB & TREE MAINTENANCE | 02-15 |
| 02935.30 - WEED CONTROL | 02-15 |
| 02945.20 - LANDSCAPE ACCESSORIES | 02-15 |
| **QUICK ESTIMATING** | **02A-16** |

© 2011 By Design & Construction Resources

# DIVISION # 02  SITE CONSTRUCTION

| | | UNIT | LABOR | MAT. | TOTAL |
|---|---|---|---|---|---|
| **02210.10** | **SOIL BORING** | | | | |
| 1000 | Borings, uncased, stable earth | | | | |
| 1020 | 2-1/2" dia. | L.F. | 28.25 | | 28.25 |
| 1040 | 4" dia. | " | 32.50 | | 32.50 |
| 1500 | Cased, including samples | | | | |
| 1520 | 2-1/2" dia. | L.F. | 37.75 | | 37.75 |
| 1540 | 4" dia. | " | 65.00 | | 65.00 |
| **02220.10** | **COMPLETE BUILDING DEMOLITION** | | | | |
| 0200 | Wood frame | C.F. | 0.32 | | 0.32 |
| 0300 | Concrete | " | 0.49 | | 0.49 |
| 0400 | Steel frame | " | 0.65 | | 0.65 |
| **02220.15** | **SELECTIVE BUILDING DEMOLITION** | | | | |
| 1000 | Partition removal | | | | |
| 1100 | Concrete block partitions | | | | |
| 1120 | 4" thick | S.F. | 2.09 | | 2.09 |
| 1140 | 8" thick | " | 2.78 | | 2.78 |
| 1160 | 12" thick | " | 3.80 | | 3.80 |
| 1200 | Brick masonry partitions | | | | |
| 1220 | 4" thick | S.F. | 2.09 | | 2.09 |
| 1240 | 8" thick | " | 2.61 | | 2.61 |
| 1260 | 12" thick | " | 3.48 | | 3.48 |
| 1280 | 16" thick | " | 5.23 | | 5.23 |
| 1380 | Cast in place concrete partitions | | | | |
| 1400 | Unreinforced | | | | |
| 1421 | 6" thick | S.F. | 15.00 | | 15.00 |
| 1423 | 8" thick | " | 16.25 | | 16.25 |
| 1425 | 10" thick | " | 19.00 | | 19.00 |
| 1427 | 12" thick | " | 22.75 | | 22.75 |
| 1440 | Reinforced | | | | |
| 1441 | 6" thick | S.F. | 17.50 | | 17.50 |
| 1443 | 8" thick | " | 22.75 | | 22.75 |
| 1445 | 10" thick | " | 25.25 | | 25.25 |
| 1447 | 12" thick | " | 30.25 | | 30.25 |
| 1500 | Terra cotta | | | | |
| 1520 | To 6" thick | S.F. | 2.09 | | 2.09 |
| 1700 | Stud partitions | | | | |
| 1720 | Metal or wood, with drywall both sides | S.F. | 2.09 | | 2.09 |
| 1740 | Metal studs, both sides, lath and plaster | " | 2.78 | | 2.78 |
| 2000 | Door and frame removal | | | | |
| 2020 | Hollow metal in masonry wall | | | | |
| 2030 | Single | | | | |
| 2040 | 2'6"x6'8" | EA. | 52.00 | | 52.00 |
| 2060 | 3'x7' | " | 70.00 | | 70.00 |
| 2070 | Double | | | | |
| 2080 | 3'x7' | EA. | 84.00 | | 84.00 |
| 2085 | 4'x8' | " | 84.00 | | 84.00 |
| 2140 | Wood in framed wall | | | | |
| 2150 | Single | | | | |
| 2160 | 2'6"x6'8" | EA. | 30.00 | | 30.00 |
| 2180 | 3'x6'8" | " | 34.75 | | 34.75 |
| 2190 | Double | | | | |
| 2200 | 2'6"x6'8" | EA. | 41.75 | | 41.75 |

# DIVISION # 02  SITE CONSTRUCTION

## 02220.15  SELECTIVE BUILDING DEMOLITION, Cont'd...

| Code | Description | UNIT | LABOR | MAT. | TOTAL |
|---|---|---|---|---|---|
| 2220 | 3'x6'8" | EA. | 46.50 | | 46.50 |
| 2240 | Remove for re-use | | | | |
| 2260 |   Hollow metal | EA. | 100 | | 100 |
| 2280 |   Wood | " | 70.00 | | 70.00 |
| 2300 | Floor removal | | | | |
| 2340 |   Brick flooring | S.F. | 1.67 | | 1.67 |
| 2360 |   Ceramic or quarry tile | " | 0.92 | | 0.92 |
| 2380 |   Terrazzo | " | 1.85 | | 1.85 |
| 2400 |   Heavy wood | " | 1.11 | | 1.11 |
| 2420 |   Residential wood | " | 1.19 | | 1.19 |
| 2440 |   Resilient tile or linoleum | " | 0.41 | | 0.41 |
| 2500 | Ceiling removal | | | | |
| 2520 |   Acoustical tile ceiling | | | | |
| 2540 |     Adhesive fastened | S.F. | 0.41 | | 0.41 |
| 2560 |     Furred and glued | " | 0.34 | | 0.34 |
| 2580 |     Suspended grid | " | 0.26 | | 0.26 |
| 2600 |   Drywall ceiling | | | | |
| 2620 |     Furred and nailed | S.F. | 0.46 | | 0.46 |
| 2640 |     Nailed to framing | " | 0.41 | | 0.41 |
| 2660 |   Plastered ceiling | | | | |
| 2680 |     Furred on framing | S.F. | 1.04 | | 1.04 |
| 2700 |     Suspended system | " | 1.39 | | 1.39 |
| 2800 | Roofing removal | | | | |
| 2820 |   Steel frame | | | | |
| 2840 |     Corrugated metal roofing | S.F. | 0.83 | | 0.83 |
| 2860 |     Built-up roof on metal deck | " | 1.39 | | 1.39 |
| 2900 |   Wood frame | | | | |
| 2920 |     Built up roof on wood deck | S.F. | 1.28 | | 1.28 |
| 2940 |     Roof shingles | " | 0.69 | | 0.69 |
| 2960 |     Roof tiles | " | 1.39 | | 1.39 |
| 8900 |   Concrete frame | C.F. | 2.78 | | 2.78 |
| 8920 |   Concrete plank | S.F. | 2.09 | | 2.09 |
| 8940 |   Built-up roof on concrete | " | 1.19 | | 1.19 |
| 9200 | Cut-outs | | | | |
| 9230 |   Concrete, elevated slabs, mesh reinforcing | | | | |
| 9240 |     Under 5 cf | C.F. | 41.75 | | 41.75 |
| 9260 |     Over 5 cf | " | 34.75 | | 34.75 |
| 9270 |   Bar reinforcing | | | | |
| 9280 |     Under 5 cf | C.F. | 70.00 | | 70.00 |
| 9290 |     Over 5 cf | " | 52.00 | | 52.00 |
| 9300 | Window removal | | | | |
| 9301 |   Metal windows, trim included | | | | |
| 9302 |     2'x3' | EA. | 41.75 | | 41.75 |
| 9304 |     2'x4' | " | 46.50 | | 46.50 |
| 9306 |     2'x6' | " | 52.00 | | 52.00 |
| 9308 |     3'x4' | " | 52.00 | | 52.00 |
| 9310 |     3'x6' | " | 60.00 | | 60.00 |
| 9312 |     3'x8' | " | 70.00 | | 70.00 |
| 9314 |     4'x4' | " | 70.00 | | 70.00 |
| 9315 |     4'x6' | " | 84.00 | | 84.00 |
| 9316 |     4'x8' | " | 100 | | 100 |
| 9317 |   Wood windows, trim included | | | | |

© 2011 By Design & Construction Resources

## DIVISION # 02 SITE CONSTRUCTION

|  |  | UNIT | LABOR | MAT. | TOTAL |
|---|---|---|---|---|---|
| **02220.15** | **SELECTIVE BUILDING DEMOLITION, Cont'd...** | | | | |
| 9318 | 2'x3' | EA. | 23.25 | | 23.25 |
| 9319 | 2'x4' | " | 24.50 | | 24.50 |
| 9320 | 2'x6' | " | 26.25 | | 26.25 |
| 9321 | 3'x4' | " | 28.00 | | 28.00 |
| 9322 | 3'x6' | " | 30.00 | | 30.00 |
| 9324 | 3'x8' | " | 32.25 | | 32.25 |
| 9325 | 6'x4' | " | 34.75 | | 34.75 |
| 9326 | 6'x6' | " | 38.00 | | 38.00 |
| 9327 | 6'x8' | " | 41.75 | | 41.75 |
| 9329 | Walls, concrete, bar reinforcing | | | | |
| 9330 | Small jobs | C.F. | 28.00 | | 28.00 |
| 9340 | Large jobs | " | 23.25 | | 23.25 |
| 9360 | Brick walls, not including toothing | | | | |
| 9390 | 4" thick | S.F. | 2.09 | | 2.09 |
| 9400 | 8" thick | " | 2.61 | | 2.61 |
| 9410 | 12" thick | " | 3.48 | | 3.48 |
| 9415 | 16" thick | " | 5.23 | | 5.23 |
| 9420 | Concrete block walls, not including toothing | | | | |
| 9440 | 4" thick | S.F. | 2.32 | | 2.32 |
| 9450 | 6" thick | " | 2.46 | | 2.46 |
| 9460 | 8" thick | " | 2.61 | | 2.61 |
| 9465 | 10" thick | " | 2.98 | | 2.98 |
| 9470 | 12" thick | " | 3.48 | | 3.48 |
| 9500 | Rubbish handling | | | | |
| 9519 | Load in dumpster or truck | | | | |
| 9520 | Minimum | C.F. | 0.92 | | 0.92 |
| 9540 | Maximum | " | 1.39 | | 1.39 |
| 9550 | For use of elevators, add | | | | |
| 9560 | Minimum | C.F. | 0.20 | | 0.20 |
| 9570 | Maximum | " | 0.41 | | 0.41 |
| 9600 | Rubbish hauling | | | | |
| 9640 | Hand loaded on trucks, 2 mile trip | C.Y. | 35.00 | | 35.00 |
| 9660 | Machine loaded on trucks, 2 mile trip | " | 22.75 | | 22.75 |
| **02225.20** | **FENCE DEMOLITION** | | | | |
| 0060 | Remove fencing | | | | |
| 0080 | Chain link, 8' high | | | | |
| 0100 | For disposal | L.F. | 2.09 | | 2.09 |
| 0200 | For reuse | " | 5.23 | | 5.23 |
| 0980 | Wood | | | | |
| 1000 | 4' high | S.F. | 1.39 | | 1.39 |
| 1960 | Masonry | | | | |
| 1980 | 8" thick | | | | |
| 2000 | 4' high | S.F. | 4.18 | | 4.18 |
| 2020 | 6' high | " | 5.23 | | 5.23 |
| **02225.50** | **SAW CUTTING PAVEMENT** | | | | |
| 0100 | Pavement, bituminous | | | | |
| 0110 | 2" thick | L.F. | 1.74 | | 1.74 |
| 0120 | 3" thick | " | 2.18 | | 2.18 |
| 0200 | Concrete pavement, with wire mesh | | | | |
| 0210 | 4" thick | L.F. | 3.36 | | 3.36 |
| 0212 | 5" thick | " | 3.64 | | 3.64 |

## DIVISION # 02  SITE CONSTRUCTION

| | | UNIT | LABOR | MAT. | TOTAL |
|---|---|---|---|---|---|
| **02225.50** | **SAW CUTTING PAVEMENT, Cont'd...** | | | | |
| 0300 | Plain concrete, unreinforced | | | | |
| 0320 | 4" thick | L.F. | 2.91 | | 2.91 |
| 0340 | 5" thick | " | 3.36 | | 3.36 |
| **02225.60** | **TORCH CUTTING** | | | | |
| 0010 | Steel plate, 1/2" thick, | L.F. | 0.90 | 0.49 | 1.39 |
| 0020 | 1" thick | " | 1.81 | 0.71 | 2.52 |
| **02230.50** | **TREE CUTTING & CLEARING** | | | | |
| 0980 | Cut trees and clear out stumps | | | | |
| 1000 | 9" to 12" dia. | EA. | 450 | | 450 |
| 1400 | To 24" dia. | " | 570 | | 570 |
| 1600 | 24" dia. and up | " | 760 | | 760 |
| **02315.10** | **BASE COURSE** | | | | |
| 1019 | Base course, crushed stone | | | | |
| 1020 | 3" thick | S.Y. | 0.61 | 3.68 | 4.29 |
| 1030 | 4" thick | " | 0.66 | 4.89 | 5.55 |
| 1040 | 6" thick | " | 0.72 | 7.31 | 8.03 |
| 2500 | Base course, bank run gravel | | | | |
| 3020 | 4" deep | S.Y. | 0.64 | 3.02 | 3.66 |
| 3040 | 6" deep | " | 0.70 | 4.62 | 5.32 |
| 4000 | Prepare and roll sub base | | | | |
| 4020 | Minimum | S.Y. | 0.61 | | 0.61 |
| 4030 | Average | " | 0.77 | | 0.77 |
| 4040 | Maximum | " | 1.02 | | 1.02 |
| **02315.20** | **BORROW** | | | | |
| 1000 | Borrow fill, F.O.B. at pit | | | | |
| 1005 | Sand, haul to site, round trip | | | | |
| 1010 | 10 mile | C.Y. | 12.25 | 18.75 | 31.00 |
| 1020 | 20 mile | " | 20.50 | 18.75 | 39.25 |
| 1030 | 30 mile | " | 30.75 | 18.75 | 49.50 |
| 3980 | Place borrow fill and compact | | | | |
| 4000 | Less than 1 in 4 slope | C.Y. | 6.16 | 18.75 | 24.91 |
| 4100 | Greater than 1 in 4 slope | " | 8.21 | 18.75 | 26.96 |
| **02315.30** | **BULK EXCAVATION** | | | | |
| 1000 | Excavation, by small dozer | | | | |
| 1020 | Large areas | C.Y. | 1.74 | | 1.74 |
| 1040 | Small areas | " | 2.91 | | 2.91 |
| 1060 | Trim banks | " | 4.37 | | 4.37 |
| 1700 | Hydraulic excavator | | | | |
| 1720 | 1 cy capacity | | | | |
| 1740 | Light material | C.Y. | 3.78 | | 3.78 |
| 1760 | Medium material | " | 4.53 | | 4.53 |
| 1780 | Wet material | " | 5.67 | | 5.67 |
| 1790 | Blasted rock | " | 6.48 | | 6.48 |
| 1800 | 1-1/2 cy capacity | | | | |
| 1820 | Light material | C.Y. | 1.54 | | 1.54 |
| 1840 | Medium material | " | 2.05 | | 2.05 |
| 1860 | Wet material | " | 2.46 | | 2.46 |
| 2000 | Wheel mounted front-end loader | | | | |
| 2020 | 7/8 cy capacity | | | | |
| 2040 | Light material | C.Y. | 3.08 | | 3.08 |

© 2011 By Design & Construction Resources

## DIVISION # 02  SITE CONSTRUCTION

| 02315.30 | BULK EXCAVATION, Cont'd... | UNIT | LABOR | MAT. | TOTAL |
|---|---|---|---|---|---|
| 2060 | Medium material | C.Y. | 3.52 | | 3.52 |
| 2080 | Wet material | " | 4.10 | | 4.10 |
| 2100 | Blasted rock | " | 4.92 | | 4.92 |
| 2300 | 2-1/2 cy capacity | | | | |
| 2320 | Light material | C.Y. | 1.44 | | 1.44 |
| 2340 | Medium material | " | 1.54 | | 1.54 |
| 2360 | Wet material | " | 1.64 | | 1.64 |
| 2380 | Blasted rock | " | 1.76 | | 1.76 |
| 2600 | Track mounted front-end loader | | | | |
| 2620 | 1-1/2 cy capacity | | | | |
| 2640 | Light material | C.Y. | 2.05 | | 2.05 |
| 2660 | Medium material | " | 2.24 | | 2.24 |
| 2680 | Wet material | " | 2.46 | | 2.46 |
| 2700 | Blasted rock | " | 2.73 | | 2.73 |
| 2720 | 2-3/4 cy capacity | | | | |
| 2740 | Light material | C.Y. | 1.23 | | 1.23 |
| 2760 | Medium material | " | 1.36 | | 1.36 |
| 2780 | Wet material | " | 1.54 | | 1.54 |
| 2790 | Blasted rock | " | 1.76 | | 1.76 |
| 4000 | Scraper -500' haul | | | | |
| 4010 | Elevated scraper, not including bulldozer, 12 c.y. | | | | |
| 4020 | Light material | C.Y. | 4.10 | | 4.10 |
| 4030 | Medium material | " | 4.48 | | 4.48 |
| 4040 | Wet material | " | 4.92 | | 4.92 |
| 4050 | Blasted rock | " | 5.47 | | 5.47 |
| 4100 | Self-propelled scraper, 14 c.y. | | | | |
| 4110 | Light material | C.Y. | 3.79 | | 3.79 |
| 4120 | Medium material | " | 4.10 | | 4.10 |
| 4130 | Wet material | " | 4.48 | | 4.48 |
| 4140 | Blasted rock | " | 4.92 | | 4.92 |
| 4200 | 1,000' haul | | | | |
| 4210 | Elevated scraper, not including bulldozer, 12 c.y. | | | | |
| 4220 | Light material | C.Y. | 4.92 | | 4.92 |
| 4230 | Medium material | " | 5.47 | | 5.47 |
| 4240 | Wet material | " | 6.16 | | 6.16 |
| 4250 | Blasted rock | " | 7.04 | | 7.04 |
| 4300 | Self-propelled scraper, 14 c.y. | | | | |
| 4310 | Light material | C.Y. | 4.48 | | 4.48 |
| 4320 | Medium material | " | 4.92 | | 4.92 |
| 4330 | Wet material | " | 5.47 | | 5.47 |
| 4340 | Blasted rock | " | 6.16 | | 6.16 |
| 4400 | 2,000' haul | | | | |
| 4410 | Elevated scraper, not including bulldozer, 12 c.y. | | | | |
| 4420 | Light material | C.Y. | 6.16 | | 6.16 |
| 4430 | Medium material | " | 7.04 | | 7.04 |
| 4440 | Wet material | " | 8.21 | | 8.21 |
| 4450 | Blasted rock | " | 9.85 | | 9.85 |
| 4510 | Self-propelled scraper, 14 c.y. | | | | |
| 4520 | Light material | C.Y. | 5.47 | | 5.47 |
| 4530 | Medium material | " | 6.16 | | 6.16 |
| 4540 | Wet material | " | 7.04 | | 7.04 |
| 4550 | Blasted rock | " | 8.21 | | 8.21 |

## DIVISION # 02 SITE CONSTRUCTION

| | | UNIT | LABOR | MAT. | TOTAL |
|---|---|---|---|---|---|
| **02315.40** | **BUILDING EXCAVATION** | | | | |
| 0090 | Structural excavation, unclassified earth | | | | |
| 0100 | 3/8 cy backhoe | C.Y. | 16.50 | | 16.50 |
| 0110 | 3/4 cy backhoe | " | 12.25 | | 12.25 |
| 0120 | 1 cy backhoe | " | 10.25 | | 10.25 |
| 0600 | Foundation backfill and compaction by machine | " | 24.75 | | 24.75 |
| **02315.45** | **HAND EXCAVATION** | | | | |
| 0980 | Excavation | | | | |
| 1000 | To 2' deep | | | | |
| 1020 | Normal soil | C.Y. | 46.50 | | 46.50 |
| 1040 | Sand and gravel | " | 41.75 | | 41.75 |
| 1060 | Medium clay | " | 52.00 | | 52.00 |
| 1080 | Heavy clay | " | 60.00 | | 60.00 |
| 1100 | Loose rock | " | 70.00 | | 70.00 |
| 1200 | To 6' deep | | | | |
| 1220 | Normal soil | C.Y. | 60.00 | | 60.00 |
| 1240 | Sand and gravel | " | 52.00 | | 52.00 |
| 1260 | Medium clay | " | 70.00 | | 70.00 |
| 1280 | Heavy clay | " | 84.00 | | 84.00 |
| 1300 | Loose rock | " | 100 | | 100 |
| 2020 | Backfilling foundation without compaction, 6" lifts | " | 26.25 | | 26.25 |
| 2200 | Compaction of backfill around structures or in trench | | | | |
| 2220 | By hand with air tamper | C.Y. | 30.00 | | 30.00 |
| 2240 | By hand with vibrating plate tamper | " | 28.00 | | 28.00 |
| 2250 | 1 ton roller | " | 43.75 | | 43.75 |
| 5400 | Miscellaneous hand labor | | | | |
| 5440 | Trim slopes, sides of excavation | S.F. | 0.06 | | 0.06 |
| 5450 | Trim bottom of excavation | " | 0.08 | | 0.08 |
| 5460 | Excavation around obstructions and services | C.Y. | 140 | | 140 |
| **02315.50** | **ROADWAY EXCAVATION** | | | | |
| 0100 | Roadway excavation | | | | |
| 0110 | 1/4 mile haul | C.Y. | 2.46 | | 2.46 |
| 0120 | 2 mile haul | " | 4.10 | | 4.10 |
| 0130 | 5 mile haul | " | 6.16 | | 6.16 |
| 3000 | Spread base course | " | 3.08 | | 3.08 |
| 3100 | Roll and compact | " | 4.10 | | 4.10 |
| **02315.60** | **TRENCHING** | | | | |
| 0100 | Trenching and continuous footing excavation | | | | |
| 0980 | By gradall | | | | |
| 1000 | 1 cy capacity | | | | |
| 1040 | Medium soil | C.Y. | 3.79 | | 3.79 |
| 1080 | Loose rock | " | 4.48 | | 4.48 |
| 1090 | Blasted rock | " | 4.74 | | 4.74 |
| 1095 | By hydraulic excavator | | | | |
| 1100 | 1/2 cy capacity | | | | |
| 1140 | Medium soil | C.Y. | 4.48 | | 4.48 |
| 1180 | Loose rock | " | 5.47 | | 5.47 |
| 1190 | Blasted rock | " | 6.16 | | 6.16 |
| 1200 | 1 cy capacity | | | | |
| 1240 | Medium soil | C.Y. | 3.08 | | 3.08 |
| 1280 | Loose rock | " | 3.52 | | 3.52 |
| 1300 | Blasted rock | " | 3.79 | | 3.79 |

© 2011 By Design & Construction Resources

# DIVISION # 02  SITE CONSTRUCTION

| | | UNIT | LABOR | MAT. | TOTAL |
|---|---|---|---|---|---|
| **02315.60** | **TRENCHING, Cont'd...** | | | | |
| 1600 | 2 cy capacity | | | | |
| 1640 | Medium soil | C.Y. | 2.59 | | 2.59 |
| 1680 | Loose rock | " | 2.89 | | 2.89 |
| 1690 | Blasted rock | " | 3.08 | | 3.08 |
| 3000 | Hand excavation | | | | |
| 3100 | Bulk, wheeled 100' | | | | |
| 3120 | Normal soil | C.Y. | 46.50 | | 46.50 |
| 3140 | Sand or gravel | " | 41.75 | | 41.75 |
| 3160 | Medium clay | " | 60.00 | | 60.00 |
| 3180 | Heavy clay | " | 84.00 | | 84.00 |
| 3200 | Loose rock | " | 100 | | 100 |
| 3300 | Trenches, up to 2' deep | | | | |
| 3320 | Normal soil | C.Y. | 52.00 | | 52.00 |
| 3340 | Sand or gravel | " | 46.50 | | 46.50 |
| 3360 | Medium clay | " | 70.00 | | 70.00 |
| 3380 | Heavy clay | " | 100 | | 100 |
| 3390 | Loose rock | " | 140 | | 140 |
| 3400 | Trenches, to 6' deep | | | | |
| 3420 | Normal soil | C.Y. | 60.00 | | 60.00 |
| 3440 | Sand or gravel | " | 52.00 | | 52.00 |
| 3460 | Medium clay | " | 84.00 | | 84.00 |
| 3480 | Heavy clay | " | 140 | | 140 |
| 3500 | Loose rock | " | 210 | | 210 |
| 3590 | Backfill trenches | | | | |
| 3600 | With compaction | | | | |
| 3620 | By hand | C.Y. | 34.75 | | 34.75 |
| 3640 | By 60 hp tracked dozer | " | 2.18 | | 2.18 |
| **02315.70** | **UTILITY EXCAVATION** | | | | |
| 2080 | Trencher, sandy clay, 8" wide trench | | | | |
| 2100 | 18" deep | L.F. | 1.94 | | 1.94 |
| 2200 | 24" deep | " | 2.18 | | 2.18 |
| 2300 | 36" deep | " | 2.49 | | 2.49 |
| 6080 | Trench backfill, 95% compaction | | | | |
| 7000 | Tamp by hand | C.Y. | 26.25 | | 26.25 |
| 7050 | Vibratory compaction | " | 21.00 | | 21.00 |
| 7060 | Trench backfilling, with borrow sand, place & compact | " | 21.00 | 18.75 | 39.75 |
| **02315.80** | **HAULING MATERIAL** | | | | |
| 0090 | Haul material by 10 cy dump truck, round trip distance | | | | |
| 0100 | 1 mile | C.Y. | 4.85 | | 4.85 |
| 0110 | 2 mile | " | 5.82 | | 5.82 |
| 0120 | 5 mile | " | 7.94 | | 7.94 |
| 0130 | 10 mile | " | 8.74 | | 8.74 |
| 0140 | 20 mile | " | 9.71 | | 9.71 |
| 0150 | 30 mile | " | 11.75 | | 11.75 |
| 2000 | Site grading, cut & fill, sandy clay, 200' haul, 75 hp dozer | " | 3.49 | | 3.49 |
| 6000 | Spread topsoil by equipment on site | " | 3.88 | | 3.88 |
| 6980 | Site grading (cut and fill to 6") less than 1 acre | | | | |
| 7000 | 75 hp dozer | C.Y. | 5.82 | | 5.82 |
| 7600 | 1.5 cy backhoe/loader | " | 8.74 | | 8.74 |
| 0010 | Blasting mats, up to 1500 c.y. | " | 95.00 | 3.02 | 98.02 |
| 0020 | Buried explosives, up to 1500 c.y. | " | 28.75 | 3.02 | 31.77 |

© 2011 By Design & Construction Resources

# DIVISION # 02  SITE CONSTRUCTION

| | | UNIT | LABOR | MAT. | TOTAL |
|---|---|---|---|---|---|
| **02340.05** | **SOIL STABILIZATION** | | | | |
| 0100 | Straw bale secured with rebar | L.F. | 1.39 | 7.54 | 8.93 |
| 0120 | Filter barrier, 18" high filter fabric | " | 4.18 | 1.82 | 6.00 |
| 0130 | Sediment fence, 36" fabric with 6" mesh | " | 5.23 | 4.32 | 9.55 |
| 1000 | Soil stabilization with tar paper, burlap, straw and stakes | S.F. | 0.05 | 0.36 | 0.41 |
| **02360.20** | **SOIL TREATMENT** | | | | |
| 1100 | Soil treatment, termite control pretreatment | | | | |
| 1120 | Under slabs | S.F. | 0.23 | 0.38 | 0.61 |
| 1140 | By walls | " | 0.27 | 0.38 | 0.65 |
| **02370.40** | **RIPRAP** | | | | |
| 0100 | Riprap | | | | |
| 0110 | Crushed stone blanket, max size 2-1/2" | TON | 65.00 | 35.25 | 100 |
| 0120 | Stone, quarry run, 300 lb. stones | " | 60.00 | 44.25 | 104 |
| 0130 | 400 lb. stones | " | 56.00 | 46.00 | 102 |
| 0140 | 500 lb. stones | " | 52.00 | 48.00 | 100 |
| 0150 | 750 lb. stones | " | 49.00 | 49.75 | 98.75 |
| 0160 | Dry concrete riprap in bags 3" thick, 80 lb. per bag | BAG | 3.26 | 5.96 | 9.22 |
| **02455.60** | **STEEL PILES** | | | | |
| 1000 | H-section piles | | | | |
| 1010 | 8x8 | | | | |
| 1020 | 36 lb/ft | | | | |
| 1021 | 30' long | L.F. | 11.25 | 15.25 | 26.50 |
| 1022 | 40' long | " | 9.00 | 15.25 | 24.25 |
| 5000 | Tapered friction piles, fluted casing, up to 50' | | | | |
| 5002 | With 4000 psi concrete no reinforcing | | | | |
| 5040 | 12" dia. | L.F. | 6.75 | 18.00 | 24.75 |
| 5060 | 14" dia. | " | 6.92 | 20.75 | 27.67 |
| **02455.65** | **STEEL PIPE PILES** | | | | |
| 1000 | Concrete filled, 3000# concrete, up to 40' | | | | |
| 1100 | 8" dia. | L.F. | 9.64 | 22.00 | 31.64 |
| 1120 | 10" dia. | " | 10.00 | 28.25 | 38.25 |
| 1140 | 12" dia. | " | 10.50 | 32.75 | 43.25 |
| 2000 | Pipe piles, non-filled | | | | |
| 2020 | 8" dia. | L.F. | 7.50 | 20.75 | 28.25 |
| 2040 | 10" dia. | " | 7.71 | 26.00 | 33.71 |
| 2060 | 12" dia. | " | 7.94 | 32.00 | 39.94 |
| 2520 | Splice | | | | |
| 2540 | 8" dia. | EA. | 84.00 | 93.00 | 177 |
| 2560 | 10" dia. | " | 84.00 | 100 | 184 |
| 2580 | 12" dia. | " | 100 | 110 | 210 |
| 2680 | Standard point | | | | |
| 2700 | 8" dia. | EA. | 84.00 | 130 | 214 |
| 2740 | 10" dia. | " | 84.00 | 160 | 244 |
| 2760 | 12" dia. | " | 100 | 180 | 280 |
| 2880 | Heavy duty point | | | | |
| 2900 | 8" dia. | EA. | 100 | 220 | 320 |
| 2920 | 10" dia. | " | 100 | 310 | 410 |
| 2940 | 12" dia. | " | 140 | 330 | 470 |
| **02455.80** | **WOOD AND TIMBER PILES** | | | | |
| 0080 | Treated wood piles, 12" butt, 8" tip | | | | |
| 0100 | 25' long | L.F. | 13.50 | 9.63 | 23.13 |
| 0110 | 30' long | " | 11.25 | 10.25 | 21.50 |

© 2011 By Design & Construction Resources

## DIVISION # 02 SITE CONSTRUCTION

| | | UNIT | LABOR | MAT. | TOTAL |
|---|---|---|---|---|---|
| **02455.80** | **WOOD AND TIMBER PILES, Cont'd...** | | | | |
| 0120 | 35' long | L.F. | 9.64 | 10.25 | 19.89 |
| 0125 | 40' long | " | 8.43 | 10.25 | 18.68 |
| **02465.50** | **PRESTRESSED PILING** | | | | |
| 0980 | Prestressed concrete piling, less than 60' long | | | | |
| 1000 | 10" sq. | L.F. | 5.62 | 13.75 | 19.37 |
| 1002 | 12" sq. | " | 5.87 | 19.00 | 24.87 |
| 1480 | Straight cylinder, less than 60' long | | | | |
| 1500 | 12" dia. | L.F. | 6.13 | 17.75 | 23.88 |
| 1540 | 14" dia. | " | 6.28 | 24.00 | 30.28 |
| **02510.10** | **WELLS** | | | | |
| 0980 | Domestic water, drilled and cased | | | | |
| 1000 | 4" dia. | L.F. | 68.00 | 27.75 | 95.75 |
| 1020 | 6" dia. | " | 75.00 | 30.50 | 106 |
| **02510.40** | **DUCTILE IRON PIPE** | | | | |
| 0990 | Ductile iron pipe, cement lined, slip-on joints | | | | |
| 1000 | 4" | L.F. | 6.30 | 13.50 | 19.80 |
| 1010 | 6" | " | 6.67 | 16.25 | 22.92 |
| 1020 | 8" | " | 7.08 | 21.25 | 28.33 |
| 1190 | Mechanical joint pipe | | | | |
| 1200 | 4" | L.F. | 8.72 | 16.00 | 24.72 |
| 1210 | 6" | " | 9.45 | 19.00 | 28.45 |
| 1220 | 8" | " | 10.25 | 25.00 | 35.25 |
| 1480 | Fittings, mechanical joint | | | | |
| 1500 | 90 degree elbow | | | | |
| 1520 | 4" | EA. | 28.00 | 190 | 218 |
| 1540 | 6" | " | 32.25 | 250 | 282 |
| 1560 | 8" | " | 41.75 | 360 | 402 |
| 1700 | 45 degree elbow | | | | |
| 1720 | 4" | EA. | 28.00 | 170 | 198 |
| 1740 | 6" | " | 32.25 | 230 | 262 |
| 1760 | 8" | " | 41.75 | 320 | 362 |
| **02510.60** | **PLASTIC PIPE** | | | | |
| 0110 | PVC, class 150 pipe | | | | |
| 0120 | 4" dia. | L.F. | 5.67 | 3.80 | 9.47 |
| 0130 | 6" dia. | " | 6.13 | 7.19 | 13.32 |
| 0140 | 8" dia. | " | 6.48 | 11.50 | 17.98 |
| 0165 | Schedule 40 pipe | | | | |
| 0170 | 1-1/2" dia. | L.F. | 2.46 | 0.95 | 3.41 |
| 0180 | 2" dia. | " | 2.61 | 1.41 | 4.02 |
| 0185 | 2-1/2" dia. | " | 2.78 | 2.15 | 4.93 |
| 0190 | 3" dia. | " | 2.98 | 2.92 | 5.90 |
| 0200 | 4" dia. | " | 3.48 | 4.13 | 7.61 |
| 0210 | 6" dia. | " | 4.18 | 7.78 | 11.96 |
| 0240 | 90 degree elbows | | | | |
| 0250 | 1" | EA. | 6.97 | 0.93 | 7.90 |
| 0260 | 1-1/2" | " | 6.97 | 1.76 | 8.73 |
| 0270 | 2" | " | 7.60 | 2.77 | 10.37 |
| 0280 | 2-1/2" | " | 8.36 | 8.44 | 16.80 |
| 0290 | 3" | " | 9.29 | 10.00 | 19.29 |
| 0300 | 4" | " | 10.50 | 18.00 | 28.50 |
| 0310 | 6" | " | 14.00 | 57.00 | 71.00 |

# DIVISION # 02 SITE CONSTRUCTION

| | | UNIT | LABOR | MAT. | TOTAL |
|---|---|---|---|---|---|
| **02510.60** | **PLASTIC PIPE, Cont'd...** | | | | |
| 0500 | Couplings | | | | |
| 0510 | 1" | EA. | 6.97 | 0.75 | 7.72 |
| 0520 | 1-1/2" | " | 6.97 | 1.07 | 8.04 |
| 0530 | 2" | " | 7.60 | 1.65 | 9.25 |
| 0540 | 2-1/2" | " | 8.36 | 3.65 | 12.01 |
| 0550 | 3" | " | 9.29 | 5.72 | 15.01 |
| 0560 | 4" | " | 10.50 | 8.27 | 18.77 |
| 0580 | 6" | " | 14.00 | 26.25 | 40.25 |
| **02530.20** | **VITRIFIED CLAY PIPE** | | | | |
| 0100 | Vitrified clay pipe, extra strength | | | | |
| 1020 | 6" dia. | L.F. | 10.25 | 5.21 | 15.46 |
| 1040 | 8" dia. | " | 10.75 | 6.24 | 16.99 |
| 1050 | 10" dia. | " | 11.25 | 9.57 | 20.82 |
| **02530.30** | **MANHOLES** | | | | |
| 0100 | Precast sections, 48" dia. | | | | |
| 0110 | Base section | EA. | 190 | 330 | 520 |
| 0120 | 1'0" riser | " | 150 | 93.00 | 243 |
| 0130 | 1'4" riser | " | 160 | 110 | 270 |
| 0140 | 2'8" riser | " | 170 | 170 | 340 |
| 0150 | 4'0" riser | " | 190 | 310 | 500 |
| 0160 | 2'8" cone top | " | 230 | 200 | 430 |
| 0170 | Precast manholes, 48" dia. | | | | |
| 0180 | 4' deep | EA. | 450 | 640 | 1,090 |
| 0200 | 6' deep | " | 570 | 970 | 1,540 |
| 0250 | 7' deep | " | 650 | 1,110 | 1,760 |
| 0260 | 8' deep | " | 760 | 1,250 | 2,010 |
| 0280 | 10' deep | " | 910 | 1,400 | 2,310 |
| 1000 | Cast-in-place, 48" dia., with frame and cover | | | | |
| 1100 | 5' deep | EA. | 1,130 | 600 | 1,730 |
| 1120 | 6' deep | " | 1,300 | 790 | 2,090 |
| 1140 | 8' deep | " | 1,510 | 1,150 | 2,660 |
| 1160 | 10' deep | " | 1,810 | 1,340 | 3,150 |
| 1480 | Brick manholes, 48" dia. with cover, 8" thick | | | | |
| 1500 | 4' deep | EA. | 510 | 640 | 1,150 |
| 1501 | 6' deep | " | 570 | 800 | 1,370 |
| 1505 | 8' deep | " | 640 | 1,020 | 1,660 |
| 1510 | 10' deep | " | 730 | 1,270 | 2,000 |
| 4200 | Frames and covers, 24" diameter | | | | |
| 4210 | 300 lb | EA. | 41.75 | 370 | 412 |
| 4220 | 400 lb | " | 46.50 | 390 | 437 |
| 4980 | Steps for manholes | | | | |
| 5000 | 7" x 9" | EA. | 8.36 | 12.50 | 20.86 |
| 5020 | 8" x 9" | " | 9.29 | 16.00 | 25.29 |
| **02530.40** | **SANITARY SEWERS** | | | | |
| 0980 | Clay | | | | |
| 1000 | 6" pipe | L.F. | 7.56 | 5.44 | 13.00 |
| 2980 | PVC | | | | |
| 3000 | 4" pipe | L.F. | 5.67 | 2.74 | 8.41 |
| 3010 | 6" pipe | " | 5.96 | 5.49 | 11.45 |

© 2011 By Design & Construction Resources

# DIVISION # 02  SITE CONSTRUCTION

| | | UNIT | LABOR | MAT. | TOTAL |
|---|---|---|---|---|---|
| **02540.10** | **DRAINAGE FIELDS** | | | | |
| 0080 | Perforated PVC pipe, for drain field | | | | |
| 0100 | 4" pipe | L.F. | 5.04 | 2.05 | 7.09 |
| 0120 | 6" pipe | " | 5.40 | 3.85 | 9.25 |
| **02540.50** | **SEPTIC TANKS** | | | | |
| 0980 | Septic tank, precast concrete | | | | |
| 1000 | 1000 gals | EA. | 380 | 750 | 1,130 |
| 1200 | 2000 gals | " | 570 | 2,420 | 2,990 |
| 1310 | Leaching pit, precast concrete, 72" diameter | | | | |
| 1320 | 3' deep | EA. | 280 | 690 | 970 |
| 1340 | 6' deep | " | 320 | 1,210 | 1,530 |
| 1360 | 8' deep | " | 380 | 1,540 | 1,920 |
| **02630.70** | **UNDERDRAIN** | | | | |
| 1480 | Drain tile, clay | | | | |
| 1500 | 6" pipe | L.F. | 5.04 | 4.52 | 9.56 |
| 1520 | 8" pipe | " | 5.27 | 7.21 | 12.48 |
| 1580 | Porous concrete, standard strength | | | | |
| 1600 | 6" pipe | L.F. | 5.04 | 4.07 | 9.11 |
| 1620 | 8" pipe | " | 5.27 | 4.40 | 9.67 |
| 1800 | Corrugated metal pipe, perforated type | | | | |
| 1810 | 6" pipe | L.F. | 5.67 | 5.64 | 11.31 |
| 1820 | 8" pipe | " | 5.96 | 6.66 | 12.62 |
| 1980 | Perforated clay pipe | | | | |
| 2000 | 6" pipe | L.F. | 6.48 | 5.44 | 11.92 |
| 2020 | 8" pipe | " | 6.67 | 7.29 | 13.96 |
| 2480 | Drain tile, concrete | | | | |
| 2500 | 6" pipe | L.F. | 5.04 | 3.23 | 8.27 |
| 2520 | 8" pipe | " | 5.27 | 5.02 | 10.29 |
| 4980 | Perforated rigid PVC underdrain pipe | | | | |
| 5000 | 4" pipe | L.F. | 3.78 | 1.91 | 5.69 |
| 5100 | 6" pipe | " | 4.53 | 3.66 | 8.19 |
| 5150 | 8" pipe | " | 5.04 | 5.60 | 10.64 |
| 6980 | Underslab drainage, crushed stone | | | | |
| 7000 | 3" thick | S.F. | 0.75 | 0.25 | 1.00 |
| 7120 | 4" thick | " | 0.87 | 0.34 | 1.21 |
| 7140 | 6" thick | " | 0.94 | 0.51 | 1.45 |
| 7180 | Plastic filter fabric for drain lines | " | 0.41 | 0.15 | 0.56 |
| **02740.20** | **ASPHALT SURFACES** | | | | |
| 0050 | Asphalt wearing surface, flexible pavement | | | | |
| 0100 | 1" thick | S.Y. | 2.25 | 3.90 | 6.15 |
| 0120 | 1-1/2" thick | " | 2.70 | 5.90 | 8.60 |
| 1000 | Binder course | | | | |
| 1010 | 1-1/2" thick | S.Y. | 2.50 | 5.59 | 8.09 |
| 1030 | 2" thick | " | 3.06 | 7.42 | 10.48 |
| 2000 | Bituminous sidewalk, no base | | | | |
| 2020 | 2" thick | S.Y. | 2.66 | 8.51 | 11.17 |
| 2040 | 3" thick | " | 2.83 | 12.75 | 15.58 |
| **02750.10** | **CONCRETE PAVING** | | | | |
| 1080 | Concrete paving, reinforced, 5000 psi concrete | | | | |
| 2000 | 6" thick | S.Y. | 21.00 | 23.75 | 44.75 |
| 2005 | 7" thick | " | 22.50 | 27.75 | 50.25 |
| 2010 | 8" thick | " | 24.00 | 31.75 | 55.75 |

# DIVISION # 02  SITE CONSTRUCTION

| | | UNIT | LABOR | MAT. | TOTAL |
|---|---|---|---|---|---|
| **02810.40** | **LAWN IRRIGATION** | | | | |
| 0480 | Residential system, complete | | | | |
| 0500 |     Minimum | ACRE | | | 15,940 |
| 0520 |     Maximum | " | | | 30,340 |
| **02820.10** | **CHAIN LINK FENCE** | | | | |
| 0230 | Chain link fence, 9 ga., galvanized, with posts 10' o.c. | | | | |
| 0250 |     4' high | L.F. | 2.98 | 6.71 | 9.69 |
| 0260 |     5' high | " | 3.80 | 8.97 | 12.77 |
| 0270 |     6' high | " | 5.23 | 10.25 | 15.48 |
| 1161 | Fabric, galvanized chain link, 2" mesh, 9 ga. | | | | |
| 1163 |     4' high | L.F. | 1.39 | 3.65 | 5.04 |
| 1164 |     5' high | " | 1.67 | 4.46 | 6.13 |
| 1165 |     6' high | " | 2.09 | 6.24 | 8.33 |
| **02820.20** | **WOOD FENCE** | | | | |
| 0010 | 4X4 posts w/2x4 horizontals, 4' -8' high | | | | |
| 0020 |     Cedar, 1x4 planks, picket | S.F. | 1.04 | 1.93 | 2.97 |
| 0030 |     1x6 planks, privacy | " | 0.83 | 3.07 | 3.90 |
| 0040 |     1x8 planks, privacy | " | 0.76 | 2.80 | 3.56 |
| 0050 |     Redwood, 1x4 planks, picket | " | 1.04 | 1.57 | 2.61 |
| 0060 |     1x6 planks, privacy | " | 0.83 | 2.91 | 3.74 |
| 0070 |     1x8 planks | " | 0.76 | 2.54 | 3.30 |
| 0080 |     Treated pine, 1x4 planks, picket | " | 1.04 | 1.54 | 2.58 |
| 0100 |     1x6 planks, privacy | " | 0.83 | 1.51 | 2.34 |
| 0110 |     1x8 planks, privacy | " | 0.76 | 1.48 | 2.24 |
| 0210 | 4' high | | | | |
| 0220 |     Composite, 1x4 planks, picket | S.F. | 1.30 | 1.69 | 2.99 |
| 0230 |     1x6 planks, privacy | " | 1.04 | 2.91 | 3.95 |
| 0240 |     1x8 planks | " | 0.87 | 2.54 | 3.41 |
| 0250 |     Vinyl, 1x4 planks, picket | " | 1.30 | 1.51 | 2.81 |
| 0260 |     1x6 planks, privacy | " | 1.04 | 2.68 | 3.72 |
| 0270 |     1x8 planks, privacy | " | 0.87 | 2.63 | 3.50 |
| 0280 |     Gate, cedar or redwood, 3' w, 1x4 planks, picket | EA. | 34.75 | 26.50 | 61.25 |
| 0290 |     1x6 planks, privacy | " | 41.75 | 73.00 | 115 |
| 0300 |     1x8 planks, privacy | " | 46.50 | 83.00 | 130 |
| **02840.40** | **PARKING BARRIERS** | | | | |
| 3010 | Bollard, conc. filled, 8' long | | | | |
| 3020 |     6" dia. | EA. | 35.50 | 410 | 446 |
| 3030 |     8" dia. | " | 44.50 | 610 | 655 |
| 3040 |     12" dia. | " | 53.00 | 780 | 833 |
| **02880.70** | **RECREATIONAL COURTS** | | | | |
| 1000 | Walls, galvanized steel | | | | |
| 1020 |     8' high | L.F. | 8.36 | 14.50 | 22.86 |
| 1040 |     10' high | " | 9.29 | 17.25 | 26.54 |
| 1060 |     12' high | " | 11.00 | 19.75 | 30.75 |
| 1200 | Vinyl coated | | | | |
| 1220 |     8' high | L.F. | 8.36 | 13.75 | 22.11 |
| 1240 |     10' high | " | 9.29 | 17.00 | 26.29 |
| 1260 |     12' high | " | 11.00 | 18.75 | 29.75 |
| 2010 | Gates, galvanized steel | | | | |
| 2200 |     Single, 3' transom | | | | |
| 2210 |         3'x7' | EA. | 210 | 340 | 550 |
| 2220 |         4'x7' | " | 240 | 360 | 600 |

© 2011 By Design & Construction Resources

# DIVISION # 02  SITE CONSTRUCTION

| | | UNIT | LABOR | MAT. | TOTAL |
|---|---|---|---|---|---|
| **02880.70** | **RECREATIONAL COURTS, Cont'd...** | | | | |
| 2230 | 5'x7' | EA. | 280 | 490 | 770 |
| 2240 | 6'x7' | " | 330 | 530 | 860 |
| 2400 | Vinyl coated | | | | |
| 2405 | Single, 3' transom | | | | |
| 2410 | 3'x7' | EA. | 210 | 660 | 870 |
| 2420 | 4'x7' | " | 240 | 720 | 960 |
| 2430 | 5'x7' | " | 280 | 720 | 1,000 |
| 2440 | 6'x7' | " | 330 | 740 | 1,070 |
| **02910.10** | **TOPSOIL** | | | | |
| 0005 | Spread topsoil, with equipment | | | | |
| 0010 | Minimum | C.Y. | 12.25 | | 12.25 |
| 0020 | Maximum | " | 15.50 | | 15.50 |
| 0080 | By hand | | | | |
| 0100 | Minimum | C.Y. | 41.75 | | 41.75 |
| 0110 | Maximum | " | 52.00 | | 52.00 |
| 0980 | Area prep. seeding (grade, rake and clean) | | | | |
| 1000 | Square yard | S.Y. | 0.33 | | 0.33 |
| 1020 | By acre | ACRE | 1,670 | | 1,670 |
| 2000 | Remove topsoil and stockpile on site | | | | |
| 2020 | 4" deep | C.Y. | 10.25 | | 10.25 |
| 2040 | 6" deep | " | 9.48 | | 9.48 |
| 2200 | Spreading topsoil from stock pile | | | | |
| 2220 | By loader | C.Y. | 11.25 | | 11.25 |
| 2240 | By hand | " | 120 | | 120 |
| 2260 | Top dress by hand | S.Y. | 1.23 | | 1.23 |
| 2280 | Place imported top soil | | | | |
| 2300 | By loader | | | | |
| 2320 | 4" deep | S.Y. | 1.23 | | 1.23 |
| 2340 | 6" deep | " | 1.36 | | 1.36 |
| 2360 | By hand | | | | |
| 2370 | 4" deep | S.Y. | 4.64 | | 4.64 |
| 2380 | 6" deep | " | 5.23 | | 5.23 |
| 5980 | Plant bed preparation, 18" deep | | | | |
| 6000 | With backhoe/loader | S.Y. | 3.08 | | 3.08 |
| 6010 | By hand | " | 6.97 | | 6.97 |
| **02920.10** | **FERTILIZING** | | | | |
| 0080 | Fertilizing (23#/1000 sf) | | | | |
| 0100 | By square yard | S.Y. | 0.13 | 0.03 | 0.16 |
| 0120 | By acre | ACRE | 680 | 160 | 840 |
| 2980 | Liming (70#/1000 sf) | | | | |
| 3000 | By square yard | S.Y. | 0.18 | 0.03 | 0.21 |
| 3020 | By acre | ACRE | 910 | 160 | 1,070 |
| **02920.30** | **SEEDING** | | | | |
| 0980 | Mechanical seeding, 175 lb/acre | | | | |
| 1000 | By square yard | S.Y. | 0.10 | 0.19 | 0.29 |
| 1020 | By acre | ACRE | 540 | 770 | 1,310 |
| 2040 | 450 lb/acre | | | | |
| 2060 | By square yard | S.Y. | 0.13 | 0.49 | 0.62 |
| 2080 | By acre | ACRE | 680 | 1,910 | 2,590 |
| 5980 | Seeding by hand, 10 lb per 100 s.y. | | | | |
| 6000 | By square yard | S.Y. | 0.13 | 0.55 | 0.68 |

# DIVISION # 02 SITE CONSTRUCTION

| | | UNIT | LABOR | MAT. | TOTAL |
|---|---|---|---|---|---|
| **02920.30** | **SEEDING, Cont'd...** | | | | |
| 6010 | By acre | ACRE | 700 | 2,130 | 2,830 |
| 8010 | Reseed disturbed areas | S.F. | 0.20 | 0.05 | 0.25 |
| **02935.10** | **SHRUB & TREE MAINTENANCE** | | | | |
| 1000 | Moving shrubs on site | | | | |
| 1220 | 3' high | EA. | 41.75 | | 41.75 |
| 1240 | 4' high | " | 46.50 | | 46.50 |
| 2000 | Moving trees on site | | | | |
| 3060 | 6' high | EA. | 50.00 | | 50.00 |
| 3080 | 8' high | " | 57.00 | | 57.00 |
| 3100 | 10' high | " | 76.00 | | 76.00 |
| 3110 | Palm trees | | | | |
| 3140 | 10' high | EA. | 76.00 | | 76.00 |
| 3144 | 40' high | " | 450 | | 450 |
| **02935.30** | **WEED CONTROL** | | | | |
| 1000 | Weed control, bromicil, 15 lb./acre, wettable powder | ACRE | 210 | 290 | 500 |
| 1100 | Vegetation control, by application of plant killer | S.Y. | 0.16 | 0.02 | 0.18 |
| 1200 | Weed killer, lawns and fields | " | 0.08 | 0.24 | 0.32 |
| **02945.20** | **LANDSCAPE ACCESSORIES** | | | | |
| 0100 | Steel edging, 3/16" x 4" | L.F. | 0.52 | 0.64 | 1.16 |
| 0200 | Landscaping stepping stones, 15"x15", white | EA. | 2.09 | 5.83 | 7.92 |
| 6000 | Wood chip mulch | C.Y. | 28.00 | 40.75 | 68.75 |
| 6010 | 2" thick | S.Y. | 0.83 | 2.49 | 3.32 |
| 6020 | 4" thick | " | 1.19 | 4.70 | 5.89 |
| 6030 | 6" thick | " | 1.52 | 7.03 | 8.55 |
| 6200 | Gravel mulch, 3/4" stone | C.Y. | 41.75 | 32.25 | 74.00 |
| 6300 | White marble chips, 1" deep | S.F. | 0.41 | 0.64 | 1.05 |
| 6980 | Peat moss | | | | |
| 7000 | 2" thick | S.Y. | 0.92 | 3.46 | 4.38 |
| 7020 | 4" thick | " | 1.39 | 6.66 | 8.05 |
| 7030 | 6" thick | " | 1.74 | 10.25 | 11.99 |
| 7980 | Landscaping timbers, treated lumber | | | | |
| 8000 | 4" x 4" | L.F. | 1.39 | 1.35 | 2.74 |
| 8020 | 6" x 6" | " | 1.49 | 2.69 | 4.18 |
| 8040 | 8" x 8" | " | 1.74 | 4.40 | 6.14 |

© 2011 By Design & Construction Resources

# DIVISION # 02 SITE CONSTRUCTION - QUICK ESTIMATING

| | | UNIT | COST |
|---|---|---|---|
| **02999.10 DEMOLITION** | | | |
| 3200 | Selective Building Removals | | |
| 3210 | No Cutting or Disposal Included | | |
| 3220 | Concrete - Hand Work | | |
| 3230 | 8" Walls - Reinforced | S.F. | 14.25 |
| 3240 | Non - Reinforced | " | 9.45 |
| 3250 | 12" Walls - Reinforced | " | 22.75 |
| 3260 | 12" Footings x 24" wide | L.F. | 20.50 |
| 3270 | x 36" wide | " | 28.25 |
| 3280 | 16" Footings x 24" wide | S.F. | 37.75 |
| 3290 | 6" Structural Slab - Reinforced | " | 8.72 |
| 3300 | 8" Structural Slab - Reinforced | " | 10.75 |
| 3310 | 4" Slab on Ground - Reinforced | " | 4.05 |
| 3320 | Non - Reinforced | " | 3.02 |
| 3330 | 6" Slab on Ground - Reinforced | " | 4.82 |
| 3340 | Non - Reinforced | " | 3.60 |
| 3350 | Stairs - Reinforced | " | 15.00 |
| 3360 | Masonry - Hand Work | | |
| 3370 | 4" Brick or Stone Walls | S.F. | 2.73 |
| 3380 | 4" Brick and 8" Backup Block or Tile | " | 5.04 |
| 3390 | 4" Block or Tile Partitions | " | 2.66 |
| 3400 | 6" Block or Tile Partitions | " | 2.90 |
| 3410 | 8" Block or Tile Partitions | " | 3.33 |
| 3420 | 12" Block or Tile Partitions | " | 4.20 |
| 3430 | Miscellaneous - Hand Work | | |
| 3440 | Acoustical Ceilings - Attached | S.F. | 0.78 |
| 3450 | Suspended (Including Grid) | " | 0.44 |
| 3460 | Asbestos - Pipe | L.F. | 57.00 |
| 3470 | Ceilings and Walls | S.F. | 19.00 |
| 3480 | Columns and Beams | " | 45.25 |
| 3490 | Tile Flooring | " | 2.11 |
| 3500 | Cabinets and Tops | L.F. | 12.50 |
| 3510 | Carpet | S.F. | 0.39 |
| 3520 | Ceramic and Quarry Tile | " | 1.51 |
| 3530 | Doors and Frames - Metal | EA. | 67.00 |
| 3540 | Wood | " | 57.00 |
| 3550 | Drywall Ceilings - Attached | S.F. | 0.94 |
| 3560 | Drywall on Wood or Metal Studs - 2 Sides | " | 1.06 |
| 3570 | Paint Removal - Doors and Windows | " | 0.94 |
| 3580 | Walls | " | 0.78 |
| 3590 | Plaster Ceilings - Attached (Including Iron) | " | 1.34 |
| 3600 | on Wood or Metal Studs | " | 1.28 |
| 3610 | Roofing - Builtup | " | 1.28 |
| 3620 | Shingles - Asphalt and Wood | " | 0.44 |
| 3630 | Terrazzo Flooring | " | 2.12 |
| 3640 | Vinyl Flooring | " | 0.44 |
| 3650 | Wall Coverings | " | 0.84 |
| 3660 | Windows | EA. | 45.25 |
| 3670 | Wood Flooring | S.F. | 0.44 |
| 4300 | Site Removals (Including Loading) | | |
| 4310 | 4" Concrete Walks - Labor Only (Non-Reinforced) | S.F. | 3.02 |
| 4320 | Machine Only (Non-Reinforced) | " | 1.00 |
| 4330 | 6" Concrete Drives - Labor Only (Non-Reinforced) | " | 3.78 |

# DIVISION # 02 SITE CONSTRUCTION - QUICK ESTIMATING

| | | UNIT | COST |
|---|---|---|---|
| **02999.10** | **DEMOLITION, Cont'd...** | | |
| 4340 | Machine Only (Reinforced) | S.F. | 1.34 |
| 4350 | 6" x 18" Concrete Curb - Machine | L.F. | 2.57 |
| 4360 | Curb and Gutter - Machine | " | 3.35 |
| 4370 | 2" Asphalt - Machine | S.F. | 0.58 |
| 4380 | Fencing - 8' Hand | L.F. | 3.46 |
| **02999.20** | **EARTHWORK** | | |
| 1000 | GRADING - Hand - 4" - Site | S.F. | 0.34 |
| 1010 | Hand – 4" Building | " | 0.58 |
| 2000 | EXCAVATION - Hand - Open - Soft (Sand) | C.Y. | 45.25 |
| 2010 | Medium (Clay) | " | 57.00 |
| 2020 | Hard (Shale) | " | 91.00 |
| 2030 | Add for Trench or Pocket | PCT. | 15.00 |
| 3000 | BACK FILL - Hand - Not Comp. (Site Borrow) | C.Y. | 20.50 |
| 4000 | BACK FILL - Hand - Comp.(Site Borrow) | | |
| 4010 | 12" Lifts - Building - No Machine | C.Y. | 35.00 |
| 4020 | With Machine | " | 28.25 |
| 4030 | 18" Lifts - Building - No Machine | " | 32.50 |
| 4040 | With Machine | " | 26.75 |
| **02999.50** | **DRAINAGE** | | |
| 4000 | BUILDING FOUNDATION DRAINAGE | | |
| 4010 | 4" Clay Pipe | L.F. | 8.90 |
| 4020 | 4" Plastic Pipe - Perforated | " | 7.17 |
| 4030 | 6" Clay Pipe | " | 10.10 |
| 4040 | 6" Plastic Pipe - Perforated | " | 11.40 |
| 4050 | Add for Porous Surround - 2' x 2' | " | 13.11 |
| **02999.60** | **PAVEMENT, CURBS AND WALKS** | | |
| 2000 | CURBS AND GUTTERS | | |
| 2100 | Concrete - Cast in Place ( Machine Placed ) | | |
| 2110 | Curb - 6" x 12" | L.F. | 20.43 |
| 2120 | 6" x 18" | " | 24.13 |
| 2130 | 6" x 24" | " | 27.72 |
| 2140 | 6" x 30" | " | 31.67 |
| 2150 | Curb and Gutter - 6" x 12" | " | 29.83 |
| 2160 | 6" x 18" | " | 35.25 |
| 2170 | 6" x 24" | " | 40.25 |
| 2180 | Add for Hand Placed | " | 9.45 |
| 2190 | Add for 2 #5 Reinf. Rods | " | 4.33 |
| 2191 | Add for Curves and Radius Work | PCT. | 40.00 |
| 2200 | Concrete Precast - 6" x 10" x 8" | L.F. | 22.36 |
| 2210 | 6" x 9" x 8" | " | 20.09 |
| 2250 | 6" x 8" | " | 17.82 |
| 2300 | Bituminous - 6" x 8" | " | 7.90 |
| 2400 | Granite - 6" x 16" | " | 64.75 |
| 2500 | Timbers - Treated - 6" x 6" | " | 14.88 |
| 2600 | Plastic - 6" x 6" | " | 19.36 |
| 3000 | WALKS | | |
| 3010 | Bituminous - 1 1/2" with 4" Sand Base | S.F. | 3.91 |
| 3020 | 2" with 4" Sand Base | " | 4.33 |
| 3030 | Concrete - 4" - Broom Finish | " | 7.17 |
| 3040 | 5" - Broom Finish | " | 8.15 |
| 3050 | 6" - Broom Finish | " | 9.22 |

© 2011 By Design & Construction Resources

## DIVISION # 02 SITE CONSTRUCTION - QUICK ESTIMATING

|  |  |  | UNIT | COST |
|---|---|---|---|---|
| **02999.60** | **PAVEMENT, CURBS AND WALKS, Cont'd...** | | | |
| 3060 | Add for 6" x 6", 10 - 10 Mesh | | S.F. | 1.67 |
| 3070 | Add for 4" Sand Base | | " | 1.44 |
| 3080 | Add for Exposed Aggregate | | " | 2.27 |
| 3090 | Crushed Rock - 4" | | " | 1.54 |
| 4000 | Brick - 4" - with 2" Sand Cushion | | " | 17.56 |
| 4010 | 4" - with 2" Mortar Setting Bed | | " | 20.72 |
| 4020 | Flagstone – 1 1/4" - with 4" Sand Cushion | | " | 28.55 |
| 4030 | 1¼" - with 2" Mortar Setting Bed | | " | 32.04 |
| 4040 | Precast Block - 1" Colored with 4" Sand Cushion | | " | 8.00 |
| 4050 | 2" Colored with 4" Sand Cushion | | " | 9.27 |
| 4060 | Wood - 2" Boards on 6" x 6" Timbers | | " | 14.13 |
| 4070 | 2" Boards on 4" x 4" Timbers | | " | 11.92 |
| 4080 | Slate - 1 1/4" - with 2" Mortar Setting Bed | | " | 38.50 |

# DIVISION # 03  CONCRETE

## TABLE OF CONTENTS  PAGE

| | |
|---|---|
| 03100.03 - FORMWORK ACCESSORIES | 03-2 |
| 03110.05 - BEAM FORMWORK | 03-2 |
| 03110.15 - COLUMN FORMWORK | 03-3 |
| 03110.18 - CURB FORMWORK | 03-3 |
| 03110.20 - ELEVATED SLAB FORMWORK | 03-3 |
| 03110.25 - EQUIPMENT PAD FORMWORK | 03-3 |
| 03110.35 - FOOTING FORMWORK | 03-3 |
| 03110.50 - GRADE BEAM FORMWORK | 03-4 |
| 03110.53 - PILE CAP FORMWORK | 03-4 |
| 03110.55 - SLAB / MAT FORMWORK | 03-4 |
| 03110.60 - STAIR FORMWORK | 03-4 |
| 03110.65 - WALL FORMWORK | 03-4 |
| 03110.70 - INSULATED CONCRETE FORMS | 03-5 |
| 03110.90 - MISCELLANEOUS FORMWORK | 03-5 |
| 03210.05 - BEAM REINFORCING | 03-6 |
| 03210.15 - COLUMN REINFORCING | 03-6 |
| 03210.20 - ELEVATED SLAB REINFORCING | 03-6 |
| 03210.25 - EQUIP. PAD REINFORCING | 03-6 |
| 03210.35 - FOOTING REINFORCING | 03-6 |
| 03210.45 - FOUNDATION REINFORCING | 03-7 |
| 03210.50 - GRADE BEAM REINFORCING | 03-7 |
| 03210.53 - PILE CAP REINFORCING | 03-7 |
| 03210.55 - SLAB / MAT REINFORCING | 03-7 |
| 03210.60 - STAIR REINFORCING | 03-8 |
| 03210.65 - WALL REINFORCING | 03-8 |
| 03250.40 - CONCRETE ACCESSORIES | 03-8 |
| 03300.10 - CONCRETE ADMIXTURES | 03-8 |
| 03350.10 - CONCRETE FINISHES | 03-8 |
| 03360.10 - PNEUMATIC CONCRETE | 03-9 |
| 03370.10 - CURING CONCRETE | 03-9 |
| 03380.05 - BEAM CONCRETE | 03-9 |
| 03380.15 - COLUMN CONCRETE | 03-9 |
| 03380.25 - EQUIPMENT PAD CONCRETE | 03-10 |
| 03380.35 - FOOTING CONCRETE | 03-10 |
| 03380.50 - GRADE BEAM CONCRETE | 03-10 |
| 03380.53 - PILE CAP CONCRETE | 03-10 |
| 03380.55 - SLAB / MAT CONCRETE | 03-10 |
| 03380.58 - SIDEWALKS | 03-11 |
| 03380.60 - STAIR CONCRETE | 03-11 |
| 03380.65 - WALL CONCRETE | 03-11 |
| 03550.10 - CONCRETE TOPPINGS | 03-12 |
| 03730.10 - CONCRETE REPAIR | 03-12 |
| QUICK ESTIMATING | 03A-14 |

© 2011 By Design & Construction Resources

# DIVISION # 03  CONCRETE

| | | UNIT | LABOR | MAT. | TOTAL |
|---|---|---|---|---|---|
| **03100.03** | **FORMWORK ACCESSORIES** | | | | |
| 1000 | Column clamps | | | | |
| 1010 | Small, adjustable, 24"x24" | EA. | | | 63.00 |
| 1020 | Medium 36"x36" | " | | | 65.00 |
| 1030 | Large 60"x60" | " | | | 66.00 |
| 2000 | Forming hangers | | | | |
| 2010 | Iron 14 ga. | EA. | | | 2.03 |
| 2020 | 22 ga. | " | | | 2.03 |
| 3000 | Snap ties | | | | |
| 3010 | Short-end with washers, 6" long | EA. | | | 1.26 |
| 3020 | 12" long | " | | | 1.43 |
| 4000 | 18" long | " | | | 1.70 |
| 4010 | 24" long | " | | | 1.83 |
| 4020 | Long-end with washers, 6' long | " | | | 1.48 |
| 4030 | 12" long | " | | | 1.65 |
| 4040 | 18" long | " | | | 1.87 |
| 4050 | 24" long | " | | | 2.09 |
| 5000 | Stakes | | | | |
| 5010 | Round, pre-drilled holes, 12" long | EA. | | | 4.52 |
| 5020 | 18" long | " | | | 5.06 |
| 5030 | 24" long | " | | | 6.49 |
| 5040 | 30" long | " | | | 8.41 |
| 5050 | 36" long | " | | | 10.25 |
| 5060 | 48" long | " | | | 13.75 |
| 5070 | I beam type, 12" long | " | | | 3.14 |
| 6000 | 18" long | " | | | 4.40 |
| 6010 | 24" long | " | | | 6.49 |
| 6020 | 30" long | " | | | 7.70 |
| 6030 | 36" long | " | | | 9.29 |
| 7000 | 48" long | " | | | 11.50 |
| 7010 | Taper ties | | | | |
| 7020 | 50K, 1-1/4" to 1", 35" long | EA. | | | 130 |
| 8000 | 45" long | " | | | 160 |
| 8010 | 55" long | " | | | 180 |
| 8020 | Walers | | | | |
| 8030 | 5" deep, 4' long | EA. | | | 190 |
| 8040 | 8' long | " | | | 250 |
| 8050 | 12' long | " | | | 420 |
| 9000 | 16' long | " | | | 540 |
| 9010 | 8" deep, 4' long | " | | | 260 |
| 9020 | 8' long | " | | | 570 |
| 9030 | 12' long | " | | | 680 |
| 9040 | 16' long | " | | | 1,080 |
| **03110.05** | **BEAM FORMWORK** | | | | |
| 1000 | Beam forms, job built | | | | |
| 1020 | Beam bottoms | | | | |
| 1040 | 1 use | S.F. | 8.89 | 4.14 | 13.03 |
| 1080 | 3 uses | " | 8.20 | 1.87 | 10.07 |
| 1120 | 5 uses | " | 7.62 | 1.41 | 9.03 |
| 2000 | Beam sides | | | | |
| 2020 | 1 use | S.F. | 5.92 | 2.95 | 8.87 |
| 2060 | 3 uses | " | 5.33 | 1.54 | 6.87 |

# DIVISION # 03 CONCRETE

| | | UNIT | LABOR | MAT. | TOTAL |
|---|---|---|---|---|---|
| **03110.05** | **BEAM FORMWORK, Cont'd...** | | | | |
| 2100 | 5 uses | S.F. | 4.85 | 1.25 | 6.10 |
| **03110.15** | **COLUMN FORMWORK** | | | | |
| 1000 | Column, square forms, job built | | | | |
| 1020 | 8" x 8" columns | | | | |
| 1040 | 1 use | S.F. | 10.75 | 3.25 | 14.00 |
| 1080 | 3 uses | " | 9.88 | 1.48 | 11.36 |
| 1120 | 5 uses | " | 9.20 | 1.15 | 10.35 |
| 1300 | 16" x 16" columns | | | | |
| 1320 | 1 use | S.F. | 8.89 | 2.83 | 11.72 |
| 1360 | 3 uses | " | 8.33 | 1.19 | 9.52 |
| 1390 | 5 uses | " | 7.84 | 0.90 | 8.74 |
| 2000 | Round fiber forms, 1 use | | | | |
| 2040 | 10" dia. | L.F. | 10.75 | 4.29 | 15.04 |
| 2120 | 18" dia. | " | 12.75 | 14.75 | 27.50 |
| 2180 | 36" dia. | " | 16.25 | 33.75 | 50.00 |
| **03110.18** | **CURB FORMWORK** | | | | |
| 0980 | Curb forms | | | | |
| 0990 | Straight, 6" high | | | | |
| 1000 | 1 use | L.F. | 5.33 | 1.90 | 7.23 |
| 1040 | 3 uses | " | 4.85 | 0.85 | 5.70 |
| 1080 | 5 uses | " | 4.44 | 0.69 | 5.13 |
| 1090 | Curved, 6" high | | | | |
| 2000 | 1 use | L.F. | 6.67 | 2.05 | 8.72 |
| 2040 | 3 uses | " | 5.92 | 0.99 | 6.91 |
| 2080 | 5 uses | " | 5.44 | 0.83 | 6.27 |
| **03110.20** | **ELEVATED SLAB FORMWORK** | | | | |
| 0100 | Elevated slab formwork | | | | |
| 1000 | Slab, with drop panels | | | | |
| 1020 | 1 use | S.F. | 4.26 | 3.42 | 7.68 |
| 1060 | 3 uses | " | 3.95 | 1.54 | 5.49 |
| 1100 | 5 uses | " | 3.68 | 1.22 | 4.90 |
| 2000 | Floor slab, hung from steel beams | | | | |
| 2020 | 1 use | S.F. | 4.10 | 2.75 | 6.85 |
| 2060 | 3 uses | " | 3.81 | 1.37 | 5.18 |
| 2100 | 5 uses | " | 3.55 | 1.01 | 4.56 |
| 3000 | Floor slab, with pans or domes | | | | |
| 3020 | 1 use | S.F. | 4.85 | 4.90 | 9.75 |
| 3060 | 3 uses | " | 4.44 | 2.97 | 7.41 |
| 3100 | 5 uses | " | 4.10 | 2.45 | 6.55 |
| 9030 | Equipment curbs, 12" high | | | | |
| 9035 | 1 use | L.F. | 5.33 | 2.53 | 7.86 |
| 9060 | 3 uses | " | 4.85 | 1.41 | 6.26 |
| 9100 | 5 uses | " | 4.44 | 1.10 | 5.54 |
| **03110.25** | **EQUIPMENT PAD FORMWORK** | | | | |
| 1000 | Equipment pad, job built | | | | |
| 1020 | 1 use | S.F. | 6.67 | 3.30 | 9.97 |
| 1040 | 2 uses | " | 6.27 | 1.98 | 8.25 |
| 1060 | 3 uses | " | 5.92 | 1.59 | 7.51 |

© 2011 By Design & Construction Resources

# DIVISION # 03 CONCRETE

| | | UNIT | LABOR | MAT. | TOTAL |
|---|---|---|---|---|---|
| **03110.35** | **FOOTING FORMWORK** | | | | |
| 2000 | Wall footings, job built, continuous | | | | |
| 2040 | 1 use | S.F. | 5.33 | 1.56 | 6.89 |
| 2060 | 3 uses | " | 4.85 | 0.90 | 5.75 |
| 2090 | 5 uses | " | 4.44 | 0.69 | 5.13 |
| 3000 | Column footings, spread | | | | |
| 3020 | 1 use | S.F. | 6.67 | 1.65 | 8.32 |
| 3060 | 3 uses | " | 5.92 | 0.88 | 6.80 |
| 3100 | 5 uses | " | 5.33 | 0.67 | 6.00 |
| **03110.50** | **GRADE BEAM FORMWORK** | | | | |
| 1000 | Grade beams, job built | | | | |
| 1020 | 1 use | S.F. | 5.33 | 2.45 | 7.78 |
| 1060 | 3 uses | " | 4.85 | 1.07 | 5.92 |
| 1100 | 5 uses | " | 4.44 | 0.74 | 5.18 |
| **03110.53** | **PILE CAP FORMWORK** | | | | |
| 1500 | Pile cap forms, job built | | | | |
| 1510 | Square | | | | |
| 1520 | 1 use | S.F. | 6.67 | 2.79 | 9.46 |
| 1560 | 3 uses | " | 5.92 | 1.28 | 7.20 |
| 1600 | 5 uses | " | 5.33 | 0.93 | 6.26 |
| **03110.55** | **SLAB / MAT FORMWORK** | | | | |
| 3000 | Mat foundations, job built | | | | |
| 3020 | 1 use | S.F. | 6.67 | 2.44 | 9.11 |
| 3060 | 3 uses | " | 5.92 | 1.03 | 6.95 |
| 3100 | 5 uses | " | 5.33 | 0.70 | 6.03 |
| 3980 | Edge forms | | | | |
| 3990 | 6" high | | | | |
| 4000 | 1 use | L.F. | 4.85 | 2.45 | 7.30 |
| 4002 | 3 uses | " | 4.44 | 1.03 | 5.47 |
| 4004 | 5 uses | " | 4.10 | 0.70 | 4.80 |
| 4014 | 5 uses | " | 4.44 | 0.64 | 5.08 |
| 5000 | Formwork for openings | | | | |
| 5020 | 1 use | S.F. | 10.75 | 3.30 | 14.05 |
| 5060 | 3 uses | " | 8.89 | 1.59 | 10.48 |
| 5100 | 5 uses | " | 7.62 | 1.02 | 8.64 |
| **03110.60** | **STAIR FORMWORK** | | | | |
| 1000 | Stairway forms, job built | | | | |
| 1020 | 1 use | S.F. | 10.75 | 4.16 | 14.91 |
| 1040 | 3 uses | " | 8.89 | 1.81 | 10.70 |
| 1060 | 5 uses | " | 7.62 | 1.39 | 9.01 |
| **03110.65** | **WALL FORMWORK** | | | | |
| 2980 | Wall forms, exterior, job built | | | | |
| 3000 | Up to 8' high wall | | | | |
| 3120 | 1 use | S.F. | 5.33 | 2.70 | 8.03 |
| 3160 | 3 uses | " | 4.85 | 1.32 | 6.17 |
| 3190 | 5 uses | " | 4.44 | 0.99 | 5.43 |
| 3200 | Over 8' high wall | | | | |
| 3220 | 1 use | S.F. | 6.67 | 2.97 | 9.64 |
| 3240 | 3 uses | " | 5.92 | 1.55 | 7.47 |
| 3290 | 5 uses | " | 5.33 | 1.22 | 6.55 |
| 5000 | Column pier and pilaster | | | | |
| 5020 | 1 use | S.F. | 10.75 | 2.97 | 13.72 |

# DIVISION # 03 CONCRETE

| | | UNIT | LABOR | MAT. | TOTAL |
|---|---|---|---|---|---|
| **03110.65** | **WALL FORMWORK, Cont'd...** | | | | |
| 5060 | 3 uses | S.F. | 8.89 | 1.63 | 10.52 |
| 5090 | 5 uses | " | 7.62 | 1.34 | 8.96 |
| 6980 | Interior wall forms | | | | |
| 7000 | Up to 8' high | | | | |
| 7020 | 1 use | S.F. | 4.85 | 2.70 | 7.55 |
| 7060 | 3 uses | " | 4.44 | 1.34 | 5.78 |
| 7100 | 5 uses | " | 4.10 | 0.96 | 5.06 |
| 7200 | Over 8' high | | | | |
| 7220 | 1 use | S.F. | 5.92 | 2.97 | 8.89 |
| 7260 | 3 uses | " | 5.33 | 1.55 | 6.88 |
| 7290 | 5 uses | " | 4.85 | 1.23 | 6.08 |
| 9000 | PVC form liner, per side, smooth finish | | | | |
| 9010 | 1 use | S.F. | 4.44 | 6.95 | 11.39 |
| 9030 | 3 uses | " | 4.10 | 3.23 | 7.33 |
| 9050 | 5 uses | " | 3.55 | 1.99 | 5.54 |
| **03110.70** | **INSULATED CONCRETE FORMS** | | | | |
| 0010 | 4" thick, straight | S.F. | 1.66 | 4.01 | 5.67 |
| 0020 | 90° corner | " | 1.66 | 4.01 | 5.67 |
| 0030 | 45° angle | " | 1.66 | 4.40 | 6.06 |
| 1000 | 6" thick, straight | " | 1.66 | 4.07 | 5.73 |
| 1010 | 90° corner | " | 1.66 | 4.07 | 5.73 |
| 1020 | 45° angle | " | 1.66 | 4.40 | 6.06 |
| 1030 | 6" thick, corbel ledge | " | 1.66 | 5.06 | 6.72 |
| 1040 | T-block | " | 1.66 | 4.54 | 6.20 |
| 2000 | 8" thick, straight | " | 1.66 | 4.18 | 5.84 |
| 2010 | 90° corner | " | 1.66 | 4.07 | 5.73 |
| 2020 | 45° angle | " | 1.66 | 4.67 | 6.33 |
| 2030 | corbel ledge | " | 1.66 | 5.22 | 6.88 |
| 2040 | T-block | " | 1.66 | 4.80 | 6.46 |
| **03110.90** | **MISCELLANEOUS FORMWORK** | | | | |
| 1200 | Keyway forms (5 uses) | | | | |
| 1220 | 2 x 4 | L.F. | 2.66 | 0.22 | 2.88 |
| 1240 | 2 x 6 | " | 2.96 | 0.33 | 3.29 |
| 1500 | Bulkheads | | | | |
| 1510 | Walls, with keyways | | | | |
| 1515 | 2 piece | L.F. | 4.85 | 3.69 | 8.54 |
| 1520 | 3 piece | " | 5.33 | 4.67 | 10.00 |
| 1560 | Elevated slab, with keyway | | | | |
| 1570 | 2 piece | L.F. | 4.44 | 4.23 | 8.67 |
| 1580 | 3 piece | " | 4.85 | 6.23 | 11.08 |
| 1600 | Ground slab, with keyway | | | | |
| 1620 | 2 piece | L.F. | 3.81 | 4.37 | 8.18 |
| 1640 | 3 piece | " | 4.10 | 5.34 | 9.44 |
| 2000 | Chamfer strips | | | | |
| 2020 | Wood | | | | |
| 2040 | 1/2" wide | L.F. | 1.18 | 0.20 | 1.38 |
| 2060 | 3/4" wide | " | 1.18 | 0.27 | 1.45 |
| 2070 | 1" wide | " | 1.18 | 0.36 | 1.54 |
| 2100 | PVC | | | | |
| 2120 | 1/2" wide | L.F. | 1.18 | 0.93 | 2.11 |
| 2140 | 3/4" wide | " | 1.18 | 1.02 | 2.20 |

© 2011 By Design & Construction Resources

# DIVISION # 03  CONCRETE

| | | UNIT | LABOR | MAT. | TOTAL |
|---|---|---|---|---|---|
| **03110.90** | **MISCELLANEOUS FORMWORK, Cont'd...** | | | | |
| 2160 | 1" wide | L.F. | 1.18 | 1.47 | 2.65 |
| 2170 | Radius | | | | |
| 2180 | 1" | L.F. | 1.27 | 1.10 | 2.37 |
| 2200 | 1-1/2" | " | 1.27 | 1.98 | 3.25 |
| 3000 | Reglets | | | | |
| 3020 | Galvanized steel, 24 ga. | L.F. | 2.13 | 1.43 | 3.56 |
| 5000 | Metal formwork | | | | |
| 5020 | Straight edge forms | | | | |
| 5080 | 8" high | L.F. | 3.81 | 26.25 | 30.06 |
| 5300 | Curb form, S-shape | | | | |
| 5310 | 12" x | | | | |
| 5340 | 2' | L.F. | 7.11 | 42.00 | 49.11 |
| 5380 | 3' | " | 5.92 | 49.75 | 55.67 |
| **03210.05** | **BEAM REINFORCING** | | | | |
| 0980 | Beam-girders | | | | |
| 1000 | #3 - #4 | TON | 1,360 | 1,310 | 2,670 |
| 1011 | #7 - #8 | " | 910 | 1,090 | 2,000 |
| 1018 | Galvanized | | | | |
| 1020 | #3 - #4 | TON | 1,360 | 2,230 | 3,590 |
| 1031 | #7 - #8 | " | 910 | 2,020 | 2,930 |
| 2000 | Bond Beams | | | | |
| 2100 | #3 - #4 | TON | 1,820 | 1,310 | 3,130 |
| 2120 | #7 - #8 | " | 1,210 | 1,090 | 2,300 |
| 2200 | Galvanized | | | | |
| 2210 | #3 - #4 | TON | 1,820 | 2,130 | 3,950 |
| 2230 | #7 - #8 | " | 1,210 | 2,020 | 3,230 |
| **03210.15** | **COLUMN REINFORCING** | | | | |
| 0980 | Columns | | | | |
| 1000 | #3 - #4 | TON | 1,560 | 1,310 | 2,870 |
| 1015 | #7 - #8 | " | 1,090 | 1,090 | 2,180 |
| 1100 | Galvanized | | | | |
| 1200 | #3 - #4 | TON | 1,560 | 2,230 | 3,790 |
| 1320 | #7 - #8 | " | 1,090 | 2,020 | 3,110 |
| **03210.20** | **ELEVATED SLAB REINFORCING** | | | | |
| 0980 | Elevated slab | | | | |
| 1000 | #3 - #4 | TON | 680 | 1,310 | 1,990 |
| 1040 | #7 - #8 | " | 550 | 1,090 | 1,640 |
| 1980 | Galvanized | | | | |
| 2000 | #3 - #4 | TON | 680 | 2,130 | 2,810 |
| 2040 | #7 - #8 | " | 550 | 2,020 | 2,570 |
| **03210.25** | **EQUIP. PAD REINFORCING** | | | | |
| 0980 | Equipment pad | | | | |
| 1000 | #3 - #4 | TON | 1,090 | 1,310 | 2,400 |
| 1040 | #7 - #8 | " | 910 | 1,090 | 2,000 |
| **03210.35** | **FOOTING REINFORCING** | | | | |
| 1000 | Footings | | | | |
| 1010 | Grade 50 | | | | |
| 1020 | #3 - #4 | TON | 910 | 1,310 | 2,220 |
| 1040 | #7 - #8 | " | 680 | 1,090 | 1,770 |
| 1055 | Grade 60 | | | | |
| 1060 | #3 - #4 | TON | 910 | 1,310 | 2,220 |

# DIVISION # 03 CONCRETE

| | | UNIT | LABOR | MAT. | TOTAL |
|---|---|---|---|---|---|
| **03210.35** | **FOOTING REINFORCING, Cont'd...** | | | | |
| 1074 | #7 - #8 | TON | 680 | 1,090 | 1,770 |
| 4980 | Straight dowels, 24" long | | | | |
| 5000 | 1" dia. (#8) | EA. | 5.45 | 4.06 | 9.51 |
| 5040 | 3/4" dia. (#6) | " | 5.45 | 3.65 | 9.10 |
| 5050 | 5/8" dia. (#5) | " | 4.54 | 3.16 | 7.70 |
| 5060 | 1/2" dia. (#4) | " | 3.89 | 2.37 | 6.26 |
| **03210.45** | **FOUNDATION REINFORCING** | | | | |
| 0980 | Foundations | | | | |
| 1000 | #3 - #4 | TON | 910 | 1,310 | 2,220 |
| 1040 | #7 - #8 | " | 680 | 1,090 | 1,770 |
| 1380 | Galvanized | | | | |
| 1400 | #3 - #4 | TON | 910 | 2,230 | 3,140 |
| 1420 | #7 - #8 | " | 680 | 2,020 | 2,700 |
| **03210.50** | **GRADE BEAM REINFORCING** | | | | |
| 0980 | Grade beams | | | | |
| 1000 | #3 - #4 | TON | 840 | 1,310 | 2,150 |
| 1040 | #7 - #8 | " | 640 | 1,090 | 1,730 |
| 1090 | Galvanized | | | | |
| 1100 | #3 - #4 | TON | 840 | 2,230 | 3,070 |
| 1140 | #7 - #8 | " | 640 | 2,020 | 2,660 |
| **03210.53** | **PILE CAP REINFORCING** | | | | |
| 0980 | Pile caps | | | | |
| 1000 | #3 - #4 | TON | 1,360 | 1,310 | 2,670 |
| 1040 | #7 - #8 | " | 1,090 | 1,090 | 2,180 |
| 1090 | Galvanized | | | | |
| 1100 | #3 - #4 | TON | 1,360 | 2,230 | 3,590 |
| 1140 | #7 - #8 | " | 1,090 | 2,020 | 3,110 |
| **03210.55** | **SLAB / MAT REINFORCING** | | | | |
| 0980 | Bars, slabs | | | | |
| 1000 | #3 - #4 | TON | 910 | 1,310 | 2,220 |
| 1040 | #7 - #8 | " | 680 | 1,090 | 1,770 |
| 1980 | Galvanized | | | | |
| 2000 | #3 - #4 | TON | 910 | 2,230 | 3,140 |
| 2020 | #5 - #6 | " | 780 | 2,100 | 2,880 |
| 2040 | #7 - #8 | " | 680 | 2,020 | 2,700 |
| 5000 | Wire mesh, slabs | | | | |
| 5010 | Galvanized | | | | |
| 5015 | 4x4 | | | | |
| 5020 | W1.4xW1.4 | S.F. | 0.36 | 0.32 | 0.68 |
| 5040 | W2.0xW2.0 | " | 0.38 | 0.41 | 0.79 |
| 5060 | W2.9xW2.9 | " | 0.41 | 0.58 | 0.99 |
| 5080 | W4.0xW4.0 | " | 0.45 | 0.87 | 1.32 |
| 5090 | 6x6 | | | | |
| 5100 | W1.4xW1.4 | S.F. | 0.27 | 0.30 | 0.57 |
| 5120 | W2.0xW2.0 | " | 0.30 | 0.41 | 0.71 |
| 5140 | W2.9xW2.9 | " | 0.32 | 0.56 | 0.88 |
| 5160 | W4.0xW4.0 | " | 0.36 | 0.61 | 0.97 |
| 5170 | Standard | | | | |
| 5175 | 2x2 | | | | |
| 5180 | W.9xW.9 | S.F. | 0.36 | 0.32 | 0.68 |
| 5185 | 4x4 | | | | |

© 2011 By Design & Construction Resources

# DIVISION # 03  CONCRETE

| | | UNIT | LABOR | MAT. | TOTAL |
|---|---|---|---|---|---|
| **03210.55** | **SLAB / MAT REINFORCING, Cont'd...** | | | | |
| 5190 | W1.4xW1.4 | S.F. | 0.36 | 0.21 | 0.57 |
| 5500 | W4.0xW4.0 | " | 0.45 | 0.58 | 1.03 |
| 5580 | 6x6 | | | | |
| 5600 | W1.4xW1.4 | S.F. | 0.27 | 0.13 | 0.40 |
| 6020 | W4.0xW4.0 | " | 0.36 | 0.39 | 0.75 |
| **03210.60** | **STAIR REINFORCING** | | | | |
| 0980 | Stairs | | | | |
| 1000 | #3 - #4 | TON | 1,090 | 1,310 | 2,400 |
| 1020 | #5 - #6 | " | 910 | 1,150 | 2,060 |
| 1980 | Galvanized | | | | |
| 2000 | #3 - #4 | TON | 1,090 | 2,230 | 3,320 |
| 2020 | #5 - #6 | " | 910 | 2,100 | 3,010 |
| **03210.65** | **WALL REINFORCING** | | | | |
| 0980 | Walls | | | | |
| 1000 | #3 - #4 | TON | 780 | 1,310 | 2,090 |
| 1040 | #7 - #8 | " | 610 | 1,090 | 1,700 |
| 1980 | Galvanized | | | | |
| 2000 | #3 - #4 | TON | 780 | 2,230 | 3,010 |
| 2040 | #7 - #8 | " | 610 | 2,020 | 2,630 |
| 8980 | Masonry wall (horizontal) | | | | |
| 9000 | #3 - #4 | TON | 2,180 | 1,310 | 3,490 |
| 9020 | #5 - #6 | " | 1,820 | 1,150 | 2,970 |
| 9030 | Galvanized | | | | |
| 9040 | #3 - #4 | TON | 2,180 | 2,230 | 4,410 |
| 9060 | #5 - #6 | " | 1,820 | 2,100 | 3,920 |
| 9180 | Masonry wall (vertical) | | | | |
| 9200 | #3 - #4 | TON | 2,730 | 1,310 | 4,040 |
| 9220 | #5 - #6 | " | 2,180 | 1,150 | 3,330 |
| 9230 | Galvanized | | | | |
| 9240 | #3 - #4 | TON | 2,730 | 2,230 | 4,960 |
| 9260 | #5 - #6 | " | 2,180 | 2,100 | 4,280 |
| **03250.40** | **CONCRETE ACCESSORIES** | | | | |
| 1000 | Expansion joint, poured | | | | |
| 1010 | Asphalt | | | | |
| 1020 | 1/2" x 1" | L.F. | 0.83 | 0.83 | 1.66 |
| 1040 | 1" x 2" | " | 0.90 | 2.59 | 3.49 |
| 1060 | Liquid neoprene, cold applied | | | | |
| 1080 | 1/2" x 1" | L.F. | 0.85 | 3.06 | 3.91 |
| 1100 | 1" x 2" | " | 0.92 | 12.75 | 13.67 |
| **03300.10** | **CONCRETE ADMIXTURES** | | | | |
| 1000 | Concrete admixtures | | | | |
| 1020 | Water reducing admixture | GAL | | | 10.25 |
| 1040 | Set retarder | " | | | 22.00 |
| 1060 | Air entraining agent | " | | | 9.62 |
| **03350.10** | **CONCRETE FINISHES** | | | | |
| 0980 | Floor finishes | | | | |
| 1000 | Broom | S.F. | 0.59 | | 0.59 |
| 1020 | Screed | " | 0.52 | | 0.52 |
| 1040 | Darby | " | 0.52 | | 0.52 |
| 1060 | Steel float | " | 0.69 | | 0.69 |
| 4000 | Wall finishes | | | | |

# DIVISION # 03  CONCRETE

| | | UNIT | LABOR | MAT. | TOTAL |
|---|---|---|---|---|---|
| **03350.10** | **CONCRETE FINISHES, Cont'd...** | | | | |
| 4020 | Burlap rub, with cement paste | S.F. | 0.69 | 0.11 | 0.80 |
| 4160 | Break ties and patch holes | " | 0.83 | | 0.83 |
| 4170 | Carborundum | | | | |
| 4180 | Dry rub | S.F. | 1.39 | | 1.39 |
| 4200 | Wet rub | " | 2.09 | | 2.09 |
| 5000 | Floor hardeners | | | | |
| 5010 | Metallic | | | | |
| 5020 | Light service | S.F. | 0.52 | 0.36 | 0.88 |
| 5040 | Heavy service | " | 0.69 | 1.10 | 1.79 |
| 5050 | Non-metallic | | | | |
| 5060 | Light service | S.F. | 0.52 | 0.18 | 0.70 |
| 5080 | Heavy service | " | 0.69 | 0.77 | 1.46 |
| **03360.10** | **PNEUMATIC CONCRETE** | | | | |
| 0100 | Pneumatic applied concrete (gunite) | | | | |
| 1035 | 2" thick | S.F. | 2.83 | 5.24 | 8.07 |
| 1040 | 3" thick | " | 3.78 | 6.44 | 10.22 |
| 1060 | 4" thick | " | 4.53 | 7.85 | 12.38 |
| 1980 | Finish surface | | | | |
| 2000 | Minimum | S.F. | 2.66 | | 2.66 |
| 2020 | Maximum | " | 5.33 | | 5.33 |
| **03370.10** | **CURING CONCRETE** | | | | |
| 1000 | Sprayed membrane | | | | |
| 1010 | Slabs | S.F. | 0.08 | 0.05 | 0.13 |
| 1020 | Walls | " | 0.10 | 0.07 | 0.17 |
| 1025 | Curing paper | | | | |
| 1030 | Slabs | S.F. | 0.11 | 0.07 | 0.18 |
| 2000 | Walls | " | 0.12 | 0.07 | 0.19 |
| 2010 | Burlap | | | | |
| 2020 | 7.5 oz. | S.F. | 0.13 | 0.06 | 0.19 |
| 2500 | 12 oz. | " | 0.14 | 0.08 | 0.22 |
| **03380.05** | **BEAM CONCRETE** | | | | |
| 0960 | Beams and girders | | | | |
| 0980 | 2500# or 3000# concrete | | | | |
| 1010 | By pump | C.Y. | 75.00 | 110 | 185 |
| 1020 | By hand buggy | " | 41.75 | 110 | 152 |
| 4000 | 5000# concrete | | | | |
| 4020 | By pump | C.Y. | 75.00 | 120 | 195 |
| 4040 | By hand buggy | " | 41.75 | 120 | 162 |
| 9460 | Bond beam, 3000# concrete | | | | |
| 9470 | By pump | | | | |
| 9480 | 8" high | | | | |
| 9500 | 4" wide | L.F. | 1.64 | 0.29 | 1.93 |
| 9520 | 6" wide | " | 1.86 | 0.71 | 2.57 |
| 9530 | 8" wide | " | 2.05 | 0.91 | 2.96 |
| 9540 | 10" wide | " | 2.28 | 1.21 | 3.49 |
| 9550 | 12" wide | " | 2.56 | 1.62 | 4.18 |
| **03380.15** | **COLUMN CONCRETE** | | | | |
| 0980 | Columns | | | | |
| 0990 | 2500# or 3000# concrete | | | | |
| 1010 | By pump | C.Y. | 69.00 | 110 | 179 |
| 3980 | 5000# concrete | | | | |

© 2011 By Design & Construction Resources

# DIVISION # 03  CONCRETE

| | | UNIT | LABOR | MAT. | TOTAL |
|---|---|---|---|---|---|
| **03380.15** | **COLUMN CONCRETE, Cont'd...** | | | | |
| 4020 | By pump | C.Y. | 69.00 | 120 | 189 |
| **03380.25** | **EQUIPMENT PAD CONCRETE** | | | | |
| 0960 | Equipment pad | | | | |
| 0980 | 2500# or 3000# concrete | | | | |
| 1000 | By chute | C.Y. | 14.00 | 110 | 124 |
| 1020 | By pump | " | 59.00 | 110 | 169 |
| 1050 | 3500# or 4000# concrete | | | | |
| 1060 | By chute | C.Y. | 14.00 | 110 | 124 |
| 1080 | By pump | " | 59.00 | 110 | 169 |
| 1110 | 5000# concrete | | | | |
| 1120 | By chute | C.Y. | 14.00 | 120 | 134 |
| 1140 | By pump | " | 59.00 | 120 | 179 |
| **03380.35** | **FOOTING CONCRETE** | | | | |
| 0980 | Continuous footing | | | | |
| 0990 | 2500# or 3000# concrete | | | | |
| 1000 | By chute | C.Y. | 14.00 | 110 | 124 |
| 1010 | By pump | " | 51.00 | 110 | 161 |
| 4000 | 5000# concrete | | | | |
| 4010 | By chute | C.Y. | 14.00 | 120 | 134 |
| 4020 | By pump | " | 51.00 | 120 | 171 |
| 4980 | Spread footing | | | | |
| 5000 | 2500# or 3000# concrete | | | | |
| 5010 | Under 5 cy | | | | |
| 5020 | By chute | C.Y. | 14.00 | 100 | 114 |
| 5040 | By pump | " | 55.00 | 100 | 155 |
| 7200 | 5000# concrete | | | | |
| 7205 | Under 5 c.y. | | | | |
| 7210 | By chute | C.Y. | 14.00 | 120 | 134 |
| 7220 | By pump | " | 55.00 | 120 | 175 |
| **03380.50** | **GRADE BEAM CONCRETE** | | | | |
| 0960 | Grade beam | | | | |
| 0980 | 2500# or 3000# concrete | | | | |
| 1000 | By chute | C.Y. | 14.00 | 100 | 114 |
| 1040 | By pump | " | 51.00 | 100 | 151 |
| 1060 | By hand buggy | " | 41.75 | 100 | 142 |
| 1150 | 5000# concrete | | | | |
| 1160 | By chute | C.Y. | 14.00 | 120 | 134 |
| 1190 | By pump | " | 51.00 | 120 | 171 |
| 1200 | By hand buggy | " | 41.75 | 120 | 162 |
| **03380.53** | **PILE CAP CONCRETE** | | | | |
| 0970 | Pile cap | | | | |
| 0980 | 2500# or 3000 concrete | | | | |
| 1000 | By chute | C.Y. | 14.00 | 110 | 124 |
| 1010 | By pump | " | 59.00 | 110 | 169 |
| 1020 | By hand buggy | " | 41.75 | 110 | 152 |
| 3980 | 5000# concrete | | | | |
| 4010 | By chute | C.Y. | 14.00 | 120 | 134 |
| 4020 | By pump | " | 59.00 | 120 | 179 |
| 4030 | By hand buggy | " | 41.75 | 120 | 162 |

## DIVISION # 03  CONCRETE

| | | UNIT | LABOR | MAT. | TOTAL |
|---|---|---|---|---|---|
| **03380.55** | **SLAB / MAT CONCRETE** | | | | |
| 0960 | Slab on grade | | | | |
| 0980 | 2500# or 3000# concrete | | | | |
| 1000 | By chute | C.Y. | 10.50 | 110 | 121 |
| 1020 | By pump | " | 29.25 | 110 | 139 |
| 1030 | By hand buggy | " | 28.00 | 110 | 138 |
| 3980 | 5000# concrete | | | | |
| 4010 | By chute | C.Y. | 10.50 | 120 | 131 |
| 4030 | By pump | " | 29.25 | 120 | 149 |
| 4040 | By hand buggy | " | 28.00 | 120 | 148 |
| **03380.58** | **SIDEWALKS** | | | | |
| 6000 | Walks, cast in place with wire mesh, base not incl. | | | | |
| 6010 | 4" thick | S.F. | 1.39 | 1.52 | 2.91 |
| 6020 | 5" thick | " | 1.67 | 2.06 | 3.73 |
| 6030 | 6" thick | " | 2.09 | 2.54 | 4.63 |
| **03380.60** | **STAIR CONCRETE** | | | | |
| 0960 | Stairs | | | | |
| 0980 | 2500# or 3000# concrete | | | | |
| 1000 | By chute | C.Y. | 14.00 | 110 | 124 |
| 1030 | By pump | " | 59.00 | 110 | 169 |
| 1040 | By hand buggy | " | 41.75 | 110 | 152 |
| 2100 | 3500# or 4000# concrete | | | | |
| 2120 | By chute | C.Y. | 14.00 | 110 | 124 |
| 2160 | By pump | " | 59.00 | 110 | 169 |
| 2180 | By hand buggy | " | 41.75 | 110 | 152 |
| 4000 | 5000# concrete | | | | |
| 4010 | By chute | C.Y. | 14.00 | 120 | 134 |
| 4030 | By pump | " | 59.00 | 120 | 179 |
| 4040 | By hand buggy | " | 41.75 | 120 | 162 |
| **03380.65** | **WALL CONCRETE** | | | | |
| 0940 | Walls | | | | |
| 0960 | 2500# or 3000# concrete | | | | |
| 0980 | To 4' | | | | |
| 1000 | By chute | C.Y. | 12.00 | 110 | 122 |
| 1010 | By pump | " | 63.00 | 110 | 173 |
| 1020 | To 8' | | | | |
| 1040 | By pump | C.Y. | 69.00 | 110 | 179 |
| 2960 | 3500# or 4000# concrete | | | | |
| 2980 | To 4' | | | | |
| 3000 | By chute | C.Y. | 12.00 | 110 | 122 |
| 3030 | By pump | " | 63.00 | 110 | 173 |
| 3060 | To 8' | | | | |
| 3100 | By pump | C.Y. | 69.00 | 110 | 179 |
| 8480 | Filled block (CMU) | | | | |
| 8490 | 3000# concrete, by pump | | | | |
| 8500 | 4" wide | S.F. | 2.93 | 0.40 | 3.33 |
| 8510 | 6" wide | " | 3.42 | 0.92 | 4.34 |
| 8520 | 8" wide | " | 4.11 | 1.44 | 5.55 |
| 8530 | 10" wide | " | 4.83 | 1.92 | 6.75 |
| 8540 | 12" wide | " | 5.87 | 2.47 | 8.34 |
| 8560 | Pilasters, 3000# concrete | C.F. | 82.00 | 5.61 | 87.61 |
| 8700 | Wall cavity, 2" thick, 3000# concrete | S.F. | 2.74 | 1.04 | 3.78 |

© 2011 By Design & Construction Resources

## DIVISION # 03  CONCRETE

| | | UNIT | LABOR | MAT. | TOTAL |
|---|---|---|---|---|---|
| **03550.10** | **CONCRETE TOPPINGS** | | | | |
| 1000 | Gypsum fill | | | | |
| 1020 | 2" thick | S.F. | 0.42 | 1.63 | 2.05 |
| 1040 | 2-1/2" thick | " | 0.43 | 1.87 | 2.30 |
| 1060 | 3" thick | " | 0.44 | 2.29 | 2.73 |
| 1080 | 3-1/2" thick | " | 0.45 | 2.62 | 3.07 |
| 1100 | 4" thick | " | 0.51 | 3.06 | 3.57 |
| 2000 | Formboard | | | | |
| 2020 | Mineral fiber board | | | | |
| 2040 | 1" thick | S.F. | 1.04 | 1.46 | 2.50 |
| 2060 | 1-1/2" thick | " | 1.19 | 3.85 | 5.04 |
| 2070 | Cement fiber board | | | | |
| 2080 | 1" thick | S.F. | 1.39 | 1.14 | 2.53 |
| 2100 | 1-1/2" thick | " | 1.60 | 1.46 | 3.06 |
| 2110 | Glass fiber board | | | | |
| 2120 | 1" thick | S.F. | 1.04 | 1.80 | 2.84 |
| 2140 | 1-1/2" thick | " | 1.19 | 2.44 | 3.63 |
| 4000 | Poured deck | | | | |
| 4010 | Vermiculite or perlite | | | | |
| 4020 | 1 to 4 mix | C.Y. | 69.00 | 160 | 229 |
| 4040 | 1 to 6 mix | " | 63.00 | 140 | 203 |
| 4050 | Vermiculite or perlite | | | | |
| 4060 | 2" thick | | | | |
| 4080 | 1 to 4 mix | S.F. | 0.43 | 1.46 | 1.89 |
| 4100 | 1 to 6 mix | " | 0.39 | 1.06 | 1.45 |
| 4200 | 3" thick | | | | |
| 4220 | 1 to 4 mix | S.F. | 0.63 | 2.00 | 2.63 |
| 4240 | 1 to 6 mix | " | 0.58 | 1.58 | 2.16 |
| 6000 | Concrete plank, lightweight | | | | |
| 6020 | 2" thick | S.F. | 3.37 | 7.95 | 11.32 |
| 6040 | 2-1/2" thick | " | 3.37 | 8.16 | 11.53 |
| 6080 | 3-1/2" thick | " | 3.75 | 8.49 | 12.24 |
| 6100 | 4" thick | " | 3.75 | 8.80 | 12.55 |
| 6500 | Channel slab, lightweight, straight | | | | |
| 6520 | 2-3/4" thick | S.F. | 3.37 | 6.41 | 9.78 |
| 6540 | 3-1/2" thick | " | 3.37 | 6.60 | 9.97 |
| 6560 | 3-3/4" thick | " | 3.37 | 7.12 | 10.49 |
| 6580 | 4-3/4" thick | " | 3.75 | 9.02 | 12.77 |
| 7000 | Gypsum plank | | | | |
| 7020 | 2" thick | S.F. | 3.37 | 2.97 | 6.34 |
| 7040 | 3" thick | " | 3.37 | 3.11 | 6.48 |
| 8000 | Cement fiber, T and G planks | | | | |
| 8020 | 1" thick | S.F. | 3.06 | 1.63 | 4.69 |
| 8040 | 1-1/2" thick | " | 3.06 | 1.73 | 4.79 |
| 8060 | 2" thick | " | 3.37 | 2.07 | 5.44 |
| 8080 | 2-1/2" thick | " | 3.37 | 2.20 | 5.57 |
| 8100 | 3" thick | " | 3.37 | 2.86 | 6.23 |
| 8120 | 3-1/2" thick | " | 3.75 | 3.30 | 7.05 |
| 8140 | 4" thick | " | 3.75 | 3.63 | 7.38 |
| **03730.10** | **CONCRETE REPAIR** | | | | |
| 0090 | Epoxy grout floor patch, 1/4" thick | S.F. | 4.18 | 6.36 | 10.54 |
| 0100 | Grout, epoxy, 2 component system | C.F. | | | 310 |

## DIVISION # 03  CONCRETE

### 03730.10  CONCRETE REPAIR, Cont'd...

| Code | Description | UNIT | LABOR | MAT. | TOTAL |
|---|---|---|---|---|---|
| 0110 | Epoxy sand | BAG | | | 20.75 |
| 0120 | Epoxy modifier | GAL | | | 130 |
| 0140 | Epoxy gel grout | S.F. | 41.75 | 3.10 | 44.85 |
| 0150 | Injection valve, 1 way, threaded plastic | EA. | 8.36 | 8.52 | 16.88 |
| 0155 | Grout crack seal, 2 component | C.F. | 41.75 | 720 | 762 |
| 0160 | Grout, non shrink | " | 41.75 | 73.00 | 115 |
| 0165 | Concrete, epoxy modified | | | | |
| 0170 |    Sand mix | C.F. | 16.75 | 120 | 137 |
| 0180 |    Gravel mix | " | 15.50 | 92.00 | 108 |
| 0190 | Concrete repair | | | | |
| 0195 |    Soffit repair | | | | |
| 0200 |      16" wide | L.F. | 8.36 | 3.63 | 11.99 |
| 0210 |      18" wide | " | 8.71 | 3.86 | 12.57 |
| 0220 |      24" wide | " | 9.29 | 4.62 | 13.91 |
| 0230 |      30" wide | " | 9.96 | 5.19 | 15.15 |
| 0240 |      32" wide | " | 10.50 | 5.54 | 16.04 |
| 0245 |    Edge repair | | | | |
| 0250 |      2" spall | L.F. | 10.50 | 1.73 | 12.23 |
| 0260 |      3" spall | " | 11.00 | 1.73 | 12.73 |
| 0270 |      4" spall | " | 11.25 | 1.84 | 13.09 |
| 0280 |      6" spall | " | 11.50 | 1.90 | 13.40 |
| 0290 |      8" spall | " | 12.25 | 2.02 | 14.27 |
| 0300 |      9" spall | " | 14.00 | 2.07 | 16.07 |
| 0330 | Crack repair, 1/8" crack | " | 4.18 | 3.40 | 7.58 |
| 5000 | Reinforcing steel repair | | | | |
| 5005 |    1 bar, 4 ft | | | | |
| 5010 |      #4 bar | L.F. | 6.82 | 0.53 | 7.35 |
| 5012 |      #5 bar | " | 6.82 | 0.72 | 7.54 |
| 5014 |      #6 bar | " | 7.27 | 0.87 | 8.14 |
| 5016 |      #8 bar | " | 7.27 | 1.59 | 8.86 |
| 5020 |      #9 bar | " | 7.79 | 2.03 | 9.82 |
| 5030 |      #11 bar | " | 7.79 | 3.17 | 10.96 |
| 7010 | Form fabric, nylon | | | | |
| 7020 |    18" diameter | L.F. | | | 13.75 |
| 7030 |    20" diameter | " | | | 14.00 |
| 7040 |    24" diameter | " | | | 23.00 |
| 7050 |    30" diameter | " | | | 23.50 |
| 7060 |    36" diameter | " | | | 27.00 |
| 7100 | Pile repairs | | | | |
| 7105 |    Polyethylene wrap | | | | |
| 7108 |      30 mil thick | | | | |
| 7110 |        60" wide | S.F. | 14.00 | 15.00 | 29.00 |
| 7120 |        72" wide | " | 16.75 | 16.25 | 33.00 |
| 7125 |      60 mil thick | | | | |
| 7130 |        60" wide | S.F. | 14.00 | 17.75 | 31.75 |
| 7140 |        80" wide | " | 19.00 | 20.50 | 39.50 |
| 8010 | Pile spall, average repair 3' | | | | |
| 8020 |    18" x 18" | EA. | 34.75 | 46.00 | 80.75 |
| 8030 |    20" x 20" | " | 41.75 | 61.00 | 103 |

© 2011 By Design & Construction Resources

# DIVISION # 03  CONCRETE - QUICK ESTIMATING

| | | UNIT | COST |
|---|---|---|---|
| **03999.10  CONCRETE** | | | |
| 1000 FOOTINGS (Incl. exc. with steel) | | | |
| 1010 | By L.F - Continuous  24" x 12"  (3 # 4 Rods) | L.F. | 27.25 |
| 1020 | 36" x 12"  (4 # 4 Rods) | " | 34.75 |
| 1030 | 20" x 10"  (2 # 5 Rods) | " | 23.25 |
| 1040 | 16" x  8"  (2 # 4 Rods) | " | 19.82 |
| 1050 | Pad  24" x 24" x 12"  (4 # 5 E.W.) | EA. | 95.25 |
| 1060 | 36" x 36" x 14"  (6 # 5 E.W.) | " | 191 |
| 1070 | 48" x 48" x 16"  (8 # 5 E.W.) | " | 340 |
| 1100 | By C.Y. - Continuous  24" x 12"  (3 # 4 Rods) | C.Y. | 340 |
| 1110 | 36" x 12"  (4 # 4 Rods) | " | 360 |
| 1120 | 20" x 10"  (2 # 5 Rods) | " | 380 |
| 1130 | 16" x  8"  (2 # 4 Rods) | " | 460 |
| 1140 | Pad  24" x 24" x 12"  (4 # 5 E.W.) | " | 580 |
| 1150 | 36" x 36" x 14"  (6 # 5 E.W.) | " | 540 |
| 1160 | 48" x 48" x 16"  (8 # 5 E.W.) | " | 520 |
| 1200 WALLS (#5 Rods 12" O.C. - 1 Face) | | | |
| 1210 | By S.F. - 8" Wall  (# 5 12" O.C. E.W.) | S.F. | 19.57 |
| 1220 | 12" Wall  (# 5 12" O.C. E.W.) | " | 21.11 |
| 1230 | 16" Wall  (# 5 12" O.C. E.W.) | " | 21.11 |
| 1300 | Add for Steel - 2 Faces - 12" Wall | " | 2.52 |
| 1310 | Add for Pilastered Wall - 24" O.C. | " | 1.20 |
| 1320 | Add for Retaining or Battered Type | " | 3.58 |
| 1330 | Add for Curved Walls | " | 6.62 |
| 1340 | By C.Y. - 8" Wall  (# 5 12" O.C. E.W.) | C.Y. | 640 |
| 1350 | 12" Wall  (# 5 12" O.C. E.W.) | " | 530 |
| 1360 | 16" Wall  (# 5 12" O.C. E.W.) | " | 480 |
| 1400 | Add for Steel - 2 Faces - 12" Wall | " | 70.25 |
| 1410 | Add for Pilastered Wall - 24" O.C. | " | 31.00 |
| 1420 | Add for Retaining or Battered Type | " | 96.25 |
| 1430 | Add for Curved Walls | " | 176 |
| 1500 COLUMNS | | | |
| 1510 | By L.F. - Square Cornered 8" x  8"  (4 # 8 Rods) | L.F. | 45.00 |
| 1520 | 12" x 12"  (6 # 8 Rods) | " | 77.00 |
| 1530 | 16" x 16"  (6 # 10 Rods) | " | 100 |
| 1540 | 20" x 20"  (8 # 20 Rods) | " | 143 |
| 1550 | 24" x 24"  (10 # 11 Rods) | " | 172 |
| 1600 | Round 8"  (4 # 8 Rods) | " | 33.00 |
| 1610 | 12"  (6 # 8 Rods) | " | 51.75 |
| 1620 | 16"  (6 # 10 Rods) | " | 71.00 |
| 1630 | 20"  (8 # 20 Rods) | " | 99.25 |
| 1640 | 24"  (10 # 11 Rods) | " | 144 |
| 1700 | By C.Y. - Sq Cornered 8" x  8"  (4 # 8 Rods) | C.Y. | 2,620 |
| 1710 | 12" x 12"  (6 # 8 Rods) | " | 2,420 |
| 1720 | 16" x 16"  (6 # 10 Rods) | " | 1,720 |
| 1730 | 20" x 20"  (8 # 20 Rods) | " | 1,530 |
| 1740 | 24" x 24"  (10 # 11 Rods) | " | 1,090 |
| 1800 | Round 8"  (4 # 8 Rods) | " | 2,420 |
| 1810 | 12"  (6 # 8 Rods) | " | 1,610 |
| 1820 | 16"  (6 # 10 Rods) | " | 1,480 |
| 1830 | 20"  (8 # 20 Rods) | " | 1,350 |
| 1840 | 24"  (10 # 11 Rods) | " | 1,290 |
| 1900 BEAMS | | | |

# DIVISION # 03  CONCRETE - QUICK ESTIMATING

| | | UNIT | COST |
|---|---|---|---|
| **03999.10** | **CONCRETE, Cont'd...** | | |
| 1910 | By L.F. - Spandrel 12" x 48" (33 # rebar) | L.F. | 173 |
| 1920 | 12" x 42" (26 # Rein. Steel) | " | 160 |
| 1930 | 12" x 36" (21 # Rein. Steel) | " | 125 |
| 1940 | 12" x 30" (15 # Rein. Steel) | " | 119 |
| 1950 | 8" x 48" (26 # Rein. Steel) | " | 155 |
| 1960 | 8" x 42" (21 # Rein. Steel) | " | 141 |
| 1970 | 8" x 36" (16 # Rein. Steel) | " | 127 |
| 2000 | Interior 16" x 30" (24 # rebar) | " | 101 |
| 2010 | 16" x 24" (20 # Rein. Steel) | " | 100 |
| 2020 | 12" x 30" (17 # Rein. Steel) | " | 117 |
| 2030 | 12" x 24" (14 # Rein. Steel) | " | 83.50 |
| 2040 | 12" x 16" (12 # Rein. Steel) | " | 71.00 |
| 2050 | 8" x 24" (13 # Rein. Steel) | " | 83.50 |
| 2060 | 8" x 16" (10 # Rein. Steel) | " | 62.75 |
| 2100 | By C.Y. - Spandrel 12" x 48" (33 # rebar) | C.Y. | 1,030 |
| 2110 | 12" x 42" (26 # Rein. Steel) | " | 1,090 |
| 2120 | 12" x 36" (21 # Rein. Steel) | " | 1,160 |
| 2130 | 12" x 30" (15 # Rein. Steel) | " | 1,220 |
| 2140 | 8" x 48" (26 # Rein. Steel) | " | 1,220 |
| 2150 | 8" x 42" (21 # Rein. Steel) | " | 1,340 |
| 2160 | 8" x 36" (16 # Rein. Steel) | " | 1,400 |
| 2200 | Interior 16" x 30" (24 # rebar) | " | 680 |
| 2210 | 16" x 24" (20 # Rein. Steel) | " | 1,000 |
| 2220 | 12" x 30" (17 # Rein. Steel) | " | 1,090 |
| 2230 | 12" x 24" (14 # Rein. Steel) | " | 1,070 |
| 2240 | 12" x 16" (12 # Rein. Steel) | " | 1,220 |
| 2250 | 8" x 24" (13 # Rein. Steel) | " | 1,350 |
| 2260 | 8" x 16" (10 # Rein. Steel) | " | 1,420 |
| 2300 | SLABS (With Reinf. Steel) | | |
| 2310 | By S.F. - Solid | | |
| 2320 | 4" Thick | S.F. | 12.21 |
| 2330 | 5" Thick | " | 14.29 |
| 2340 | 6" Thick | " | 15.72 |
| 2350 | 7" Thick | " | 17.52 |
| 2360 | 8" Thick | " | 16.79 |
| 2400 | Deduct for Post Tensioned Slabs | " | 1.05 |
| 2410 | Pan | " | |
| 2420 | Joist -20" Pan - 10" x 2" | " | 16.12 |
| 2430 | 12" x 2" | " | 18.14 |
| 2440 | 30" Pan - 10" x 2 1/2" | " | 16.25 |
| 2450 | 12" x 2 1/2" | " | 18.14 |
| 2500 | Dome -19" x 19" - 10" x 2" | " | 17.80 |
| 2510 | 12" x 2" | " | 18.38 |
| 2520 | 30" x 30" - 10" x 2 1/2" | " | 15.69 |
| 2530 | 12" x 2 1/2" | " | 17.41 |
| 2600 | By C.Y. - Solid | | |
| 2610 | 4" Thick | C.Y. | 930 |
| 2620 | 5" Thick | " | 890 |
| 2630 | 6" Thick | " | 860 |
| 2640 | 8" Thick | " | 830 |
| 2700 | COMBINED COLUMNS, BEAMS AND SLABS | | |
| 2710 | 20' Span | S.F. | 24.75 |

© 2011 By Design & Construction Resources

# DIVISION # 03  CONCRETE - QUICK ESTIMATING

### 03999.10  CONCRETE, Cont'd...

| Code | Description | UNIT | COST |
|------|-------------|------|------|
| 2720 | 30' Span | S.F. | 26.00 |
| 2730 | 40' Span | " | 27.50 |
| 2740 | 50' Span | " | 30.00 |
| 2750 | 60' Span | " | 50.75 |
| 2800 | STAIRS (Including Landing) | | |
| 2810 | By EA. - 4' Wide 10' Floor Heights 16 Risers | EA. | 220 |
| 2820 | 5' Wide 10' Floor Heights 16 Risers | " | 240 |
| 2830 | 6' Wide 10' Floor Heights 16 Risers | " | 300 |
| 2840 | By C.Y. - 4' Wide 10' Floor Heights 16 Risers | C.Y. | 1,350 |
| 2850 | 5' Wide 10' Floor Heights 16 Risers | " | 1,390 |
| 2860 | 6' Wide 10' Floor Heights 16 Risers | " | 1,370 |
| 2900 | SLABS ON GROUND | | |
| 2910 | 4" Concrete Slab | | |
| 2920 | (6 6/10 - 10 Mesh - 5 1/2 Sack Concrete, | | |
| 2930 | Trowel Finished, Cured & Truck Chuted) | S.F. | 4.15 |
| 2940 | Add per Inch of Concrete | " | 0.69 |
| 2950 | Add per Sack of Cement | " | 0.18 |
| 2960 | Deduct for Float Finish | " | 0.09 |
| 2970 | Deduct for Brush or Broom Finish | " | 0.07 |
| 3000 | Add for Runway and Buggied Concrete | " | 0.27 |
| 3010 | Add for Vapor Barrier (4 mil) | " | 0.19 |
| 3020 | Add for Sub - Floor Fill (4" sand/gravel) | " | 0.59 |
| 3030 | Add for Change to 6 6/8 - 8 Mesh | " | 0.10 |
| 3040 | Add for Change to 6 6/6 - 6 Mesh | " | 0.19 |
| 3050 | Add for Sloped Slab | " | 0.25 |
| 3060 | Add for Edge Strip (sidewalk area) | " | 0.27 |
| 3100 | Add for ½" Expansion Joint (20' O.C.) | " | 0.09 |
| 3110 | Add for Control Joints (keyed/ dep.) | " | 0.21 |
| 3120 | Add for Control Joints (joint filled) | " | 0.22 |
| 3130 | Add for Control Joints - Saw Cut (20' O.C.) | " | 0.38 |
| 3140 | Add for Floor Hardener (1 coat) | " | 0.18 |
| 3150 | Add for Exposed Aggregate - Washed Added | " | 0.52 |
| 3200 | Retarding Added | " | 0.49 |
| 3210 | Seeding Added | " | 0.51 |
| 3220 | Add for Light Weight Aggregates | " | 0.52 |
| 3230 | Add for Heavy Weight Aggregates | " | 0.36 |
| 3240 | Add for Winter Production Loss/Cost | " | 0.45 |
| 3300 | TOPPING SLABS | | |
| 3310 | 2" Concrete | S.F. | 3.54 |
| 3320 | 3" Concrete | " | 4.42 |
| 3330 | No Mesh or Hoisting | | |
| 3400 | PADS & PLATFORMS (Including Form Work & Reinforcing) | | |
| 3410 | 4" | S.F. | 8.66 |
| 3420 | 6" | " | 10.92 |
| 3500 | PRECAST CONCRETE ITEMS | | |
| 3510 | Curbs 6" x 10" x 8" | L.F. | 14.68 |
| 3520 | Sills & Stools 6" | " | 33.25 |
| 3530 | Splash Blocks 3" x 16" | EA. | 80.00 |
| 3600 | MISCELLANEOUS ADDITIONS TO ABOVE CONCRETE | | |
| 3610 | Abrasives - Carborundum - Grits | S.F. | 1.13 |
| 3620 | Strips | L.F. | 3.74 |
| 3630 | Bushhammer - Green Concrete | S.F. | 2.51 |

## DIVISION # 03  CONCRETE - QUICK ESTIMATING

### 03999.10  CONCRETE, Cont'd...

| Code | Description | UNIT | COST |
|---|---|---|---|
| 3640 | Cured Concrete | S.F. | 3.38 |
| 3650 | Chamfers - Plastic 3/4" | L.F. | 1.32 |
| 3660 | Wood 3/4" | " | 0.78 |
| 3670 | Metal 3/4" | " | 1.44 |
| 3680 | Colors Dust On | S.F. | 1.05 |
| 3690 | Integral (Top 1") | " | 1.79 |
| 3700 | Control Joints - Asphalt 1/2" x 4" | L.F. | 1.11 |
| 3710 | 1/2" x 6" | " | 1.28 |
| 3720 | PolyFoam 1/2" x 4" | " | 1.40 |
| 3730 | Dovetail Slots 22 Ga | " | 1.95 |
| 3740 | 24 Ga | " | 1.25 |
| 3800 | Hardeners Acrylic and Urethane | S.F. | 0.37 |
| 3810 | Epoxy | " | 0.48 |
| 3820 | Joint Sealers Epoxy | L.F. | 4.48 |
| 3830 | Rubber Asphalt | " | 2.34 |
| 3840 | Moisture Proofing - Polyethylene 4 mil | S.F. | 0.24 |
| 3850 | 6 mil | " | 0.28 |
| 3900 | Non-Shrink Grouts - Non - Metallic | C.F. | 51.75 |
| 3910 | Aluminum Oxide | " | 37.75 |
| 3920 | Iron Oxide | " | 55.25 |
| 4000 | Reglets Flashing | L.F. | 3.46 |
| 4010 | Sand Blast - Light | S.F. | 1.78 |
| 4020 | Heavy | " | 3.47 |
| 4030 | Shelf Angle Inserts 5/8" | L.F. | 12.56 |
| 4040 | Stair Nosings Steel - Galvanized | " | 9.04 |
| 4050 | Tongue & Groove Joint Forms - Asphalt 5 1/2" | " | 2.71 |
| 4060 | Wood 5 1/2" | " | 2.21 |
| 4070 | Metal 5 1/2" | " | 2.82 |
| 4100 | Treads - Extruded Aluminum | " | 11.91 |
| 4110 | Cast Iron | " | 13.77 |
| 4120 | Water Stops Center Bulb - Rubber - 6" | " | 14.05 |
| 4130 | 9" | " | 26.50 |
| 4140 | Polyethylene - 6" | " | 3.86 |
| 4150 | 9" | " | 3.91 |

© 2011 By Design & Construction Resources

**Design & Construction Resources**

# DIVISION # 04  MASONRY

## TABLE OF CONTENTS

| | PAGE |
|---|---|
| 04100.10 - MASONRY GROUT | 04-2 |
| 04150.10 - MASONRY ACCESSORIES | 04-2 |
| 04150.20 - MASONRY CONTROL JOINTS | 04-4 |
| 04150.50 - MASONRY FLASHING | 04-4 |
| 04210.10 - BRICK MASONRY | 04-4 |
| 04210.20 - STRUCTURAL TILE | 04-5 |
| 04210.60 - PAVERS, MASONRY | 04-6 |
| 04220.10 - CONCRETE MASONRY UNITS | 04-6 |
| 04220.90 - BOND BEAMS & LINTELS | 04-8 |
| 04240.10 - CLAY TILE | 04-9 |
| 04270.10 - GLASS BLOCK | 04-10 |
| 04295.10 - PARGING / MASONRY PLASTER | 04-10 |
| 04400.10 - STONE | 04-10 |
| **QUICK ESTIMATING** | 04A-13 |

© 2011 By Design & Construction Resources

## DIVISION # 04 MASONRY

| | | UNIT | LABOR | MAT. | TOTAL |
|---|---|---|---|---|---|
| **04100.10** | **MASONRY GROUT** | | | | |
| 0100 | Grout, non shrink, non-metallic, trowelable | C.F. | 1.51 | 4.95 | 6.46 |
| 2110 | Grout door frame, hollow metal | | | | |
| 2120 | Single | EA. | 57.00 | 12.25 | 69.25 |
| 2140 | Double | " | 60.00 | 17.25 | 77.25 |
| 2980 | Grout-filled concrete block (CMU) | | | | |
| 3000 | 4" wide | S.F. | 1.89 | 0.33 | 2.22 |
| 3020 | 6" wide | " | 2.06 | 0.86 | 2.92 |
| 3040 | 8" wide | " | 2.26 | 1.27 | 3.53 |
| 3060 | 12" wide | " | 2.38 | 2.09 | 4.47 |
| 3070 | Grout-filled individual CMU cells | | | | |
| 3090 | 4" wide | L.F. | 1.13 | 0.27 | 1.40 |
| 3100 | 6" wide | " | 1.13 | 0.37 | 1.50 |
| 3120 | 8" wide | " | 1.13 | 0.49 | 1.62 |
| 3140 | 10" wide | " | 1.29 | 0.61 | 1.90 |
| 3160 | 12" wide | " | 1.29 | 0.74 | 2.03 |
| 4000 | Bond beams or lintels, 8" deep | | | | |
| 4010 | 6" thick | L.F. | 1.86 | 0.74 | 2.60 |
| 4020 | 8" thick | " | 2.05 | 0.99 | 3.04 |
| 4040 | 10" thick | " | 2.28 | 1.24 | 3.52 |
| 4060 | 12" thick | " | 2.56 | 1.48 | 4.04 |
| 5000 | Cavity walls | | | | |
| 5020 | 2" thick | S.F. | 2.74 | 0.82 | 3.56 |
| 5040 | 3" thick | " | 2.74 | 1.24 | 3.98 |
| 5060 | 4" thick | " | 2.93 | 1.65 | 4.58 |
| 5080 | 6" thick | " | 3.42 | 2.47 | 5.89 |
| **04150.10** | **MASONRY ACCESSORIES** | | | | |
| 0200 | Foundation vents | EA. | 20.25 | 32.25 | 52.50 |
| 1010 | Bar reinforcing | | | | |
| 1015 | Horizontal | | | | |
| 1020 | #3 - #4 | Lb. | 2.03 | 0.60 | 2.63 |
| 1030 | #5 - #6 | " | 1.69 | 0.60 | 2.29 |
| 1035 | Vertical | | | | |
| 1040 | #3 - #4 | Lb. | 2.54 | 0.60 | 3.14 |
| 1050 | #5 - #6 | " | 2.03 | 0.60 | 2.63 |
| 1100 | Horizontal joint reinforcing | | | | |
| 1105 | Truss type | | | | |
| 1110 | 4" wide, 6" wall | L.F. | 0.20 | 0.19 | 0.39 |
| 1120 | 6" wide, 8" wall | " | 0.21 | 0.19 | 0.40 |
| 1130 | 8" wide, 10" wall | " | 0.22 | 0.24 | 0.46 |
| 1140 | 10" wide, 12" wall | " | 0.23 | 0.24 | 0.47 |
| 1150 | 12" wide, 14" wall | " | 0.24 | 0.29 | 0.53 |
| 1155 | Ladder type | | | | |
| 1160 | 4" wide, 6" wall | L.F. | 0.20 | 0.14 | 0.34 |
| 1170 | 6" wide, 8" wall | " | 0.21 | 0.16 | 0.37 |
| 1180 | 8" wide, 10" wall | " | 0.22 | 0.17 | 0.39 |
| 1190 | 10" wide, 12" wall | " | 0.22 | 0.20 | 0.42 |
| 2000 | Rectangular wall ties | | | | |
| 2005 | 3/16" dia., galvanized | | | | |
| 2010 | 2" x 6" | EA. | 0.84 | 0.36 | 1.20 |
| 2020 | 2" x 8" | " | 0.84 | 0.39 | 1.23 |
| 2040 | 2" x 10" | " | 0.84 | 0.45 | 1.29 |

# DIVISION # 04  MASONRY

| | | UNIT | LABOR | MAT. | TOTAL |
|---|---|---|---|---|---|
| **04150.10** | **MASONRY ACCESSORIES, Cont'd...** | | | | |
| 2050 | 2" x 12" | EA. | 0.84 | 0.50 | 1.34 |
| 2060 | 4" x 6" | " | 1.01 | 0.41 | 1.42 |
| 2070 | 4" x 8" | " | 1.01 | 0.47 | 1.48 |
| 2080 | 4" x 10" | " | 1.01 | 0.61 | 1.62 |
| 2090 | 4" x 12" | " | 1.01 | 0.70 | 1.71 |
| 2095 | 1/4" dia., galvanized | | | | |
| 2100 | 2" x 6" | EA. | 0.84 | 0.68 | 1.52 |
| 2110 | 2" x 8" | " | 0.84 | 0.76 | 1.60 |
| 2120 | 2" x 10" | " | 0.84 | 0.86 | 1.70 |
| 2130 | 2" x 12" | " | 0.84 | 0.99 | 1.83 |
| 2140 | 4" x 6" | " | 1.01 | 0.78 | 1.79 |
| 2150 | 4" x 8" | " | 1.01 | 0.86 | 1.87 |
| 2160 | 4" x 10" | " | 1.01 | 0.99 | 2.00 |
| 2170 | 4" x 12" | " | 1.01 | 1.03 | 2.04 |
| 2200 | "Z" type wall ties, galvanized | | | | |
| 2215 | 6" long | | | | |
| 2220 | 1/8" dia. | EA. | 0.84 | 0.32 | 1.16 |
| 2230 | 3/16" dia. | " | 0.84 | 0.34 | 1.18 |
| 2240 | 1/4" dia. | " | 0.84 | 0.36 | 1.20 |
| 2245 | 8" long | | | | |
| 2250 | 1/8" dia. | EA. | 0.84 | 0.34 | 1.18 |
| 2260 | 3/16" dia. | " | 0.84 | 0.36 | 1.20 |
| 2270 | 1/4" dia. | " | 0.84 | 0.39 | 1.23 |
| 2275 | 10" long | | | | |
| 2280 | 1/8" dia. | EA. | 0.84 | 0.36 | 1.20 |
| 2290 | 3/16" dia. | " | 0.84 | 0.41 | 1.25 |
| 2300 | 1/4" dia. | " | 0.84 | 0.47 | 1.31 |
| 3000 | Dovetail anchor slots | | | | |
| 3015 | Galvanized steel, filled | | | | |
| 3020 | 24 ga. | L.F. | 1.27 | 0.82 | 2.09 |
| 3040 | 20 ga. | " | 1.27 | 1.72 | 2.99 |
| 3060 | 16 oz. copper, foam filled | " | 1.27 | 2.03 | 3.30 |
| 3100 | Dovetail anchors | | | | |
| 3115 | 16 ga. | | | | |
| 3120 | 3-1/2" long | EA. | 0.84 | 0.25 | 1.09 |
| 3140 | 5-1/2" long | " | 0.84 | 0.30 | 1.14 |
| 3150 | 12 ga. | | | | |
| 3160 | 3-1/2" long | EA. | 0.84 | 0.33 | 1.17 |
| 3180 | 5-1/2" long | " | 0.84 | 0.55 | 1.39 |
| 3200 | Dovetail, triangular galvanized ties, 12 ga. | | | | |
| 3220 | 3" x 3" | EA. | 0.84 | 0.56 | 1.40 |
| 3240 | 5" x 5" | " | 0.84 | 0.60 | 1.44 |
| 3260 | 7" x 7" | " | 0.84 | 0.68 | 1.52 |
| 3280 | 7" x 9" | " | 0.84 | 0.72 | 1.56 |
| 3400 | Brick anchors | | | | |
| 3420 | Corrugated, 3-1/2" long | | | | |
| 3440 | 16 ga. | EA. | 0.84 | 0.22 | 1.06 |
| 3460 | 12 ga. | " | 0.84 | 0.38 | 1.22 |
| 3500 | Non-corrugated, 3-1/2" long | | | | |
| 3520 | 16 ga. | EA. | 0.84 | 0.30 | 1.14 |
| 3540 | 12 ga. | " | 0.84 | 0.55 | 1.39 |
| 3580 | Cavity wall anchors, corrugated, galvanized | | | | |

© 2011 By Design & Construction Resources

## DIVISION # 04  MASONRY

| | | UNIT | LABOR | MAT. | TOTAL |
|---|---|---|---|---|---|
| **04150.10** | **MASONRY ACCESSORIES, Cont'd...** | | | | |
| 3600 | 5" long | | | | |
| 3620 | 16 ga. | EA. | 0.84 | 0.68 | 1.52 |
| 3640 | 12 ga. | " | 0.84 | 1.01 | 1.85 |
| 3660 | 7" long | | | | |
| 3680 | 28 ga. | EA. | 0.84 | 0.74 | 1.58 |
| 3700 | 24 ga. | " | 0.84 | 0.94 | 1.78 |
| 3720 | 22 ga. | " | 0.84 | 0.96 | 1.80 |
| 3740 | 16 ga. | " | 0.84 | 1.08 | 1.92 |
| 3800 | Mesh ties, 16 ga., 3" wide | | | | |
| 3820 | 8" long | EA. | 0.84 | 0.91 | 1.75 |
| 3840 | 12" long | " | 0.84 | 1.01 | 1.85 |
| 3860 | 20" long | " | 0.84 | 1.39 | 2.23 |
| 3900 | 24" long | " | 0.84 | 1.54 | 2.38 |
| **04150.20** | **MASONRY CONTROL JOINTS** | | | | |
| 1000 | Control joint, cross shaped PVC | L.F. | 1.27 | 2.17 | 3.44 |
| 1010 | Closed cell joint filler | | | | |
| 1020 | 1/2" | L.F. | 1.27 | 0.38 | 1.65 |
| 1040 | 3/4" | " | 1.27 | 0.77 | 2.04 |
| 1070 | Rubber, for | | | | |
| 1080 | 4" wall | L.F. | 1.27 | 2.50 | 3.77 |
| 1090 | 6" wall | " | 1.34 | 3.10 | 4.44 |
| 1100 | 8" wall | " | 1.41 | 3.74 | 5.15 |
| 1110 | PVC, for | | | | |
| 1120 | 4" wall | L.F. | 1.27 | 1.30 | 2.57 |
| 1140 | 6" wall | " | 1.34 | 2.20 | 3.54 |
| 1160 | 8" wall | " | 1.41 | 3.33 | 4.74 |
| **04150.50** | **MASONRY FLASHING** | | | | |
| 0080 | Through-wall flashing | | | | |
| 1000 | 5 oz. coated copper | S.F. | 4.24 | 3.35 | 7.59 |
| 1020 | 0.030" elastomeric | " | 3.39 | 1.10 | 4.49 |
| **04210.10** | **BRICK MASONRY** | | | | |
| 0100 | Standard size brick, running bond | | | | |
| 1000 | Face brick, red (6.4/sf) | | | | |
| 1020 | Veneer | S.F. | 8.48 | 5.39 | 13.87 |
| 1030 | Cavity wall | " | 7.27 | 5.39 | 12.66 |
| 1040 | 9" solid wall | " | 14.50 | 10.75 | 25.25 |
| 1200 | Common brick (6.4/sf) | | | | |
| 1210 | Select common for veneers | S.F. | 8.48 | 3.52 | 12.00 |
| 1215 | Back-up | | | | |
| 1220 | 4" thick | S.F. | 6.36 | 3.16 | 9.52 |
| 1230 | 8" thick | " | 10.25 | 6.33 | 16.58 |
| 1235 | Firewall | | | | |
| 1240 | 12" thick | S.F. | 17.00 | 10.25 | 27.25 |
| 1250 | 16" thick | " | 23.25 | 13.75 | 37.00 |
| 1300 | Glazed brick (7.4/sf) | | | | |
| 1310 | Veneer | S.F. | 9.25 | 14.75 | 24.00 |
| 1400 | Buff or gray face brick (6.4/sf) | | | | |
| 1410 | Veneer | S.F. | 8.48 | 6.27 | 14.75 |
| 1420 | Cavity wall | " | 7.27 | 6.27 | 13.54 |
| 1500 | Jumbo or oversize brick (3/sf) | | | | |
| 1510 | 4" veneer | S.F. | 5.09 | 4.12 | 9.21 |

## DIVISION # 04  MASONRY

| | | UNIT | LABOR | MAT. | TOTAL |
|---|---|---|---|---|---|
| **04210.10** | **BRICK MASONRY, Cont'd...** | | | | |
| 1530 | 4" back-up | S.F. | 4.24 | 4.12 | 8.36 |
| 1540 | 8" back-up | " | 7.27 | 4.78 | 12.05 |
| 1550 | 12" firewall | " | 12.75 | 6.43 | 19.18 |
| 1560 | 16" firewall | " | 17.00 | 9.07 | 26.07 |
| 1600 | Norman brick, red face, (4.5/sf) | | | | |
| 1620 | 4" veneer | S.F. | 6.36 | 5.94 | 12.30 |
| 1640 | Cavity wall | " | 5.65 | 5.94 | 11.59 |
| 3000 | Chimney, standard brick, including flue | | | | |
| 3020 | 16" x 16" | L.F. | 51.00 | 25.25 | 76.25 |
| 3040 | 16" x 20" | " | 51.00 | 43.00 | 94.00 |
| 3060 | 16" x 24" | " | 51.00 | 45.75 | 96.75 |
| 3080 | 20" x 20" | " | 64.00 | 35.75 | 99.75 |
| 3100 | 20" x 24" | " | 64.00 | 48.25 | 112 |
| 3120 | 20" x 32" | " | 73.00 | 54.00 | 127 |
| 4000 | Window sill, face brick on edge | " | 12.75 | 2.97 | 15.72 |
| **04210.20** | **STRUCTURAL TILE** | | | | |
| 5000 | Structural glazed tile | | | | |
| 5010 | 6T series, 5-1/2" x 12" | | | | |
| 5020 | Glazed on one side | | | | |
| 5040 | 2" thick | S.F. | 5.09 | 9.90 | 14.99 |
| 5060 | 4" thick | " | 5.09 | 12.00 | 17.09 |
| 5080 | 6" thick | " | 5.65 | 19.00 | 24.65 |
| 5100 | 8" thick | " | 6.36 | 23.25 | 29.61 |
| 5200 | Glazed on two sides | | | | |
| 5220 | 4" thick | S.F. | 6.36 | 17.50 | 23.86 |
| 5240 | 6" thick | " | 7.27 | 24.25 | 31.52 |
| 5500 | Special shapes | | | | |
| 5510 | Group 1 | S.F. | 10.25 | 10.25 | 20.50 |
| 5520 | Group 2 | " | 10.25 | 13.00 | 23.25 |
| 5530 | Group 3 | " | 10.25 | 17.00 | 27.25 |
| 5540 | Group 4 | " | 10.25 | 34.25 | 44.50 |
| 5550 | Group 5 | " | 10.25 | 41.75 | 52.00 |
| 5600 | Fire rated | | | | |
| 5620 | 4" thick, 1 hr rating | S.F. | 5.09 | 18.00 | 23.09 |
| 5640 | 6" thick, 2 hr rating | " | 5.65 | 22.00 | 27.65 |
| 6000 | 8W series, 8" x 16" | | | | |
| 6010 | Glazed on one side | | | | |
| 6020 | 2" thick | S.F. | 3.39 | 10.25 | 13.64 |
| 6040 | 4" thick | " | 3.39 | 11.00 | 14.39 |
| 6060 | 6" thick | " | 3.91 | 18.00 | 21.91 |
| 6080 | 8" thick | " | 3.91 | 19.75 | 23.66 |
| 6100 | Glazed on two sides | | | | |
| 6120 | 4" thick | S.F. | 4.24 | 17.25 | 21.49 |
| 6140 | 6" thick | " | 5.09 | 24.25 | 29.34 |
| 6160 | 8" thick | " | 5.09 | 29.50 | 34.59 |
| 6200 | Special shapes | | | | |
| 6220 | Group 1 | S.F. | 7.27 | 15.50 | 22.77 |
| 6230 | Group 2 | " | 7.27 | 19.00 | 26.27 |
| 6240 | Group 3 | " | 7.27 | 20.75 | 28.02 |
| 6250 | Group 4 | " | 7.27 | 34.50 | 41.77 |
| 6260 | Group 5 | " | 7.27 | 44.00 | 51.27 |

© 2011 By Design & Construction Resources

## DIVISION # 04  MASONRY

| | | UNIT | LABOR | MAT. | TOTAL |
|---|---|---|---|---|---|
| **04210.20** | **STRUCTURAL TILE, Cont'd...** | | | | |
| 6270 | Fire rated | | | | |
| 6290 | 4" thick, 1 hr rating | S.F. | 7.27 | 26.00 | 33.27 |
| 6300 | 6" thick, 2 hr rating | " | 7.27 | 31.25 | 38.52 |
| **04210.60** | **PAVERS, MASONRY** | | | | |
| 4000 | Brick walk laid on sand, sand joints | | | | |
| 4020 | Laid flat, (4.5 per sf) | S.F. | 5.65 | 3.78 | 9.43 |
| 4040 | Laid on edge, (7.2 per sf) | " | 8.48 | 6.05 | 14.53 |
| 5000 | Precast concrete patio blocks | | | | |
| 5005 | 2" thick | | | | |
| 5010 | Natural | S.F. | 1.69 | 2.68 | 4.37 |
| 5020 | Colors | " | 1.69 | 3.74 | 5.43 |
| 5080 | Exposed aggregates, local aggregate | | | | |
| 5100 | Natural | S.F. | 1.69 | 8.08 | 9.77 |
| 5120 | Colors | " | 1.69 | 8.08 | 9.77 |
| 5130 | Granite or limestone aggregate | " | 1.69 | 8.44 | 10.13 |
| 5140 | White tumblestone aggregate | " | 1.69 | 6.05 | 7.74 |
| 6000 | Stone pavers, set in mortar | | | | |
| 6005 | Bluestone | | | | |
| 6008 | 1" thick | | | | |
| 6010 | Irregular | S.F. | 12.75 | 6.14 | 18.89 |
| 6020 | Snapped rectangular | " | 10.25 | 9.35 | 19.60 |
| 6060 | 1-1/2" thick, random rectangular | " | 12.75 | 10.75 | 23.50 |
| 6070 | 2" thick, random rectangular | " | 14.50 | 12.75 | 27.25 |
| 6090 | Slate | | | | |
| 6100 | Natural cleft | | | | |
| 6110 | Irregular, 3/4" thick | S.F. | 14.50 | 7.71 | 22.21 |
| 6115 | Random rectangular | | | | |
| 6120 | 1-1/4" thick | S.F. | 12.75 | 16.75 | 29.50 |
| 6130 | 1-1/2" thick | " | 14.25 | 18.75 | 33.00 |
| 7000 | Granite blocks | | | | |
| 7010 | 3" thick, 3" to 6" wide | | | | |
| 7020 | 4" to 12" long | S.F. | 17.00 | 11.00 | 28.00 |
| 7030 | 6" to 15" long | " | 14.50 | 7.15 | 21.65 |
| 9000 | Flagstone pavers | | | | |
| 9010 | Random sizes, 1-4 s.f., tumbled cobble | S.F. | 10.25 | 15.50 | 25.75 |
| 9020 | Tumbled patio | " | 10.25 | 16.50 | 26.75 |
| 9040 | Saw-cut Flagstone Tiles | | | | |
| 9060 | 12"x12", assorted colors | S.F. | 7.27 | 14.25 | 21.52 |
| 9080 | 18"x18", assorted colors | " | 6.36 | 14.25 | 20.61 |
| 9100 | 24"x24", assorted colors | " | 5.65 | 14.25 | 19.90 |
| 9800 | Crushed stone, white marble, 3" thick | " | 0.83 | 1.70 | 2.53 |
| **04220.10** | **CONCRETE MASONRY UNITS** | | | | |
| 0110 | Hollow, load bearing | | | | |
| 0120 | 4" | S.F. | 3.77 | 1.47 | 5.24 |
| 0140 | 6" | " | 3.91 | 2.16 | 6.07 |
| 0160 | 8" | " | 4.24 | 2.48 | 6.72 |
| 0180 | 10" | " | 4.62 | 3.43 | 8.05 |
| 0190 | 12" | " | 5.09 | 3.93 | 9.02 |
| 0280 | Solid, load bearing | | | | |
| 0300 | 4" | S.F. | 3.77 | 2.31 | 6.08 |
| 0320 | 6" | " | 3.91 | 2.60 | 6.51 |

© 2011 By Design & Construction Resources

# DIVISION # 04 MASONRY

## 04220.10 CONCRETE MASONRY UNITS, Cont'd...

| | | UNIT | LABOR | MAT. | TOTAL |
|---|---|---|---|---|---|
| 0340 | 8" | S.F. | 4.24 | 3.54 | 7.78 |
| 0360 | 10" | " | 4.62 | 3.78 | 8.40 |
| 0380 | 12" | " | 5.09 | 5.61 | 10.70 |
| 0480 | Back-up block, 8" x 16" | | | | |
| 0500 | 2" | S.F. | 2.90 | 1.55 | 4.45 |
| 0540 | 4" | " | 2.99 | 1.61 | 4.60 |
| 0560 | 6" | " | 3.18 | 2.36 | 5.54 |
| 0580 | 8" | " | 3.39 | 2.71 | 6.10 |
| 0600 | 10" | " | 3.63 | 3.75 | 7.38 |
| 0620 | 12" | " | 3.91 | 4.30 | 8.21 |
| 0980 | Foundation wall, 8" x 16" | | | | |
| 1000 | 6" | S.F. | 3.63 | 2.36 | 5.99 |
| 1030 | 8" | " | 3.91 | 2.71 | 6.62 |
| 1040 | 10" | " | 4.24 | 3.75 | 7.99 |
| 1050 | 12" | " | 4.62 | 4.31 | 8.93 |
| 1055 | Solid | | | | |
| 1060 | 6" | S.F. | 3.91 | 2.85 | 6.76 |
| 1070 | 8" | " | 4.24 | 3.89 | 8.13 |
| 1080 | 10" | " | 4.62 | 4.15 | 8.77 |
| 1100 | 12" | " | 5.09 | 6.16 | 11.25 |
| 1480 | Exterior, styrofoam inserts, std weight, 8" x 16" | | | | |
| 1500 | 6" | S.F. | 3.91 | 4.35 | 8.26 |
| 1530 | 8" | " | 4.24 | 4.70 | 8.94 |
| 1540 | 10" | " | 4.62 | 6.09 | 10.71 |
| 1550 | 12" | " | 5.09 | 8.36 | 13.45 |
| 1580 | Lightweight | | | | |
| 1600 | 6" | S.F. | 3.91 | 4.85 | 8.76 |
| 1660 | 8" | " | 4.24 | 5.45 | 9.69 |
| 1680 | 10" | " | 4.62 | 5.80 | 10.42 |
| 1700 | 12" | " | 5.09 | 7.65 | 12.74 |
| 1980 | Acoustical slotted block | | | | |
| 2000 | 4" | S.F. | 4.62 | 5.05 | 9.67 |
| 2020 | 6" | " | 4.62 | 5.30 | 9.92 |
| 2040 | 8" | " | 5.09 | 6.61 | 11.70 |
| 2050 | Filled cavities | | | | |
| 2060 | 4" | S.F. | 5.65 | 5.41 | 11.06 |
| 2070 | 6" | " | 5.99 | 6.24 | 12.23 |
| 2080 | 8" | " | 6.36 | 8.00 | 14.36 |
| 4000 | Hollow, split face | | | | |
| 4020 | 4" | S.F. | 3.77 | 3.46 | 7.23 |
| 4030 | 6" | " | 3.91 | 4.01 | 7.92 |
| 4040 | 8" | " | 4.24 | 4.21 | 8.45 |
| 4080 | 10" | " | 4.62 | 4.71 | 9.33 |
| 4100 | 12" | " | 5.09 | 5.03 | 10.12 |
| 4480 | Split rib profile | | | | |
| 4500 | 4" | S.F. | 4.62 | 4.21 | 8.83 |
| 4520 | 6" | " | 4.62 | 4.89 | 9.51 |
| 4540 | 8" | " | 5.09 | 5.32 | 10.41 |
| 4560 | 10" | " | 5.09 | 5.82 | 10.91 |
| 4580 | 12" | " | 5.09 | 6.31 | 11.40 |
| 4980 | High strength block, 3500 psi | | | | |
| 5000 | 2" | S.F. | 3.77 | 1.63 | 5.40 |

© 2011 By Design & Construction Resources

## DIVISION # 04 MASONRY

### 04220.10 CONCRETE MASONRY UNITS, Cont'd...

| Code | Description | UNIT | LABOR | MAT. | TOTAL |
|---|---|---|---|---|---|
| 5020 | 4" | S.F. | 3.91 | 2.04 | 5.95 |
| 5030 | 6" | " | 3.91 | 2.44 | 6.35 |
| 5040 | 8" | " | 4.24 | 2.76 | 7.00 |
| 5050 | 10" | " | 4.62 | 3.21 | 7.83 |
| 5060 | 12" | " | 5.09 | 3.81 | 8.90 |
| 5500 | Solar screen concrete block | | | | |
| 5505 |   4" thick | | | | |
| 5510 |     6" x 6" | S.F. | 11.25 | 3.89 | 15.14 |
| 5520 |     8" x 8" | " | 10.25 | 4.65 | 14.90 |
| 5530 |     12" x 12" | " | 7.83 | 4.76 | 12.59 |
| 5540 |   8" thick | | | | |
| 5550 |     8" x 16" | S.F. | 7.27 | 4.76 | 12.03 |
| 7000 | Glazed block | | | | |
| 7020 |   Cove base, glazed 1 side, 2" | L.F. | 5.65 | 10.50 | 16.15 |
| 7030 |     4" | " | 5.65 | 10.75 | 16.40 |
| 7040 |     6" | " | 6.36 | 11.00 | 17.36 |
| 7050 |     8" | " | 6.36 | 11.75 | 18.11 |
| 7055 |   Single face | | | | |
| 7060 |     2" | S.F. | 4.24 | 11.00 | 15.24 |
| 7080 |     4" | " | 4.24 | 13.50 | 17.74 |
| 7090 |     6" | " | 4.62 | 14.50 | 19.12 |
| 7100 |     8" | " | 5.09 | 15.25 | 20.34 |
| 7105 |     10" | " | 5.65 | 17.25 | 22.90 |
| 7110 |     12" | " | 5.99 | 18.25 | 24.24 |
| 7115 |   Double face | | | | |
| 7120 |     4" | S.F. | 5.36 | 16.25 | 21.61 |
| 7140 |     6" | " | 5.65 | 19.25 | 24.90 |
| 7160 |     8" | " | 6.36 | 20.25 | 26.61 |
| 7180 |   Corner or bullnose | | | | |
| 7200 |     2" | EA. | 6.36 | 11.00 | 17.36 |
| 7240 |     4" | " | 7.27 | 14.00 | 21.27 |
| 7260 |     6" | " | 7.27 | 17.25 | 24.52 |
| 7280 |     8" | " | 8.48 | 18.75 | 27.23 |
| 7290 |     10" | " | 9.25 | 20.25 | 29.50 |
| 7300 |     12" | " | 10.25 | 22.00 | 32.25 |
| 9500 | Gypsum unit masonry | | | | |
| 9510 |   Partition blocks (12"x30") | | | | |
| 9515 |     Solid | | | | |
| 9520 |       2" | S.F. | 2.03 | 1.11 | 3.14 |
| 9525 |     Hollow | | | | |
| 9530 |       3" | S.F. | 2.03 | 1.12 | 3.15 |
| 9540 |       4" | " | 2.12 | 1.28 | 3.40 |
| 9550 |       6" | " | 2.31 | 1.37 | 3.68 |
| 9900 | Vertical reinforcing | | | | |
| 9920 |   4' o.c., add 5% to labor | | | | |
| 9940 |   2'8" o.c., add 15% to labor | | | | |
| 9960 |   Interior partitions, add 10% to labor | | | | |

### 04220.90 BOND BEAMS & LINTELS

| Code | Description | UNIT | LABOR | MAT. | TOTAL |
|---|---|---|---|---|---|
| 0980 | Bond beam, no grout or reinforcement | | | | |
| 0990 |   8" x 16" x | | | | |
| 1000 |     4" thick | L.F. | 3.91 | 1.46 | 5.37 |

## DIVISION # 04  MASONRY

| | | UNIT | LABOR | MAT. | TOTAL |
|---|---|---|---|---|---|
| **04220.90** | **BOND BEAMS & LINTELS, Cont'd...** | | | | |
| 1040 | 6" thick | L.F. | 4.07 | 2.24 | 6.31 |
| 1060 | 8" thick | " | 4.24 | 2.56 | 6.80 |
| 1080 | 10" thick | " | 4.42 | 3.17 | 7.59 |
| 1100 | 12" thick | " | 4.62 | 3.60 | 8.22 |
| 6000 | Beam lintel, no grout or reinforcement | | | | |
| 6010 | 8" x 16" x | | | | |
| 6020 | 10" thick | L.F. | 5.09 | 5.86 | 10.95 |
| 6040 | 12" thick | " | 5.65 | 7.44 | 13.09 |
| 6080 | Precast masonry lintel | | | | |
| 7000 | 6 lf, 8" high x | | | | |
| 7020 | 4" thick | L.F. | 8.48 | 5.36 | 13.84 |
| 7040 | 6" thick | " | 8.48 | 6.85 | 15.33 |
| 7060 | 8" thick | " | 9.25 | 7.75 | 17.00 |
| 7080 | 10" thick | " | 9.25 | 9.25 | 18.50 |
| 7090 | 10 lf, 8" high x | | | | |
| 7100 | 4" thick | L.F. | 5.09 | 6.74 | 11.83 |
| 7120 | 6" thick | " | 5.09 | 8.31 | 13.40 |
| 7140 | 8" thick | " | 5.65 | 9.25 | 14.90 |
| 7160 | 10" thick | " | 5.65 | 12.50 | 18.15 |
| 8000 | Steel angles and plates | | | | |
| 8010 | Minimum | Lb. | 0.72 | 1.04 | 1.76 |
| 8020 | Maximum | " | 1.27 | 1.54 | 2.81 |
| 8200 | Various size angle lintels | | | | |
| 8205 | 1/4" stock | | | | |
| 8210 | 3" x 3" | L.F. | 3.18 | 5.39 | 8.57 |
| 8220 | 3" x 3-1/2" | " | 3.18 | 5.94 | 9.12 |
| 8225 | 3/8" stock | | | | |
| 8230 | 3" x 4" | L.F. | 3.18 | 9.35 | 12.53 |
| 8240 | 3-1/2" x 4" | " | 3.18 | 9.82 | 13.00 |
| 8250 | 4" x 4" | " | 3.18 | 10.75 | 13.93 |
| 8260 | 5" x 3-1/2" | " | 3.18 | 11.50 | 14.68 |
| 8262 | 6" x 3-1/2" | " | 3.18 | 12.75 | 15.93 |
| 8265 | 1/2" stock | | | | |
| 8280 | 6" x 4" | L.F. | 3.18 | 14.25 | 17.43 |
| **04240.10** | **CLAY TILE** | | | | |
| 0100 | Hollow clay tile, for back-up, 12" x 12" | | | | |
| 1000 | Scored face | | | | |
| 1010 | Load bearing | | | | |
| 1020 | 4" thick | S.F. | 3.63 | 6.56 | 10.19 |
| 1040 | 6" thick | " | 3.77 | 7.65 | 11.42 |
| 1060 | 8" thick | " | 3.91 | 9.53 | 13.44 |
| 1080 | 10" thick | " | 4.07 | 11.75 | 15.82 |
| 1100 | 12" thick | " | 4.24 | 20.00 | 24.24 |
| 2000 | Non-load bearing | | | | |
| 2020 | 3" thick | S.F. | 3.51 | 12.75 | 16.26 |
| 2040 | 4" thick | " | 3.63 | 6.16 | 9.79 |
| 2060 | 6" thick | " | 3.77 | 7.12 | 10.89 |
| 2080 | 8" thick | " | 3.91 | 9.08 | 12.99 |
| 2100 | 12" thick | " | 4.24 | 13.00 | 17.24 |
| 4100 | Partition, 12" x 12" | | | | |
| 4150 | In walls | | | | |

## DIVISION # 04  MASONRY

| | | UNIT | LABOR | MAT. | TOTAL |
|---|---|---|---|---|---|
| **04240.10** | **CLAY TILE, Cont'd...** | | | | |
| 4201 | 3" thick | S.F. | 4.24 | 5.32 | 9.56 |
| 4210 | 4" thick | " | 4.24 | 6.17 | 10.41 |
| 4220 | 6" thick | " | 4.42 | 6.79 | 11.21 |
| 4230 | 8" thick | " | 4.62 | 8.91 | 13.53 |
| 4240 | 10" thick | " | 4.84 | 10.50 | 15.34 |
| 4250 | 12" thick | " | 5.09 | 15.50 | 20.59 |
| 4300 | Clay tile floors | | | | |
| 4320 | 4" thick | S.F. | 2.82 | 6.16 | 8.98 |
| 4330 | 6" thick | " | 2.99 | 7.65 | 10.64 |
| 4340 | 8" thick | " | 3.18 | 9.53 | 12.71 |
| 4350 | 10" thick | " | 3.39 | 11.75 | 15.14 |
| 4360 | 12" thick | " | 3.63 | 17.50 | 21.13 |
| 6000 | Terra cotta | | | | |
| 6020 | Coping, 10" or 12" wide, 3" thick | L.F. | 10.25 | 14.75 | 25.00 |
| **04270.10** | **GLASS BLOCK** | | | | |
| 1000 | Glass block, 4" thick | | | | |
| 1040 | 6" x 6" | S.F. | 17.00 | 27.50 | 44.50 |
| 1060 | 8" x 8" | " | 12.75 | 17.25 | 30.00 |
| 1080 | 12" x 12" | " | 10.25 | 22.00 | 32.25 |
| 8980 | Replacement glass blocks, 4" x 8" x 8" | | | | |
| 9100 | Minimum | S.F. | 51.00 | 21.00 | 72.00 |
| 9120 | Maximum | " | 100 | 26.75 | 127 |
| **04295.10** | **PARGING / MASONRY PLASTER** | | | | |
| 0080 | Parging | | | | |
| 0100 | 1/2" thick | S.F. | 3.39 | 0.29 | 3.68 |
| 0200 | 3/4" thick | " | 4.24 | 0.37 | 4.61 |
| 0300 | 1" thick | " | 5.09 | 0.50 | 5.59 |
| **04400.10** | **STONE** | | | | |
| 0160 | Rubble stone | | | | |
| 0180 | Walls set in mortar | | | | |
| 0200 | 8" thick | S.F. | 12.75 | 15.00 | 27.75 |
| 0220 | 12" thick | " | 20.25 | 18.25 | 38.50 |
| 0420 | 18" thick | " | 25.50 | 24.00 | 49.50 |
| 0440 | 24" thick | " | 34.00 | 30.25 | 64.25 |
| 0445 | Dry set wall | | | | |
| 0450 | 8" thick | S.F. | 8.48 | 17.00 | 25.48 |
| 0455 | 12" thick | " | 12.75 | 19.00 | 31.75 |
| 0460 | 18" thick | " | 17.00 | 26.50 | 43.50 |
| 0465 | 24" thick | " | 20.25 | 32.25 | 52.50 |
| 0480 | Cut stone | | | | |
| 0490 | Imported marble | | | | |
| 0510 | Facing panels | | | | |
| 0520 | 3/4" thick | S.F. | 20.25 | 33.25 | 53.50 |
| 0530 | 1-1/2" thick | " | 23.25 | 52.00 | 75.25 |
| 0540 | 2-1/4" thick | " | 28.25 | 63.00 | 91.25 |
| 0600 | Base | | | | |
| 0610 | 1" thick | | | | |
| 0620 | 4" high | L.F. | 25.50 | 16.50 | 42.00 |
| 0640 | 6" high | " | 25.50 | 20.00 | 45.50 |
| 0700 | Columns, solid | | | | |
| 0720 | Plain faced | C.F. | 340 | 120 | 460 |

## DIVISION # 04 MASONRY

| | | UNIT | LABOR | MAT. | TOTAL |
|---|---|---|---|---|---|
| **04400.10** | **STONE, Cont'd...** | | | | |
| 0740 | Fluted | C.F. | 340 | 320 | 660 |
| 0780 | Flooring, travertine, minimum | S.F. | 7.83 | 16.00 | 23.83 |
| 0800 | Average | " | 10.25 | 21.50 | 31.75 |
| 0820 | Maximum | " | 11.25 | 39.25 | 50.50 |
| 1000 | Domestic marble | | | | |
| 1020 | Facing panels | | | | |
| 1040 | 7/8" thick | S.F. | 20.25 | 31.75 | 52.00 |
| 1060 | 1-1/2" thick | " | 23.25 | 47.75 | 71.00 |
| 1080 | 2-1/4" thick | " | 28.25 | 58.00 | 86.25 |
| 1500 | Stairs | | | | |
| 1510 | 12" treads | L.F. | 25.50 | 28.50 | 54.00 |
| 1520 | 6" risers | " | 17.00 | 21.00 | 38.00 |
| 1525 | Thresholds, 7/8" thick, 3' long, 4" to 6" wide | | | | |
| 1530 | Plain | EA. | 42.50 | 27.00 | 69.50 |
| 1540 | Beveled | " | 42.50 | 30.00 | 72.50 |
| 1545 | Window sill | | | | |
| 1550 | 6" wide, 2" thick | L.F. | 20.25 | 15.25 | 35.50 |
| 1555 | Stools | | | | |
| 1560 | 5" wide, 7/8" thick | L.F. | 20.25 | 22.25 | 42.50 |
| 1620 | Limestone panels up to 12' x 5', smooth finish | | | | |
| 1630 | 2" thick | S.F. | 9.07 | 29.75 | 38.82 |
| 1650 | 3" thick | " | 9.07 | 34.75 | 43.82 |
| 1660 | 4" thick | " | 9.07 | 49.75 | 58.82 |
| 1760 | Miscellaneous limestone items | | | | |
| 1770 | Steps, 14" wide, 6" deep | L.F. | 34.00 | 63.00 | 97.00 |
| 1780 | Coping, smooth finish | C.F. | 17.00 | 88.00 | 105 |
| 1790 | Sills, lintels, jambs, smooth finish | " | 20.25 | 88.00 | 108 |
| 1800 | Granite veneer facing panels, polished | | | | |
| 1810 | 7/8" thick | | | | |
| 1820 | Black | S.F. | 20.25 | 46.25 | 66.50 |
| 1840 | Gray | " | 20.25 | 36.25 | 56.50 |
| 1850 | Base | | | | |
| 1860 | 4" high | L.F. | 10.25 | 19.50 | 29.75 |
| 1870 | 6" high | " | 11.25 | 23.50 | 34.75 |
| 1880 | Curbing, straight, 6" x 16" | " | 37.75 | 21.50 | 59.25 |
| 1890 | Radius curbs, radius over 5' | " | 50.00 | 26.25 | 76.25 |
| 1900 | Ashlar veneer | | | | |
| 1905 | 4" thick, random | S.F. | 20.25 | 35.75 | 56.00 |
| 1910 | Pavers, 4" x 4" split | | | | |
| 1915 | Gray | S.F. | 10.25 | 35.00 | 45.25 |
| 1920 | Pink | " | 10.25 | 34.50 | 44.75 |
| 1930 | Black | " | 10.25 | 34.00 | 44.25 |
| 2000 | Slate, panels | | | | |
| 2010 | 1" thick | S.F. | 20.25 | 25.00 | 45.25 |
| 2020 | 2" thick | " | 23.25 | 34.00 | 57.25 |
| 2030 | Sills or stools | | | | |
| 2040 | 1" thick | | | | |
| 2060 | 6" wide | L.F. | 20.25 | 11.75 | 32.00 |
| 2080 | 10" wide | " | 22.25 | 19.00 | 41.25 |
| 2100 | 2" thick | | | | |
| 2120 | 6" wide | L.F. | 23.25 | 19.00 | 42.25 |
| 2140 | 10" wide | " | 25.50 | 31.50 | 57.00 |

© 2011 By Design & Construction Resources

## DIVISION # 04 MASONRY

### 04400.10 STONE, Cont'd...

| | | UNIT | LABOR | MAT. | TOTAL |
|---|---|---|---|---|---|
| 2200 | Simulated masonry | | | | |
| 2210 | Cultured stone veneer, 1-3/4" thick | | | | |
| 2220 | Ledgestone, large-pattern | S.F. | 5.09 | 9.35 | 14.44 |
| 2230 | Small-pattern | " | 6.78 | 9.35 | 16.13 |
| 2240 | Drystack | " | 5.78 | 9.35 | 15.13 |
| 2250 | Castlestone | " | 5.19 | 9.35 | 14.54 |
| 2260 | Fieldstone | " | 5.65 | 9.35 | 15.00 |
| 2270 | Limestone | " | 4.62 | 9.35 | 13.97 |
| 2280 | Split-face | " | 5.09 | 9.35 | 14.44 |
| 2290 | Stream stone (river rock) | " | 5.36 | 9.35 | 14.71 |
| 0030 | Flagstone, strip veneer, random lengths | | | | |
| 0040 | 1" to 2-1/2" high | S.F. | 5.65 | 9.35 | 15.00 |
| 0050 | 2" to 4" high | " | 4.62 | 9.35 | 13.97 |
| 0060 | 5" to 6" high | " | 4.07 | 9.35 | 13.42 |
| 0070 | 7" to 8" high | " | 3.39 | 9.35 | 12.74 |

# DIVISION # 04 MASONRY - QUICK ESTIMATING

| Code | Description | UNIT | COST |
|---|---|---|---|
| **04999.10** | **MASONRY** | | |
| 1000 | BRICK MASONRY | | |
| 1100 | Conventional (Modular Size) | | |
| 1110 | Running Bond - 8" x 2 2/3" x 4" | S.F. | 17.45 |
| 1120 | Common Bond - 6 Course Header | " | 20.34 |
| 1130 | Stack Bond | " | 17.79 |
| 1140 | Dutch & English Bond - Every Other Course Header | " | 26.25 |
| 1150 | Every Course Header | " | 29.00 |
| 1160 | Flemish Bond - Every Other Course Header | " | 19.85 |
| 1170 | Every Course Header | " | 23.60 |
| 1200 | Add: If Scaffold Needed | " | 0.88 |
| 1210 | Add: For each 10' of Floor Hgt. or Floor (3%) | " | 0.49 |
| 1220 | Add: Piers and Corbels (15% to Labor) | " | 2.51 |
| 1230 | Add: Sills and Soldiers (20% to Labor) | " | 2.39 |
| 1240 | Add: Floor Brick (10% to Labor) | " | 1.74 |
| 1300 | Add: Weave & Herringbone Patterns (20% to Labor) | " | 2.38 |
| 1310 | Add: Stack Bond (8% to Labor) | " | 1.39 |
| 1320 | Add: Circular or Radius Work 20% to Labor) | " | 3.64 |
| 1330 | Add: Rock Faced & Slurried Face (10% to Labor) | " | 1.74 |
| 1340 | Add: Arches (75% to Labor) | " | 5.37 |
| 1350 | Add: For Winter Work (below 40°) | " | 1.74 |
| 1400 | Production Loss (10% to Labor) | " | 1.74 |
| 1410 | Enclosures - Wall Area Conventional | " | 1.74 |
| 1420 | Heat and Fuel - Wall Area Conventional | " | 0.36 |
| 1500 | Econo - 8" x 4" x 3" | " | 14.44 |
| 1600 | Panel - 8" x 8" x 4" | " | 11.33 |
| 1700 | Norman - 12" x 2 2/3" x 4" | " | 14.46 |
| 1800 | King Size - 10" x 2 5/8" x 4" | " | 12.57 |
| 1900 | Norwegian - 12" x 3 1/5" x 4" | " | 12.10 |
| 2000 | Saxon-Utility - 12" x 4" x 3" | " | 11.35 |
| 2010 | 12" x 4" x 4" | " | 11.40 |
| 2020 | 12" x 4" x 6" | " | 14.39 |
| 2030 | 12" x 4" x 8" | " | 17.11 |
| 2200 | Adobe - 12" x 3" x 4" | " | 19.72 |
| 2300 | COATED BRICK (Ceramic) | " | 23.46 |
| 2400 | COMMON BRICK (Clay, Concrete and Sand Lime) | " | 13.38 |
| 2500 | FIRE BRICK -Light Duty | " | 21.87 |
| 2510 | Heavy Duty | " | 27.75 |
| 2520 | Deduct for Residential Work - All Above - 5% | | |
| **04999.20** | **CONCRETE BLOCK** | | |
| 1000 | CONVENTIONAL (Struck 2 Sides - Partitions) | | |
| 1010 | 12" x 8" x 16" Plain | S.F. | 9.25 |
| 1020 | Bond Beam (with Fill-Reinforcing) | " | 12.24 |
| 1030 | 12" x 8" x 8" Half Block | " | 11.03 |
| 1040 | Double End - Header | " | 9.48 |
| 1050 | 8" x 8" x 16" Plain | " | 8.07 |
| 1060 | Bond Beam (with Fill-Reinforcing) | " | 9.90 |
| 1070 | 8" x 8" x 8" Half Block | " | 7.91 |
| 1080 | Double End - Header | " | 8.40 |
| 1090 | 6 "x 8" x 16" Plain | " | 7.53 |
| 2000 | Bond Beam (with Fill-Reinforcing) | " | 8.45 |
| 2010 | Half Block | " | 7.42 |

© 2011 By Design & Construction Resources

# DIVISION # 04  MASONRY - QUICK ESTIMATING

| Code | Description | UNIT | COST |
|---|---|---|---|
| **04999.20** | **CONCRETE BLOCK, Cont'd...** | | |
| 2020 | 4" x 8" x 16" Plain | S.F. | 7.29 |
| 2030 | Half Block | " | 6.36 |
| 2040 | 16" x 8" x 16" Plain | " | 10.49 |
| 2050 | Half Block | " | 9.99 |
| 2060 | 14" x 8" x 16" Plain | " | 9.95 |
| 2070 | Half Block | " | 9.46 |
| 2080 | 10" x 8" x 16" Plain | " | 8.62 |
| 3000 | Bond Beam (with Fill-Reinforcing) | " | 9.93 |
| 3010 | Half Block | " | 9.67 |
| 3020 | Deduct: Block Struck or Cleaned One Side | " | 0.30 |
| 3030 | Deduct: Block Not Struck or Cleaned Two Sides | " | 0.48 |
| 3040 | Deduct: Clean One Side Only | " | 0.21 |
| 3050 | Deduct: Lt. Wt. Block (Labor Only) | " | 0.18 |
| 4000 | Add: Jamb and Sash Block | " | 0.51 |
| 4010 | Add: Bullnose Block | " | 0.75 |
| 4020 | Add: Pilaster, Pier, Pedestal Work | " | 0.84 |
| 4030 | Add: Stack Bond Work | " | 0.31 |
| 4040 | Add: Radius or Circular Work | " | 1.56 |
| 5000 | Add: If Scaffold Needed | " | 0.86 |
| 5010 | Add: Winter Production Cost (10% Labor) | " | 0.50 |
| 5020 | Add: Winter Enclosing - Wall Area | " | 0.50 |
| 5030 | Add: Winter Heating - Wall Area | " | 0.46 |
| 5040 | Add: Core & Beam Filling - See 0411 (Page 4A-18) | | |
| 5050 | Add: Insulation - See 0412 (Page 4A-18) | | |
| 6000 | Deduct for Residential Work - 5% | | |
| 8010 | SCREEN WALL - 4" x 12" x 12" | S.F. | 7.21 |
| 8020 | BURNISHED - 12" x 8" x 16" | " | 13.50 |
| 8030 | 8" x 8" x 16" | " | 12.58 |
| 8040 | 6" x 8" x 16" | " | 11.49 |
| 8050 | 4" x 8" x 16" | " | 10.78 |
| 8060 | 2" x 8" x 16" | " | 9.71 |
| 8070 | Add for Shapes | " | 2.92 |
| 8080 | Add for 2 Faced Finish | " | 4.22 |
| 8090 | Add for Scored Finish - 1 Face | " | 1.02 |
| 8100 | PREFACED UNITS -12" x 8" x 16" Stretcher | " | 18.87 |
| 8110 | (Ceramic Glazed) 12" x 8" x 16" Glazed 2 Face | " | 25.25 |
| 8120 | 8" x 8" x 16" Stretcher | " | 17.59 |
| 8130 | Glazed 2 Face | " | 24.01 |
| 8140 | 6" x 8" x 16" Stretcher | " | 15.77 |
| 8150 | Glazed 2 Face | " | 23.94 |
| 8160 | 4" x 8" x 16" Stretcher | " | 16.54 |
| 8170 | Glazed 2 Face | " | 22.99 |
| 8180 | 2" x 8" x 16" Stretcher | " | 16.41 |
| 8190 | 4" x 16" x 16" Stretcher | " | 42.25 |
| 8200 | Add for Base, Caps, Jambs, Headers, Lintels | " | 4.73 |
| 8210 | Add for Scored Block | " | 1.40 |
| **04999.30** | **CLAY BACKING AND PARTITION TILE** | | |
| 0010 | 3" x 12" x 12" | S.F. | 6.29 |
| 0020 | 4" x 12" x 12" | " | 6.74 |
| 0030 | 6" x 12" x 12" | " | 8.02 |
| 0040 | 8" x 12" x 12" | " | 8.79 |

# DIVISION # 04 MASONRY - QUICK ESTIMATING

| | | UNIT | COST |
|---|---|---|---|
| **04999.40** | **CLAY FACING TILE (GLAZED)** | | |
| 1000 | 6T or 5" x 12" - SERIES | | |
| 1010 | 2" x 5 1/3" x 12" Soap Stretcher (Solid Back) | S.F. | 22.99 |
| 1020 | 4" x 5 1/2" x 12" 1 Face Stretcher | " | 24.62 |
| 1030 | 2 Face Stretcher | " | 29.00 |
| 1040 | 6" x 5 1/3" x 12" 1 Face Stretcher | " | 29.50 |
| 1050 | 8" x 5 1/3" x 12" 1 Face Stretcher | " | 16.79 |
| 2000 | 8W or 8" x 16" - SERIES | | |
| 2010 | 2" x 8" x 16" Soap Stretcher (Solid Back) | S.F. | 17.50 |
| 2020 | 4" x 8" x 16" 1 Face Stretcher | " | 17.97 |
| 2030 | 2 Face Stretcher | " | 23.71 |
| 2040 | 6" x 8" x 16" 1 Face Stretcher | " | 21.07 |
| 2050 | 8" x 8" x 16" 1 Face Stretcher | " | 22.22 |
| 2060 | Add for Shapes (Average) | PCT. | 50.00 |
| 2070 | Add for Designer Colors | " | 20.00 |
| 2080 | Add for Less than Truckload Lots | " | 10.00 |
| 2090 | Add for Base Only | " | 25.00 |
| **04999.50** | **GLASS UNITS** | | |
| 0010 | 4" x 8" x 4" | S.F. | 58.25 |
| 0020 | 6" x 6" x 4" | " | 62.00 |
| 0030 | 8" x 8" x 4" | " | 37.75 |
| 0040 | 12" x 12" x 4" | " | 38.00 |
| **04999.60** | **TERRA-COTTA** | | |
| 0010 | Unglazed | S.F. | 13.09 |
| 0020 | Glazed | " | 17.59 |
| 0030 | Colored Glazed | " | 21.07 |
| **04999.70** | **FLUE LINING** | | |
| 0010 | 8" x 12" | S.F. | 21.84 |
| 0020 | 12" x 12" | " | 23.62 |
| 0030 | 16" x 16" | " | 37.75 |
| 0040 | 18" x 18" | " | 38.50 |
| 0050 | 20" x 20" | " | 75.75 |
| 0060 | 24" x 24" | " | 96.50 |
| **04999.80** | **NATURAL STONE** | | |
| 1000 | CUT STONE BY S.F. | | |
| 1010 | Limestone- Indiana and Alabama - 3" | S.F. | 43.50 |
| 1020 | 4" | " | 47.75 |
| 1030 | Minnesota, Wisc, Texas, etc.- 3" | " | 48.50 |
| 1040 | 4" | " | 55.75 |
| 1200 | Marble - 2" | " | 60.25 |
| 1210 | 3" | " | 64.00 |
| 1300 | Granite - 2" | " | 56.25 |
| 1310 | 3" | " | 60.75 |
| 1400 | Slate - 1 1/2" | " | 60.25 |
| 2000 | Ashlar - 4" Sawed Bed | | |
| 2100 | Limestone- Indiana - Random | S.F. | 34.00 |
| 2110 | Coursed - 2" - 5" - 8" | " | 32.75 |
| 2120 | Minnesota, Alabama, Wisconsin, etc. | | |
| 2130 | Split Face - Random | S.F. | 34.00 |
| 2140 | Coursed | " | 38.50 |
| 2150 | Sawed or Planed Face - Random | " | 36.75 |
| 2160 | Coursed | " | 39.00 |

© 2011 By Design & Construction Resources

## DIVISION # 04  MASONRY - QUICK ESTIMATING

| | | UNIT | COST |
|---|---|---|---|
| **04999.80** | **NATURAL STONE, Cont'd...** | | |
| 2200 | Marble - Sawed - Random | S.F. | 48.25 |
| 2210 | Coursed | " | 49.00 |
| 2300 | Granite - Bushhammered - Random | " | 49.25 |
| 2310 | Coursed | " | 54.75 |
| 2400 | Quartzite | " | 38.00 |
| 3000 | ROUGH STONE | | |
| 3100 | Rubble and Flagstone | S.F. | 34.75 |
| 3200 | Field Stone or Boulders | " | 32.75 |
| 3300 | Light Weight Boulders (Igneous) | | |
| 3310 | 2" to 4" Veneer - Sawed Back | S.F. | 28.25 |
| 3320 | 3" to 10" Boulders | " | 29.75 |
| 3330 | CUT STONE BY C.F | | |
| 3400 | Limestone- Indiana and Alabama - 3" | C.F. | 187 |
| 3410 | 4" | " | 138 |
| 3420 | Minnesota, Wisc, Texas, etc.- 3" | " | 196 |
| 3430 | 4" | " | 184 |
| 3500 | Marble - 2" | " | 420 |
| 3510 | 3" | " | 260 |
| 3600 | Granite - 2" | " | 390 |
| 3610 | 3" | " | 260 |
| 3700 | Slate - 1 1/2" | " | 400 |
| 3800 | ASHLAR Limestone- Indiana - Random | " | 101 |
| 3810 | Coursed - 2" - 5" - 8" | " | 101 |
| 3820 | Split Face - Random | " | 102 |
| 3830 | Coursed | " | 126 |
| 3840 | Sawed or Planed Face - Random | " | 125 |
| 3850 | Coursed | " | 127 |
| 3900 | Marble - Sawed - Random | " | 155 |
| 3910 | Coursed | " | 156 |
| 4000 | Granite - Bushhammered - Random | " | 158 |
| 4010 | Coursed | " | 162 |
| 4100 | Quartzite | " | 125 |
| 4200 | ROUGH STONE, Rubble and Flagstone | " | 102 |
| 4300 | Field Stone or Boulders | " | 101 |
| **04999.90** | **PRECAST VENEERS AND SIMULATED MASONRY** | | |
| 1000 | ARCHITECTURAL PRECAST STONE | | |
| 1005 | Limestone | S.F. | 42.75 |
| 1010 | Marble | " | 51.00 |
| 2010 | PRECAST CONCRETE | " | 34.75 |
| 3010 | MOSAIC GRANITE PANELS | " | 48.00 |
| **04999.91** | **MORTAR** | | |
| 0010 | Portland Cement and Lime Mortar - Labor in Unit Costs | S.F. | 128 |
| 0020 | Masonry Cement Mortar - Labor in Unit Costs | " | 123 |
| 0030 | Mortar for Standard Brick - Material Only | " | 0.53 |
| **04999.92** | **CORE FILLING FOR REINFORCED CONCRETE** | | |
| 1010 | Add to Block Prices in 0402.0 (Job Mixed) | | |
| 1020 | 12" x 8" x 16" Plain (includes #4 Rod 16" O.C. Vertical) | S.F. | 3.99 |
| 1030 | Bond Beam (includes 2 #4 Rods) | " | 4.70 |
| 1040 | 8" x 8" x 6" Plain (includes #4 Rod 16" O.C. Vertical) | " | 2.43 |
| 1050 | Bond Beam (includes 2 #4 Rods) | " | 1.98 |
| 1060 | 6" x 8" x 16" Plain | " | 2.15 |

# DIVISION # 04 MASONRY - QUICK ESTIMATING

| | | UNIT | COST |
|---|---|---|---|
| **04999.92** | **CORE FILLING FOR REINFORCED CONCRETE BLOCK, Cont'd...** | | |
| 1070 | Bond Beam (includes 1 #4 Rod ) | S.F. | 1.11 |
| 1080 | 10" x 8" x 16"  Bond Beam (includes 2 #4 Rods) | " | 4.26 |
| 1090 | 14" x 8" x 16"  Bond Beam (includes 2 #4 Rods) | " | 4.87 |
| **04999.93** | **CORE AND CAVITY FILL FOR INSULATED** | | |
| 2100 | LOOSE | | |
| 2110 | Core Fill - Expanded Styrene | | |
| 2120 | 12" x 8" x 16"  Concrete Block | S.F. | 1.50 |
| 2130 | 10" x 8" x 16"  Concrete Block | " | 1.33 |
| 2140 | 8" x 8" x 16"  Concrete Block | " | 0.95 |
| 2150 | 6" x 8" x 16"  Concrete Block | " | 0.82 |
| 2160 | 8" Brick - Jumbo - Thru the Wall | " | 0.72 |
| 2170 | 6" Brick - Jumbo - Thru the Wall | " | 0.58 |
| 2180 | 4" Brick - Jumbo | " | 0.50 |
| 2190 | Cavity Fill - per Inch | | |
| 2200 | Expanded Styrene | S.F. | 0.64 |
| 2210 | Mica | " | 1.07 |
| 2220 | Fiber Glass | " | 0.66 |
| 2230 | Rock Wool | " | 0.66 |
| 2240 | Cellulose | " | 0.65 |
| 2300 | RIGID - Fiber Glass - 3# Density, 1" | " | 1.11 |
| 2310 | 2"1.58   - | | |
| 2320 | Expanded Styrene - Molded - 1# Density, 1" | S.F. | 0.82 |
| 2330 | 2" | " | 1.22 |
| 2340 | Extruded - 2#  Density, 1" | " | 1.17 |
| 2350 | 2" | " | 1.78 |
| 2360 | Expanded Urethane - 1" | " | 1.26 |
| 2370 | 2" | " | 1.67 |
| 2380 | Perlite - 1" | " | 1.22 |
| 2390 | 2" | " | 1.89 |
| 2400 | Add for Embedded Water Type | " | 1.89 |
| 2410 | Add for Glued Applications | " | 0.07 |
| **04999.95** | **CLEANING AND POINTING** | | |
| 4010 | Brick and Stone - Acid or Chemicals | S.F. | 0.90 |
| 4020 | Soap and Water | " | 0.84 |
| 4030 | Block & Facing Tile - 1 Face (Incl. Hollow Metal Frames) | " | 0.47 |
| 4040 | Point with White Cement | " | 1.79 |
| **04999.97** | **SCAFFOLD** | | |
| 7100 | EQUIPMENT, TOOLS AND BLADES | | |
| 7110 | Percentage of Labor as an average | PCT. | 7.00 |
| 7120 | See Division 1 for Rental Rates & New Costs | | |
| 7200 | SCAFFOLD- Tubular Frame - to 40 feet - Exterior | S.F. | 1.12 |
| 7210 | Tubular Frame - to 16 feet - Interior | " | 1.07 |
| 7220 | Swing Stage - 40 feet and up | " | 1.18 |

© 2011 By Design & Construction Resources

**Design & Construction Resources**

# DIVISION # 05  METALS

## TABLE OF CONTENTS — PAGE

| | |
|---|---|
| 05050.10 - STRUCTURAL WELDING | 05-2 |
| 05050.30 - MECHANICAL ANCHORS | 05-2 |
| 05050.90 - METAL ANCHORS | 05-4 |
| 05050.95 - METAL LINTELS | 05-4 |
| 05120.10 - STRUCTURAL STEEL | 05-4 |
| 05410.10 - METAL FRAMING | 05-4 |
| 05510.10 - STAIRS | 05-5 |
| 05515.10 - LADDERS | 05-6 |
| 05520.10 - RAILINGS | 05-6 |
| 05580.10 - METAL SPECIALTIES | 05-6 |
| 05700.10 - ORNAMENTAL METAL | 05-7 |
| **QUICK ESTIMATING** | 05A-8 |

© 2011 By Design & Construction Resources

# DIVISION # 05 METALS

| | | UNIT | LABOR | MAT. | TOTAL |
|---|---|---|---|---|---|
| **05050.10** | **STRUCTURAL WELDING** | | | | |
| 0080 | Welding | | | | |
| 0100 | Single pass | | | | |
| 0120 | 1/8" | L.F. | 2.95 | 0.33 | 3.28 |
| 0140 | 3/16" | " | 3.93 | 0.55 | 4.48 |
| 0160 | 1/4" | " | 4.91 | 0.77 | 5.68 |
| **05050.30** | **MECHANICAL ANCHORS** | | | | |
| 0010 | Drop-in, stainless steel, for masonry, 3/8" | EA. | | | 0.97 |
| 0020 | 1/2" | " | | | 1.07 |
| 0030 | Hollow wall, for use in gypsum drywall, 6-32"x | | | | |
| 0040 | 1-1/4" | EA. | | | 0.33 |
| 0050 | 1-1/2" | " | | | 0.38 |
| 0060 | 1-3/4" | " | | | 0.35 |
| 0070 | 2" | " | | | 0.33 |
| 0080 | 2-3/8" | " | | | 0.35 |
| 1000 | Concrete anchor, 3/16"x | | | | |
| 1010 | 1-1/4" | EA. | | | 0.44 |
| 1020 | 1-3/4" | " | | | 0.55 |
| 1030 | 2-3/4" | " | | | 0.55 |
| 1040 | 1/4"x | | | | |
| 1050 | 1-1/4" | EA. | | | 0.55 |
| 1060 | 2-1/4" | " | | | 0.66 |
| 1070 | 2-3/4" | " | | | 0.71 |
| 1080 | Toggle anchor, 5/8" | " | | | 1.50 |
| 2000 | 3/4" | " | | | 1.50 |
| 2010 | Toggle bolts, 1/8"x | | | | |
| 2020 | 2" | EA. | | | 0.27 |
| 2030 | 3" | " | | | 0.27 |
| 2040 | 4" | " | | | 0.27 |
| 2050 | 3/16"x | | | | |
| 2060 | 2" | EA. | | | 0.55 |
| 2070 | 3" | " | | | 0.55 |
| 2080 | 4" | " | | | 0.55 |
| 2090 | 1/4"x | | | | |
| 3000 | 2" | EA. | | | 0.80 |
| 3010 | 3" | " | | | 0.80 |
| 3020 | 4" | " | | | 0.80 |
| 3030 | 6" | " | | | 1.61 |
| 3050 | Sleeve anchor, 3/8"x | | | | |
| 3060 | 1-7/8" | EA. | | | 0.37 |
| 3070 | 2-1/4" | " | | | 0.42 |
| 3080 | 3" | " | | | 0.48 |
| 3090 | 1/4x2-1/4" | " | | | 0.43 |
| 4000 | 1/2"x | | | | |
| 4010 | 2-1/4" | EA. | | | 0.48 |
| 4020 | 3" | " | | | 0.54 |
| 4030 | 4" | " | | | 0.72 |
| 4040 | 5/8"x | | | | |
| 4050 | 2-1/4" | EA. | | | 0.84 |
| 4060 | 4-1/4" | " | | | 0.84 |
| 4070 | 6" | " | | | 0.90 |
| 4080 | Machine screw, corrosion resistant, for use in masonry, 5/8"x | | | | |

© 2011 By Design & Construction Resources

## DIVISION # 05  METALS

| 05050.30 | MECHANICAL ANCHORS, Cont'd... | UNIT | LABOR | MAT. | TOTAL |
|---|---|---|---|---|---|
| 4090 | 2" | EA. | | | 0.90 |
| 5000 | 4" | " | | | 1.37 |
| 5010 | 6" | " | | | 2.32 |
| 5020 | 8" | " | | | 3.36 |
| 5030 | Wedge anchor, 1/4"x2-1/4" | " | | | 0.48 |
| 5040 | 3/8"x | | | | |
| 5050 | 2-1/4" | EA. | | | 0.44 |
| 5060 | 3" | " | | | 0.56 |
| 5070 | 4" | " | | | 0.63 |
| 5080 | 5" | " | | | 0.75 |
| 5090 | 1/2"x | | | | |
| 6000 | 2-1/2" | EA. | | | 0.60 |
| 6010 | 3-1/4" | " | | | 1.11 |
| 6020 | 4-1/4" | " | | | 1.32 |
| 6030 | 5-1/2" | " | | | 1.64 |
| 6040 | 5/8"x | | | | |
| 6050 | 6" | EA. | | | 2.36 |
| 6060 | 7" | " | | | 2.77 |
| 6070 | 8" | " | | | 3.18 |
| 6080 | Spring wing, toggle bolt, for use in hollow walls, 1/8"x | | | | |
| 6090 | 2" | EA. | | | 0.39 |
| 7000 | 3" | " | | | 0.39 |
| 7010 | 4" | " | | | 0.39 |
| 7020 | 3/16"x | | | | |
| 7030 | 2" | EA. | | | 0.55 |
| 7040 | 3" | " | | | 0.55 |
| 7050 | 4" | " | | | 0.55 |
| 7060 | 5" | " | | | 0.55 |
| 7070 | 1/4"x | | | | |
| 7080 | 2" | EA. | | | 0.80 |
| 7090 | 3" | " | | | 0.80 |
| 8000 | 4" | " | | | 0.80 |
| 8010 | 3/8"x6" | " | | | 1.61 |
| 8020 | Stud anchor, 1-1/4" | " | | | 0.55 |
| 8030 | 3/4" | " | | | 0.55 |
| 8040 | Hex bolt, zinc plated, 3/4"x | | | | |
| 8050 | 4" | EA. | | | 2.72 |
| 8060 | 6" | " | | | 3.36 |
| 8070 | 8" | " | | | 3.99 |
| 8080 | 1/2"x | | | | |
| 8090 | 4" | EA. | | | 0.94 |
| 9000 | 6" | " | | | 1.46 |
| 9010 | 8" | " | | | 1.86 |
| 9020 | Lag screw, 1/4"x | | | | |
| 9030 | 2" | EA. | | | 0.19 |
| 9040 | 4" | " | | | 0.42 |
| 9050 | 6" | " | | | 0.67 |
| 9060 | Machine screw, zinc plated, 5/8"x | | | | |
| 9070 | 4" | EA. | | | 1.21 |
| 9100 | 6" | " | | | 2.04 |
| 9110 | 8" | " | | | 2.96 |
| 9120 | Ribbed plastic anchor 5/8"x | | | | |

© 2011 By Design & Construction Resources

## DIVISION # 05 METALS

| | | UNIT | LABOR | MAT. | TOTAL |
|---|---|---|---|---|---|
| **05050.30** | **MECHANICAL ANCHORS, Cont'd...** | | | | |
| 9130 | 1-1/4" | EA. | | | 0.25 |
| 9140 | 1-1/2" | " | | | 0.36 |
| **05050.90** | **METAL ANCHORS** | | | | |
| 1000 | Anchor bolts | | | | |
| 1020 | 3/8" x | | | | |
| 1040 | 8" long | EA. | | | 0.97 |
| 1080 | 12" long | " | | | 1.16 |
| 1090 | 1/2" x | | | | |
| 1100 | 8" long | EA. | | | 1.46 |
| 1140 | 12" long | " | | | 1.70 |
| 1170 | 5/8" x | | | | |
| 1180 | 8" long | EA. | | | 1.36 |
| 1220 | 12" long | " | | | 1.60 |
| 1270 | 3/4" x | | | | |
| 1280 | 8" long | EA. | | | 1.94 |
| 1300 | 12" long | " | | | 2.18 |
| 4480 | Non-drilling anchor | | | | |
| 4500 | 1/4" | EA. | | | 0.64 |
| 4540 | 3/8" | " | | | 0.80 |
| 4560 | 1/2" | " | | | 1.23 |
| 7000 | Self-drilling anchor | | | | |
| 7020 | 1/4" | EA. | | | 1.62 |
| 7060 | 3/8" | " | | | 2.44 |
| 7080 | 1/2" | " | | | 3.25 |
| **05050.95** | **METAL LINTELS** | | | | |
| 0080 | Lintels, steel | | | | |
| 0100 | Plain | Lb. | 1.47 | 1.33 | 2.80 |
| 0120 | Galvanized | " | 1.47 | 2.00 | 3.47 |
| **05120.10** | **STRUCTURAL STEEL** | | | | |
| 0100 | Beams and girders, A-36 | | | | |
| 0120 | Welded | TON | 680 | 2,650 | 3,330 |
| 0140 | Bolted | " | 610 | 2,590 | 3,200 |
| 0180 | Columns | | | | |
| 0185 | Pipe | | | | |
| 0190 | 6" dia. | Lb. | 0.67 | 1.49 | 2.16 |
| 1300 | Structural tube | | | | |
| 1310 | 6" square | | | | |
| 1320 | Light sections | TON | 1,350 | 3,480 | 4,830 |
| **05410.10** | **METAL FRAMING** | | | | |
| 0100 | Furring channel, galvanized | | | | |
| 0110 | Beams and columns, 3/4" | | | | |
| 0120 | 12" o.c. | S.F. | 5.90 | 0.39 | 6.29 |
| 0140 | 16" o.c. | " | 5.36 | 0.30 | 5.66 |
| 0150 | Walls, 3/4" | | | | |
| 0160 | 12" o.c. | S.F. | 2.95 | 0.39 | 3.34 |
| 0170 | 16" o.c. | " | 2.45 | 0.30 | 2.75 |
| 0172 | 24" o.c. | " | 1.96 | 0.22 | 2.18 |
| 0173 | 1-1/2" | | | | |
| 0174 | 12" o.c. | S.F. | 2.95 | 0.66 | 3.61 |
| 0175 | 16" o.c. | " | 2.45 | 0.49 | 2.94 |
| 0176 | 24" o.c. | " | 1.96 | 0.34 | 2.30 |

# DIVISION # 05 METALS

| | | UNIT | LABOR | MAT. | TOTAL |
|---|---|---|---|---|---|
| **05410.10** | **METAL FRAMING, Cont'd...** | | | | |
| 0177 | Stud, load bearing | | | | |
| 0178 | 16" o.c. | | | | |
| 0179 | 16 ga. | | | | |
| 0180 | 2-1/2" | S.F. | 2.62 | 1.21 | 3.83 |
| 0190 | 3-5/8" | " | 2.62 | 1.43 | 4.05 |
| 0200 | 4" | " | 2.62 | 1.48 | 4.10 |
| 0220 | 6" | " | 2.95 | 1.87 | 4.82 |
| 0280 | 18 ga. | | | | |
| 0300 | 2-1/2" | S.F. | 2.62 | 0.99 | 3.61 |
| 0310 | 3-5/8" | " | 2.62 | 1.21 | 3.83 |
| 0320 | 4" | " | 2.62 | 1.26 | 3.88 |
| 0330 | 6" | " | 2.95 | 1.59 | 4.54 |
| 0350 | 8" | " | 2.95 | 1.92 | 4.87 |
| 0360 | 20 ga. | | | | |
| 0370 | 2-1/2" | S.F. | 2.62 | 0.55 | 3.17 |
| 0390 | 3-5/8" | " | 2.62 | 0.66 | 3.28 |
| 0400 | 4" | " | 2.62 | 0.71 | 3.33 |
| 0420 | 6" | " | 2.95 | 0.88 | 3.83 |
| 0440 | 8" | " | 2.95 | 1.04 | 3.99 |
| 0480 | 24" o.c. | | | | |
| 0490 | 16 ga. | | | | |
| 0500 | 2-1/2" | S.F. | 2.26 | 0.82 | 3.08 |
| 0510 | 3-5/8" | " | 2.26 | 0.99 | 3.25 |
| 0520 | 4" | " | 2.26 | 1.04 | 3.30 |
| 0530 | 6" | " | 2.45 | 1.26 | 3.71 |
| 0540 | 8" | " | 2.45 | 1.59 | 4.04 |
| 0545 | 18 ga. | | | | |
| 0550 | 2-1/2" | S.F. | 2.26 | 0.66 | 2.92 |
| 0560 | 3-5/8" | " | 2.26 | 0.77 | 3.03 |
| 0570 | 4" | " | 2.26 | 0.82 | 3.08 |
| 0580 | 6" | " | 2.45 | 1.04 | 3.49 |
| 0590 | 8" | " | 2.45 | 1.26 | 3.71 |
| 0595 | 20 ga. | | | | |
| 0600 | 2-1/2" | S.F. | 2.26 | 0.44 | 2.70 |
| 0610 | 3-5/8" | " | 2.26 | 0.49 | 2.75 |
| 0620 | 4" | " | 2.26 | 0.55 | 2.81 |
| 0630 | 6" | " | 2.45 | 0.71 | 3.16 |
| 0640 | 8" | " | 2.45 | 0.88 | 3.33 |
| **05510.10** | **STAIRS** | | | | |
| 1000 | Stock unit, steel, complete, per riser | | | | |
| 1010 | Tread | | | | |
| 1020 | 3'-6" wide | EA. | 74.00 | 140 | 214 |
| 1040 | 4' wide | " | 84.00 | 160 | 244 |
| 1060 | 5' wide | " | 98.00 | 180 | 278 |
| 1200 | Metal pan stair, cement filled, per riser | | | | |
| 1220 | 3'-6" wide | EA. | 59.00 | 150 | 209 |
| 1240 | 4' wide | " | 66.00 | 170 | 236 |
| 1260 | 5' wide | " | 74.00 | 190 | 264 |
| 1280 | Landing, steel pan | S.F. | 14.75 | 58.00 | 72.75 |
| 1300 | Cast iron tread, steel stringers, stock units, per riser | | | | |
| 1310 | Tread | | | | |

© 2011 By Design & Construction Resources

# DIVISION # 05  METALS

| | | UNIT | LABOR | MAT. | TOTAL |
|---|---|---|---|---|---|
| **05510.10** | **STAIRS, Cont'd...** | | | | |
| 1320 | 3'-6" wide | EA. | 74.00 | 260 | 334 |
| 1340 | 4' wide | " | 84.00 | 300 | 384 |
| 1360 | 5' wide | " | 98.00 | 360 | 458 |
| 1400 | Stair treads, abrasive, 12" x 3'-6" | | | | |
| 1410 | Cast iron | | | | |
| 1420 | 3/8" | EA. | 29.50 | 140 | 170 |
| 1440 | 1/2" | " | 29.50 | 180 | 210 |
| 1450 | Cast aluminum | | | | |
| 1460 | 5/16" | EA. | 29.50 | 170 | 200 |
| 1480 | 3/8" | " | 29.50 | 180 | 210 |
| 1500 | 1/2" | " | 29.50 | 210 | 240 |
| **05515.10** | **LADDERS** | | | | |
| 0100 | Ladder, 18" wide | | | | |
| 0110 | With cage | L.F. | 39.25 | 94.00 | 133 |
| 0120 | Without cage | " | 29.50 | 59.00 | 88.50 |
| **05520.10** | **RAILINGS** | | | | |
| 0080 | Railing, pipe | | | | |
| 0090 | 1-1/4" diameter, welded steel | | | | |
| 0095 | 2-rail | | | | |
| 0100 | Primed | L.F. | 11.75 | 29.75 | 41.50 |
| 0120 | Galvanized | " | 11.75 | 38.00 | 49.75 |
| 0130 | 3-rail | | | | |
| 0140 | Primed | L.F. | 14.75 | 38.00 | 52.75 |
| 0160 | Galvanized | " | 14.75 | 49.25 | 64.00 |
| 0170 | Wall mounted, single rail, welded steel | | | | |
| 0180 | Primed | L.F. | 9.07 | 19.75 | 28.82 |
| 0200 | Galvanized | " | 9.07 | 25.75 | 34.82 |
| 0210 | 1-1/2" diameter, welded steel | | | | |
| 0215 | 2-rail | | | | |
| 0220 | Primed | L.F. | 11.75 | 32.25 | 44.00 |
| 0240 | Galvanized | " | 11.75 | 41.75 | 53.50 |
| 0245 | 3-rail | | | | |
| 0250 | Primed | L.F. | 14.75 | 40.50 | 55.25 |
| 0260 | Galvanized | " | 14.75 | 53.00 | 67.75 |
| 0270 | Wall mounted, single rail, welded steel | | | | |
| 0280 | Primed | L.F. | 9.07 | 21.50 | 30.57 |
| 0300 | Galvanized | " | 9.07 | 28.00 | 37.07 |
| 0960 | 2" diameter, welded steel | | | | |
| 0980 | 2-rail | | | | |
| 1000 | Primed | L.F. | 13.00 | 40.50 | 53.50 |
| 1020 | Galvanized | " | 13.00 | 53.00 | 66.00 |
| 1030 | 3-rail | | | | |
| 1040 | Primed | L.F. | 16.75 | 51.00 | 67.75 |
| 1070 | Galvanized | " | 16.75 | 66.00 | 82.75 |
| 1075 | Wall mounted, single rail, welded steel | | | | |
| 1080 | Primed | L.F. | 9.83 | 23.25 | 33.08 |
| 1100 | Galvanized | " | 9.83 | 30.25 | 40.08 |
| **05580.10** | **METAL SPECIALTIES** | | | | |
| 0060 | Kick plate | | | | |
| 0080 | 4" high x 1/4" thick | | | | |
| 0100 | Primed | L.F. | 11.75 | 7.70 | 19.45 |

© 2011 By Design & Construction Resources

# DIVISION # 05 METALS

| | | UNIT | LABOR | MAT. | TOTAL |
|---|---|---|---|---|---|
| **05580.10** | **METAL SPECIALTIES, Cont'd...** | | | | |
| 0120 | Galvanized | L.F. | 11.75 | 8.74 | 20.49 |
| 0130 | 6" high x 1/4" thick | | | | |
| 0140 | Primed | L.F. | 13.00 | 7.92 | 20.92 |
| 0160 | Galvanized | " | 13.00 | 9.40 | 22.40 |
| 0200 | Fire Escape (10'-12' high) | | | | |
| 0210 | Landing with fixed stair, 3'-6" wide | EA. | 1,180 | 5,060 | 6,240 |
| 0220 | 4'-6" wide | " | 1,180 | 5,720 | 6,900 |
| **05700.10** | **ORNAMENTAL METAL** | | | | |
| 1020 | Railings, square bars, 6" o.c., shaped top rails | | | | |
| 1040 | Steel | L.F. | 29.50 | 88.00 | 118 |
| 1060 | Aluminum | " | 29.50 | 110 | 140 |
| 1080 | Bronze | " | 39.25 | 190 | 229 |
| 1100 | Stainless steel | " | 39.25 | 180 | 219 |
| 1200 | Laminated metal or wood handrails | | | | |
| 1220 | 2-1/2" round or oval shape | L.F. | 29.50 | 280 | 310 |
| 2020 | Grilles and louvers | | | | |
| 2040 | Fixed type louvers | | | | |
| 2060 | 4 through 10 sf | S.F. | 9.83 | 28.25 | 38.08 |
| 2080 | Over 10 sf | " | 7.37 | 33.25 | 40.62 |
| 2200 | Movable type louvers | | | | |
| 2220 | 4 through 10 sf | S.F. | 9.83 | 33.25 | 43.08 |
| 2240 | Over 10 sf | " | 7.37 | 36.75 | 44.12 |
| 3000 | Aluminum louvers | | | | |
| 3010 | Residential use, fixed type, with screen | | | | |
| 3020 | 8" x 8" | EA. | 29.50 | 17.25 | 46.75 |
| 3060 | 12" x 12" | " | 29.50 | 19.00 | 48.50 |
| 3080 | 12" x 18" | " | 29.50 | 22.75 | 52.25 |
| 3100 | 14" x 24" | " | 29.50 | 32.75 | 62.25 |
| 3120 | 18" x 24" | " | 29.50 | 36.75 | 66.25 |
| 3140 | 30" x 24" | " | 32.75 | 50.00 | 82.75 |

© 2011 By Design & Construction Resources

# DIVISION # 05 METALS - QUICK ESTIMATING

| | | UNIT | COST |
|---|---|---|---|
| **05999.10** | **STRUCTURAL STEEL FRAME** | | |
| 1000 | To 30 Ton 20' Span | S.F. | 11.25 |
| 1010 | 24' Span | " | 11.87 |
| 1020 | 28' Span | " | 11.99 |
| 1030 | 32' Span | " | 14.38 |
| 1040 | 36' Span | " | 16.03 |
| 2010 | 44' Span | " | 18.27 |
| 2020 | 48' Span | " | 19.62 |
| 2030 | 52' Span | " | 21.90 |
| 2050 | 60' Span | " | 25.46 |
| 3000 | Deduct for Over 30 Ton | PCT. | 5.00 |
| **05999.40** | **OPEN WEB JOISTS** | | |
| 1000 | To 20 Ton, 20' Span | S.F. | 4.17 |
| 1010 | 24' Span | " | 4.20 |
| 1030 | 32' Span | " | 4.29 |
| 2000 | 40' Span | " | 4.93 |
| 2010 | 48' Span | " | 5.82 |
| 2030 | 56' Span | " | 6.78 |
| 2040 | 60' Span | " | 7.28 |
| 3000 | Deduct for Over 20 Ton | PCT. | 10.00 |
| **05999.50** | **METAL DECKING** | | |
| 1000 | 1/2" Deep - Ribbed - Baked Enamel - 18 Ga | S.F. | 4.43 |
| 1020 | 22 Ga | " | 3.73 |
| 2000 | 3" Deep - Ribbed - Baked Enamel - 18 Ga | " | 8.83 |
| 2020 | 22 Ga | " | 7.77 |
| 3000 | 4 1/2" Deep - Ribbed - Baked Enamel - 16 Ga | " | 11.62 |
| 3010 | 18 Ga | " | 10.04 |
| 3020 | 20 Ga | " | 9.35 |
| 4000 | 3" Deep - Cellular - 18 Ga | " | 11.34 |
| 4010 | 16 Ga | " | 13.99 |
| 4020 | 4 1/2" Deep - Cellular - 18 Ga | " | 16.03 |
| 4030 | 16 Ga | " | 18.36 |
| 4040 | Add for Galvanized | PCT | 16.50 |
| 4050 | Corrugated Black Standard .015 | S.F. | 2.27 |
| 4060 | Heavy Duty - 26 Ga | " | 2.45 |
| 4070 | S. Duty - 24 Ga | " | 3.21 |
| 4080 | 22 Ga | " | 3.33 |
| 5000 | Add for Galvanized | PCT | 15.00 |
| **05999.60** | **METAL SIDING AND ROOFING** | | |
| 1000 | Aluminum- Anodized | S.F. | 5.66 |
| 1010 | Porcelainized | " | 11.25 |
| 1020 | Corrugated | " | 3.83 |
| 1030 | Enamel, Baked Ribbed | " | 5.99 |
| 1040 | 24 Ga Ribbed | " | 4.10 |
| 1050 | Acrylic | " | 7.01 |
| 2000 | Porcelain Ribbed | " | 7.74 |
| 2010 | Galvanized- Corrugated | " | 3.87 |
| 2020 | Plastic Faced | " | 8.41 |
| 2030 | Protected Metal | " | 10.25 |
| 2040 | Add for Liner Panels | " | 3.18 |
| 2050 | Add for Insulation | " | 0.51 |

© 2011 By Design & Construction Resources

# DIVISION # 06  WOOD AND PLASTICS

## TABLE OF CONTENTS

| | PAGE |
|---|---|
| 06110.10 - BLOCKING | 06-2 |
| 06110.20 - CEILING FRAMING | 06-2 |
| 06110.30 - FLOOR FRAMING | 06-2 |
| 06110.40 - FURRING | 06-3 |
| 06110.50 - ROOF FRAMING | 06-3 |
| 06110.60 - SLEEPERS | 06-5 |
| 06110.65 - SOFFITS | 06-5 |
| 06110.70 - WALL FRAMING | 06-5 |
| 06115.10 - FLOOR SHEATHING | 06-6 |
| 06115.20 - ROOF SHEATHING | 06-6 |
| 06115.30 - WALL SHEATHING | 06-6 |
| 06125.10 - WOOD DECKING | 06-7 |
| 06130.10 - HEAVY TIMBER | 06-7 |
| 06190.20 - WOOD TRUSSES | 06-8 |
| 06190.30 - LAMINATED BEAMS | 06-8 |
| 06200.10 - FINISH CARPENTRY | 06-9 |
| 06220.10 - MILLWORK | 06-11 |
| 06300.10 - WOOD TREATMENT | 06-11 |
| 06430.10 - STAIRWORK | 06-12 |
| 06440.10 - COLUMNS | 06-12 |
| **QUICK ESTIMATING** | **06A-13** |

© 2011 By Design & Construction Resources

## DIVISION # 06 WOOD AND PLASTICS

| | | | UNIT | LABOR | MAT. | TOTAL |
|---|---|---|---|---|---|---|
| **06110.10** | **BLOCKING** | | | | | |
| 1215 | Wood construction | | | | | |
| 1220 | Walls | | | | | |
| 1230 | 2x4 | | L.F. | 2.96 | 0.38 | 3.34 |
| 1240 | 2x6 | | " | 3.33 | 0.58 | 3.91 |
| 1250 | 2x8 | | " | 3.55 | 0.77 | 4.32 |
| 1260 | 2x10 | | " | 3.81 | 1.02 | 4.83 |
| 1270 | 2x12 | | " | 4.10 | 1.32 | 5.42 |
| 1280 | Ceilings | | | | | |
| 1290 | 2x4 | | L.F. | 3.33 | 0.38 | 3.71 |
| 1300 | 2x6 | | " | 3.81 | 0.58 | 4.39 |
| 1310 | 2x8 | | " | 4.10 | 0.77 | 4.87 |
| 1320 | 2x10 | | " | 4.44 | 1.02 | 5.46 |
| 1330 | 2x12 | | " | 4.85 | 1.32 | 6.17 |
| **06110.20** | **CEILING FRAMING** | | | | | |
| 1000 | Ceiling joists | | | | | |
| 1070 | 16" o.c. | | | | | |
| 1080 | 2x4 | | S.F. | 1.02 | 0.46 | 1.48 |
| 1090 | 2x6 | | " | 1.06 | 0.69 | 1.75 |
| 1100 | 2x8 | | " | 1.11 | 0.97 | 2.08 |
| 1110 | 2x10 | | " | 1.16 | 1.10 | 2.26 |
| 1120 | 2x12 | | " | 1.21 | 2.06 | 3.27 |
| 1130 | 24" o.c. | | | | | |
| 1140 | 2x4 | | S.F. | 0.84 | 0.33 | 1.17 |
| 1150 | 2x6 | | " | 0.88 | 0.55 | 1.43 |
| 1160 | 2x8 | | " | 0.93 | 0.82 | 1.75 |
| 1170 | 2x10 | | " | 0.98 | 0.97 | 1.95 |
| 1180 | 2x12 | | " | 1.04 | 2.47 | 3.51 |
| 1200 | Headers and nailers | | | | | |
| 1210 | 2x4 | | L.F. | 1.72 | 0.38 | 2.10 |
| 1220 | 2x6 | | " | 1.77 | 0.58 | 2.35 |
| 1230 | 2x8 | | " | 1.90 | 0.77 | 2.67 |
| 1240 | 2x10 | | " | 2.05 | 1.02 | 3.07 |
| 1250 | 2x12 | | " | 2.22 | 1.26 | 3.48 |
| 1300 | Sister joists for ceilings | | | | | |
| 1310 | 2x4 | | L.F. | 3.81 | 0.38 | 4.19 |
| 1320 | 2x6 | | " | 4.44 | 0.58 | 5.02 |
| 1330 | 2x8 | | " | 5.33 | 0.77 | 6.10 |
| 1340 | 2x10 | | " | 6.67 | 1.02 | 7.69 |
| 1350 | 2x12 | | " | 8.89 | 1.26 | 10.15 |
| **06110.30** | **FLOOR FRAMING** | | | | | |
| 1000 | Floor joists | | | | | |
| 1180 | 16" o.c. | | | | | |
| 1190 | 2x6 | | S.F. | 0.88 | 0.60 | 1.48 |
| 1200 | 2x8 | | " | 0.90 | 0.84 | 1.74 |
| 1220 | 2x10 | | " | 0.92 | 1.03 | 1.95 |
| 1230 | 2x12 | | " | 0.95 | 1.28 | 2.23 |
| 1240 | 2x14 | | " | 0.98 | 2.86 | 3.84 |
| 1250 | 3x6 | | " | 0.92 | 1.98 | 2.90 |
| 1260 | 3x8 | | " | 0.95 | 2.53 | 3.48 |
| 1270 | 3x10 | | " | 0.98 | 3.19 | 4.17 |
| 1280 | 3x12 | | " | 1.02 | 3.85 | 4.87 |

## DIVISION # 06  WOOD AND PLASTICS

### 06110.30  FLOOR FRAMING, Cont'd...

| | | UNIT | LABOR | MAT. | TOTAL |
|---|---|---|---|---|---|
| 1290 | 3x14 | S.F. | 1.06 | 4.56 | 5.62 |
| 1300 | 4x6 | " | 0.92 | 2.53 | 3.45 |
| 1310 | 4x8 | " | 0.95 | 3.46 | 4.41 |
| 1320 | 4x10 | " | 0.98 | 4.29 | 5.27 |
| 1330 | 4x12 | " | 1.02 | 5.06 | 6.08 |
| 1340 | 4x14 | " | 1.06 | 6.05 | 7.11 |
| 2000 | Sister joists for floors | | | | |
| 2010 | 2x4 | L.F. | 3.33 | 0.38 | 3.71 |
| 2020 | 2x6 | " | 3.81 | 0.58 | 4.39 |
| 2030 | 2x8 | " | 4.44 | 0.77 | 5.21 |
| 2040 | 2x10 | " | 5.33 | 1.02 | 6.35 |
| 2050 | 2x12 | " | 6.67 | 1.32 | 7.99 |
| 2060 | 3x6 | " | 5.33 | 1.92 | 7.25 |
| 2070 | 3x8 | " | 5.92 | 2.36 | 8.28 |
| 2080 | 3x10 | " | 6.67 | 3.13 | 9.80 |
| 2090 | 3x12 | " | 7.62 | 3.79 | 11.41 |
| 2100 | 4x6 | " | 5.33 | 2.47 | 7.80 |
| 2110 | 4x8 | " | 5.92 | 3.30 | 9.22 |
| 2120 | 4x10 | " | 6.67 | 4.29 | 10.96 |
| 2130 | 4x12 | " | 7.62 | 4.78 | 12.40 |

### 06110.40  FURRING

| | | UNIT | LABOR | MAT. | TOTAL |
|---|---|---|---|---|---|
| 1100 | Furring, wood strips | | | | |
| 1102 | Walls | | | | |
| 1105 | On masonry or concrete walls | | | | |
| 1107 | 1x2 furring | | | | |
| 1110 | 12" o.c. | S.F. | 1.66 | 0.30 | 1.96 |
| 1120 | 16" o.c. | " | 1.52 | 0.26 | 1.78 |
| 1130 | 24" o.c. | " | 1.40 | 0.25 | 1.65 |
| 1135 | 1x3 furring | | | | |
| 1140 | 12" o.c. | S.F. | 1.66 | 0.38 | 2.04 |
| 1150 | 16" o.c. | " | 1.52 | 0.35 | 1.87 |
| 1160 | 24" o.c. | " | 1.40 | 0.27 | 1.67 |
| 1165 | On wood walls | | | | |
| 1167 | 1x2 furring | | | | |
| 1170 | 12" o.c. | S.F. | 1.18 | 0.30 | 1.48 |
| 1180 | 16" o.c. | " | 1.06 | 0.26 | 1.32 |
| 1190 | 24" o.c. | " | 0.97 | 0.24 | 1.21 |
| 1195 | 1x3 furring | | | | |
| 1200 | 12" o.c. | S.F. | 1.18 | 0.39 | 1.57 |
| 1210 | 16" o.c. | " | 1.06 | 0.33 | 1.39 |
| 1220 | 24" o.c. | " | 0.97 | 0.27 | 1.24 |

### 06110.50  ROOF FRAMING

| | | UNIT | LABOR | MAT. | TOTAL |
|---|---|---|---|---|---|
| 1000 | Roof framing | | | | |
| 1005 | Rafters, gable end | | | | |
| 1008 | 0-2 pitch (flat to 2-in-12) | | | | |
| 1070 | 16" o.c. | | | | |
| 1080 | 2x6 | S.F. | 0.95 | 0.69 | 1.64 |
| 1090 | 2x8 | " | 0.98 | 0.96 | 1.94 |
| 1100 | 2x10 | " | 1.02 | 1.10 | 2.12 |
| 1110 | 2x12 | " | 1.06 | 2.03 | 3.09 |
| 1120 | 24" o.c. | | | | |

© 2011 By Design & Construction Resources

## DIVISION # 06  WOOD AND PLASTICS

| 06110.50 | ROOF FRAMING, Cont'd... | UNIT | LABOR | MAT. | TOTAL |
|---|---|---|---|---|---|
| 1130 | 2x6 | S.F. | 0.80 | 0.38 | 1.18 |
| 1140 | 2x8 | " | 0.83 | 0.80 | 1.63 |
| 1150 | 2x10 | " | 0.86 | 0.93 | 1.79 |
| 1160 | 2x12 | " | 0.88 | 1.65 | 2.53 |
| 1165 | 4-6 pitch (4-in-12 to 6-in-12) | | | | |
| 1220 | 16" o.c. | | | | |
| 1230 | 2x6 | S.F. | 0.98 | 0.69 | 1.67 |
| 1240 | 2x8 | " | 1.02 | 1.10 | 2.12 |
| 1250 | 2x10 | " | 1.06 | 1.26 | 2.32 |
| 1260 | 2x12 | " | 1.11 | 1.87 | 2.98 |
| 1270 | 24" o.c. | | | | |
| 1280 | 2x6 | S.F. | 0.83 | 0.55 | 1.38 |
| 1290 | 2x8 | " | 0.86 | 0.93 | 1.79 |
| 1300 | 2x10 | " | 0.92 | 0.99 | 1.91 |
| 1310 | 2x12 | " | 1.02 | 1.54 | 2.56 |
| 1315 | 8-12 pitch (8-in-12 to 12-in-12) | | | | |
| 1380 | 16" o.c. | | | | |
| 1390 | 2x6 | S.F. | 1.02 | 0.77 | 1.79 |
| 1400 | 2x8 | " | 1.06 | 1.23 | 2.29 |
| 1410 | 2x10 | " | 1.11 | 1.37 | 2.48 |
| 1420 | 2x12 | " | 1.16 | 1.98 | 3.14 |
| 1430 | 24" o.c. | | | | |
| 1440 | 2x6 | S.F. | 0.86 | 0.60 | 1.46 |
| 1450 | 2x8 | " | 0.88 | 0.97 | 1.85 |
| 1460 | 2x10 | " | 0.92 | 1.10 | 2.02 |
| 1470 | 2x12 | " | 0.95 | 1.76 | 2.71 |
| 2000 | Ridge boards | | | | |
| 2010 | 2x6 | L.F. | 2.66 | 0.58 | 3.24 |
| 2020 | 2x8 | " | 2.96 | 0.77 | 3.73 |
| 2030 | 2x10 | " | 3.33 | 1.02 | 4.35 |
| 2040 | 2x12 | " | 3.81 | 1.32 | 5.13 |
| 3000 | Hip rafters | | | | |
| 3010 | 2x6 | L.F. | 1.90 | 0.58 | 2.48 |
| 3020 | 2x8 | " | 1.97 | 0.77 | 2.74 |
| 3030 | 2x10 | " | 2.05 | 1.02 | 3.07 |
| 3040 | 2x12 | " | 2.13 | 1.32 | 3.45 |
| 3180 | Jack rafters | | | | |
| 3190 | 4-6 pitch (4-in-12 to 6-in-12) | | | | |
| 3200 | 16" o.c. | | | | |
| 3210 | 2x6 | S.F. | 1.56 | 0.71 | 2.27 |
| 3220 | 2x8 | " | 1.61 | 1.10 | 2.71 |
| 3230 | 2x10 | " | 1.72 | 1.26 | 2.98 |
| 3240 | 2x12 | " | 1.77 | 1.87 | 3.64 |
| 3250 | 24" o.c. | | | | |
| 3260 | 2x6 | S.F. | 1.21 | 0.55 | 1.76 |
| 3270 | 2x8 | " | 1.24 | 0.93 | 2.17 |
| 3280 | 2x10 | " | 1.30 | 1.10 | 2.40 |
| 3290 | 2x12 | " | 1.33 | 1.59 | 2.92 |
| 3295 | 8-12 pitch (8-in-12 to 12-in-12) | | | | |
| 3300 | 16" o.c. | | | | |
| 3310 | 2x6 | S.F. | 1.66 | 1.10 | 2.76 |
| 3320 | 2x8 | " | 1.72 | 1.37 | 3.09 |

© 2011 By Design & Construction Resources

## DIVISION # 06 WOOD AND PLASTICS

### 06110.50 ROOF FRAMING, Cont'd...

| Code | Description | UNIT | LABOR | MAT. | TOTAL |
|---|---|---|---|---|---|
| 3330 | 2x10 | S.F. | 1.77 | 1.98 | 3.75 |
| 3340 | 2x12 | " | 1.84 | 2.75 | 4.59 |
| 3350 | 24" o.c. | | | | |
| 3360 | 2x6 | S.F. | 1.27 | 0.88 | 2.15 |
| 3370 | 2x8 | " | 1.30 | 1.10 | 2.40 |
| 3380 | 2x10 | " | 1.33 | 1.76 | 3.09 |
| 3390 | 2x12 | " | 1.36 | 2.53 | 3.89 |
| 4980 | Sister rafters | | | | |
| 5000 | 2x4 | L.F. | 3.81 | 0.38 | 4.19 |
| 5010 | 2x6 | " | 4.44 | 0.58 | 5.02 |
| 5020 | 2x8 | " | 5.33 | 0.77 | 6.10 |
| 5030 | 2x10 | " | 6.67 | 1.02 | 7.69 |
| 5040 | 2x12 | " | 8.89 | 1.32 | 10.21 |
| 5050 | Fascia boards | | | | |
| 5060 | 2x4 | L.F. | 2.66 | 0.38 | 3.04 |
| 5070 | 2x6 | " | 2.66 | 0.58 | 3.24 |
| 5080 | 2x8 | " | 2.96 | 0.77 | 3.73 |
| 5090 | 2x10 | " | 2.96 | 1.02 | 3.98 |
| 5100 | 2x12 | " | 3.33 | 1.32 | 4.65 |
| 7980 | Cant strips | | | | |
| 7985 | Fiber | | | | |
| 8000 | 3x3 | L.F. | 1.52 | 0.30 | 1.82 |
| 8020 | 4x4 | " | 1.61 | 0.42 | 2.03 |
| 8030 | Wood | | | | |
| 8040 | 3x3 | L.F. | 1.61 | 1.59 | 3.20 |

### 06110.60 SLEEPERS

| Code | Description | UNIT | LABOR | MAT. | TOTAL |
|---|---|---|---|---|---|
| 0960 | Sleepers, over concrete | | | | |
| 1090 | 16" o.c. | | | | |
| 1100 | 1x2 | S.F. | 1.06 | 0.19 | 1.25 |
| 1120 | 1x3 | " | 1.06 | 0.28 | 1.34 |
| 1140 | 2x4 | " | 1.27 | 0.59 | 1.86 |
| 1160 | 2x6 | " | 1.33 | 0.88 | 2.21 |

### 06110.65 SOFFITS

| Code | Description | UNIT | LABOR | MAT. | TOTAL |
|---|---|---|---|---|---|
| 0980 | Soffit framing | | | | |
| 1000 | 2x3 | L.F. | 3.81 | 0.30 | 4.11 |
| 1020 | 2x4 | " | 4.10 | 0.38 | 4.48 |
| 1030 | 2x6 | " | 4.44 | 0.57 | 5.01 |
| 1040 | 2x8 | " | 4.85 | 0.79 | 5.64 |

### 06110.70 WALL FRAMING

| Code | Description | UNIT | LABOR | MAT. | TOTAL |
|---|---|---|---|---|---|
| 0960 | Framing wall, studs | | | | |
| 1110 | 16" o.c. | | | | |
| 1120 | 2x3 | S.F. | 0.83 | 0.33 | 1.16 |
| 1140 | 2x4 | " | 0.83 | 0.46 | 1.29 |
| 1150 | 2x6 | " | 0.88 | 0.66 | 1.54 |
| 1160 | 2x8 | " | 0.92 | 1.03 | 1.95 |
| 1165 | 24" o.c. | | | | |
| 1170 | 2x3 | S.F. | 0.72 | 0.25 | 0.97 |
| 1180 | 2x4 | " | 0.72 | 0.35 | 1.07 |
| 1190 | 2x6 | " | 0.76 | 0.55 | 1.31 |
| 1200 | 2x8 | " | 0.78 | 0.71 | 1.49 |
| 1480 | Plates, top or bottom | | | | |

© 2011 By Design & Construction Resources

## DIVISION # 06  WOOD AND PLASTICS

| | | UNIT | LABOR | MAT. | TOTAL |
|---|---|---|---|---|---|
| **06110.70** | **WALL FRAMING, Cont'd...** | | | | |
| 1500 | 2x3 | L.F. | 1.56 | 0.30 | 1.86 |
| 1510 | 2x4 | " | 1.66 | 0.38 | 2.04 |
| 1520 | 2x6 | " | 1.77 | 0.57 | 2.34 |
| 1530 | 2x8 | " | 1.90 | 0.79 | 2.69 |
| 2000 | Headers, door or window | | | | |
| 2044 | 2x8 | | | | |
| 2046 | Single | | | | |
| 2050 | 4' long | EA. | 33.25 | 3.38 | 36.63 |
| 2060 | 8' long | " | 41.00 | 6.76 | 47.76 |
| 2065 | Double | | | | |
| 2070 | 4' long | EA. | 38.00 | 6.76 | 44.76 |
| 2080 | 8' long | " | 48.50 | 13.50 | 62.00 |
| 2134 | 2x12 | | | | |
| 2138 | Single | | | | |
| 2140 | 6' long | EA. | 41.00 | 7.42 | 48.42 |
| 2150 | 12' long | " | 53.00 | 14.50 | 67.50 |
| 2155 | Double | | | | |
| 2160 | 6' long | EA. | 48.50 | 14.50 | 63.00 |
| 2170 | 12' long | " | 59.00 | 29.00 | 88.00 |
| **06115.10** | **FLOOR SHEATHING** | | | | |
| 1980 | Sub-flooring, plywood, CDX | | | | |
| 2000 | 1/2" thick | S.F. | 0.66 | 0.41 | 1.07 |
| 2020 | 5/8" thick | " | 0.76 | 0.59 | 1.35 |
| 2080 | 3/4" thick | " | 0.88 | 1.10 | 1.98 |
| 2090 | Structural plywood | | | | |
| 2100 | 1/2" thick | S.F. | 0.66 | 0.66 | 1.32 |
| 2120 | 5/8" thick | " | 0.76 | 1.04 | 1.80 |
| 2140 | 3/4" thick | " | 0.82 | 1.10 | 1.92 |
| 5990 | Underlayment | | | | |
| 6000 | Hardboard, 1/4" tempered | S.F. | 0.66 | 0.61 | 1.27 |
| 6010 | Plywood, CDX | | | | |
| 6020 | 3/8" thick | S.F. | 0.66 | 0.63 | 1.29 |
| 6040 | 1/2" thick | " | 0.71 | 0.75 | 1.46 |
| 6060 | 5/8" thick | " | 0.76 | 0.88 | 1.64 |
| 6080 | 3/4" thick | " | 0.82 | 1.10 | 1.92 |
| **06115.20** | **ROOF SHEATHING** | | | | |
| 0080 | Sheathing | | | | |
| 0090 | Plywood, CDX | | | | |
| 1000 | 3/8" thick | S.F. | 0.68 | 0.63 | 1.31 |
| 1020 | 1/2" thick | " | 0.71 | 0.75 | 1.46 |
| 1040 | 5/8" thick | " | 0.76 | 0.88 | 1.64 |
| 1060 | 3/4" thick | " | 0.82 | 1.10 | 1.92 |
| 1080 | Structural plywood | | | | |
| 2040 | 3/8" thick | S.F. | 0.68 | 0.40 | 1.08 |
| 2060 | 1/2" thick | " | 0.71 | 0.52 | 1.23 |
| 2080 | 5/8" thick | " | 0.76 | 0.63 | 1.39 |
| 2100 | 3/4" thick | " | 0.82 | 0.77 | 1.59 |
| **06115.30** | **WALL SHEATHING** | | | | |
| 0980 | Sheathing | | | | |
| 0990 | Plywood, CDX | | | | |
| 1000 | 3/8" thick | S.F. | 0.79 | 0.63 | 1.42 |

## DIVISION # 06 WOOD AND PLASTICS

| | | UNIT | LABOR | MAT. | TOTAL |
|---|---|---|---|---|---|
| **06115.30** | **WALL SHEATHING, Cont'd...** | | | | |
| 1020 | 1/2" thick | S.F. | 0.82 | 0.75 | 1.57 |
| 1040 | 5/8" thick | " | 0.88 | 0.88 | 1.76 |
| 1060 | 3/4" thick | " | 0.97 | 1.10 | 2.07 |
| 3000 | Waferboard | | | | |
| 3020 | 3/8" thick | S.F. | 0.79 | 0.40 | 1.19 |
| 3040 | 1/2" thick | " | 0.82 | 0.52 | 1.34 |
| 3060 | 5/8" thick | " | 0.88 | 0.63 | 1.51 |
| 3080 | 3/4" thick | " | 0.97 | 0.70 | 1.67 |
| 4100 | Structural plywood | | | | |
| 4120 | 3/8" thick | S.F. | 0.79 | 0.63 | 1.42 |
| 4140 | 1/2" thick | " | 0.82 | 0.75 | 1.57 |
| 4160 | 5/8" thick | " | 0.88 | 0.88 | 1.76 |
| 4180 | 3/4" thick | " | 0.97 | 0.75 | 1.72 |
| 7000 | Gypsum, 1/2" thick | " | 0.82 | 0.40 | 1.22 |
| 8000 | Asphalt impregnated fiberboard, 1/2" thick | " | 0.82 | 0.99 | 1.81 |
| **06125.10** | **WOOD DECKING** | | | | |
| 0090 | Decking, T&G solid | | | | |
| 0095 | Cedar | | | | |
| 0100 | 3" thick | S.F. | 1.33 | 8.80 | 10.13 |
| 0120 | 4" thick | " | 1.42 | 11.00 | 12.42 |
| 1030 | Fir | | | | |
| 1040 | 3" thick | S.F. | 1.33 | 3.85 | 5.18 |
| 1060 | 4" thick | " | 1.42 | 4.67 | 6.09 |
| 1080 | Southern yellow pine | | | | |
| 2000 | 3" thick | S.F. | 1.52 | 3.85 | 5.37 |
| 2020 | 4" thick | " | 1.64 | 4.07 | 5.71 |
| 3120 | White pine | | | | |
| 3140 | 3" thick | S.F. | 1.33 | 4.67 | 6.00 |
| 3160 | 4" thick | " | 1.42 | 6.32 | 7.74 |
| **06130.10** | **HEAVY TIMBER** | | | | |
| 1000 | Mill framed structures | | | | |
| 1010 | Beams to 20' long | | | | |
| 1020 | Douglas fir | | | | |
| 1040 | 6x8 | L.F. | 6.85 | 6.12 | 12.97 |
| 1042 | 6x10 | " | 7.08 | 7.22 | 14.30 |
| 1044 | 6x12 | " | 7.61 | 8.64 | 16.25 |
| 1046 | 6x14 | " | 7.90 | 10.25 | 18.15 |
| 1048 | 6x16 | " | 8.22 | 11.25 | 19.47 |
| 1060 | 8x10 | " | 7.08 | 9.58 | 16.66 |
| 1070 | 8x12 | " | 7.61 | 11.25 | 18.86 |
| 1080 | 8x14 | " | 7.90 | 13.00 | 20.90 |
| 1090 | 8x16 | " | 8.22 | 14.75 | 22.97 |
| 1380 | Columns to 12' high | | | | |
| 1400 | Douglas fir | | | | |
| 1420 | 6x6 | L.F. | 10.25 | 4.40 | 14.65 |
| 1440 | 8x8 | " | 10.25 | 7.54 | 17.79 |
| 1460 | 10x10 | " | 11.50 | 13.25 | 24.75 |
| 1480 | 12x12 | " | 11.50 | 16.25 | 27.75 |
| 2000 | Posts, treated | | | | |
| 2100 | 4x4 | L.F. | 2.13 | 1.51 | 3.64 |
| 2120 | 6x6 | " | 2.66 | 4.40 | 7.06 |

© 2011 By Design & Construction Resources

# DIVISION # 06  WOOD AND PLASTICS

| | | UNIT | LABOR | MAT. | TOTAL |
|---|---|---|---|---|---|
| **06190.20** | **WOOD TRUSSES** | | | | |
| 0960 | Truss, fink, 2x4 members | | | | |
| 0980 | 3-in-12 slope | | | | |
| 1030 | 5-in-12 slope | | | | |
| 1040 | 24' span | EA. | 60.00 | 95.00 | 155 |
| 1050 | 28' span | " | 62.00 | 100 | 162 |
| 1055 | 30' span | " | 64.00 | 110 | 174 |
| 1060 | 32' span | " | 64.00 | 110 | 174 |
| 1070 | 40' span | " | 69.00 | 160 | 229 |
| 1074 | Gable, 2x4 members | | | | |
| 1078 | 5-in-12 slope | | | | |
| 1080 | 24' span | EA. | 60.00 | 110 | 170 |
| 1100 | 28' span | " | 62.00 | 130 | 192 |
| 1120 | 30' span | " | 64.00 | 140 | 204 |
| 1160 | 36' span | " | 66.00 | 150 | 216 |
| 1180 | 40' span | " | 69.00 | 170 | 239 |
| 1190 | King post type, 2x4 members | | | | |
| 2000 | 4-in-12 slope | | | | |
| 2040 | 16' span | EA. | 56.00 | 66.00 | 122 |
| 2060 | 18' span | " | 57.00 | 72.00 | 129 |
| 2080 | 24' span | " | 60.00 | 77.00 | 137 |
| 2120 | 30' span | " | 64.00 | 100 | 164 |
| 2160 | 38' span | " | 66.00 | 130 | 196 |
| 2180 | 42' span | " | 71.00 | 160 | 231 |
| **06190.30** | **LAMINATED BEAMS** | | | | |
| 0010 | Parallel strand beams 3-1/2" wide x | | | | |
| 0020 | 9-1/2" | L.F. | 2.93 | 8.80 | 11.73 |
| 0030 | 11-1/4" | " | 3.04 | 9.35 | 12.39 |
| 0040 | 11-7/8" | " | 3.16 | 9.90 | 13.06 |
| 0050 | 14" | " | 3.73 | 12.50 | 16.23 |
| 0060 | 16" | " | 4.11 | 14.75 | 18.86 |
| 0070 | 18" | " | 4.56 | 17.50 | 22.06 |
| 1000 | Laminated veneer beams, 1-3/4" wide x | | | | |
| 1010 | 11-7/8" | L.F. | 3.16 | 5.99 | 9.15 |
| 1020 | 14" | " | 3.73 | 7.48 | 11.21 |
| 1030 | 16" | " | 4.11 | 7.37 | 11.48 |
| 1040 | 18" | " | 4.56 | 9.35 | 13.91 |
| 2000 | Laminated strand beams, 1-3/4" wide x | | | | |
| 2010 | 9-1/2" | L.F. | 2.93 | 3.85 | 6.78 |
| 2020 | 11-7/8" | " | 3.16 | 4.40 | 7.56 |
| 2030 | 14" | " | 3.73 | 5.17 | 8.90 |
| 2040 | 16" | " | 4.11 | 5.94 | 10.05 |
| 2050 | 3-1/2" wide x | | | | |
| 2060 | 9-1/2" | L.F. | 2.93 | 6.76 | 9.69 |
| 2070 | 11-7/8" | " | 3.16 | 8.80 | 11.96 |
| 2080 | 14" | " | 3.73 | 10.25 | 13.98 |
| 2090 | 16" | " | 4.11 | 12.25 | 16.36 |
| 3000 | Gluelam beam, 3-1/2" wide x | | | | |
| 3010 | 10" | L.F. | 2.93 | 10.25 | 13.18 |
| 3020 | 12" | " | 3.42 | 12.00 | 15.42 |
| 3030 | 15" | " | 3.91 | 14.25 | 18.16 |
| 3040 | 5-1/2" wide x | | | | |

## DIVISION # 06 WOOD AND PLASTICS

| | | UNIT | LABOR | MAT. | TOTAL |
|---|---|---|---|---|---|
| **06190.30** | **LAMINATED BEAMS, Cont'd...** | | | | |
| 3050 | 10" | L.F. | 2.93 | 16.50 | 19.43 |
| 3060 | 16" | " | 4.11 | 25.75 | 29.86 |
| 3070 | 20" | " | 4.83 | 30.50 | 35.33 |
| **06200.10** | **FINISH CARPENTRY** | | | | |
| 0070 | Mouldings and trim | | | | |
| 0980 | Apron, flat | | | | |
| 1000 | 9/16 x 2 | L.F. | 2.66 | 1.43 | 4.09 |
| 1010 | 9/16 x 3-1/2 | " | 2.80 | 3.30 | 6.10 |
| 1015 | Base | | | | |
| 1020 | Colonial | | | | |
| 1022 | 7/16 x 2-1/4 | L.F. | 2.66 | 1.70 | 4.36 |
| 1024 | 7/16 x 3 | " | 2.66 | 2.20 | 4.86 |
| 1026 | 7/16 x 3-1/4 | " | 2.66 | 2.25 | 4.91 |
| 1028 | 9/16 x 3 | " | 2.80 | 2.20 | 5.00 |
| 1030 | 9/16 x 3-1/4 | " | 2.80 | 2.31 | 5.11 |
| 1034 | 11/16 x 2-1/4 | " | 2.96 | 2.42 | 5.38 |
| 1035 | Ranch | | | | |
| 1036 | 7/16 x 2-1/4 | L.F. | 2.66 | 1.87 | 4.53 |
| 1038 | 7/16 x 3-1/4 | " | 2.66 | 2.20 | 4.86 |
| 1039 | 9/16 x 2-1/4 | " | 2.80 | 2.03 | 4.83 |
| 1041 | 9/16 x 3 | " | 2.80 | 2.20 | 5.00 |
| 1043 | 9/16 x 3-1/4 | " | 2.80 | 2.25 | 5.05 |
| 1050 | Casing | | | | |
| 1060 | 11/16 x 2-1/2 | L.F. | 2.42 | 1.76 | 4.18 |
| 1070 | 11/16 x 3-1/2 | " | 2.54 | 1.98 | 4.52 |
| 1180 | Chair rail | | | | |
| 1200 | 9/16 x 2-1/2 | L.F. | 2.66 | 1.87 | 4.53 |
| 1210 | 9/16 x 3-1/2 | " | 2.66 | 2.58 | 5.24 |
| 1250 | Closet pole | | | | |
| 1300 | 1-1/8" dia. | L.F. | 3.55 | 1.26 | 4.81 |
| 1310 | 1-5/8" dia. | " | 3.55 | 1.87 | 5.42 |
| 1340 | Cove | | | | |
| 1500 | 9/16 x 1-3/4 | L.F. | 2.66 | 1.43 | 4.09 |
| 1510 | 11/16 x 2-3/4 | " | 2.66 | 2.20 | 4.86 |
| 1550 | Crown | | | | |
| 1600 | 9/16 x 1-5/8 | L.F. | 3.55 | 1.87 | 5.42 |
| 1620 | 11/16 x 3-5/8 | " | 4.44 | 2.20 | 6.64 |
| 1640 | 11/16 x 5-1/4 | " | 5.33 | 3.68 | 9.01 |
| 1680 | Drip cap | | | | |
| 1700 | 1-1/16 x 1-5/8 | L.F. | 2.66 | 1.98 | 4.64 |
| 1780 | Glass bead | | | | |
| 1800 | 3/8 x 3/8 | L.F. | 3.33 | 0.71 | 4.04 |
| 1840 | 5/8 x 5/8 | " | 3.33 | 0.93 | 4.26 |
| 1860 | 3/4 x 3/4 | " | 3.33 | 1.10 | 4.43 |
| 1880 | Half round | | | | |
| 1900 | 1/2 | L.F. | 2.13 | 0.82 | 2.95 |
| 1910 | 5/8 | " | 2.13 | 1.10 | 3.23 |
| 1920 | 3/4 | " | 2.13 | 1.48 | 3.61 |
| 1980 | Lattice | | | | |
| 2000 | 1/4 x 7/8 | L.F. | 2.13 | 0.66 | 2.79 |
| 2010 | 1/4 x 1-1/8 | " | 2.13 | 0.71 | 2.84 |

## DIVISION # 06  WOOD AND PLASTICS

### 06200.10  FINISH CARPENTRY, Cont'd...

| Code | Description | UNIT | LABOR | MAT. | TOTAL |
|---|---|---|---|---|---|
| 2030 | 1/4 x 1-3/4 | L.F. | 2.13 | 0.85 | 2.98 |
| 2040 | 1/4 x 2 | " | 2.13 | 0.99 | 3.12 |
| 2080 | Ogee molding | | | | |
| 2100 | 5/8 x 3/4 | L.F. | 2.66 | 1.32 | 3.98 |
| 2110 | 11/16 x 1-1/8 | " | 2.66 | 3.08 | 5.74 |
| 2120 | 11/16 x 1-3/8 | " | 2.66 | 2.42 | 5.08 |
| 2180 | Parting bead | | | | |
| 2200 | 3/8 x 7/8 | L.F. | 3.33 | 1.10 | 4.43 |
| 2300 | Quarter round | | | | |
| 2301 | 1/4 x 1/4 | L.F. | 2.13 | 0.38 | 2.51 |
| 2303 | 3/8 x 3/8 | " | 2.13 | 0.55 | 2.68 |
| 2305 | 1/2 x 1/2 | " | 2.13 | 0.71 | 2.84 |
| 2307 | 11/16 x 11/16 | " | 2.32 | 0.71 | 3.03 |
| 2309 | 3/4 x 3/4 | " | 2.32 | 1.32 | 3.64 |
| 2311 | 1-1/16 x 1-1/16 | " | 2.42 | 1.04 | 3.46 |
| 2380 | Railings, balusters | | | | |
| 2400 | 1-1/8 x 1-1/8 | L.F. | 5.33 | 3.52 | 8.85 |
| 2410 | 1-1/2 x 1-1/2 | " | 4.85 | 4.12 | 8.97 |
| 2480 | Screen moldings | | | | |
| 2500 | 1/4 x 3/4 | L.F. | 4.44 | 0.88 | 5.32 |
| 2510 | 5/8 x 5/16 | " | 4.44 | 1.10 | 5.54 |
| 2580 | Shoe | | | | |
| 2600 | 7/16 x 11/16 | L.F. | 2.13 | 1.10 | 3.23 |
| 2605 | Sash beads | | | | |
| 2620 | 1/2 x 7/8 | L.F. | 4.44 | 1.43 | 5.87 |
| 2640 | 5/8 x 7/8 | " | 4.85 | 1.54 | 6.39 |
| 2760 | Stop | | | | |
| 2780 | 5/8 x 1-5/8 | | | | |
| 2800 | Colonial | L.F. | 3.33 | 0.77 | 4.10 |
| 2810 | Ranch | " | 3.33 | 0.77 | 4.10 |
| 2880 | Stools | | | | |
| 2900 | 11/16 x 2-1/4 | L.F. | 5.92 | 3.35 | 9.27 |
| 2910 | 11/16 x 2-1/2 | " | 5.92 | 3.52 | 9.44 |
| 2920 | 11/16 x 5-1/4 | " | 6.67 | 3.63 | 10.30 |
| 4000 | Exterior trim, casing, select pine, 1x3 | " | 2.66 | 2.42 | 5.08 |
| 4010 | Douglas fir | | | | |
| 4020 | 1x3 | L.F. | 2.66 | 1.15 | 3.81 |
| 4040 | 1x4 | " | 2.66 | 1.43 | 4.09 |
| 4060 | 1x6 | " | 2.96 | 1.87 | 4.83 |
| 4100 | 1x8 | " | 3.33 | 2.58 | 5.91 |
| 5000 | Cornices, white pine, #2 or better | | | | |
| 5040 | 1x4 | L.F. | 2.66 | 0.88 | 3.54 |
| 5080 | 1x8 | " | 3.13 | 1.76 | 4.89 |
| 5120 | 1x12 | " | 3.55 | 2.80 | 6.35 |
| 8600 | Shelving, pine | | | | |
| 8620 | 1x8 | L.F. | 4.10 | 1.26 | 5.36 |
| 8640 | 1x10 | " | 4.26 | 1.65 | 5.91 |
| 8660 | 1x12 | " | 4.44 | 2.09 | 6.53 |
| 8800 | Plywood shelf, 3/4", with edge band, 12" wide | " | 5.33 | 2.25 | 7.58 |
| 8840 | Adjustable shelf, and rod, 12" wide | | | | |
| 8860 | 3' to 4' long | EA. | 13.25 | 18.00 | 31.25 |
| 8880 | 5' to 8' long | " | 17.75 | 33.75 | 51.50 |

# DIVISION # 06 WOOD AND PLASTICS

| | | UNIT | LABOR | MAT. | TOTAL |
|---|---|---|---|---|---|
| **06200.10** | **FINISH CARPENTRY, Cont'd...** | | | | |
| 8900 | Prefinished wood shelves with brackets and supports | | | | |
| 8905 | 8" wide | | | | |
| 8910 | 3' long | EA. | 13.25 | 53.00 | 66.25 |
| 8922 | 4' long | " | 13.25 | 61.00 | 74.25 |
| 8924 | 6' long | " | 13.25 | 88.00 | 101 |
| 8930 | 10" wide | | | | |
| 8940 | 3' long | EA. | 13.25 | 58.00 | 71.25 |
| 8942 | 4' long | " | 13.25 | 85.00 | 98.25 |
| 8946 | 6' long | " | 13.25 | 95.00 | 108 |
| **06220.10** | **MILLWORK** | | | | |
| 0070 | Countertop, laminated plastic | | | | |
| 0080 | 25" x 7/8" thick | | | | |
| 0099 | Minimum | L.F. | 13.25 | 14.00 | 27.25 |
| 0100 | Average | " | 17.75 | 26.75 | 44.50 |
| 0110 | Maximum | " | 21.25 | 39.25 | 60.50 |
| 0115 | 25" x 1-1/4" thick | | | | |
| 0120 | Minimum | L.F. | 17.75 | 17.00 | 34.75 |
| 0130 | Average | " | 21.25 | 34.00 | 55.25 |
| 0140 | Maximum | " | 26.75 | 51.00 | 77.75 |
| 0160 | Add for cutouts | EA. | 33.25 | | 33.25 |
| 0165 | Backsplash, 4" high, 7/8" thick | L.F. | 10.75 | 18.75 | 29.50 |
| 2000 | Plywood, sanded, A-C | | | | |
| 2020 | 1/4" thick | S.F. | 1.77 | 1.21 | 2.98 |
| 2040 | 3/8" thick | " | 1.90 | 1.32 | 3.22 |
| 2060 | 1/2" thick | " | 2.05 | 1.48 | 3.53 |
| 2070 | A-D | | | | |
| 2080 | 1/4" thick | S.F. | 1.77 | 1.15 | 2.92 |
| 2090 | 3/8" thick | " | 1.90 | 1.32 | 3.22 |
| 2100 | 1/2" thick | " | 2.05 | 1.43 | 3.48 |
| 2500 | Base cab., 34-1/2" high, 24" deep, hardwood | | | | |
| 2540 | Minimum | L.F. | 21.25 | 180 | 201 |
| 2560 | Average | " | 26.75 | 210 | 237 |
| 2580 | Maximum | " | 35.50 | 240 | 276 |
| 2600 | Wall cabinets | | | | |
| 2640 | Minimum | L.F. | 17.75 | 56.00 | 73.75 |
| 2660 | Average | " | 21.25 | 76.00 | 97.25 |
| 2680 | Maximum | " | 26.75 | 95.00 | 122 |
| **06300.10** | **WOOD TREATMENT** | | | | |
| 1000 | Creosote preservative treatment | | | | |
| 1020 | 8 lb/cf | B.F. | | | 0.60 |
| 1040 | 10 lb/cf | " | | | 0.71 |
| 1060 | Salt preservative treatment | | | | |
| 1070 | Oil borne | | | | |
| 1080 | Minimum | B.F. | | | 0.55 |
| 1100 | Maximum | " | | | 0.77 |
| 1120 | Water borne | | | | |
| 1140 | Minimum | B.F. | | | 0.38 |
| 1150 | Maximum | " | | | 0.60 |
| 1200 | Fire retardant treatment | | | | |
| 1220 | Minimum | B.F. | | | 0.77 |
| 1240 | Maximum | " | | | 0.93 |

© 2011 By Design & Construction Resources

## DIVISION # 06 WOOD AND PLASTICS

| | | UNIT | LABOR | MAT. | TOTAL |
|---|---|---|---|---|---|
| **06300.10** | **WOOD TREATMENT, Cont'd...** | | | | |
| 1300 | Kiln dried, softwood, add to framing costs | | | | |
| 1320 | 1" thick | B.F. | | | 0.27 |
| 1360 | 3" thick | " | | | 0.49 |
| **06430.10** | **STAIRWORK** | | | | |
| 0080 | Risers, 1x8, 42" wide | | | | |
| 0100 | White oak | EA. | 26.75 | 39.50 | 66.25 |
| 0120 | Pine | " | 26.75 | 35.25 | 62.00 |
| 0130 | Treads, 1-1/16" x 9-1/2" x 42" | | | | |
| 0140 | White oak | EA. | 33.25 | 47.25 | 80.50 |
| **06440.10** | **COLUMNS** | | | | |
| 0980 | Column, hollow, round wood | | | | |
| 0990 | 12" diameter | | | | |
| 1000 | 10' high | EA. | 76.00 | 700 | 776 |
| 1080 | 16' high | " | 110 | 1,270 | 1,380 |
| 2000 | 24" diameter | | | | |
| 2020 | 16' high | EA. | 110 | 2,890 | 3,000 |
| 2060 | 20' high | " | 120 | 4,040 | 4,160 |
| 2100 | 24' high | " | 130 | 4,640 | 4,770 |

# DIVISION # 06  WOOD AND PLASTICS - QUICK ESTIMATING

| Code | Description | UNIT | COST |
|---|---|---|---|
| **06999.10** | **ROUGH CARPENTRY** | | |
| 1000 | LIGHT FRAMING AND SHEATHING | | |
| 1100 | Joists and Headers - Floor Area - 16" O.C. | | |
| 1110 | 2" x 6" Joists - with Headers & Bridging | S.F. | 2.94 |
| 1120 | 2" x 8" Joists | " | 3.62 |
| 1130 | 2" x 10" Joists | " | 4.03 |
| 1140 | 2" x 12" Joists | " | 4.80 |
| 1150 | Add for Ceiling Joists, 2nd Floor and Above | " | 0.11 |
| 1160 | Add for Sloped Installation | " | 0.18 |
| 1200 | Studs, Plates and Framing - 8' Wall Height - 16" O.C. | " | 1.76 |
| 1210 | 2" x 3" Stud Wall - Non-Bearing (Single Top Plate) | | |
| 1220 | 2" x 4" Stud Wall - Bearing (Double Top Plate) | S.F. | 2.12 |
| 1230 | 2" x 4" Stud Wall - Non-Bearing (Single Top Plate) | " | 1.56 |
| 1240 | 2" x 6" Stud Wall - Bearing (Double Top Plate) | " | 2.87 |
| 1250 | 2" x 6" Stud Wall - Non-Bearing (Single Top Plate) | " | 2.12 |
| 1300 | Add for Stud Wall - 12" O.C. | " | 0.10 |
| 1310 | Deduct for Stud Wall - 24" O.C. | " | 0.26 |
| 1320 | Add for Bolted Plates or Sills | " | 0.15 |
| 1330 | Add for Each Foot Above 8' | " | 0.09 |
| 1340 | Add to Above for Fire Stops, Fillers and Nailers | " | 0.56 |
| 1350 | Add for Soffits and Suspended Framing | " | 0.77 |
| 1360 | Bridging - 1" x 3" Wood Diagonal | EA. | 2.98 |
| 1370 | 2" x 8" Solid | " | 3.32 |
| 1400 | Rafters | | |
| 1410 | 2" x 4" Rafter (Incl Bracing) 3 - 12 Slope | S.F. | 2.17 |
| 1420 | 4 - 12 Slope | " | 2.17 |
| 1430 | 5 - 12 Slope | " | 2.45 |
| 1440 | 6 - 12 Slope | " | 2.89 |
| 1500 | Add for Hip-and-Valley Type | " | 0.57 |
| 1510 | Add for 1' 0" Overhang - Total Area of Roof | " | 0.22 |
| 1520 | 2" x 6" Rafter (Incl Bracing) 3-12 Slope | " | 2.74 |
| 1530 | 4-12 Slope | " | 2.77 |
| 1540 | 5-12 Slope | " | 2.85 |
| 1550 | 6-12 Slope | " | 3.00 |
| 1560 | Add for Hip - and - Valley Type | " | 0.63 |
| 1600 | Stairs | EA. | 550 |
| 1700 | Sub Floor Sheathing (Structural) | | |
| 1710 | 1" x 8" and 1" x 10" #3 Pine | S.F. | 1.93 |
| 1720 | 1/2" x 4' x 8' CD Plywood - Exterior | " | 1.55 |
| 1730 | 5/8" x 4' x 8' | " | 1.88 |
| 1740 | 3/4" x 4' x 8' | " | 2.52 |
| 1800 | Floor Sheathing (Over Sub Floor) | | |
| 1810 | 3/8" x 4' x 8' CD Plywood | S.F. | 1.44 |
| 1820 | 1/2" x 4' x 8' | " | 1.72 |
| 1830 | 5/8" x 4' x 8' | " | 2.25 |
| 1840 | 1/2" x 4' x 8' Particle Board | " | 1.78 |
| 1850 | 5/8" x 4' x 8' | " | 2.10 |
| 1860 | 3/4" x 4' x 8' | " | 2.57 |
| 1900 | Wall Sheathing | | |
| 1910 | 1' x 8" and 1" x 10" - #3 Pine | S.F. | 1.97 |
| 1920 | 3/8" x 4' x 8' CD Plywood - Exterior | " | 1.47 |
| 1930 | 1/2" x 4' x 8' | " | 1.73 |
| 1940 | 5/8" x 4' x 8' | " | 2.37 |

© 2011 By Design & Construction Resources

# DIVISION # 06  WOOD AND PLASTICS - QUICK ESTIMATING

| | | UNIT | COST |
|---|---|---|---|
| **06999.10** | **ROUGH CARPENTRY, Cont'd...** | | |
| 1950 | 3/4" x 4' x 8' | S.F. | 2.65 |
| 1960 | 25/32" x 4' x 8' Fiber Board - Impregnated | " | 1.65 |
| 1970 | 1" x 2' x 8' T&G Styrofoam | " | 1.45 |
| 1980 | 2" x 2' x 8' | " | 2.14 |
| 2000 | Roof Sheathing - Flat Construction | | |
| 2010 | 1" x 6" and 1" x 8" - #3 Pine | S.F. | 2.45 |
| 2020 | 1/2" x 4' x 8' CD Plywood - Exterior | " | 2.27 |
| 2030 | 5/8" x 4' x 8' | " | 1.99 |
| 2040 | 3/4" x 4' x 8' | " | 2.66 |
| 2050 | Add for Sloped Roof Construction (to 5-12 slope) | " | 0.23 |
| 2060 | Add for Steep Sloped Construction (over 5-12 slope) | " | 0.42 |
| 2070 | Add to Above Sheathing | | |
| 2080 | AC or AD Plywood | S.F. | 0.42 |
| 2090 | 10' Length Plywood | " | 0.31 |
| 2100 | HEAVY FRAMING | | |
| 2200 | Columns and Beams - 16' Span Average - Floor Area | S.F. | 8.45 |
| 2210 | 20' Span | " | 8.78 |
| 2220 | 24' Span | " | 10.36 |
| 2300 | Deck 2" x 6" T&G - Fir Random Construction Grade | " | 5.12 |
| 2310 | 3" x 6" T&G - Fir Random Construction Grade | " | 6.82 |
| 2320 | 4" x 6" | " | 8.45 |
| 2330 | 2" x 6" T&G - Red Cedar | " | 5.38 |
| 2340 | Add for D Grade Cedar | " | 2.11 |
| 2350 | 2" x 6" T&G - Panelized Fir | " | 4.55 |
| 3000 | MISCELLANEOUS CARPENTRY | | |
| 3100 | Blocking and Bucks (2" x 4" and 2" x 6") | | |
| 3110 | Doors & Windows - Nailed to Concrete or Masonry | EA. | 58.25 |
| 3120 | Bolted to Concrete or Masonry | " | 64.25 |
| 3130 | Doors & Windows - Nailed to Concrete or Masonry | B.F. | 2.83 |
| 3140 | Bolted to Concrete or Masonry | " | 3.90 |
| 3150 | Roof Edges - Nailed to Wood | " | 2.26 |
| 3160 | Bolted to Concrete (Incl. bolts) | " | 3.37 |
| 3200 | Grounds and Furring | | |
| 3210 | 1" x 6" Fastened to Wood | L.F. | 1.76 |
| 3220 | 1" x 4" | " | 1.32 |
| 3230 | 1" x 3" | " | 1.20 |
| 3240 | 1" x 3" Fastened to Concrete/Masonry - Nailed | " | 1.86 |
| 3250 | Gun Driven | " | 1.69 |
| 3260 | PreClipped | " | 2.11 |
| 3270 | 2" x 2" Suspended Framing | " | 1.86 |
| 3280 | Not Suspended Framing | " | 1.61 |
| 3300 | Grounds and Furring | | |
| 3310 | 1" x 6" Fastened to Wood | B.F. | 3.54 |
| 3320 | 1" x 4" | " | 4.20 |
| 3330 | 1" x 3" | " | 4.72 |
| 3340 | 1" x 3" Fastened to Concrete/Masonry - Nailed | " | 7.08 |
| 3400 | Gun Driven | " | 6.73 |
| 3410 | PreClipped | " | 8.25 |
| 3420 | 2" x 2" Suspended Framing | " | 5.52 |
| 3430 | Not Suspended Framing | " | 4.77 |
| 3440 | Cant Strips | | |
| 3450 | 4" x 4" Treated and Nailed | S.F. | 2.12 |

# DIVISION # 06  WOOD AND PLASTICS - QUICK ESTIMATING

| | | UNIT | COST |
|---|---|---|---|
| **06999.10** | **ROUGH CARPENTRY, Cont'd...** | | |
| 3460 | Treated and Bolted (Including Bolts) | S.F. | 3.07 |
| 3470 | 6" x 6" Treated and Nailed | " | 4.24 |
| 3480 | Treated and Bolted (Including Bolts) | " | 5.40 |
| 3600 | Building Papers and Sealers | | |
| 3610 | 15" Felt | S.F. | 0.29 |
| 3620 | Polyethylene - 4 mil | " | 0.24 |
| 3630 | 6 mil | " | 0.27 |
| 3640 | Sill Sealer | " | 1.05 |
| **06999.20** | **FINISH CARPENTRY** | | |
| 1000 | FINISH SIDINGS AND FACING MATERIALS (Exterior) TO % | | |
| 1100 | Boards and Beveled Sidings | | |
| 1200 | Cedar Beveled - Clear Heart 1/2" x 4" | S.F. | 6.66 |
| 1210 | 1/2" x 6" | " | 5.85 |
| 1220 | 1/2" x 8" | " | 5.00 |
| 1300 | Rough Sawn 7/8" x 8" | " | 5.10 |
| 1310 | 7/8" x 10" | " | 5.27 |
| 1320 | 7/8" x 12" | " | 5.27 |
| 1330 | 3/4" x 12" | " | 4.58 |
| 1400 | Redwood Beveled - Clear Heart | | |
| 1410 | 1/2" x 6" | S.F. | 6.40 |
| 1430 | 5/8" x 10" | " | 6.51 |
| 1440 | 3/4" x 6" | " | 6.86 |
| 1450 | 3/4" x 8" | " | 7.50 |
| 1500 | 3/4" x 6" Board - Clear | " | 3.86 |
| 1510 | 3/4" Tongue & Groove | " | 6.18 |
| 1520 | 1" Rustic Beveled - 6" and 8" | " | 6.69 |
| 1530 | 5/4" Rustic Beveled - 6" and 8" | " | 6.69 |
| 1540 | Add for Metal Corners | EA. | 1.86 |
| 1550 | Add for Mitering Corners | " | 3.91 |
| 1600 | Plywood Fir AC Smooth -One Side 1/4" | S.F. | 2.34 |
| 1610 | 3/8" | " | 2.48 |
| 1620 | 1/2" | " | 2.54 |
| 1630 | 5/8" | " | 2.68 |
| 1640 | 3/4" | " | 3.00 |
| 1650 | 5/8" - Grooved and Rough Faced | " | 3.08 |
| 1700 | Cedar - Rough Sawn 3/8" | " | 3.00 |
| 1710 | 5/8" | " | 3.08 |
| 1720 | 3/4" | " | 3.65 |
| 1730 | 5/8" - Grooved and Rough Faced | " | 3.65 |
| 1740 | Add for Wood Batten Strips, 1" x 2" - 4' O.C. | " | 0.48 |
| 1750 | Add for Splines | " | 0.48 |
| 1800 | Hardboard - Paneling and Lap Siding (Primed) | | |
| 1810 | 3/8" Rough Textured Paneling - 4' x 8' | S.F. | 2.47 |
| 1820 | 7/16" Grooved - 4' x 8' | " | 2.34 |
| 1830 | 7/16" Stucco Board Paneling | " | 2.59 |
| 1840 | 7/16" x 8" Lap Siding | " | 2.96 |
| 1860 | Add for Pre-Finishing | " | 0.24 |
| 1900 | Shingles | | |
| 1910 | Wood - 16" Red Cedar - 12" to Weather - #1 | S.F. | 4.86 |
| 1920 | #2 | " | 3.83 |
| 1930 | #3 | " | 3.59 |

*© 2011 By Design & Construction Resources*

# DIVISION # 06  WOOD AND PLASTICS - QUICK ESTIMATING

| | | UNIT | COST |
|---|---|---|---|
| **06999.20** | **FINISH CARPENTRY, Cont'd...** | | |
| 1940 | Red Cedar Hand Splits - #1, 24" - 1/2" to 3/4" | S.F. | 4.07 |
| 1950 | 24" - 3/4" to 1 1/4" | " | 4.55 |
| 1960 | #2 | " | 4.07 |
| 1970 | #3 | " | 3.83 |
| 2000 | Add for Fire Retardant | " | 0.58 |
| 2010 | Add for 3/8" Backer Board | " | 0.97 |
| 2020 | Add for Metal Corners | EA. | 1.88 |
| 2030 | Add for Ridges, Hips and Corners | L.F. | 5.01 |
| 2040 | Add for 8" to Weather | PCT. | 25.00 |
| 2100 | Facia - Pine #2 1" x 8" | L.F. | 2.37 |
| 2110 | Cedar #3 1" x 8" | " | 3.74 |
| 2120 | Redwood - Clear 1" x 8" | " | 4.99 |
| 2130 | Plywood 5/8" - ACX 1" x 8" | " | 2.45 |
| 2140 | Facia - Pine #2 1" x 8" | S.F. | 3.55 |
| 2200 | Cedar #3 1" x 8" | " | 5.25 |
| 2210 | Redwood - Clear 1" x 8" | " | 7.64 |
| 2220 | Plywood 5/8" - ACX 1" x 8" | " | 3.62 |
| 2300 | FINISH WALLS (Interior) (15% Added for Waste) | " | 3.94 |
| 2400 | Boards, Cedar - #3 1" x 6" and 1" x 8" | " | 3.94 |
| 2410 | Knotty 1" x 6" and 1" x 8" | " | 4.18 |
| 2420 | D Grade 1" x 6" and 1" x 8" | " | 5.08 |
| 2430 | Aromatic 1" x 6" and 1" x 8" | " | 5.25 |
| 2440 | Redwood - Construction 1" x 6" and 1" x 8" | " | 6.28 |
| 2450 | Clear 1" x 6" and 1" x 8" | " | 6.51 |
| 2460 | Fir - Beaded 5/8" x 4" | " | 5.59 |
| 2470 | Pine - #2 1" x 6" and 1" x 8" | " | 7.05 |
| 2500 | Hardboard (Paneling) Tempered - 1/8" | " | 5.13 |
| 2510 | 1/4" | " | 3.92 |
| 2600 | Plywood (Prefinished Paneling) 1/4" Birch - Natural | " | 1.64 |
| 2610 | 3/4" Birch - Natural | " | 1.79 |
| 2620 | 1/4" Birch - White | " | 3.43 |
| 2630 | 1/4" Oak - Rotary Cut | " | 4.52 |
| 2640 | 3/4" | " | 5.89 |
| 2700 | 1/4" Oak - White | " | 4.33 |
| 2710 | 1/4" Mahogany (Lauan) | " | 5.41 |
| 2720 | 3/4" | " | 7.22 |
| 2730 | 3/4" Mahogany (African) | " | 3.41 |
| 2740 | 1/4" Walnut | " | 4.87 |
| 2800 | Gypsum Board (Paneling) | " | 5.96 |
| 2810 | Prefinished | " | 6.55 |
| 2820 | Red Oak Plastic | | |
| **06999.30** | **MILLWORK & CUSTOM WOODWORK** | | |
| 1000 | CUSTOM CABINET WORK (Red Oak or Birch) | | |
| 1010 | Base Cabinets - Avg. 35" H x 24" D with Drawer | L.F. | 350 |
| 1020 | Sink Fronts | " | 137 |
| 1030 | Corner Cabinets | " | 280 |
| 1040 | Add per Drawer | " | 59.00 |
| 1050 | Upper Cabinets - Avg. 30" High x 12" Deep | " | 178 |
| 2000 | Utility Cabinets - Avg. 84" High x 24" Deep | " | 420 |
| 2010 | China or Corner Cabinets - 84" High | EA. | 800 |
| 2020 | Oven Cabinets - 84" High x 24" Deep | " | 470 |

# DIVISION # 06 WOOD AND PLASTICS - QUICK ESTIMATING

| | | UNIT | COST |
|---|---|---|---|
| **06999.30** | **MILLWORK & CUSTOM WOODWORK, Cont'd...** | | |
| 2030 | Vanity Cabinets - Avg. 30" High x 21" Deep | EA. | 280 |
| 2040 | Deduct for Prefinishing wood | PCT. | 10.00 |
| 2050 | Base Cabinets - Avg. 35" H x 24" D with Drawer | EA. | 209 |
| 2060 | Sink Fronts | L.F. | 137 |
| 2070 | Corner Cabinets | " | 300 |
| 2080 | Add per Drawer | " | 60.00 |
| 2090 | Upper Cabinets - Avg. 30" High x 12" Deep | " | 175 |
| 3000 | Utility Cabinets - Avg. 84" High x 24" Deep | " | 420 |
| 3010 | China or Corner Cabinets - 84" High | " | 810 |
| 3020 | Oven Cabinets - 84" High x 24" Deep | " | 470 |
| 3030 | Vanity Cabinets - Avg. 30" High x 21" Deep | " | 280 |
| 4000 | COUNTER TOPS - 25" | | |
| 4010 | Plastic Laminated with 4" Back Splash | L.F. | 79.75 |
| 4020 | Deduct for No Back Splash | " | 13.47 |
| 4030 | Granite - 1 1/4" - Artificial | " | 144 |
| 4040 | 3/4" - Artificial | " | 113 |
| 4050 | Marble | " | 138 |
| 4070 | Wood Cutting Block | " | 138 |
| 5000 | Stainless Steel | " | 194 |
| 5010 | Polyester-Acrylic Solid Surface | " | 220 |
| 5020 | Quartz | " | 124 |
| 5030 | Plastic (Polymer) | " | 84.75 |
| 6000 | CUSTOM DOOR FRAMES - Including 2 Sides Trim | | |
| 6010 | Birch | EA. | 380 |
| 6020 | Fir | " | 220 |
| 6030 | Poplar | " | 230 |
| 6040 | Oak | " | 420 |
| 6050 | Pine | " | 310 |
| 6060 | Walnut | " | 500 |
| 8000 | MOULDINGS AND TRIM | | |
| 8010 | Apron 7/16" x 2" | L.F. | 2.93 |
| 8020 | Astragal 1 3/4" x 2 1/4" | " | 6.92 |
| 8030 | Base 7/16" x 2 3/4" | " | 4.19 |
| 8050 | Base Shoe 7/16" x 2 3/4" | " | 3.35 |
| 8060 | Batten Strip 5/8" x 1 5/8" | " | 2.89 |
| 8070 | Brick Mould 1 1/14" x 2" | " | 3.36 |
| 9080 | Casing 11/16" x 2 1/4" | " | 3.64 |
| 9100 | Chair Rail 5/8" x 1 3/4" | " | 3.81 |
| 9110 | Closet Rod 1 5/16" | " | 3.97 |
| 9120 | Corner Bead 1 1/8" x 1 1/8" | " | 5.03 |
| 9130 | Cove Moulding 3/4" x 3/4" | " | 3.14 |
| 9140 | Crown Moulding 9/16" x 3 5/8" | " | 4.66 |
| 9160 | Drip Cap | " | 3.76 |
| 9170 | Half Round 1/2" x 1" | " | 4.02 |
| 9180 | Hand Rail 1 5/8" x 1 3/4" | " | 5.63 |
| 9190 | Hook Strip 5/8" x 2 1/2" | " | 3.24 |
| 9200 | Picture Mould 3/4" x 1 1/2" | " | 3.59 |
| 9210 | Quarter Round 3/4" x 3/4" | " | 2.55 |
| 9220 | 1/2" x 1/2" | " | 1.97 |
| 9230 | Sill 3/4" x 2 1/2" | " | 4.29 |
| 9240 | Stool 11/16 x 2 1/2" | " | 5.15 |
| 9250 | BIRCH | | |

© 2011 By Design & Construction Resources

# DIVISION # 06  WOOD AND PLASTICS - QUICK ESTIMATING

| | UNIT | COST |
|---|---|---|
| **06999.30  MILLWORK & CUSTOM WOODWORK, Cont'd...** | | |
| 9260  STAIRS (Treads, Risers, Skirt Boards) | L.F. | 47.75 |
| 9270  SHELVING (12" Deep) | S.F. | 50.25 |
| 9280  CUSTOM PANELING | " | 34.50 |
| 9290 OAK | | |
| 9300  STAIRS (Treads, Risers, Skirt Boards) | L.F. | 37.00 |
| 9310  SHELVING (12" Deep) | S.F. | 45.00 |
| 9320  CUSTOM PANELING | " | 25.75 |
| 9330  THRESHOLDS - 3/4" x 3 1/2" | L.F. | 24.50 |
| 9340 PINE | | |
| 9350  STAIRS (Treads, Risers, Skirt Boards) | L.F. | 27.75 |
| 9360  SHELVING (12" Deep) | " | 31.00 |
| 9370  CUSTOM PANELING | S.F. | 21.29 |
| **06999.40  GLUE LAMINATE** | | |
| 0010  Arches 80' Span | S.F. | 12.37 |
| 0020  Beams & Purlins 40' Span | " | 8.57 |
| 0030  Deck Fir - 3" x 6" | " | 10.21 |
| 0040        4" x 6" | " | 10.99 |
| 0050  Deck Cedar - 3" x 6" | " | 13.19 |
| 0060        4" x 6" | " | 14.85 |
| 0070  Deck Pine - 3" x 6" | " | 8.96 |
| **06999.50  PREFABRICATED WOOD COMPONENTS** | | |
| 1000  WOOD TRUSSED RAFTERS | | |
| 1010   24" O.C. - 4 -12 Pitch | | |
| 2000     Span To 16' w/ Supports | EA. | 168 |
| 2010     20' | " | 172 |
| 2030     24' | " | 200 |
| 2050     28' | " | 210 |
| 2070     32' | " | 260 |
| 3000   Add for 5-12 Pitch | PCT. | 5.00 |
| 3010   Add for 6-12 Pitch | " | 10.00 |
| 3020   Add for Scissor Truss | EA. | 36.50 |
| 3030   Add for Gable End 24' | " | 79.00 |
| 3040     Span To 16' w/ Supports | S.F. | 5.19 |
| 3050     20' | " | 4.20 |
| 3070     24' | " | 3.98 |
| 3100     28' | " | 4.01 |
| 3120     32' | " | 4.50 |
| 5000   Add for 5-12 Pitch | PCT. | 15.00 |
| 5010   Add for 6-12 Pitch | " | 25.00 |
| 5020   Add for Scissor Truss | S.F. | 29.00 |
| 5030   Add for Gable End 24' | " | 0.52 |
| 6000  WOOD FLOOR TRUSS JOISTS (TJI) | | |
| 6010   Open Web - Wood or Metal - 24" O.C. | | |
| 6020     Up To 23' Span x 12" Single | L.F. | 10.43 |
| 6030     To 24' Span x 15" Cord | " | 10.69 |
| 6050     To 30' Span x 21" | " | 11.65 |
| 6060     To 25' Span x 15" Double | " | 10.15 |
| 6070     To 30' Span x 18" Cord | " | 10.74 |
| 6080     To 36' Span x 21" | " | 12.00 |
| 7000   Plywood Web - 24" O.C. | | |
| 7010     Up To 15' x 9 1/2" | L.F. | 6.75 |

# DIVISION # 06  WOOD AND PLASTICS - QUICK ESTIMATING

| | | UNIT | COST |
|---|---|---|---|
| **06999.50** | **PREFABRICATED WOOD COMPONENTS, Cont'd...** | | |
| 7030 | To 21' x 14" | L.F. | 7.50 |
| 7040 | To 22' x 16" | " | 8.46 |
| 8000 | Open Web - Wood or Metal - 24" O.C. | | |
| 8010 | Up To 23' Span x 12" Single | S.F. | 5.15 |
| 8020 | To 24' Span x 15" Cord | " | 4.24 |
| 8030 | To 27' Span x 18" | " | 5.48 |
| 8040 | To 30' Span x 21" | " | 5.82 |
| 8050 | To 25' Span x 15" Double | " | 5.08 |
| 8060 | To 30' Span x 18" Cord | " | 5.19 |
| 8070 | To 36' Span x 21" | " | 5.88 |
| 8500 | Plywood Web - 24" O.C. | | |
| 8510 | Up To 15' x 9 1/2" | S.F. | 3.41 |
| 8520 | To 19' x 11 7/8" | " | 3.40 |
| 8530 | To 21' x 14" | " | 3.81 |
| 8540 | To 22' x 16" | " | 4.20 |
| **06999.51** | **LAMINATED VENEER STRUCTURAL BEAMS** | | |
| 0005 | Micro Lam - Plywood - 24" O.C. | | |
| 0010 | 9 1/2" x 1 3/4" | L.F. | 10.10 |
| 0020 | 11 7/8" x 1 3/4" | " | 10.95 |
| 0030 | 14" x 1 3/4" | " | 12.99 |
| 0040 | 16" x 1 3/4" | " | 14.36 |
| 1000 | Glue Lam- Dimension Lumber- 24" O.C. | | |
| 1010 | 9" x 3 1/2" | L.F. | 18.99 |
| 1020 | 12" x 3 1/2" | " | 23.25 |
| 1040 | 9" x 5 1/2" | " | 28.00 |
| 1050 | 12" x 5 1/2" | " | 33.75 |
| 1070 | 18" x 5 1/2" | " | 52.00 |
| 2000 | Add for Architectural Grade | PCT. | 25.00 |
| 2010 | Add for 6 3/4" | " | 40.00 |
| 3000 | Micro Lam - Plywood - 24" O.C. | | |
| 3010 | 9 1/2" x 1 3/4" | S.F. | 5.10 |
| 3020 | 11 7/8" x 1 3/4" | " | 5.47 |
| 3040 | 16" x 1 3/4" | " | 7.12 |
| 4000 | Glue Lam - Dimension Lumber - 24" O.C. | | |
| 4010 | 9" x 3 1/2" | S.F. | 9.44 |
| 4020 | 12" x 3 1/2" | " | 11.66 |
| 4040 | 9" x 5 1/2" | " | 14.00 |
| 4050 | 12" x 5 1/2" | " | 16.97 |
| 4070 | 18" x 5 1/2" | " | 26.00 |
| **06999.60** | **WOOD TREATMENTS** | | |
| 0010 | PRESERVATIVES – PRESSURE TREATED | | |
| 0020 | Dimensions | B.F. | 0.29 |
| 0030 | Timbers | " | 0.44 |
| 0040 | FIRE RETARDENTS | | |
| 0050 | Dimensions & Timbers | B.F. | 0.55 |
| **06999.70** | **ROUGH HARDWARE** | | |
| 1000 | NAILS | B.F. | 0.03 |
| 2000 | JOIST HANGERS | EA. | 3.59 |
| 3000 | BOLTS - 5/8" x 12" | " | 4.72 |

© 2011 By Design & Construction Resources

**Design & Construction Resources**

## DIVISION # 07 THERMAL AND MOISTURE

### TABLE OF CONTENTS — PAGE

| Section | Page |
|---|---|
| 07100.10 - WATERPROOFING | 07-2 |
| 07160.10 - BITUMINOUS DAMPPROOFING | 07-2 |
| 07190.10 - VAPOR BARRIERS | 07-2 |
| 07210.10 - BATT INSULATION | 07-2 |
| 07210.20 - BOARD INSULATION | 07-3 |
| 07210.60 - LOOSE FILL INSULATION | 07-3 |
| 07210.70 - SPRAYED INSULATION | 07-3 |
| 07310.10 - ASPHALT SHINGLES | 07-3 |
| 07310.50 - METAL SHINGLES | 07-3 |
| 07310.60 - SLATE SHINGLES | 07-4 |
| 07310.70 - WOOD SHINGLES | 07-4 |
| 07310.80 - WOOD SHAKES | 07-4 |
| 07310.90 - CLAY TILE ROOF (assorted colors) | 07-4 |
| 07460.10 - METAL SIDING PANELS | 07-4 |
| 07460.50 - PLASTIC SIDING | 07-5 |
| 07460.60 - PLYWOOD SIDING | 07-5 |
| 07460.80 - WOOD SIDING | 07-5 |
| 07510.10 - BUILT-UP ASPHALT ROOFING | 07-6 |
| 07530.10 - SINGLE-PLY ROOFING | 07-6 |
| 07610.10 - METAL ROOFING | 07-6 |
| 07620.10 - FLASHING AND TRIM | 07-6 |
| 07620.20 - GUTTERS AND DOWNSPOUTS | 07-7 |
| 07810.10 - PLASTIC SKYLIGHTS | 07-8 |
| 07920.10 - CAULKING | 07-8 |
| **QUICK ESTIMATING** | 07A-9 |

*© 2011 By Design & Construction Resources*

# DIVISION # 07  THERMAL AND MOISTURE

| | | UNIT | LABOR | MAT. | TOTAL |
|---|---|---|---|---|---|
| **07100.10** | **WATERPROOFING** | | | | |
| 0100 | Membrane waterproofing, elastomeric | | | | |
| 1020 | Butyl | | | | |
| 1040 | 1/32" thick | S.F. | 1.67 | 1.05 | 2.72 |
| 1060 | 1/16" thick | " | 1.74 | 1.37 | 3.11 |
| 1140 | Neoprene | | | | |
| 1160 | 1/32" thick | S.F. | 1.67 | 1.80 | 3.47 |
| 1180 | 1/16" thick | " | 1.74 | 2.94 | 4.68 |
| 1260 | Plastic vapor barrier (polyethylene) | | | | |
| 1280 | 4 mil | S.F. | 0.16 | 0.04 | 0.20 |
| 1300 | 6 mil | " | 0.16 | 0.06 | 0.22 |
| 1320 | 10 mil | " | 0.20 | 0.09 | 0.29 |
| 1400 | Bituminous membrane, asphalt felt, 15 lb. | | | | |
| 1440 | One ply | S.F. | 1.04 | 0.62 | 1.66 |
| 1460 | Two ply | " | 1.26 | 0.73 | 1.99 |
| 1480 | Three ply | " | 1.49 | 0.91 | 2.40 |
| **07160.10** | **BITUMINOUS DAMPPROOFING** | | | | |
| 0100 | Building paper, asphalt felt | | | | |
| 0120 | 15 lb | S.F. | 1.67 | 0.16 | 1.83 |
| 0140 | 30 lb | " | 1.74 | 0.30 | 2.04 |
| 1000 | Asphalt, troweled, cold, primer plus | | | | |
| 1020 | 1 coat | S.F. | 1.39 | 0.68 | 2.07 |
| 1040 | 2 coats | " | 2.09 | 1.43 | 3.52 |
| 1060 | 3 coats | " | 2.61 | 2.04 | 4.65 |
| 1200 | Fibrous asphalt, hot troweled, primer plus | | | | |
| 1220 | 1 coat | S.F. | 1.67 | 0.68 | 2.35 |
| 1240 | 2 coats | " | 2.32 | 1.43 | 3.75 |
| 1260 | 3 coats | " | 2.98 | 2.04 | 5.02 |
| **07190.10** | **VAPOR BARRIERS** | | | | |
| 0980 | Vapor barrier, polyethylene | | | | |
| 1000 | 2 mil | S.F. | 0.20 | 0.01 | 0.21 |
| 1010 | 6 mil | " | 0.20 | 0.05 | 0.25 |
| 1020 | 8 mil | " | 0.23 | 0.06 | 0.29 |
| 1040 | 10 mil | " | 0.23 | 0.07 | 0.30 |
| **07210.10** | **BATT INSULATION** | | | | |
| 0980 | Ceiling, fiberglass, unfaced | | | | |
| 1000 | 3-1/2" thick, R11 | S.F. | 0.49 | 0.38 | 0.87 |
| 1020 | 6" thick, R19 | " | 0.55 | 0.50 | 1.05 |
| 1030 | 9" thick, R30 | " | 0.64 | 1.00 | 1.64 |
| 1035 | Suspended ceiling, unfaced | | | | |
| 1040 | 3-1/2" thick, R11 | S.F. | 0.46 | 0.38 | 0.84 |
| 1060 | 6" thick, R19 | " | 0.52 | 0.50 | 1.02 |
| 1070 | 9" thick, R30 | " | 0.59 | 1.00 | 1.59 |
| 1075 | Crawl space, unfaced | | | | |
| 1080 | 3-1/2" thick, R11 | S.F. | 0.64 | 0.38 | 1.02 |
| 1100 | 6" thick, R19 | " | 0.69 | 0.50 | 1.19 |
| 1120 | 9" thick, R30 | " | 0.76 | 1.00 | 1.76 |
| 2000 | Wall, fiberglass | | | | |
| 2010 | Paper backed | | | | |
| 2020 | 2" thick, R7 | S.F. | 0.44 | 0.25 | 0.69 |
| 2040 | 3" thick, R8 | " | 0.46 | 0.27 | 0.73 |
| 2060 | 4" thick, R11 | " | 0.49 | 0.45 | 0.94 |

# DIVISION # 07  THERMAL AND MOISTURE

| | | UNIT | LABOR | MAT. | TOTAL |
|---|---|---|---|---|---|
| **07210.10** | **BATT INSULATION, Cont'd...** | | | | |
| 2080 | 6" thick, R19 | S.F. | 0.52 | 0.67 | 1.19 |
| 2090 | Foil backed, 1 side | | | | |
| 2100 | 2" thick, R7 | S.F. | 0.44 | 0.58 | 1.02 |
| 2120 | 3" thick, R11 | " | 0.46 | 0.61 | 1.07 |
| 2140 | 4" thick, R14 | " | 0.49 | 0.64 | 1.13 |
| 2160 | 6" thick, R21 | " | 0.52 | 0.84 | 1.36 |
| **07210.20** | **BOARD INSULATION** | | | | |
| 2200 | Perlite board, roof | | | | |
| 2220 | 1.00" thick, R2.78 | S.F. | 0.34 | 0.58 | 0.92 |
| 2240 | 1.50" thick, R4.17 | " | 0.36 | 0.90 | 1.26 |
| 2580 | Rigid urethane | | | | |
| 2600 | 1" thick, R6.67 | S.F. | 0.34 | 1.03 | 1.37 |
| 2640 | 1.50" thick, R11.11 | " | 0.36 | 1.40 | 1.76 |
| 2780 | Polystyrene | | | | |
| 2800 | 1.0" thick, R4.17 | S.F. | 0.34 | 0.41 | 0.75 |
| 2820 | 1.5" thick, R6.26 | " | 0.36 | 0.63 | 0.99 |
| **07210.60** | **LOOSE FILL INSULATION** | | | | |
| 1000 | Blown-in type | | | | |
| 1010 | Fiberglass | | | | |
| 1020 | 5" thick, R11 | S.F. | 0.34 | 0.36 | 0.70 |
| 1040 | 6" thick, R13 | " | 0.41 | 0.41 | 0.82 |
| 1060 | 9" thick, R19 | " | 0.59 | 0.50 | 1.09 |
| **07210.70** | **SPRAYED INSULATION** | | | | |
| 1000 | Foam, sprayed on | | | | |
| 1010 | Polystyrene | | | | |
| 1020 | 1" thick, R4 | S.F. | 0.41 | 0.61 | 1.02 |
| 1040 | 2" thick, R8 | " | 0.55 | 1.19 | 1.74 |
| 1050 | Urethane | | | | |
| 1060 | 1" thick, R4 | S.F. | 0.41 | 0.58 | 0.99 |
| 1080 | 2" thick, R8 | " | 0.55 | 1.11 | 1.66 |
| **07310.10** | **ASPHALT SHINGLES** | | | | |
| 1000 | Standard asphalt shingles, strip shingles | | | | |
| 1020 | 210 lb/square | SQ. | 51.00 | 68.00 | 119 |
| 1040 | 235 lb/square | " | 57.00 | 72.00 | 129 |
| 1060 | 240 lb/square | " | 64.00 | 75.00 | 139 |
| 1080 | 260 lb/square | " | 73.00 | 110 | 183 |
| 1100 | 300 lb/square | " | 85.00 | 120 | 205 |
| 1120 | 385 lb/square | " | 100 | 160 | 260 |
| 5980 | Roll roofing, mineral surface | | | | |
| 6000 | 90 lb | SQ. | 36.50 | 41.75 | 78.25 |
| 6020 | 110 lb | " | 42.50 | 69.00 | 112 |
| 6040 | 140 lb | " | 51.00 | 72.00 | 123 |
| **07310.50** | **METAL SHINGLES** | | | | |
| 0980 | Aluminum, .020" thick | | | | |
| 1000 | Plain | SQ. | 100 | 260 | 360 |
| 1020 | Colors | " | 100 | 280 | 380 |
| 1960 | Steel, galvanized | | | | |
| 1980 | 26 ga. | | | | |
| 2000 | Plain | SQ. | 100 | 260 | 360 |
| 2020 | Colors | " | 100 | 340 | 440 |
| 2030 | 24 ga. | | | | |

© 2011 By Design & Construction Resources

# DIVISION # 07  THERMAL AND MOISTURE

| | | UNIT | LABOR | MAT. | TOTAL |
|---|---|---|---|---|---|
| **07310.50** | **METAL SHINGLES, Cont'd...** | | | | |
| 2040 | Plain | SQ. | 100 | 280 | 380 |
| 2060 | Colors | " | 100 | 350 | 450 |
| **07310.60** | **SLATE SHINGLES** | | | | |
| 0960 | Slate shingles | | | | |
| 0980 | Pennsylvania | | | | |
| 1000 | Ribbon | SQ. | 250 | 630 | 880 |
| 1020 | Clear | " | 250 | 810 | 1,060 |
| 1030 | Vermont | | | | |
| 1040 | Black | SQ. | 250 | 680 | 930 |
| 1060 | Gray | " | 250 | 750 | 1,000 |
| 1070 | Green | " | 250 | 760 | 1,010 |
| 1080 | Red | " | 250 | 1,380 | 1,630 |
| **07310.70** | **WOOD SHINGLES** | | | | |
| 1000 | Wood shingles, on roofs | | | | |
| 1010 | White cedar, #1 shingles | | | | |
| 1020 | 4" exposure | SQ. | 170 | 230 | 400 |
| 1040 | 5" exposure | " | 130 | 210 | 340 |
| 1050 | #2 shingles | | | | |
| 1060 | 4" exposure | SQ. | 170 | 160 | 330 |
| 1080 | 5" exposure | " | 130 | 140 | 270 |
| 1090 | Resquared and rebutted | | | | |
| 1100 | 4" exposure | SQ. | 170 | 210 | 380 |
| 1120 | 5" exposure | " | 130 | 170 | 300 |
| 1140 | On walls | | | | |
| 1150 | White cedar, #1 shingles | | | | |
| 1160 | 4" exposure | SQ. | 250 | 230 | 480 |
| 1180 | 5" exposure | " | 200 | 210 | 410 |
| 1200 | 6" exposure | " | 170 | 170 | 340 |
| 1210 | #2 shingles | | | | |
| 1220 | 4" exposure | SQ. | 250 | 160 | 410 |
| 1240 | 5" exposure | " | 200 | 140 | 340 |
| 1260 | 6" exposure | " | 170 | 120 | 290 |
| 1300 | Add for fire retarding | " | | | 110 |
| **07310.80** | **WOOD SHAKES** | | | | |
| 2010 | Shakes, hand split, 24" red cedar, on roofs | | | | |
| 2020 | 5" exposure | SQ. | 250 | 260 | 510 |
| 2040 | 7" exposure | " | 200 | 250 | 450 |
| 2060 | 9" exposure | " | 170 | 230 | 400 |
| 2080 | On walls | | | | |
| 2100 | 6" exposure | SQ. | 250 | 250 | 500 |
| 2120 | 8" exposure | " | 200 | 240 | 440 |
| 2140 | 10" exposure | " | 170 | 220 | 390 |
| 3000 | Add for fire retarding | " | | | 75.00 |
| **07310.90** | **CLAY TILE ROOF (assorted colors)** | | | | |
| 1010 | Spanish tile, terracota | SQ. | 130 | 390 | 520 |
| 1020 | Mission tile, terracota | " | 170 | 820 | 990 |
| 1030 | French tile, rustic blue, green patina | " | 150 | 950 | 1,100 |
| **07460.10** | **METAL SIDING PANELS** | | | | |
| 1000 | Aluminum siding panels | | | | |
| 1020 | Corrugated | | | | |
| 1030 | Plain finish | | | | |

# DIVISION # 07 THERMAL AND MOISTURE

| | | UNIT | LABOR | MAT. | TOTAL |
|---|---|---|---|---|---|
| **07460.10** | **METAL SIDING PANELS, Cont'd...** | | | | |
| 1040 | .024" | S.F. | 2.36 | 2.03 | 4.39 |
| 1060 | .032" | " | 2.36 | 2.40 | 4.76 |
| 1070 | Painted finish | | | | |
| 1080 | .024" | S.F. | 2.36 | 2.54 | 4.90 |
| 1100 | .032" | " | 2.36 | 2.90 | 5.26 |
| 2000 | Steel siding panels | | | | |
| 2040 | Corrugated | | | | |
| 2080 | 22 ga. | S.F. | 3.93 | 2.25 | 6.18 |
| 2100 | 24 ga. | " | 3.93 | 2.05 | 5.98 |
| **07460.50** | **PLASTIC SIDING** | | | | |
| 1000 | Horizontal vinyl siding, solid | | | | |
| 1010 | 8" wide | | | | |
| 1020 | Standard | S.F. | 2.05 | 1.23 | 3.28 |
| 1040 | Insulated | " | 2.05 | 1.49 | 3.54 |
| 1050 | 10" wide | | | | |
| 1060 | Standard | S.F. | 1.90 | 1.27 | 3.17 |
| 1080 | Insulated | " | 1.90 | 1.52 | 3.42 |
| 8500 | Vinyl moldings for doors and windows | L.F. | 2.13 | 0.79 | 2.92 |
| **07460.60** | **PLYWOOD SIDING** | | | | |
| 1000 | Rough sawn cedar, 3/8" thick | S.F. | 1.77 | 1.79 | 3.56 |
| 1020 | Fir, 3/8" thick | " | 1.77 | 0.99 | 2.76 |
| 1980 | Texture 1-11, 5/8" thick | | | | |
| 2000 | Cedar | S.F. | 1.90 | 2.42 | 4.32 |
| 2020 | Fir | " | 1.90 | 1.69 | 3.59 |
| 2040 | Redwood | " | 1.82 | 2.59 | 4.41 |
| 2060 | Southern Yellow Pine | " | 1.90 | 1.37 | 3.27 |
| **07460.80** | **WOOD SIDING** | | | | |
| 1000 | Beveled siding, cedar | | | | |
| 1010 | A grade | | | | |
| 1040 | 1/2 x 8 | S.F. | 2.13 | 4.42 | 6.55 |
| 1060 | 3/4 x 10 | " | 1.77 | 5.68 | 7.45 |
| 1070 | Clear | | | | |
| 1100 | 1/2 x 8 | S.F. | 2.13 | 4.92 | 7.05 |
| 1120 | 3/4 x 10 | " | 1.77 | 6.60 | 8.37 |
| 1130 | B grade | | | | |
| 1160 | 1/2 x 8 | S.F. | 21.25 | 5.25 | 26.50 |
| 1180 | 3/4 x 10 | " | 1.77 | 4.95 | 6.72 |
| 2000 | Board and batten | | | | |
| 2010 | Cedar | | | | |
| 2020 | 1x6 | S.F. | 2.66 | 5.12 | 7.78 |
| 2040 | 1x8 | " | 2.13 | 4.66 | 6.79 |
| 2060 | 1x10 | " | 1.90 | 4.21 | 6.11 |
| 2080 | 1x12 | " | 1.72 | 3.77 | 5.49 |
| 2090 | Pine | | | | |
| 2100 | 1x6 | S.F. | 2.66 | 1.29 | 3.95 |
| 2120 | 1x8 | " | 2.13 | 1.26 | 3.39 |
| 2140 | 1x10 | " | 1.90 | 1.21 | 3.11 |
| 2160 | 1x12 | " | 1.72 | 1.12 | 2.84 |
| 3000 | Tongue and groove | | | | |
| 3010 | Cedar | | | | |
| 3020 | 1x4 | S.F. | 2.96 | 4.80 | 7.76 |

## DIVISION # 07 THERMAL AND MOISTURE

| | | UNIT | LABOR | MAT. | TOTAL |
|---|---|---|---|---|---|
| **07460.80** | **WOOD SIDING, Cont'd...** | | | | |
| 3040 | 1x6 | S.F. | 2.80 | 4.63 | 7.43 |
| 3060 | 1x8 | " | 2.66 | 4.33 | 6.99 |
| 3080 | 1x10 | " | 2.54 | 4.26 | 6.80 |
| 3090 | Pine | | | | |
| 3100 | 1x4 | S.F. | 2.96 | 1.44 | 4.40 |
| 3120 | 1x6 | " | 2.80 | 1.36 | 4.16 |
| 3140 | 1x8 | " | 2.66 | 1.27 | 3.93 |
| 3160 | 1x10 | " | 2.54 | 1.21 | 3.75 |
| **07510.10** | **BUILT-UP ASPHALT ROOFING** | | | | |
| 0980 | Built-up roofing, asphalt felt, including gravel | | | | |
| 1000 | 2 ply | SQ. | 130 | 80.00 | 210 |
| 1500 | 3 ply | " | 170 | 110 | 280 |
| 2000 | 4 ply | " | 200 | 160 | 360 |
| 2195 | Cant strip, 4" x 4" | | | | |
| 2200 | Treated wood | L.F. | 1.45 | 2.11 | 3.56 |
| 2260 | Foamglass | " | 1.27 | 1.81 | 3.08 |
| 8000 | New gravel for built-up roofing, 400 lb/sq | SQ. | 100 | 32.00 | 132 |
| **07530.10** | **SINGLE-PLY ROOFING** | | | | |
| 2000 | Elastic sheet roofing | | | | |
| 2060 | Neoprene, 1/16" thick | S.F. | 0.63 | 2.83 | 3.46 |
| 2115 | PVC | | | | |
| 2120 | 45 mil | S.F. | 0.63 | 2.03 | 2.66 |
| 2200 | Flashing | | | | |
| 2220 | Pipe flashing, 90 mil thick | | | | |
| 2260 | 1" pipe | EA. | 12.75 | 28.50 | 41.25 |
| 2360 | Neoprene flashing, 60 mil thick strip | | | | |
| 2380 | 6" wide | L.F. | 4.24 | 1.73 | 5.97 |
| 2390 | 12" wide | " | 6.37 | 3.42 | 9.79 |
| **07610.10** | **METAL ROOFING** | | | | |
| 1000 | Sheet metal roofing, copper, 16 oz, batten seam | SQ. | 340 | 1,200 | 1,540 |
| 1020 | Standing seam | " | 320 | 1,170 | 1,490 |
| 2000 | Aluminum roofing, natural finish | | | | |
| 2005 | Corrugated, on steel frame | | | | |
| 2010 | .0175" thick | SQ. | 150 | 120 | 270 |
| 2040 | .0215" thick | " | 150 | 160 | 310 |
| 2060 | .024" thick | " | 150 | 190 | 340 |
| 2080 | .032" thick | " | 150 | 240 | 390 |
| 2100 | V-beam, on steel frame | | | | |
| 2120 | .032" thick | SQ. | 150 | 250 | 400 |
| 2130 | .040" thick | " | 150 | 270 | 420 |
| 2140 | .050" thick | " | 150 | 340 | 490 |
| 2200 | Ridge cap | | | | |
| 2220 | .019" thick | L.F. | 1.69 | 3.85 | 5.54 |
| 2500 | Corrugated galvanized steel roofing, on steel frame | | | | |
| 2520 | 28 ga. | SQ. | 150 | 200 | 350 |
| 2540 | 26 ga. | " | 150 | 230 | 380 |
| 2550 | 24 ga. | " | 150 | 260 | 410 |
| 2560 | 22 ga. | " | 150 | 290 | 440 |

# DIVISION # 07 THERMAL AND MOISTURE

| | | UNIT | LABOR | MAT. | TOTAL |
|---|---|---|---|---|---|
| **07620.10** | **FLASHING AND TRIM** | | | | |
| 0050 | Counter flashing | | | | |
| 0060 | Aluminum, .032" | S.F. | 5.09 | 1.58 | 6.67 |
| 0100 | Stainless steel, .015" | " | 5.09 | 5.06 | 10.15 |
| 0105 | Copper | | | | |
| 0110 | 16 oz. | S.F. | 5.09 | 7.49 | 12.58 |
| 0112 | 20 oz. | " | 5.09 | 8.89 | 13.98 |
| 0114 | 24 oz. | " | 5.09 | 10.75 | 15.84 |
| 0116 | 32 oz. | " | 5.09 | 13.25 | 18.34 |
| 0118 | Valley flashing | | | | |
| 0120 | Aluminum, .032" | S.F. | 3.18 | 1.58 | 4.76 |
| 0130 | Stainless steel, .015 | " | 3.18 | 5.06 | 8.24 |
| 0135 | Copper | | | | |
| 0140 | 16 oz. | S.F. | 3.18 | 7.49 | 10.67 |
| 0160 | 20 oz. | " | 4.24 | 8.89 | 13.13 |
| 0180 | 24 oz. | " | 3.18 | 10.75 | 13.93 |
| 0200 | 32 oz. | " | 3.18 | 13.25 | 16.43 |
| 0380 | Base flashing | | | | |
| 0400 | Aluminum, .040" | S.F. | 4.24 | 2.60 | 6.84 |
| 0410 | Stainless steel, .018" | " | 4.24 | 6.05 | 10.29 |
| 0415 | Copper | | | | |
| 0420 | 16 oz. | S.F. | 4.24 | 7.49 | 11.73 |
| 0422 | 20 oz. | " | 3.18 | 8.89 | 12.07 |
| 0424 | 24 oz. | " | 4.24 | 10.75 | 14.99 |
| 0426 | 32 oz. | " | 4.24 | 13.25 | 17.49 |
| **07620.20** | **GUTTERS AND DOWNSPOUTS** | | | | |
| 1500 | Copper gutter and downspout | | | | |
| 1520 | Downspouts, 16 oz. copper | | | | |
| 1530 | Round | | | | |
| 1540 | 3" dia. | L.F. | 3.39 | 10.50 | 13.89 |
| 1550 | 4" dia. | " | 3.39 | 13.00 | 16.39 |
| 1800 | Gutters, 16 oz. copper | | | | |
| 1810 | Half round | | | | |
| 1820 | 4" wide | L.F. | 5.09 | 9.38 | 14.47 |
| 1840 | 5" wide | " | 5.66 | 11.50 | 17.16 |
| 1860 | Type K | | | | |
| 1880 | 4" wide | L.F. | 5.09 | 10.50 | 15.59 |
| 1890 | 5" wide | " | 5.66 | 11.00 | 16.66 |
| 3000 | Aluminum gutter and downspout | | | | |
| 3005 | Downspouts | | | | |
| 3010 | 2" x 3" | L.F. | 3.39 | 1.15 | 4.54 |
| 3030 | 3" x 4" | " | 3.64 | 1.58 | 5.22 |
| 3035 | 4" x 5" | " | 3.92 | 1.75 | 5.67 |
| 3038 | Round | | | | |
| 3040 | 3" dia. | L.F. | 3.39 | 1.94 | 5.33 |
| 3050 | 4" dia. | " | 3.64 | 2.48 | 6.12 |
| 3240 | Gutters, stock units | | | | |
| 3260 | 4" wide | L.F. | 5.36 | 1.88 | 7.24 |
| 3270 | 5" wide | " | 5.66 | 2.24 | 7.90 |
| 4101 | Galvanized steel gutter and downspout | | | | |
| 4111 | Downspouts, round corrugated | | | | |
| 4121 | 3" dia. | L.F. | 3.39 | 1.94 | 5.33 |

© 2011 By Design & Construction Resources

# DIVISION # 07 THERMAL AND MOISTURE

| | | UNIT | LABOR | MAT. | TOTAL |
|---|---|---|---|---|---|
| **07620.20** | **GUTTERS AND DOWNSPOUTS, Cont'd...** | | | | |
| 4131 | 4" dia. | L.F. | 3.39 | 2.61 | 6.00 |
| 4141 | 5" dia. | " | 3.64 | 3.88 | 7.52 |
| 4151 | 6" dia. | " | 3.64 | 5.15 | 8.79 |
| 4161 | Rectangular | | | | |
| 4171 | 2" x 3" | L.F. | 3.39 | 1.75 | 5.14 |
| 4191 | 3" x 4" | " | 3.18 | 2.51 | 5.69 |
| 4201 | 4" x 4" | " | 3.18 | 3.15 | 6.33 |
| 4300 | Gutters, stock units | | | | |
| 4310 | 5" wide | | | | |
| 4320 | Plain | L.F. | 5.66 | 1.69 | 7.35 |
| 4330 | Painted | " | 5.66 | 1.84 | 7.50 |
| 4335 | 6" wide | | | | |
| 4340 | Plain | L.F. | 5.99 | 2.36 | 8.35 |
| 4360 | Painted | " | 5.99 | 2.65 | 8.64 |
| **07810.10** | **PLASTIC SKYLIGHTS** | | | | |
| 1030 | Single thickness, not including mounting curb | | | | |
| 1040 | 2' x 4' | EA. | 64.00 | 360 | 424 |
| 1050 | 4' x 4' | " | 85.00 | 490 | 575 |
| 1060 | 5' x 5' | " | 130 | 650 | 780 |
| 1070 | 6' x 8' | " | 170 | 1,390 | 1,560 |
| **07920.10** | **CAULKING** | | | | |
| 0100 | Caulk exterior, two component | | | | |
| 0120 | 1/4 x 1/2 | L.F. | 2.66 | 0.39 | 3.05 |
| 0140 | 3/8 x 1/2 | " | 2.96 | 0.60 | 3.56 |
| 0160 | 1/2 x 1/2 | " | 3.33 | 0.82 | 4.15 |
| 0220 | Caulk interior, single component | | | | |
| 0240 | 1/4 x 1/2 | L.F. | 2.54 | 0.26 | 2.80 |
| 0260 | 3/8 x 1/2 | " | 2.80 | 0.37 | 3.17 |
| 0280 | 1/2 x 1/2 | " | 3.13 | 0.49 | 3.62 |

# DIVISION # 07 THERMAL AND MOISTURE - QUICK ESTIMATING

| | | UNIT | COST |
|---|---|---|---|
| **07999.10** | **WATERPROOFING** | | |
| 0010 | 1-Ply Membrane Felt 15# | S.F. | 1.72 |
| 0020 | 2-Ply Membrane Felt 15# | " | 2.62 |
| 0030 | Hydrolithic | " | 2.83 |
| 0040 | Elastomeric Rubberized Asphalt with Poly Sheet | " | 2.62 |
| 0060 | Metallic Oxide 3-Coat | " | 4.48 |
| 0070 | Vinyl Plastic | " | 3.13 |
| 0080 | Bentonite 3/8" - Trowel | " | 2.66 |
| 0090 | 5/8" - Panels | " | 3.02 |
| **07999.20** | **DAMPPROOFING** | | |
| 0010 | Asphalt Trowel Mastic 1/16" | S.F. | 1.06 |
| 0020 | 1/8" | " | 1.42 |
| 0030 | Spray Liquid 1-Coat | " | 0.66 |
| 0040 | 2-Coat | " | 0.92 |
| 0050 | Brush Liquid 2-Coat | " | 1.03 |
| 1000 | Hot Mop 1-Coat and Primer | " | 1.72 |
| 1010 | 1 Fibrous Asphalt | " | 1.88 |
| 1020 | Cementitious Per Coat 1/2" Coat | " | 1.10 |
| 1030 | Silicone 1-Coat | " | 0.72 |
| 1040 | 2-Coat | " | 1.27 |
| 1050 | Add for Scaffold and Lift Operations | " | 0.65 |
| **07999.30** | **BUILDING INSULATION** | | |
| 1000 | FLEXIBLE | | |
| 1010 | Fiberglass 2 1/4" R 7.40 | S.F. | 0.77 |
| 1020 | 3 1/2" R 11.00 | " | 0.90 |
| 1040 | 6" R 19.00 | " | 1.13 |
| 1060 | 12" R 38.00 | " | 1.57 |
| 1100 | Add for Ceiling Work | " | 0.10 |
| 1110 | Add for Paper Faced | " | 0.12 |
| 1120 | Add for Polystyrene Barrier (2m) | " | 0.12 |
| 1130 | Add for Scaffold Work | " | 0.77 |
| 1200 | RIGID | | |
| 1300 | Fiberglass 1" R 4.35 3# Density | S.F. | 1.19 |
| 1310 | 1 1/2" R 6.52 3# Density | " | 1.53 |
| 1320 | 2" R 8.70 3# Density | " | 1.81 |
| 1400 | Styrene, Molded 1" R 4.3.5 | " | 5.72 |
| 1410 | 1 1/2" R 6.52 | " | 1.01 |
| 1420 | 2" R 7.69 | " | 1.36 |
| 1430 | 2" T&G R 7.69 | " | 1.75 |
| 1500 | Styrene, Extruded 1" R 5.40 | " | 1.24 |
| 1510 | 1 1/2" R 6.52 | " | 1.46 |
| 1520 | 2" R 7.69 | " | 1.57 |
| 1530 | 2" T&G R 7.69 | " | 1.75 |
| 1600 | Perlite 1" R 2.78 | " | 1.24 |
| 1610 | 2" R 5.56 | " | 1.98 |
| 1700 | Urethane 1" R 6.67 | " | 1.46 |
| 1710 | 2" R 13.34 | " | 1.87 |
| 1720 | Add for Glued Applications | " | 0.10 |
| 1800 | LOOSE 1" Styrene R 3.8 | " | 0.87 |
| 1810 | 1" Fiberglass R 2.2 | " | 0.84 |
| 1820 | 1" Rock Wool R 2.9 | " | 0.86 |
| 1830 | 1" Cellulose R 3.7 | " | 0.82 |

© 2011 By Design & Construction Resources

# DIVISION # 07  THERMAL AND MOISTURE - QUICK ESTIMATING

| | | UNIT | COST |
|---|---|---|---|
| **07999.30** | **BUILDING INSULATION, Cont'd...** | | |
| 1900 | FOAMED Urethane Per Inch | S.F. | 2.30 |
| 2000 | SPRAYED Cellulose Per Inch | " | 1.54 |
| 2100 | Polystyrene | " | 1.84 |
| 2200 | Urethane | " | 2.61 |
| 2300 | ALUMINUM PAPER | " | 0.70 |
| 2400 | VINYL FACED FIBERGLASS | " | 2.09 |
| **07999.80** | **SHINGLE ROOFING** | | |
| 1000 | ASPHALT SHINGLES 235# Seal Down | S.F. | 1.38 |
| 1010 | 300# Laminated | " | 1.56 |
| 1020 | 325# Fire Resistant | " | 2.25 |
| 1030 | Timberline | " | 2.21 |
| 1040 | 340# Tab Lock | " | 2.61 |
| 2000 | ASPHALT ROLL  90# | " | 0.76 |
| 3000 | FIBERGLASS SHINGLES 215# | " | 1.34 |
| 3010 | 250# | " | 1.51 |
| 4000 | RED CEDAR 16" x  5" to Weather #1 Grade | " | 4.03 |
| 4010 | #2 Grade | " | 3.57 |
| 4020 | #3 Grade | " | 2.55 |
| 4030 | 24" x 10" to Weather - Hand Splits - 1/2" x 3/4" # | " | 13.00 |
| 4040 | 3/4" x 1 1/4" # | " | 13.11 |
| 4050 | Add for Fire Retardant | " | 1.01 |
| 5000 | METAL Aluminum 020 mil | " | 4.32 |
| 6000 | Anodized 020 Mil | " | 5.01 |
| 7000 | Steel, Enameled Colored | " | 6.44 |
| 8000 | Galvanized Colored | " | 5.57 |
| 9000 | Add to Above for 15# Felt Underlayment | | |
| 9010 | Add for Base Starter | S.F. | 0.79 |
| 9020 | Add for Ice & Water Starter | " | 1.31 |
| 9030 | Add for Boston Ridge | " | 2.96 |
| 9040 | Add for Removal & Haul Away | " | 1.13 |
| 9050 | Add for Pitches Over 5-12 each Pitch Increase | " | 0.06 |
| 9060 | Add for Chimneys, Skylights and Bay Windows | EA. | 85.00 |
| **07999.90** | **BUILT-UP ROOFING** | | |
| 1000 | MEMBRANE | | |
| 1010 | 3-Ply Asphalt & Gravel - R 10.0 | S.F. | 720 |
| 1020 | R 16.6 | " | 740 |
| 1030 | 4-Ply - R 10.0 | " | 740 |
| 1040 | R 16.6 | " | 760 |
| 1050 | 5-Ply - R 10.0 | " | 780 |
| 1060 | R 16.6 | " | 810 |
| 2000 | Add for Sheet Rock over Steel Deck - 5/8" | " | 152 |
| 2010 | Add for Fiberglass Insulation | " | 51.75 |
| 2020 | Add for Pitch and Gravel | " | 79.75 |
| 2030 | Add for Sloped Roofs | " | 56.00 |
| 2040 | Add for Thermal Barrier | " | 43.25 |
| 2050 | Add for Upside Down Roofing System | " | 152 |
| 3000 | SINGLE-PLY - 60M Butylene Roofing & Gravel Ballast - R 10.0 | " | 540 |
| 3010 | Mech. Fastened - R 10.0 | " | 520 |
| 3020 | PVC & EPDM Roofing & Gravel Ballast - R 10.0 | " | 500 |
| 3030 | Mech. Fastened - R 10.0 | " | 520 |
| 3040 | Blocking and Cants Not Included | | |

# DIVISION # 08  DOORS AND WINDOWS

## TABLE OF CONTENTS

| | PAGE |
|---|---|
| 08110.10 - METAL DOORS | 08-2 |
| 08110.40 - METAL DOOR FRAMES | 08-2 |
| 08210.10 - WOOD DOORS | 08-3 |
| 08210.90 - WOOD FRAMES | 08-5 |
| 08300.10 - SPECIAL DOORS | 08-6 |
| 08410.10 - STOREFRONTS | 08-8 |
| 08510.10 - STEEL WINDOWS | 08-8 |
| 08520.10 - ALUMINUM WINDOWS | 08-8 |
| 08600.10 - WOOD WINDOWS | 08-9 |
| 08710.10 - HINGES | 08-10 |
| 08710.20 - LOCKSETS | 08-10 |
| 08710.30 - CLOSERS | 08-11 |
| 08710.40 - DOOR TRIM | 08-11 |
| 08710.60 - WEATHERSTRIPPING | 08-11 |
| 08810.10 - GLAZING | 08-12 |
| 08910.10 - GLAZED CURTAIN WALLS | 08-13 |
| **QUICK ESTIMATING** | **08A-15** |

© 2011 By Design & Construction Resources

# DIVISION # 08  DOORS AND WINDOWS

| | | UNIT | LABOR | MAT. | TOTAL |
|---|---|---|---|---|---|
| **08110.10** | **METAL DOORS** | | | | |
| 1000 | Flush hollow metal, std. duty, 20 ga., 1-3/8" thick | | | | |
| 1020 | 2-6 x 6-8 | EA. | 59.00 | 300 | 359 |
| 1080 | 3-0 x 6-8 | " | 59.00 | 360 | 419 |
| 1090 | 1-3/4" thick | | | | |
| 1100 | 2-6 x 6-8 | EA. | 59.00 | 360 | 419 |
| 1150 | 3-0 x 6-8 | " | 59.00 | 410 | 469 |
| 1200 | 2-6 x 7-0 | " | 59.00 | 390 | 449 |
| 1240 | 3-0 x 7-0 | " | 59.00 | 430 | 489 |
| 2110 | Heavy duty, 20 ga., unrated, 1-3/4" | | | | |
| 2130 | 2-8 x 6-8 | EA. | 59.00 | 390 | 449 |
| 2135 | 3-0 x 6-8 | " | 59.00 | 420 | 479 |
| 2140 | 2-8 x 7-0 | " | 59.00 | 450 | 509 |
| 2150 | 3-0 x 7-0 | " | 59.00 | 430 | 489 |
| 2200 | 18 ga., 1-3/4", unrated door | | | | |
| 2210 | 2-0 x 7-0 | EA. | 59.00 | 420 | 479 |
| 2235 | 2-6 x 7-0 | " | 59.00 | 420 | 479 |
| 2260 | 3-0 x 7-0 | " | 59.00 | 470 | 529 |
| 2270 | 3-4 x 7-0 | " | 59.00 | 480 | 539 |
| 2310 | 2", unrated door | | | | |
| 2320 | 2-0 x 7-0 | EA. | 67.00 | 460 | 527 |
| 2340 | 2-6 x 7-0 | " | 67.00 | 460 | 527 |
| 2360 | 3-0 x 7-0 | " | 67.00 | 520 | 587 |
| 2370 | 3-4 x 7-0 | " | 67.00 | 530 | 597 |
| 2400 | Galvanized metal door | | | | |
| 2410 | 3-0 x 7-0 | EA. | 67.00 | 500 | 567 |
| 2450 | For lead lining in doors | " | | | 970 |
| 2460 | For sound attenuation | " | | | 88.00 |
| 4280 | Vision glass | | | | |
| 4300 | 8" x 8" | EA. | 67.00 | 100 | 167 |
| 4320 | 8" x 48" | " | 67.00 | 150 | 217 |
| 4340 | Fixed metal louver | " | 53.00 | 230 | 283 |
| 4350 | For fire rating, add | | | | |
| 4370 | 3 hr door | EA. | | | 390 |
| 4380 | 1-1/2 hr door | " | | | 160 |
| 4400 | 3/4 hr door | " | | | 81.00 |
| 4430 | 1' extra height, add to material, 20% | | | | |
| 4440 | 1'6" extra height, add to material, 60% | | | | |
| 4470 | For dutch doors with shelf, add to material, 100% | | | | |
| 5000 | Stainless steel, general application | | | | |
| 5010 | 3'x7' | EA. | 590 | 1,620 | 2,210 |
| 5020 | 5'X7' | " | 790 | 2,690 | 3,480 |
| 6000 | Heavy impact, s-core, 18 ga., stainless | | | | |
| 6010 | 3'x7' | EA. | 590 | 1,960 | 2,550 |
| 6020 | 5'X7' | " | 790 | 3,270 | 4,060 |
| **08110.40** | **METAL DOOR FRAMES** | | | | |
| 1000 | Hollow metal, stock, 18 ga., 4-3/4" x 1-3/4" | | | | |
| 1020 | 2-0 x 7-0 | EA. | 67.00 | 140 | 207 |
| 1060 | 2-6 x 7-0 | " | 67.00 | 160 | 227 |
| 1100 | 3-0 x 7-0 | " | 67.00 | 160 | 227 |
| 1120 | 4-0 x 7-0 | " | 89.00 | 180 | 269 |
| 1140 | 5-0 x 7-0 | " | 89.00 | 190 | 279 |

## DIVISION # 08  DOORS AND WINDOWS

| | | UNIT | LABOR | MAT. | TOTAL |
|---|---|---|---|---|---|
| **08110.40** | **METAL DOOR FRAMES, Cont'd...** | | | | |
| 1160 | 6-0 x 7-0 | EA. | 89.00 | 230 | 319 |
| 1500 | 16 ga., 6-3/4" x 1-3/4" | | | | |
| 1520 | 2-0 x 7-0 | EA. | 74.00 | 160 | 234 |
| 1535 | 2-6 x 7-0 | " | 74.00 | 160 | 234 |
| 1550 | 3-0 x 7-0 | " | 74.00 | 170 | 244 |
| 1560 | 4-0 x 7-0 | " | 98.00 | 200 | 298 |
| 1580 | 6-0 x 7-0 | " | 98.00 | 230 | 328 |
| **08210.10** | **WOOD DOORS** | | | | |
| 0980 | Solid core, 1-3/8" thick | | | | |
| 1000 | Birch faced | | | | |
| 1020 | 2-4 x 7-0 | EA. | 67.00 | 150 | 217 |
| 1060 | 3-0 x 7-0 | " | 67.00 | 160 | 227 |
| 1070 | 3-4 x 7-0 | " | 67.00 | 310 | 377 |
| 1080 | 2-4 x 6-8 | " | 67.00 | 150 | 217 |
| 1090 | 2-6 x 6-8 | " | 67.00 | 150 | 217 |
| 1100 | 3-0 x 6-8 | " | 67.00 | 160 | 227 |
| 1120 | Lauan faced | | | | |
| 1140 | 2-4 x 6-8 | EA. | 67.00 | 140 | 207 |
| 1180 | 3-0 x 6-8 | " | 67.00 | 150 | 217 |
| 1200 | 3-4 x 6-8 | " | 67.00 | 160 | 227 |
| 1300 | Tempered hardboard faced | | | | |
| 1320 | 2-4 x 7-0 | EA. | 67.00 | 170 | 237 |
| 1360 | 3-0 x 7-0 | " | 67.00 | 210 | 277 |
| 1380 | 3-4 x 7-0 | " | 67.00 | 210 | 277 |
| 1420 | Hollow core, 1-3/8" thick | | | | |
| 1440 | Birch faced | | | | |
| 1460 | 2-4 x 7-0 | EA. | 67.00 | 140 | 207 |
| 1500 | 3-0 x 7-0 | " | 67.00 | 150 | 217 |
| 1520 | 3-4 x 7-0 | " | 67.00 | 160 | 227 |
| 1600 | Lauan faced | | | | |
| 1620 | 2-4 x 6-8 | EA. | 67.00 | 58.00 | 125 |
| 1630 | 2-6 x 6-8 | " | 67.00 | 63.00 | 130 |
| 1660 | 3-0 x 6-8 | " | 67.00 | 82.00 | 149 |
| 1680 | 3-4 x 6-8 | " | 67.00 | 91.00 | 158 |
| 1740 | Tempered hardboard faced | | | | |
| 1770 | 2-6 x 7-0 | EA. | 67.00 | 77.00 | 144 |
| 1800 | 3-0 x 7-0 | " | 67.00 | 90.00 | 157 |
| 1820 | 3-4 x 7-0 | " | 67.00 | 98.00 | 165 |
| 1900 | Solid core, 1-3/4" thick | | | | |
| 1920 | Birch faced | | | | |
| 1940 | 2-4 x 7-0 | EA. | 67.00 | 230 | 297 |
| 1950 | 2-6 x 7-0 | " | 67.00 | 240 | 307 |
| 1970 | 3-0 x 7-0 | " | 67.00 | 230 | 297 |
| 1980 | 3-4 x 7-0 | " | 67.00 | 240 | 307 |
| 2000 | Lauan faced | | | | |
| 2020 | 2-4 x 7-0 | EA. | 67.00 | 160 | 227 |
| 2030 | 2-6 x 7-0 | " | 67.00 | 180 | 247 |
| 2060 | 3-4 x 7-0 | " | 67.00 | 200 | 267 |
| 2080 | 3-0 x 7-0 | " | 67.00 | 220 | 287 |
| 2140 | Tempered hardboard faced | | | | |
| 2170 | 2-6 x 7-0 | EA. | 67.00 | 230 | 297 |

© 2011 By Design & Construction Resources

## DIVISION # 08  DOORS AND WINDOWS

### 08210.10  WOOD DOORS, Cont'd...

| | | UNIT | LABOR | MAT. | TOTAL |
|---|---|---|---|---|---|
| 2190 | 3-0 x 7-0 | EA. | 67.00 | 270 | 337 |
| 2200 | 3-4 x 7-0 | " | 67.00 | 290 | 357 |
| 2250 | Hollow core, 1-3/4" thick | | | | |
| 2270 |   Birch faced | | | | |
| 2295 |     2-6 x 7-0 | EA. | 67.00 | 160 | 227 |
| 2320 |     3-0 x 7-0 | " | 67.00 | 170 | 237 |
| 2340 |     3-4 x 7-0 | " | 67.00 | 180 | 247 |
| 2400 |   Lauan faced | | | | |
| 2430 |     2-6 x 6-8 | EA. | 67.00 | 110 | 177 |
| 2460 |     3-0 x 6-8 | " | 67.00 | 100 | 167 |
| 2480 |     3-4 x 6-8 | " | 67.00 | 110 | 177 |
| 2520 |   Tempered hardboard | | | | |
| 2550 |     2-6 x 7-0 | EA. | 67.00 | 93.00 | 160 |
| 2580 |     3-0 x 7-0 | " | 67.00 | 100 | 167 |
| 2600 |     3-4 x 7-0 | " | 67.00 | 110 | 177 |
| 2620 |   Add-on, louver | " | 53.00 | 35.00 | 88.00 |
| 2640 |   Glass | " | 53.00 | 110 | 163 |
| 2700 | Exterior doors, 3-0 x 7-0 x 2-1/2", solid core | | | | |
| 2710 |   Carved | | | | |
| 2720 |     One face | EA. | 130 | 1,330 | 1,460 |
| 2740 |     Two faces | " | 130 | 1,830 | 1,960 |
| 3000 | Closet doors, 1-3/4" thick | | | | |
| 3001 |   Bi-fold or bi-passing, includes frame and trim | | | | |
| 3020 |     Paneled | | | | |
| 3040 |       4-0 x 6-8 | EA. | 89.00 | 460 | 549 |
| 3060 |       6-0 x 6-8 | " | 89.00 | 520 | 609 |
| 3070 |     Louvered | | | | |
| 3080 |       4-0 x 6-8 | EA. | 89.00 | 320 | 409 |
| 3100 |       6-0 x 6-8 | " | 89.00 | 380 | 469 |
| 3130 |     Flush | | | | |
| 3140 |       4-0 x 6-8 | EA. | 89.00 | 230 | 319 |
| 3160 |       6-0 x 6-8 | " | 89.00 | 300 | 389 |
| 3170 |     Primed | | | | |
| 3180 |       4-0 x 6-8 | EA. | 89.00 | 260 | 349 |
| 3200 |       6-0 x 6-8 | " | 89.00 | 290 | 379 |
| 3210 | French Door, Dual-Tempered, Clear-Glass, 6'-8' | | | | |
| 3220 |   24"x80"x1-3/4" | EA. | 110 | 370 | 480 |
| 3230 |     with Low-E glass | " | 110 | 500 | 610 |
| 3240 |   30"x80"x1-3/4" | " | 110 | 420 | 530 |
| 3250 |     with Low-E glass | " | 110 | 500 | 610 |
| 3260 |   42"x80"x1-3/4" | " | 110 | 550 | 660 |
| 3270 |     with Low-E glass | " | 110 | 660 | 770 |
| 3280 |   24"x96"x1-3/4" | " | 110 | 440 | 550 |
| 3290 |     with Low-E glass | " | 110 | 550 | 660 |
| 3310 |   32"x96"x1-3/4" | " | 110 | 490 | 600 |
| 3320 |     with Low-E glass | " | 110 | 610 | 720 |
| 3330 | French door, 10-lite, 1-3/4' thick, 6'-8" high | | | | |
| 3340 |   24" wide | EA. | 110 | 390 | 500 |
| 3350 |   30" wide | " | 110 | 480 | 590 |
| 3360 |   36" wide | " | 110 | 490 | 600 |
| 3370 |   96" high, 24" wide | " | 110 | 500 | 610 |
| 3380 |     30" wide | " | 110 | 600 | 710 |

## DIVISION # 08  DOORS AND WINDOWS

| | | UNIT | LABOR | MAT. | TOTAL |
|---|---|---|---|---|---|
| **08210.10** | **WOOD DOORS, Cont'd...** | | | | |
| 3390 | 36" wide | EA. | 110 | 780 | 890 |
| 3400 | French door, 1-lite, 1-3/4' thick, 6'-8" high | | | | |
| 3410 | 48" wide | EA. | 110 | 1,380 | 1,490 |
| 3420 | 56" wide | " | 110 | 1,650 | 1,760 |
| 3430 | 60" wide | " | 110 | 1,930 | 2,040 |
| 3440 | 72" wide | " | 110 | 1,810 | 1,920 |
| 3500 | Fiberglass, single door, 6'-8" high | | | | |
| 3510 | 2-4" wide | EA. | 67.00 | 200 | 267 |
| 3520 | 2-6" wide | " | 67.00 | 300 | 367 |
| 3530 | 2-8" wide | " | 67.00 | 300 | 367 |
| 3540 | 3-0" wide | " | 67.00 | 370 | 437 |
| 3550 | 8'-0" high | | | | |
| 3560 | 2-4" wide | EA. | 67.00 | 400 | 467 |
| 3570 | 2-6" wide | " | 67.00 | 500 | 567 |
| 3580 | 2-8" wide | " | 67.00 | 600 | 667 |
| 3590 | 3-0" wide | " | 67.00 | 600 | 667 |
| 3600 | Fiberglass, double door, 6'-8" high | | | | |
| 3610 | 56" wide | EA. | 110 | 700 | 810 |
| 3620 | 60" wide | " | 110 | 800 | 910 |
| 3630 | 64" wide | " | 110 | 830 | 940 |
| 3640 | 72" wide | " | 110 | 950 | 1,060 |
| 3650 | 8'-0" high | | | | |
| 3700 | 56" wide | EA. | 110 | 260 | 370 |
| 3710 | 60" wide | " | 110 | 270 | 380 |
| 3720 | 64" wide | " | 110 | 290 | 400 |
| 3730 | 72" wide | " | 110 | 310 | 420 |
| 3740 | Metal clad, double door, 6'-8" high | | | | |
| 3750 | 56" wide | EA. | 110 | 280 | 390 |
| 3760 | 60" wide | " | 110 | 290 | 400 |
| 3770 | 64" wide | " | 110 | 300 | 410 |
| 3780 | 72" wide | " | 110 | 310 | 420 |
| 3790 | 8'-0" high | | | | |
| 3800 | 56" wide | EA. | 110 | 470 | 580 |
| 3810 | 60" wide | " | 110 | 500 | 610 |
| 3820 | 64" wide | " | 110 | 550 | 660 |
| 3830 | 72" wide | " | 110 | 600 | 710 |
| 3840 | For outswinging doors, add min. | " | | | 66.00 |
| 3850 | Maximum | " | | | 140 |
| **08210.90** | **WOOD FRAMES** | | | | |
| 0080 | Frame, interior, pine | | | | |
| 0100 | 2-6 x 6-8 | EA. | 76.00 | 78.00 | 154 |
| 0160 | 3-0 x 6-8 | " | 76.00 | 87.00 | 163 |
| 0180 | 5-0 x 6-8 | " | 76.00 | 91.00 | 167 |
| 0200 | 6-0 x 6-8 | " | 76.00 | 96.00 | 172 |
| 0220 | 2-6 x 7-0 | " | 76.00 | 89.00 | 165 |
| 0260 | 3-0 x 7-0 | " | 76.00 | 100 | 176 |
| 0280 | 5-0 x 7-0 | " | 110 | 120 | 230 |
| 0300 | 6-0 x 7-0 | " | 110 | 120 | 230 |
| 1000 | Exterior, custom, with threshold, including trim | | | | |
| 1040 | Walnut | | | | |
| 1060 | 3-0 x 7-0 | EA. | 130 | 340 | 470 |

© 2011 By Design & Construction Resources

# DIVISION # 08  DOORS AND WINDOWS

|  |  | UNIT | LABOR | MAT. | TOTAL |
|---|---|---|---|---|---|
| **08210.90** | **WOOD FRAMES, Cont'd...** |  |  |  |  |
| 1080 | 6-0 x 7-0 | EA. | 130 | 390 | 520 |
| 1090 | Oak |  |  |  |  |
| 1100 | 3-0 x 7-0 | EA. | 130 | 310 | 440 |
| 1120 | 6-0 x 7-0 | " | 130 | 360 | 490 |
| 1200 | Pine |  |  |  |  |
| 1240 | 2-6 x 7-0 | EA. | 110 | 130 | 240 |
| 1300 | 3-0 x 7-0 | " | 110 | 140 | 250 |
| 1320 | 3-4 x 7-0 | " | 110 | 160 | 270 |
| 1340 | 6-0 x 7-0 | " | 180 | 170 | 350 |
| 3000 | Fire-rated wood jambs |  |  |  |  |
| 3010 | 20-Minute, positive or neutral pressure, 3/4" | L.F. | 4.44 | 8.80 | 13.24 |
| 3020 | 45-60-minute | " | 4.44 | 9.90 | 14.34 |
| 3030 | 90-minute | " | 4.44 | 11.00 | 15.44 |
| 3040 | 120-minute | " | 4.44 | 13.25 | 17.69 |
| **08300.10** | **SPECIAL DOORS** |  |  |  |  |
| 1000 | Vault door and frame, class 5, steel | EA. | 530 | 6,550 | 7,080 |
| 1480 | Overhead door, coiling insulated |  |  |  |  |
| 1500 | Chain gear, no frame, 12' x 12' | EA. | 670 | 3,410 | 4,080 |
| 2000 | Aluminum, bronze glass panels, 12-9 x 13-0 | " | 530 | 3,850 | 4,380 |
| 2200 | Garage, flush, ins. metal, primed, 9-0 x 7-0 | " | 180 | 1,040 | 1,220 |
| 3000 | Sliding fire doors, motorized, fusible link, 3 hr. |  |  |  |  |
| 3040 | 3-0 x 6-8 | EA. | 1,070 | 3,900 | 4,970 |
| 3060 | 3-8 x 6-8 | " | 1,070 | 3,900 | 4,970 |
| 3080 | 4-0 x 8-0 | " | 1,070 | 4,240 | 5,310 |
| 3100 | 5-0 x 8-0 | " | 1,070 | 4,280 | 5,350 |
| 3200 | Metal clad doors, including electric motor |  |  |  |  |
| 3210 | Light duty |  |  |  |  |
| 3220 | Minimum | S.F. | 8.89 | 43.00 | 51.89 |
| 3240 | Maximum | " | 21.25 | 69.00 | 90.25 |
| 3250 | Heavy duty |  |  |  |  |
| 3260 | Minimum | S.F. | 26.75 | 67.00 | 93.75 |
| 3280 | Maximum | " | 33.25 | 110 | 143 |
| 3500 | Counter doors, (roll-up shutters), std, manual |  |  |  |  |
| 3510 | Opening, 4' high |  |  |  |  |
| 3520 | 4' wide | EA. | 440 | 1,300 | 1,740 |
| 3540 | 6' wide | " | 440 | 1,760 | 2,200 |
| 3560 | 8' wide | " | 490 | 1,980 | 2,470 |
| 3580 | 10' wide | " | 670 | 2,200 | 2,870 |
| 3590 | 14' wide | " | 670 | 2,750 | 3,420 |
| 3595 | 6' high |  |  |  |  |
| 3600 | 4' wide | EA. | 440 | 1,540 | 1,980 |
| 3620 | 6' wide | " | 490 | 2,010 | 2,500 |
| 3630 | 8' wide | " | 530 | 2,200 | 2,730 |
| 3640 | 10' wide | " | 670 | 2,480 | 3,150 |
| 3650 | 14' wide | " | 760 | 2,810 | 3,570 |
| 3660 | For stainless steel, add to material, 40% |  |  |  |  |
| 3670 | For motor operator, add | EA. |  |  | 1,520 |
| 3800 | Service doors, (roll up shutters), std, manual |  |  |  |  |
| 3810 | Opening |  |  |  |  |
| 3820 | 8' high x 8' wide | EA. | 300 | 1,650 | 1,950 |
| 3840 | 12' high x 12' wide | " | 670 | 2,310 | 2,980 |

## DIVISION # 08  DOORS AND WINDOWS

|  |  | UNIT | LABOR | MAT. | TOTAL |
|---|---|---|---|---|---|
| **08300.10** | **SPECIAL DOORS, Cont'd...** | | | | |
| 3860 | 16' high x 14' wide | EA. | 890 | 4,240 | 5,130 |
| 3870 | 20' high x 14' wide | " | 1,330 | 4,790 | 6,120 |
| 3880 | 24' high x 16' wide | " | 1,190 | 7,810 | 9,000 |
| 3890 | For motor operator | | | | |
| 3900 | Up to 12-0 x 12-0, add | EA. | | | 1,550 |
| 3920 | Over 12-0 x 12-0, add | " | | | 1,980 |
| 4040 | Roll-up doors | | | | |
| 4050 | 13-0 high x 14-0 wide | EA. | 760 | 1,400 | 2,160 |
| 4060 | 12-0 high x 14-0 wide | " | 760 | 1,790 | 2,550 |
| 5200 | Sectional wood overhead, frames not incl. | | | | |
| 5220 | Commercial grade, HD, 1-3/4" thick, manual | | | | |
| 5240 | 8' x 8' | EA. | 440 | 1,030 | 1,470 |
| 5260 | 10' x 10' | " | 490 | 1,480 | 1,970 |
| 5280 | 12' x 12' | " | 530 | 1,930 | 2,460 |
| 5290 | Chain hoist | | | | |
| 5300 | 12' x 16' high | EA. | 890 | 2,860 | 3,750 |
| 5320 | 14' x 14' high | " | 670 | 3,140 | 3,810 |
| 5340 | 20' x 8' high | " | 1,070 | 2,690 | 3,760 |
| 5360 | 16' high | " | 1,330 | 6,050 | 7,380 |
| 5990 | Sectional metal overhead doors, complete | | | | |
| 6000 | Residential grade, manual | | | | |
| 6020 | 9' x 7' | EA. | 210 | 710 | 920 |
| 6040 | 16' x 7' | " | 270 | 1,270 | 1,540 |
| 6100 | Commercial grade | | | | |
| 6120 | 8' x 8' | EA. | 440 | 820 | 1,260 |
| 6140 | 10' x 10' | " | 490 | 1,090 | 1,580 |
| 6160 | 12' x 12' | " | 530 | 1,810 | 2,340 |
| 6180 | 20' x 14', with chain hoist | " | 1,070 | 4,350 | 5,420 |
| 6400 | Sliding glass doors | | | | |
| 6420 | Tempered plate glass, 1/4" thick | | | | |
| 6430 | 6' wide | | | | |
| 6440 | Economy grade | EA. | 180 | 1,070 | 1,250 |
| 6450 | Premium grade | " | 180 | 1,220 | 1,400 |
| 6455 | 12' wide | | | | |
| 6460 | Economy grade | EA. | 270 | 1,500 | 1,770 |
| 6465 | Premium grade | " | 270 | 2,250 | 2,520 |
| 6470 | Insulating glass, 5/8" thick | | | | |
| 6475 | 6' wide | | | | |
| 6480 | Economy grade | EA. | 180 | 1,320 | 1,500 |
| 6500 | Premium grade | " | 180 | 1,690 | 1,870 |
| 6505 | 12' wide | | | | |
| 6510 | Economy grade | EA. | 270 | 1,640 | 1,910 |
| 6515 | Premium grade | " | 270 | 2,630 | 2,900 |
| 6520 | 1" thick | | | | |
| 6525 | 6' wide | | | | |
| 6530 | Economy grade | EA. | 180 | 1,660 | 1,840 |
| 6540 | Premium grade | " | 180 | 1,910 | 2,090 |
| 6545 | 12' wide | | | | |
| 6550 | Economy grade | EA. | 270 | 2,570 | 2,840 |
| 6560 | Premium grade | " | 270 | 3,760 | 4,030 |
| 6600 | Added costs | | | | |
| 6620 | Custom quality, add to material, 30% | | | | |

© 2011 By Design & Construction Resources

## DIVISION # 08  DOORS AND WINDOWS

| | | UNIT | LABOR | MAT. | TOTAL |
|---|---|---|---|---|---|
| **08300.10** | **SPECIAL DOORS, Cont'd...** | | | | |
| 6630 | Tempered glass, 6' wide, add | S.F. | | | 4.62 |
| 6880 | Residential storm door | | | | |
| 6900 | Minimum | EA. | 89.00 | 160 | 249 |
| 6920 | Average | " | 89.00 | 220 | 309 |
| 6940 | Maximum | " | 130 | 480 | 610 |
| **08410.10** | **STOREFRONTS** | | | | |
| 0135 | Storefront, aluminum and glass | | | | |
| 0140 | Minimum | S.F. | 7.37 | 24.00 | 31.37 |
| 0150 | Average | " | 8.42 | 35.75 | 44.17 |
| 0160 | Maximum | " | 9.83 | 72.00 | 81.83 |
| 1020 | Entrance doors, premium, closers, panic dev.,etc. | | | | |
| 1030 | 1/2" thick glass | | | | |
| 1040 | 3' x 7' | EA. | 490 | 3,190 | 3,680 |
| 1060 | 6' x 7' | " | 740 | 5,450 | 6,190 |
| 1065 | 3/4" thick glass | | | | |
| 1070 | 3' x 7' | EA. | 490 | 3,300 | 3,790 |
| 1080 | 6' x 7' | " | 740 | 5,500 | 6,240 |
| 1085 | 1" thick glass | | | | |
| 1090 | 3' x 7' | EA. | 490 | 3,580 | 4,070 |
| 1100 | 6' x 7' | " | 740 | 6,330 | 7,070 |
| 1150 | Revolving doors | | | | |
| 1151 | 7'diameter, 7' high | | | | |
| 1160 | Minimum | EA. | 5,670 | 24,920 | 30,590 |
| 1170 | Average | " | 9,070 | 31,350 | 40,420 |
| 1180 | Maximum | " | 11,340 | 40,460 | 51,800 |
| **08510.10** | **STEEL WINDOWS** | | | | |
| 0100 | Steel windows, primed | | | | |
| 1000 | Casements | | | | |
| 1010 | Operable | | | | |
| 1020 | Minimum | S.F. | 3.47 | 37.00 | 40.47 |
| 1040 | Maximum | " | 3.93 | 55.00 | 58.93 |
| 1060 | Fixed sash | " | 2.95 | 29.50 | 32.45 |
| 1080 | Double hung | " | 3.27 | 55.00 | 58.27 |
| 1100 | Industrial windows | | | | |
| 1120 | Horizontally pivoted sash | S.F. | 3.93 | 52.00 | 55.93 |
| 1130 | Fixed sash | " | 3.27 | 40.75 | 44.02 |
| 1135 | Security sash | | | | |
| 1140 | Operable | S.F. | 3.93 | 65.00 | 68.93 |
| 1150 | Fixed | " | 3.27 | 57.00 | 60.27 |
| 1155 | Picture window | " | 3.27 | 27.75 | 31.02 |
| 1160 | Projecting sash | | | | |
| 1170 | Minimum | S.F. | 3.68 | 48.00 | 51.68 |
| 1180 | Maximum | " | 3.68 | 59.00 | 62.68 |
| 1930 | Mullions | L.F. | 2.95 | 12.75 | 15.70 |
| **08520.10** | **ALUMINUM WINDOWS** | | | | |
| 0110 | Jalousie | | | | |
| 0120 | 3-0 x 4-0 | EA. | 74.00 | 320 | 394 |
| 0140 | 3-0 x 5-0 | " | 74.00 | 370 | 444 |
| 0220 | Fixed window | | | | |
| 0240 | 6 sf to 8 sf | S.F. | 8.42 | 15.75 | 24.17 |
| 0250 | 12 sf to 16 sf | " | 6.55 | 14.00 | 20.55 |

© 2011 By Design & Construction Resources

# DIVISION # 08  DOORS AND WINDOWS

| | | UNIT | LABOR | MAT. | TOTAL |
|---|---|---|---|---|---|
| **08520.10** | **ALUMINUM WINDOWS, Cont'd...** | | | | |
| 0255 | Projecting window | | | | |
| 0260 | 6 sf to 8 sf | S.F. | 14.75 | 35.00 | 49.75 |
| 0270 | 12 sf to 16 sf | " | 9.83 | 31.50 | 41.33 |
| 0275 | Horizontal sliding | | | | |
| 0280 | 6 sf to 8 sf | S.F. | 7.37 | 22.75 | 30.12 |
| 0290 | 12 sf to 16 sf | " | 5.90 | 21.00 | 26.90 |
| 1140 | Double hung | | | | |
| 1160 | 6 sf to 8 sf | S.F. | 11.75 | 31.50 | 43.25 |
| 1180 | 10 sf to 12 sf | " | 9.83 | 28.00 | 37.83 |
| 3010 | Storm window, 0.5 cfm, up to | | | | |
| 3020 | 60 u.i. (united inches) | EA. | 29.50 | 74.00 | 104 |
| 3060 | 80 u.i. | " | 29.50 | 84.00 | 114 |
| 3080 | 90 u.i. | " | 32.75 | 86.00 | 119 |
| 3100 | 100 u.i. | " | 32.75 | 88.00 | 121 |
| 3110 | 2.0 cfm, up to | | | | |
| 3120 | 60 u.i. | EA. | 29.50 | 95.00 | 125 |
| 3160 | 80 u.i. | " | 29.50 | 98.00 | 128 |
| 3180 | 90 u.i. | " | 32.75 | 110 | 143 |
| 3200 | 100 u.i. | " | 32.75 | 110 | 143 |
| **08600.10** | **WOOD WINDOWS** | | | | |
| 0980 | Double hung | | | | |
| 0990 | 24" x 36" | | | | |
| 1000 | Minimum | EA. | 53.00 | 220 | 273 |
| 1002 | Average | " | 67.00 | 320 | 387 |
| 1004 | Maximum | " | 89.00 | 430 | 519 |
| 1010 | 24" x 48" | | | | |
| 1020 | Minimum | EA. | 53.00 | 250 | 303 |
| 1022 | Average | " | 67.00 | 370 | 437 |
| 1024 | Maximum | " | 89.00 | 520 | 609 |
| 1030 | 30" x 48" | | | | |
| 1040 | Minimum | EA. | 59.00 | 270 | 329 |
| 1042 | Average | " | 76.00 | 380 | 456 |
| 1044 | Maximum | " | 110 | 540 | 650 |
| 1050 | 30" x 60" | | | | |
| 1060 | Minimum | EA. | 59.00 | 290 | 349 |
| 1062 | Average | " | 76.00 | 470 | 546 |
| 1064 | Maximum | " | 110 | 570 | 680 |
| 1160 | Casement | | | | |
| 1180 | 1 leaf, 22" x 38" high | | | | |
| 1220 | Minimum | EA. | 53.00 | 320 | 373 |
| 1222 | Average | " | 67.00 | 390 | 457 |
| 1224 | Maximum | " | 89.00 | 450 | 539 |
| 1230 | 2 leaf, 50" x 50" high | | | | |
| 1240 | Minimum | EA. | 67.00 | 850 | 917 |
| 1242 | Average | " | 89.00 | 1,110 | 1,199 |
| 1244 | Maximum | " | 130 | 1,280 | 1,410 |
| 1250 | 3 leaf, 71" x 62" high | | | | |
| 1260 | Minimum | EA. | 67.00 | 1,410 | 1,477 |
| 1262 | Average | " | 89.00 | 1,430 | 1,519 |
| 1264 | Maximum | " | 130 | 1,720 | 1,850 |
| 1290 | 5 leaf, 119" x 75" high | | | | |

© 2011 By Design & Construction Resources

# DIVISION # 08 DOORS AND WINDOWS

|  |  | UNIT | LABOR | MAT. | TOTAL |
|---|---|---|---|---|---|
| **08600.10** | **WOOD WINDOWS, Cont'd...** | | | | |
| 1300 | Minimum | EA. | 76.00 | 2,420 | 2,496 |
| 1302 | Average | " | 110 | 2,610 | 2,720 |
| 1304 | Maximum | " | 180 | 3,340 | 3,520 |
| 1360 | Picture window, fixed glass, 54" x 54" high | | | | |
| 1400 | Minimum | EA. | 67.00 | 500 | 567 |
| 1422 | Average | " | 76.00 | 560 | 636 |
| 1424 | Maximum | " | 89.00 | 1,000 | 1,089 |
| 1430 | 68" x 55" high | | | | |
| 1440 | Minimum | EA. | 67.00 | 900 | 967 |
| 1442 | Average | " | 76.00 | 1,030 | 1,106 |
| 1444 | Maximum | " | 89.00 | 1,360 | 1,449 |
| 1480 | Sliding, 40" x 31" high | | | | |
| 1520 | Minimum | EA. | 53.00 | 300 | 353 |
| 1522 | Average | " | 67.00 | 450 | 517 |
| 1524 | Maximum | " | 89.00 | 540 | 629 |
| 1530 | 52" x 39" high | | | | |
| 1540 | Minimum | EA. | 67.00 | 370 | 437 |
| 1542 | Average | " | 76.00 | 550 | 626 |
| 1544 | Maximum | " | 89.00 | 620 | 709 |
| 1550 | 64" x 72" high | | | | |
| 1560 | Minimum | EA. | 67.00 | 570 | 637 |
| 1562 | Average | " | 89.00 | 910 | 999 |
| 1564 | Maximum | " | 110 | 1,010 | 1,120 |
| 1760 | Awning windows | | | | |
| 1780 | 34" x 21" high | | | | |
| 1800 | Minimum | EA. | 53.00 | 310 | 363 |
| 1822 | Average | " | 67.00 | 360 | 427 |
| 1824 | Maximum | " | 89.00 | 420 | 509 |
| 1880 | 48" x 27" high | | | | |
| 1900 | Minimum | EA. | 59.00 | 390 | 449 |
| 1902 | Average | " | 76.00 | 470 | 546 |
| 1904 | Maximum | " | 110 | 540 | 650 |
| 1920 | 60" x 36" high | | | | |
| 1940 | Minimum | EA. | 67.00 | 410 | 477 |
| 1942 | Average | " | 89.00 | 730 | 819 |
| 1944 | Maximum | " | 110 | 820 | 930 |
| 8000 | Window frame, milled | | | | |
| 8010 | Minimum | L.F. | 10.75 | 5.80 | 16.55 |
| 8020 | Average | " | 13.25 | 6.47 | 19.72 |
| 8030 | Maximum | " | 17.75 | 9.74 | 27.49 |
| **08710.10** | **HINGES** | | | | |
| 1200 | Hinges | | | | |
| 1250 | 3 x 3 butts, steel, interior, plain bearing | PAIR | | | 20.75 |
| 1260 | 4 x 4 butts, steel, standard | " | | | 30.50 |
| 1270 | 5 x 4-1/2 butts, bronze/s. steel, heavy duty | " | | | 79.00 |
| 1290 | Pivot hinges | | | | |
| 1300 | Top pivot | EA. | | | 88.00 |
| 1310 | Intermediate pivot | " | | | 94.00 |
| 1320 | Bottom pivot | " | | | 180 |

# DIVISION # 08 DOORS AND WINDOWS

| | | UNIT | LABOR | MAT. | TOTAL |
|---|---|---|---|---|---|
| **08710.20** | **LOCKSETS** | | | | |
| 1280 | Latchset, heavy duty | | | | |
| 1300 |    Cylindrical | EA. | 33.25 | 190 | 223 |
| 1320 |    Mortise | " | 53.00 | 200 | 253 |
| 1325 | Lockset, heavy duty | | | | |
| 1330 |    Cylindrical | EA. | 33.25 | 300 | 333 |
| 1350 |    Mortise | " | 53.00 | 340 | 393 |
| 2200 | Preassembled locks and latches, brass | | | | |
| 2220 |    Latchset, passage or closet latch | EA. | 44.50 | 270 | 315 |
| 2225 |    Lockset | | | | |
| 2230 |       Privacy (bath or bathroom) | EA. | 44.50 | 330 | 375 |
| 2240 |       Entry lock | " | 44.50 | 470 | 515 |
| 2285 |    Lockset | | | | |
| 2290 |       Privacy (bath or bedroom) | EA. | 44.50 | 210 | 255 |
| 2300 |       Entry lock | " | 44.50 | 240 | 285 |
| **08710.30** | **CLOSERS** | | | | |
| 2600 | Door closers | | | | |
| 2610 |    Standard | EA. | 67.00 | 220 | 287 |
| 2620 |    Heavy duty | " | 67.00 | 260 | 327 |
| **08710.40** | **DOOR TRIM** | | | | |
| 1600 | Panic device | | | | |
| 1610 |    Mortise | EA. | 130 | 780 | 910 |
| 1620 |    Vertical rod | " | 130 | 1,170 | 1,300 |
| 1630 |    Labeled, rim type | " | 130 | 810 | 940 |
| 1640 |    Mortise | " | 130 | 1,060 | 1,190 |
| 1650 |    Vertical rod | " | 130 | 1,130 | 1,260 |
| 2300 | Door plates | | | | |
| 2305 |    Kick plate, aluminum, 3 beveled edges | | | | |
| 2310 |       10" x 28" | EA. | 26.75 | 26.50 | 53.25 |
| 2340 |       10" x 38" | " | 26.75 | 34.25 | 61.00 |
| 2350 |    Push plate, 4" x 16" | | | | |
| 2360 |       Aluminum | EA. | 10.75 | 22.00 | 32.75 |
| 2371 |       Bronze | " | 10.75 | 84.00 | 94.75 |
| 2380 |       Stainless steel | " | 10.75 | 67.00 | 77.75 |
| 2385 |    Armor plate, 40" x 34" | " | 21.25 | 77.00 | 98.25 |
| 2388 |    Pull handle, 4" x 16" | | | | |
| 2390 |       Aluminum | EA. | 10.75 | 94.00 | 105 |
| 2400 |       Bronze | " | 10.75 | 180 | 191 |
| 2420 |       Stainless steel | " | 10.75 | 140 | 151 |
| 2425 |    Hasp assembly | | | | |
| 2430 |       3" | EA. | 8.89 | 4.40 | 13.29 |
| 2440 |       4-1/2" | " | 11.75 | 5.50 | 17.25 |
| 2450 |       6" | " | 15.25 | 8.74 | 23.99 |
| **08710.60** | **WEATHERSTRIPPING** | | | | |
| 0100 | Weatherstrip, head and jamb, metal strip, neoprene bulb | | | | |
| 0140 |    Standard duty | L.F. | 2.96 | 4.95 | 7.91 |
| 0160 |    Heavy duty | " | 3.33 | 5.50 | 8.83 |
| 3980 |    Spring type | | | | |
| 4000 |       Metal doors | EA. | 130 | 55.00 | 185 |
| 4010 |       Wood doors | " | 180 | 55.00 | 235 |
| 4020 |    Sponge type with adhesive backing | " | 53.00 | 51.00 | 104 |
| 4500 | Thresholds | | | | |

© 2011 By Design & Construction Resources

## DIVISION # 08 DOORS AND WINDOWS

| | | UNIT | LABOR | MAT. | TOTAL |
|---|---|---|---|---|---|
| **08710.60** | **WEATHERSTRIPPING, Cont'd...** | | | | |
| 4510 | Bronze | L.F. | 13.25 | 53.00 | 66.25 |
| 4515 | Aluminum | | | | |
| 4520 | Plain | L.F. | 13.25 | 36.50 | 49.75 |
| 4525 | Vinyl insert | " | 13.25 | 39.25 | 52.50 |
| 4530 | Aluminum with grit | " | 13.25 | 37.50 | 50.75 |
| 4533 | Steel | | | | |
| 4535 | Plain | L.F. | 13.25 | 29.75 | 43.00 |
| 4540 | Interlocking | " | 44.50 | 39.50 | 84.00 |
| **08810.10** | **GLAZING** | | | | |
| 0800 | Sheet glass, 1/8" thick | S.F. | 3.27 | 7.70 | 10.97 |
| 1020 | Plate glass, bronze or grey, 1/4" thick | " | 5.36 | 11.25 | 16.61 |
| 1040 | Clear | " | 5.36 | 8.80 | 14.16 |
| 1060 | Polished | " | 5.36 | 10.50 | 15.86 |
| 1980 | Plexiglass | | | | |
| 2000 | 1/8" thick | S.F. | 5.36 | 4.95 | 10.31 |
| 2020 | 1/4" thick | " | 3.27 | 8.91 | 12.18 |
| 3000 | Float glass, clear | | | | |
| 3010 | 3/16" thick | S.F. | 4.91 | 5.99 | 10.90 |
| 3020 | 1/4" thick | " | 5.36 | 6.10 | 11.46 |
| 3040 | 3/8" thick | " | 7.37 | 12.25 | 19.62 |
| 3100 | Tinted glass, polished plate, twin ground | | | | |
| 3120 | 3/16" thick | S.F. | 4.91 | 8.25 | 13.16 |
| 3130 | 1/4" thick | " | 5.36 | 8.25 | 13.61 |
| 3140 | 3/8" thick | " | 7.37 | 13.25 | 20.62 |
| 5000 | Insulated glass, bronze or gray | | | | |
| 5020 | 1/2" thick | S.F. | 9.83 | 15.25 | 25.08 |
| 5040 | 1" thick | " | 14.75 | 18.25 | 33.00 |
| 5100 | Spandrel, polished, 1 side, 1/4" thick | " | 5.36 | 12.25 | 17.61 |
| 6000 | Tempered glass (safety) | | | | |
| 6010 | Clear sheet glass | | | | |
| 6020 | 1/8" thick | S.F. | 3.27 | 8.41 | 11.68 |
| 6030 | 3/16" thick | " | 4.53 | 10.25 | 14.78 |
| 6040 | Clear float glass | | | | |
| 6050 | 1/4" thick | S.F. | 4.91 | 8.80 | 13.71 |
| 6060 | 5/16" thick | " | 5.90 | 15.75 | 21.65 |
| 6070 | 3/8" thick | " | 7.37 | 19.25 | 26.62 |
| 6080 | 1/2" thick | " | 9.83 | 26.25 | 36.08 |
| 6800 | Insulating glass, two lites, clear float glass | | | | |
| 6840 | 1/2" thick | S.F. | 9.83 | 12.00 | 21.83 |
| 6850 | 5/8" thick | " | 11.75 | 13.75 | 25.50 |
| 6860 | 3/4" thick | " | 14.75 | 15.25 | 30.00 |
| 6870 | 7/8" thick | " | 16.75 | 16.00 | 32.75 |
| 6880 | 1" thick | " | 19.75 | 21.25 | 41.00 |
| 6885 | Glass seal edge | | | | |
| 6890 | 3/8" thick | S.F. | 9.83 | 10.00 | 19.83 |
| 6895 | Tinted glass | | | | |
| 6900 | 1/2" thick | S.F. | 9.83 | 20.50 | 30.33 |
| 6910 | 1" thick | " | 19.75 | 22.00 | 41.75 |
| 6920 | Tempered, clear | | | | |
| 6930 | 1" thick | S.F. | 19.75 | 40.25 | 60.00 |
| 7200 | Plate mirror glass | | | | |

© 2011 By Design & Construction Resources

## DIVISION # 08  DOORS AND WINDOWS

| | | UNIT | LABOR | MAT. | TOTAL |
|---|---|---|---|---|---|
| **08810.10** | **GLAZING, Cont'd...** | | | | |
| 7205 | 1/4" thick | | | | |
| 7210 | 15 sf | S.F. | 5.90 | 10.50 | 16.40 |
| 7220 | Over 15 sf | " | 5.36 | 9.68 | 15.04 |
| 9650 | Sand-Blasted Glass | | | | |
| 9660 | 3/16" Float glass, full sandblast, no custom decoration | S.F. | 4.91 | 10.50 | 15.41 |
| 9670 | 3/8" Float glass, full sandblast, no custom decoration | " | 5.90 | 12.25 | 18.15 |
| 9680 | Beveled glass | | | | |
| 9690 | commercial standard grade | S.F. | 5.90 | 130 | 136 |
| **08910.10** | **GLAZED CURTAIN WALLS** | | | | |
| 1000 | Curtain wall, aluminum system, framing sections | | | | |
| 1005 | 2" x 3" | | | | |
| 1010 | Jamb | L.F. | 4.91 | 11.25 | 16.16 |
| 1020 | Horizontal | " | 4.91 | 11.50 | 16.41 |
| 1030 | Mullion | " | 4.91 | 15.25 | 20.16 |
| 1035 | 2" x 4" | | | | |
| 1040 | Jamb | L.F. | 7.37 | 15.25 | 22.62 |
| 1060 | Horizontal | " | 7.37 | 15.75 | 23.12 |
| 1070 | Mullion | " | 7.37 | 15.25 | 22.62 |
| 1080 | 3" x 5-1/2" | | | | |
| 1090 | Jamb | L.F. | 7.37 | 20.25 | 27.62 |
| 1100 | Horizontal | " | 7.37 | 22.50 | 29.87 |
| 1110 | Mullion | " | 7.37 | 20.25 | 27.62 |
| 1115 | 4" corner mullion | " | 9.83 | 27.00 | 36.83 |
| 1120 | Coping sections | | | | |
| 1130 | 1/8" x 8" | L.F. | 9.83 | 28.25 | 38.08 |
| 1140 | 1/8" x 9" | " | 9.83 | 28.25 | 38.08 |
| 1150 | 1/8" x 12-1/2" | " | 11.75 | 29.00 | 40.75 |
| 1160 | Sill section | | | | |
| 1170 | 1/8" x 6" | L.F. | 5.90 | 27.75 | 33.65 |
| 1180 | 1/8" x 7" | " | 5.90 | 28.00 | 33.90 |
| 1190 | 1/8" x 8-1/2" | " | 5.90 | 28.50 | 34.40 |
| 1200 | Column covers, aluminum | | | | |
| 1210 | 1/8" x 26" | L.F. | 14.75 | 27.75 | 42.50 |
| 1220 | 1/8" x 34" | " | 15.50 | 28.00 | 43.50 |
| 1230 | 1/8" x 38" | " | 15.50 | 28.25 | 43.75 |
| 1500 | Doors | | | | |
| 1600 | Aluminum framed, standard hardware | | | | |
| 1620 | Narrow stile | | | | |
| 1630 | 2-6 x 7-0 | EA. | 300 | 630 | 930 |
| 1640 | 3-0 x 7-0 | " | 300 | 630 | 930 |
| 1660 | 3-6 x 7-0 | " | 300 | 660 | 960 |
| 1700 | Wide stile | | | | |
| 1720 | 2-6 x 7-0 | EA. | 300 | 1,080 | 1,380 |
| 1730 | 3-0 x 7-0 | " | 300 | 1,160 | 1,460 |
| 1750 | 3-6 x 7-0 | " | 300 | 1,250 | 1,550 |
| 1800 | Flush panel doors, to match adjacent wall panels | | | | |
| 1810 | 2-6 x 7-0 | EA. | 370 | 910 | 1,280 |
| 1820 | 3-0 x 7-0 | " | 370 | 960 | 1,330 |
| 1840 | 3-6 x 7-0 | " | 370 | 990 | 1,360 |
| 2100 | Wall panel, insulated | | | | |
| 2120 | "U"=.08 | S.F. | 4.91 | 11.50 | 16.41 |

© 2011 By Design & Construction Resources

# DIVISION # 08 DOORS AND WINDOWS

## 08910.10 GLAZED CURTAIN WALLS, Cont'd...

| | | UNIT | LABOR | MAT. | TOTAL |
|---|---|---|---|---|---|
| 2140 | "U"=.10 | S.F. | 4.91 | 10.75 | 15.66 |
| 2160 | "U"=.15 | " | 4.91 | 9.76 | 14.67 |
| 3000 | Window wall system, complete | | | | |
| 3010 | Minimum | S.F. | 5.90 | 30.25 | 36.15 |
| 3030 | Average | " | 6.55 | 48.25 | 54.80 |
| 3050 | Maximum | " | 8.42 | 110 | 118 |
| 4860 | Added costs | | | | |
| 4870 | For bronze, add 20% to material | | | | |
| 4880 | For stainless steel, add 50% to material | | | | |

# DIVISION # 08 DOORS AND WINDOWS - QUICK ESTIMATING

| | | UNIT | COST |
|---|---|---|---|
| **08999.10** | **DOORS** | | |
| 0900 | HOLLOW METAL | | |
| 1000 | CUSTOM FRAMES (16 ga) | | |
| 1010 | 2'6" x 6'8" x 4 3/4" | EA. | 339 |
| 1020 | 2'8" x 6'8" x 4 3/4" | " | 350 |
| 1030 | 3'0" x 6'8" x 4 3/4" | " | 380 |
| 1040 | 3'4" x 6'8" x 4 3/4" | " | 390 |
| 2000 | Add for A, B or C Label | " | 42.50 |
| 2010 | Add for Side Lights | " | 197 |
| 2020 | Add for Frames over 7'0" - Height | " | 78.75 |
| 2030 | Add for Frames over 6 3/4" - Width | " | 68.75 |
| 3000 | CUSTOM DOORS (1 3/8" or 1 3/4") (18 ga) | | |
| 3010 | 2'6" x 6'8" x 1 3/4" | EA. | 500 |
| 3020 | 2'8" x 6'8" x 1 3/4" | " | 520 |
| 3030 | 3'0" x 6'8" x 1 3/4" | " | 540 |
| 3040 | 3'4" x 6'8" x 1 3/4" | " | 550 |
| 4000 | Add for 16 ga | " | 78.75 |
| 4010 | Add for B and C Label | " | 34.50 |
| 4020 | Add for Vision Panels or Lights | " | 138 |
| 5000 | STOCK FRAMES (16 ga) | | |
| 5010 | 2'6" x 6'8" or 7'0" x 4 3/4" | EA. | 225 |
| 5020 | 2'8" x 6'8" or 7'0" x 4 3/4" | " | 236 |
| 5030 | 3'0" x 6'8" or 7'0" x 4 3/4" | " | 246 |
| 5040 | 3'4" x 6'8" or 7'0" x 4 3/4" | " | 266 |
| 5050 | Add for A, B or C Label | " | 41.00 |
| 6000 | STOCK DOORS (1 3/8" or 1 3/4" - 18 ga) | | |
| 6010 | 2'6" x 6'8" or 7'0" | EA. | 530 |
| 6020 | 2'8" x 6'8" or 7'0" | " | 550 |
| 6030 | 3'0" x 6'8" or 7'0" | " | 550 |
| 6040 | 3'4" x 6'8" or 7'0" | " | 600 |
| 6050 | Add for B or C Label | " | 32.25 |
| **08999.20** | **WOOD DOORS (Incl. butts and locksets)** | | |
| 1000 | FLUSH DOORS - No Label - Paint Grade | | |
| 2000 | Birch - 7 Ply 2'4" x 6'8" x 1 3/8" -Hollow Core | EA. | 225 |
| 2010 | 2'6" x 6'8" x 1 3/8" | " | 225 |
| 2020 | 2'8" x 6'8" x 1 3/8" | " | 246 |
| 2030 | 3'0" x 6'8" x 1 3/8" | " | 236 |
| 2040 | 2'4" x 6'8" x 1 3/4" | " | 246 |
| 2050 | 2'6" x 6'8" x 1 3/4" | " | 246 |
| 2060 | 2'8" x 6'8" x 1 3/4" | " | 256 |
| 2070 | 3'0" x 6'8" x 1 3/4" | " | 266 |
| 2080 | 3'4" x 6'8" x 1 3/4" | " | 266 |
| 2090 | 3'6" x 6'8" x 1 3/4" | " | 266 |
| 3000 | Birch - 7 Ply 2'4" x 6'8" x 1 3/8" -Solid Core | " | 266 |
| 3010 | 2'6" x 6'8" x 1 3/8" | " | 266 |
| 3020 | 2'8" x 6'8" x 1 3/8" | " | 306 |
| 3030 | 3'0" x 6'8" x 1 3/8" | " | 306 |
| 3040 | 2'4" x 6'8" x 1 3/4" | " | 306 |
| 3050 | 2'6" x 6'8" x 1 3/4" | " | 306 |
| 3060 | 2'8" x 6'8" x 1 3/4" | " | 331 |
| 3070 | 3'0" x 6'8" x 1 3/4" | " | 331 |
| 3080 | 3'4" x 6'8" x 1 3/4" | " | 341 |

© 2011 By Design & Construction Resources

## DIVISION # 08  DOORS AND WINDOWS - QUICK ESTIMATING

**08999.20  WOOD DOORS (Incl. butts and locksets), Cont'd...**

| Code | Description | UNIT | COST |
|---|---|---|---|
| 3090 | 3'6" x 6'8" x 1 3/4"E | EA. | 390 |
| 4000 | Add for Stain Grade | " | 43.25 |
| 4010 | Add for 5 Ply | " | 93.25 |
| 4020 | Add for Jamb & Trim - Solid - Knock Down | " | 96.25 |
| 4030 | Add for Jamb & Trim - Veneer - Knock Down | " | 64.00 |
| 4040 | Add for Red Oak - Rotary Cut | " | 38.75 |
| 4050 | Add for Red Oak - Plain Sliced | " | 52.25 |
| 5000 | Deduct for Lauan | " | 41.72 |
| 5010 | Add for Architectural Grade - 7 Ply | " | 90.75 |
| 5020 | Add for Vinyl Overlay | " | 70.00 |
| 5030 | Add for 7' - 0" Doors | " | 30.72 |
| 5040 | Add for Lite Cutouts with Metal Frame | " | 102 |
| 5050 | Add for Wood Louvres | " | 155 |
| 5060 | Add for Transom Panels & Side Panels | " | 197 |
| 6000 | LABELED - 1 3/4" - Paint Grade | | |
| 6010 | 2'6" x 6'8" - Birch - 20 Min. | EA. | 341 |
| 6020 | 2'8" x 6'8" | " | 321 |
| 6030 | 3'0" x 6'8" | " | 331 |
| 6040 | 3'4" x 6'8" | " | 370 |
| 6050 | 3'6" x 6'8" | " | 420 |
| 7000 | 2'6" x 6'8" - Birch - 45 Min | " | 350 |
| 7010 | 2'8" x 6'8" | " | 370 |
| 7020 | 3'0" x 6'8" | " | 380 |
| 7030 | 3'4" x 6'8" | " | 400 |
| 7040 | 3'6" x 6'8" | " | 410 |
| 8000 | 2'6" x 6'8" - Birch - 60 Min | " | 470 |
| 8010 | 2'8" x 6'8" | " | 500 |
| 8020 | 3'0" x 6'8" | " | 510 |
| 8030 | 3'4" x 6'8" | " | 540 |
| 8040 | 3'6" x 6'8" | " | 431 |
| 9000 | PANEL DOORS | | |
| 9010 | Exterior - 1 3/4" -Pine | | |
| 9020 | 2'8" x 6'8" | EA. | 810 |
| 9030 | 3'0" x 6'8" | " | 780 |
| 9040 | Interior - 1 3/8" -Pine | | |
| 9050 | 2'6" x 6'8" | EA. | 410 |
| 9060 | 2'8" x 6'8" | " | 430 |
| 9070 | 3'0" x 6'8" | " | 460 |
| 9080 | Add for Sidelights | " | 360 |
| 9140 | Exterior - 1 3/4"- Birch/ Oak | | |
| 9150 | 2'8" x 6'8" | EA. | 850 |
| 9160 | 3'0" x 6'8" | " | 840 |
| 9170 | Interior - 1 3/8" | | |
| 9180 | 2'6" x 6'8" | EA. | 560 |
| 9190 | 2'8" x 6'8" | " | 580 |
| 9200 | 3'0" x 6'8" | " | 620 |
| 9210 | Add for Sidelights | " | 560 |
| 9212 | LOUVERED DOORS - 1 3/8" -Pine | | |
| 9213 | 2'0" x 6'8" | EA. | 300 |
| 9214 | 2'6" x 6'8" | " | 350 |
| 9215 | 2'8" x 6'8" | " | 370 |
| 9216 | 3'0" x 6'8" | " | 390 |

# DIVISION # 08 DOORS AND WINDOWS - QUICK ESTIMATING

| | | UNIT | COST |
|---|---|---|---|
| **08999.20** | **WOOD DOORS (Incl. butts and locksets), Cont'd...** | | |
| 9220 | Birch/Oak - 1 3/8" | | |
| 9230 | 2'0" x 6'8" | EA. | 660 |
| 9240 | 2'6" x 6'8" | " | 670 |
| 9250 | 2'8" x 6'8" | " | 700 |
| 9260 | 3'0" x 6'8" | " | 710 |
| 9270 | BI-FOLD with hdwr. 1 3/8" - Flush | | |
| 9280 | Birch/Oak, 2'0" x 6'8" | EA. | 226 |
| 9290 | 2'4" x 6'8" | " | 251 |
| 9300 | 2'6" x 6'8" | " | 271 |
| 9320 | Lauan, 2'0" x 6'8" | " | 226 |
| 9330 | 2'4" x 6'8" | " | 236 |
| 9340 | 2'6" x 6'8" | " | 246 |
| 9350 | Add for Prefinished | " | 28.72 |
| 9360 | CAFE DOORS - 1 1/8" - Pair | | |
| 9370 | 2'6" x 3'8" | EA. | 460 |
| 9380 | 2'8" x 3'8" | " | 470 |
| 9390 | 3'0" x 3'8" | " | 490 |
| 9400 | FRENCH DOORS - 1 3/8" -Pine | | |
| 9410 | 2'6" x 3'8" | EA. | 610 |
| 9420 | 2'8" x 3'8" | " | 620 |
| 9430 | 3'0" x 3'8" | " | 650 |
| 9440 | 2'6" x 3'8" -Birch/Oak | " | 800 |
| 9450 | 2'8" x 3'8" | " | 810 |
| 9460 | 3'0" x 3'8" | " | 820 |
| 9470 | DUTCH DOORS | | |
| 9480 | 2'6" x 3'8" | EA. | 900 |
| 9490 | 2'8" x 3'8" | " | 1,000 |
| 9500 | 3'0" x 3'8" | " | 1,260 |
| 9510 | PREHUNG DOORS (INCL. TRIM) | | |
| 9520 | Exterior, entrance - 1 3/4" | | |
| 9530 | Panel - 2'8" x 6'8" | EA. | 780 |
| 9540 | 3'0" x 6'8" | " | 860 |
| 9550 | 3'0" x 7'0" | " | 950 |
| 9560 | Add for Insulation | " | 266 |
| 9570 | Add for Side Lights | " | 326 |
| 9580 | Interior - 1 3/8" | | |
| 9590 | Flush, H.C. - 2'6" x 6'8" -Birch/Oak | EA. | 420 |
| 9600 | 2'8" x 6'8" | " | 430 |
| 9610 | 3'0" x 6'8"Each | " | 450 |
| 9620 | Flush, H.C. - 2'6" x 6'8" -Lauan | " | 331 |
| 9630 | 2'8" x 6'8" | " | 360 |
| 9640 | 3'0" x 6'8"Each | " | 360 |
| 9650 | Add for Int. Panel Door | " | 301 |
| **08999.30** | **SPECIAL DOORS** | | |
| 1000 | BI-FOLDING - PREHUNG, 1 3/8" | | |
| 1020 | Wood - 2 Door - 2'0" x 6'8" -Oak/flush | EA. | 331 |
| 1030 | 2'6" x 6'8" | " | 370 |
| 1040 | 3'0" x 6'8" | " | 390 |
| 1050 | 4 Door - 4'0" x 6'8" | " | 420 |
| 1060 | 5'0" x 6'8" | " | 430 |
| 1070 | 6'0" x 6'8" | " | 510 |

© 2011 By Design & Construction Resources

# DIVISION # 08  DOORS AND WINDOWS - QUICK ESTIMATING

|  |  | UNIT | COST |
|---|---|---|---|
| **08999.30** | **SPECIAL DOORS, Cont'd...** | | |
| 1080 | Add for Prefinished | EA. | 39.75 |
| 1090 | Add for Jambs and Casings | " | 97.25 |
| 2000 | Wood - 2 Door - 2'0" x 6'8" Pine/Panel | " | 650 |
| 2010 | 2'6" x 6'8" | " | 660 |
| 2020 | 3'0" x 6'8" | " | 780 |
| 2030 | 4 Door - 4'0" x 6'8" | " | 980 |
| 2040 | 5'0" x 6'8" | " | 1,060 |
| 2050 | 6'0" x 6'8" | " | 1,280 |
| 3000 | Metal - 2 Door - 2'0" x 6'8" | " | 207 |
| 3010 | 2'6" x 6'8" | " | 207 |
| 3020 | 3'0" x 6'8" | " | 256 |
| 3030 | 4 Door - 4'0" x 6'8" | " | 276 |
| 3040 | 5'0" x 6'8" | " | 301 |
| 3050 | 6'0" x 6'8" | " | 321 |
| 3060 | Add for Plastic Overlay | " | 46.25 |
| 3070 | Add for Louvre or Decorative Type | " | 240 |
| 4000 | Leaded Mirror (Based on 2-Panel Unit) | | |
| 4010 | 4'0" x 6'8" | EA. | 950 |
| 4020 | 5'0" x 6'8" | " | 1,090 |
| 4030 | 6'0" x 6'8" | " | 1,090 |
| 7000 | ROLLING - DOORS & GRILLES | | |
| 7010 | Doors - 8' x 8' | EA. | 3,780 |
| 7020 | 10' x 10' | " | 3,960 |
| 7030 | Grilles - 6'-8" x 3'-2" | " | 1,320 |
| 7040 | 6'-8" x 4'-2" | " | 1,480 |
| 8000 | SHOWER DOORS - 28" x 66" | " | 390 |
| 9000 | SLIDING OR PATIO DOORS | | |
| 9010 | Metal (Aluminum) - Including Glass Thresholds & Screen | | |
| 9020 | Opening 8'0" x 6'8" | EA. | 2,100 |
| 9030 | 8'0" x 8'0" | " | 2,380 |
| 9040 | Wood | | |
| 9050 | Vinyl Clad 6'0" x 6'10" | EA. | 2,620 |
| 9060 | 8'0" x 6'10" | " | 2,880 |
| 9070 | Pine - Prefinished 6'0" x 6'10" | " | 2,600 |
| 9080 | 8'0" x 6'10" | " | 2,890 |
| 9090 | Add for Grilles | " | 420 |
| 9100 | Add for Triple Glazing | " | 276 |
| 9110 | Add for Screen | " | 197 |
| 9120 | SOUND REDUCTION - Metal | " | 2,530 |
| 9130 | Wood | " | 1,650 |
| 9200 | VAULT DOORS - 6'6" x 2'2" with Frame - 2 hour | " | 4,300 |
| **08999.50** | **METAL WINDOWS** | | |
| 1000 | EACH, 2'4" x 4'6" - ALUMINUM WINDOWS | | |
| 1010 | Casement and Awning | EA. | 495 |
| 1020 | Sliding or Horizontal | " | 407 |
| 1030 | Double and Single-Hung | " | 437 |
| 1040 | or Vertical Sliding | | 350 |
| 1050 | Projected | EA. | 465 |
| 1060 | Add for Screens | " | 66.86 |
| 1070 | Add for Storms | " | 118 |
| 1080 | Add for Insulated Glass | " | 102 |

# DIVISION # 08  DOORS AND WINDOWS - QUICK ESTIMATING

| | | UNIT | COST |
|---|---|---|---|
| **08999.50** | **METAL WINDOWS, Cont'd...** | | |
| 2000 | ALUMINUM SASH | | |
| 2010 | Casement | EA. | 427 |
| 2020 | Sliding | " | 377 |
| 2030 | Single-Hung | " | 377 |
| 2040 | Projected | " | 315 |
| 2050 | Fixed | " | 325 |
| 3000 | STEEL WINDOWS | | |
| 3010 | Double-Hung | EA. | 831 |
| 3020 | Projected | " | 801 |
| 4000 | STEEL SASH | | |
| 4010 | Casement | EA. | 616 |
| 4020 | Double-Hung | " | 676 |
| 4030 | Projected | " | 525 |
| 4040 | Fixed | " | 525 |
| 5000 | By S.F., 2'4" x 4'6" - ALUMINUM WINDOWS | | |
| 5010 | Casement and Awning | S.F. | 46.23 |
| 5020 | Sliding or Horizontal | " | 36.29 |
| 5030 | Double and Single-Hung | " | 40.92 |
| 5040 | or Vertical Sliding | " | 33.50 |
| 5050 | Projected | " | 46.05 |
| 5060 | Add for Screens | " | 6.54 |
| 5070 | Add for Storms | " | 11.89 |
| 5080 | Add for Insulated Glass | " | 9.93 |
| 6000 | ALUMINUM SASH | | |
| 6010 | Casement | S.F. | 43.21 |
| 6020 | Sliding | " | 36.54 |
| 6030 | Single-Hung | " | 36.54 |
| 6040 | Projected | " | 31.02 |
| 6050 | Fixed | " | 32.19 |
| 7000 | STEEL WINDOWS | | |
| 7010 | Double-Hung | S.F. | 68.14 |
| 7020 | Projected | " | 64.72 |
| 8000 | STEEL SASH | | |
| 8010 | Casement | S.F. | 52.58 |
| 8020 | Double-Hung | " | 64.72 |
| 8030 | Projected | " | 45.04 |
| 8040 | Fixed | " | 46.51 |
| **08999.60** | **WOOD WINDOWS** | | |
| 1000 | BASEMENT OR UTILITY | | |
| 1020 | Prefinished with Screen, 2'8" x 1'4" | EA. | 255 |
| 1030 | 2'8" x 2'0" | " | 297 |
| 1040 | Add for Double Glazing or Storm | " | 65.50 |
| 2000 | CASEMENT OR AWNING | | |
| 2010 | Operating Units - Insulating Glass | | |
| 2020 | Single 2'4" x 4'0" | EA. | 720 |
| 2030 | 2'4" x 5'0" | " | 680 |
| 3000 | Double with Screen 4'0" x 4'0" (2 units) | " | 920 |
| 3010 | 4'0" x 5'0" (2 units) | " | 1,180 |
| 3020 | Triple with Screen 6'0" x 4'0" (3 units) | " | 1,610 |
| 3030 | 6'0" x 5'0" (3 units) | " | 1,620 |
| 4000 | Fixed Units - Insulating Glass | | |

*© 2011 By Design & Construction Resources*

# DIVISION # 08  DOORS AND WINDOWS - QUICK ESTIMATING

|  |  | UNIT | COST |
|---|---|---|---|
| **08999.60** | **WOOD WINDOWS, Cont'd...** | | |
| 4010 | Single 2'4" x 4'0" | EA. | 570 |
| 4020 | 2'4" x 5'0" | " | 640 |
| 4030 | Picture 4'0" x 4'6" | " | 790 |
| 4040 | 4'0" x 6'0" | " | 940 |
| 5000 | DOUBLE HUNG - Insul. Glass - 2'6" x 3'6" | " | 610 |
| 5010 | 2'6" x 4'2" | " | 610 |
| 5020 | 3'2" x 3'6" | " | 630 |
| 5030 | 3'2" x 4'2" | " | 700 |
| 5040 | Add for Triple Glazing | " | 98.75 |
| 6000 | GLIDER - & Insul. Glass with Screen - 4'0" x 3'6" | " | 1,430 |
| 6010 | 5'0" x 4'0" | " | 1,610 |
| 8000 | PICTURE WINDOWS | | |
| 8010 | 9'6" x 4'10" | EA. | 3,000 |
| 8020 | 9'6" x 5'6" | " | 2,290 |
| 9000 | CASEMENT - Insulating Glass | | |
| 9010 | 30° - 5'10" x 4'2" - (3 units) | EA. | 2,170 |
| 9015 | 7'10" x 4'2" - (4 units) | " | 2,630 |
| 9020 | 5'10" x 5'2" - (3 units) | " | 2,270 |
| 9030 | 7'10" x 5'2" - (4 units) | " | 2,580 |
| 9040 | 45° - 5'4" x 4'2" - (3 units) | " | 2,160 |
| 9050 | 7'4" x 4'2" - (4 units) | " | 2,380 |
| 9060 | 5'4" x 5'2" - (3 units) | " | 2,520 |
| 9070 | 7'4" x 5'2" - (4 units) | " | 2,840 |
| 9100 | CASEMENT BOW WINDOWS - Insulating Glass | | |
| 9110 | 6'2" x 4'2" - (3 units) | EA. | 2,180 |
| 9120 | 8'2" x 4'2" - (4 units) | " | 2,880 |
| 9130 | 6'2" x 5'2" - (3 units) | " | 2,430 |
| 9140 | 8'2" x 5'2" - (4 units) | " | 3,170 |
| 9150 | Add for Triple Glazing - per unit | " | 81.75 |
| 9160 | Add for Bronze Glazing - per unit | " | 81.75 |
| 9170 | Deduct for Primed Only - per unit | " | 20.51 |
| 9180 | Add for Screens - per unit | " | 25.18 |
| 9200 | 90° BOX BAY WINDOWS - Insulating Glass 4'8" x 4'2" | " | 2,880 |
| 9210 | 6'8" x 4'2" | " | 3,660 |
| 9220 | 6'8" x 5'2" | " | 3,800 |
| 9300 | ROOF WINDOWS 1'10" x 3'10"-Fixed | " | 840 |
| 9310 | 2'4" x 3'10" | " | 960 |
| 9320 | 3'8" x 3'10" | " | 1,190 |
| 9400 | ROOF WINDOWS 1'10" x 3'10"-Movable | " | 1,130 |
| 9410 | 2'4" x 3'10" | " | 1,390 |
| 9420 | 3'8" x 3'10" | " | 1,600 |
| 9500 | CIRCULAR TOPS & ROUNDS - 4'0" | " | 900 |
| 9510 | 6'0" | " | 2,010 |
| **08999.70** | **SPECIAL WINDOWS** | | |
| 1000 | LIGHT-PROOF WINDOWS | S.F. | 53.50 |
| 2000 | PASS WINDOWS | " | 41.35 |
| 3000 | DETENTION WINDOWS | " | 56.00 |
| 4000 | VENETIAN BLIND WINDOWS (ALUMINUM) | " | 46.82 |
| 5000 | SOUND-CONTROL WINDOWS | " | 45.64 |

# DIVISION # 08 DOORS AND WINDOWS - QUICK ESTIMATING

| | | UNIT | COST |
|---|---|---|---|
| **08999.80** | **DOOR AND WINDOW ACCESSORIES** | | |
| 1000 | STORMS AND SCREENS | | |
| 1010 | Windows | | |
| 1020 | Screen Only - Wood - 3' x 5' | EA. | 148 |
| 1030 | Aluminum - 3' x 5' | " | 163 |
| 1040 | Storm & Screen Combination - Aluminum | " | 185 |
| 1050 | Doors | " | |
| 1060 | Screen Only - Wood | " | 345 |
| 1070 | Aluminum - 3' x 6' - 8' | " | 345 |
| 1080 | Storm & Screen Combination - Aluminum | " | 406 |
| 1090 | Wood 1 1/8" | " | 461 |
| 2000 | DETENTION SCREENS | | |
| 2010 | Example: 4' 0" x 7' 0" | EA. | 1,020 |
| 3000 | DOOR OPENING ASSEMBLIES | | |
| 3010 | Floor or Overhead Electric Eye Units | | |
| 3020 | Swing - Single 3' x 7' Door - Hydraulic | EA. | 5,670 |
| 3030 | Double 6' x 7' Door - Hydraulic | " | 9,010 |
| 3040 | Sliding - Single 3' x 7' Door - Hydraulic | " | 6,940 |
| 3050 | Double 5' x 7' Doors - Hydraulic | " | 8,970 |
| 3060 | Industrial Doors - 10' x 8' | " | 10,090 |
| 4000 | SHUTTERS | | |
| 4010 | 16" x 1 1/8" x 48" | EA. | 160 |
| 4020 | 16" x 1 1/8" x 60" | " | 185 |
| 4030 | 16" x 1 1/8" x 72" | " | 215 |
| **08999.90** | **FINISH HARDWARE** | | |
| 1000 | BUTT HINGES - Painted | | |
| 1010 | 3" x 3" | EA. | 35.25 |
| 1020 | 3 1/2" x 3 1/2" | " | 37.00 |
| 1030 | 4" x 4" | " | 39.50 |
| 1040 | 4 1/2" x 4 1/2" | " | 43.00 |
| 1050 | 4" x 4" Ball Bearing | " | 65.00 |
| 1060 | 4 1/2" x 4 1/2" Ball Bearing | " | 69.00 |
| 2000 | Bronze | | |
| 2010 | 3" x 3" | EA. | 37.00 |
| 2020 | 3 1/2" x 3 1/2" | " | 37.75 |
| 2030 | 4" x 4" | " | 39.50 |
| 2040 | 4 1/2" x 4 1/2" | " | 45.75 |
| 2050 | 4" x 4" Ball Bearing | " | 67.00 |
| 2060 | 4 1/2" x 4 1/2" Ball Bearing | " | 76.00 |
| 3000 | Chrome | | |
| 3010 | 3" x 3" | EA. | 39.50 |
| 3020 | 3 1/2" x 3 1/2" | " | 42.25 |
| 3030 | 4" x 4" | " | 44.00 |
| 3040 | 4 1/2" x 4 1/2" | " | 53.00 |
| 3050 | 4" x 4" Ball Bearing | " | 76.00 |
| 3060 | 4 1/2" x 4 1/2" Ball Bearing | " | 80.00 |
| 5000 | CLOSERS - SURFACE MOUNTED - 3' - 0" Door | " | 261 |
| 5010 | 3' - 4" | " | 271 |
| 5020 | 3' - 8" | " | 281 |
| 5030 | 4' - 0" | " | 350 |
| 6000 | CLOSERS - CONCEALED - Interior | " | 430 |
| 6010 | Exterior Each | " | 580 |

© 2011 By Design & Construction Resources

# DIVISION # 08 DOORS AND WINDOWS - QUICK ESTIMATING

## 08999.90 FINISH HARDWARE, Cont'd...

| | | | |
|---|---|---|---|
| 6020 | Add for Fusible Link - Electric | EA. | 251 |
| 6030 | CLOSERS - FLOOR HINGES - Interior | " | 650 |
| 6040 | Exterior | " | 980 |
| 6050 | Add for Hold Open Feature | " | 102 |
| 6060 | Add for Double Acting Feature | " | 330 |
| 7000 | DEAD BOLT LOCK - Cylinder - Outside Key | " | 221 |
| 7010 | Cylinder - Double Key | " | 310 |
| 7020 | Flush - Push/ Pull | " | 85.25 |
| 8000 | EXIT DEVICES (PANIC) - Surface | " | 940 |
| 8010 | Mortise Lock | " | 1,190 |
| 8020 | Concealed | " | 2,970 |
| 8030 | Handicap (ADA) Automatic | " | 2,190 |
| 9000 | HINGES, SPRING (PAINTED) - 6" Single Acting | " | 160 |
| 9010 | 6" Double Acting | " | 195 |
| 9101 | LATCHSETS - Bronze or Chrome | " | 261 |
| 9102 | Stainless Steel | " | 290 |
| 9200 | LOCKSETS - Mortise - Bronze or Chrome - H.D. | " | 350 |
| 9210 | Mortise - Bronze or Chrome - S.D. | " | 281 |
| 9220 | Stainless Steel | " | 460 |
| 9230 | Cylindrical - Bronze or Chrome | " | 310 |
| 9240 | Stainless Steel | " | 360 |
| 9300 | LEVER HANDICAP - Latch Set | " | 360 |
| 9310 | Lock Set | " | 430 |
| 9400 | PLATES - Kick - 8" x 34" - Aluminum | " | 112 |
| 9410 | Bronze | " | 104 |
| 9420 | Push - 6" x 15" - Aluminum | " | 74.75 |
| 9430 | Bronze | " | 106 |
| 9440 | Push & Pull Combination - Aluminum | " | 123 |
| 9450 | Bronze | " | 177 |
| 9500 | STOPS AND HOLDERS | | |
| 9510 | Holder - Magnetic (No Electric) | EA. | 251 |
| 9520 | Bumper | " | 59.00 |
| 9530 | Overhead - Bronze, Chrome or Aluminum | " | 137 |
| 9540 | Wall Stops | " | 52.00 |
| 9550 | Floor Stops | " | 64.75 |

## 08999.91 WEATHERSTRIPPING

| Code | Description | Unit | Cost |
|---|---|---|---|
| 1000 | ASTRAGALS - Aluminum - 1/8" x 2" | EA. | 78.50 |
| 1010 | Painted Steel | " | 70.50 |
| 2000 | DOORS (WOOD) - Interlocking | " | 113 |
| 2010 | Spring Bronze | " | 122 |
| 2020 | Add for Metal Doors | " | 56.25 |
| 3000 | SWEEPS - 36" WOOD DOORS - Aluminum | " | 32.00 |
| 3010 | Vinyl | " | 31.75 |
| 4000 | THRESHOLDS - Aluminum - 4" x 1/2" | " | 67.50 |
| 4010 | Bronze 4" x 1/2" | " | 85.25 |
| 4020 | 5 1/2" x 1/2" | " | 90.50 |
| 5000 | WINDOWS (WOOD) - Interlocking | " | 96.00 |
| 5010 | Spring Bronze | " | 113 |

© 2011 By Design & Construction Resources

# DIVISION # 09  FINISHES

## TABLE OF CONTENTS

| | PAGE |
|---|---|
| 09110.10 - METAL STUDS | 09-2 |
| 09205.10 - GYPSUM LATH | 09-2 |
| 09205.20 - METAL LATH | 09-3 |
| 09205.60 - PLASTER ACCESSORIES | 09-3 |
| 09210.10 - PLASTER | 09-3 |
| 09220.10 - PORTLAND CEMENT PLASTER | 09-3 |
| 09250.10 - GYPSUM BOARD | 09-4 |
| 09310.10 - CERAMIC TILE | 09-4 |
| 09330.10 - QUARRY TILE | 09-5 |
| 09410.10 - TERRAZZO | 09-5 |
| 09510.10 - CEILINGS AND WALLS | 09-6 |
| 09550.10 - WOOD FLOORING | 09-6 |
| 09550.20 - BAMBOO FLOORING | 09-7 |
| 09630.10 - UNIT MASONRY FLOORING | 09-7 |
| 09660.10 - RESILIENT TILE FLOORING | 09-7 |
| 09665.10 - RESILIENT SHEET FLOORING | 09-8 |
| 09678.10 - RESILIENT BASE AND ACCESSORIES | 09-8 |
| 09682.10 - CARPET PADDING | 09-8 |
| 09685.10 - CARPET | 09-8 |
| 09905.10 - PAINTING PREPARATION | 09-8 |
| 09910.05 - EXT. PAINTING, SITEWORK | 09-9 |
| 09910.15 - EXT. PAINTING, BUILDINGS | 09-11 |
| 09910.35 - INT. PAINTING, BUILDINGS | 09-12 |
| 09955.10 - WALL COVERING | 09-13 |

© 2011 By Design & Construction Resources

## DIVISION # 09 FINISHES

| | | UNIT | LABOR | MAT. | TOTAL |
|---|---|---|---|---|---|
| **09110.10** | **METAL STUDS** | | | | |
| 0060 | Studs, non load bearing, galvanized | | | | |
| 0130 | 3-5/8", 20 ga. | | | | |
| 0140 | 12" o.c. | S.F. | 1.33 | 0.85 | 2.18 |
| 0142 | 16" o.c. | " | 1.06 | 0.66 | 1.72 |
| 0144 | 24" o.c. | " | 0.88 | 0.49 | 1.37 |
| 0170 | 25 ga. | | | | |
| 0180 | 12" o.c. | S.F. | 1.33 | 0.57 | 1.90 |
| 0182 | 16" o.c. | " | 1.06 | 0.46 | 1.52 |
| 0184 | 24" o.c. | " | 0.88 | 0.35 | 1.23 |
| 0210 | 6", 20 ga. | | | | |
| 0220 | 12" o.c. | S.F. | 1.66 | 1.19 | 2.85 |
| 0222 | 16" o.c. | " | 1.33 | 0.88 | 2.21 |
| 0224 | 24" o.c. | " | 1.11 | 0.71 | 1.82 |
| 0230 | 25 ga. | | | | |
| 0240 | 12" o.c. | S.F. | 1.66 | 0.78 | 2.44 |
| 0242 | 16" o.c. | " | 1.33 | 0.61 | 1.94 |
| 0244 | 24" o.c. | " | 1.11 | 0.46 | 1.57 |
| 0980 | Load bearing studs, galvanized | | | | |
| 0990 | 3-5/8", 16 ga. | | | | |
| 1000 | 12" o.c. | S.F. | 1.33 | 1.55 | 2.88 |
| 1020 | 16" o.c. | " | 1.06 | 1.43 | 2.49 |
| 1110 | 18 ga. | | | | |
| 1130 | 12" o.c. | S.F. | 0.88 | 1.11 | 1.99 |
| 1140 | 16" o.c. | " | 1.06 | 1.21 | 2.27 |
| 1980 | 6", 16 ga. | | | | |
| 2000 | 12" o.c. | S.F. | 1.66 | 2.07 | 3.73 |
| 2001 | 16" o.c. | " | 1.33 | 1.87 | 3.20 |
| 3000 | Furring | | | | |
| 3160 | On beams and columns | | | | |
| 3170 | 7/8" channel | L.F. | 3.55 | 0.55 | 4.10 |
| 3180 | 1-1/2" channel | " | 4.10 | 0.66 | 4.76 |
| 4460 | On ceilings | | | | |
| 4470 | 3/4" furring channels | | | | |
| 4480 | 12" o.c. | S.F. | 2.22 | 0.39 | 2.61 |
| 4490 | 16" o.c. | " | 2.13 | 0.30 | 2.43 |
| 4495 | 24" o.c. | " | 1.90 | 0.22 | 2.12 |
| 4500 | 1-1/2" furring channels | | | | |
| 4520 | 12" o.c. | S.F. | 2.42 | 0.66 | 3.08 |
| 4540 | 16" o.c. | " | 2.22 | 0.49 | 2.71 |
| 4560 | 24" o.c. | " | 2.05 | 0.34 | 2.39 |
| 5000 | On walls | | | | |
| 5020 | 3/4" furring channels | | | | |
| 5050 | 12" o.c. | S.F. | 1.77 | 0.39 | 2.16 |
| 5100 | 16" o.c. | " | 1.66 | 0.30 | 1.96 |
| 5150 | 24" o.c. | " | 1.56 | 0.22 | 1.78 |
| 5200 | 1-1/2" furring channels | | | | |
| 5210 | 12" o.c. | S.F. | 1.90 | 0.66 | 2.56 |
| 5220 | 16" o.c. | " | 1.77 | 0.49 | 2.26 |
| 5230 | 24" o.c. | " | 1.66 | 0.34 | 2.00 |

## DIVISION # 09 FINISHES

| Code | Description | UNIT | LABOR | MAT. | TOTAL |
|---|---|---|---|---|---|
| **09205.10** | **GYPSUM LATH** | | | | |
| 1070 | Gypsum lath, 1/2" thick | | | | |
| 1090 |    Clipped | S.Y. | 2.96 | 7.20 | 10.16 |
| 1110 |    Nailed | " | 3.33 | 7.20 | 10.53 |
| **09205.20** | **METAL LATH** | | | | |
| 0960 | Diamond expanded, galvanized | | | | |
| 0980 |    2.5 lb., on walls | | | | |
| 1010 |      Nailed | S.Y. | 6.67 | 4.22 | 10.89 |
| 1030 |      Wired | " | 7.62 | 4.22 | 11.84 |
| 1040 |    On ceilings | | | | |
| 1050 |      Nailed | S.Y. | 7.62 | 4.22 | 11.84 |
| 1070 |      Wired | " | 8.89 | 4.22 | 13.11 |
| 2230 | Stucco lath | | | | |
| 2240 |    1.8 lb. | S.Y. | 6.67 | 4.96 | 11.63 |
| 2300 |    3.6 lb. | " | 6.67 | 5.56 | 12.23 |
| 2310 |    Paper backed | | | | |
| 2320 |      Minimum | S.Y. | 5.33 | 3.85 | 9.18 |
| 2400 |      Maximum | " | 7.62 | 6.21 | 13.83 |
| **09205.60** | **PLASTER ACCESSORIES** | | | | |
| 0120 | Expansion joint, 3/4", 26 ga., galv. | L.F. | 1.33 | 1.48 | 2.81 |
| 2000 | Plaster corner beads, 3/4", galvanized | " | 1.52 | 0.41 | 1.93 |
| 2020 | Casing bead, expanded flange, galvanized | " | 1.33 | 0.56 | 1.89 |
| 2100 | Expanded wing, 1-1/4" wide, galvanized | " | 1.33 | 0.66 | 1.99 |
| 2500 | Joint clips for lath | EA. | 0.26 | 0.17 | 0.43 |
| 2580 | Metal base, galvanized, 2-1/2" high | L.F. | 1.77 | 0.75 | 2.52 |
| 2600 | Stud clips for gypsum lath | EA. | 0.26 | 0.17 | 0.43 |
| 2700 | Tie wire galvanized, 18 ga., 25 lb. hank | " | | | 47.00 |
| 8000 | Sound deadening board, 1/4" | S.F. | 0.88 | 0.31 | 1.19 |
| **09210.10** | **PLASTER** | | | | |
| 0980 | Gypsum plaster, trowel finish, 2 coats | | | | |
| 1000 |    Ceilings | S.Y. | 15.50 | 6.20 | 21.70 |
| 1020 |    Walls | " | 14.75 | 6.20 | 20.95 |
| 1030 |    3 coats | | | | |
| 1040 |      Ceilings | S.Y. | 21.75 | 8.60 | 30.35 |
| 1060 |      Walls | " | 19.25 | 8.60 | 27.85 |
| 7000 | On columns, add to installation, 50% | " | | | |
| 7020 | Chases, fascia, and soffits, add to installation, 50% | " | | | |
| 7040 | Beams, add to installation, 50% | " | | | |
| **09220.10** | **PORTLAND CEMENT PLASTER** | | | | |
| 2980 | Stucco, portland, gray, 3 coat, 1" thick | | | | |
| 3000 |    Sand finish | S.Y. | 21.75 | 7.75 | 29.50 |
| 3020 |    Trowel finish | " | 22.75 | 7.75 | 30.50 |
| 3030 |    White cement | | | | |
| 3040 |      Sand finish | S.Y. | 22.75 | 8.85 | 31.60 |
| 3060 |      Trowel finish | " | 25.00 | 8.85 | 33.85 |
| 3980 | Scratch coat | | | | |
| 4000 |    For ceramic tile | S.Y. | 4.98 | 2.81 | 7.79 |
| 4020 |    For quarry tile | " | 4.98 | 2.81 | 7.79 |
| 5000 | Portland cement plaster | | | | |
| 5020 |    2 coats, 1/2" | S.Y. | 9.96 | 5.58 | 15.54 |
| 5040 |    3 coats, 7/8" | " | 12.50 | 6.66 | 19.16 |

© 2011 By Design & Construction Resources

## DIVISION # 09  FINISHES

### 09250.10  GYPSUM BOARD

| Code | Description | UNIT | LABOR | MAT. | TOTAL |
|------|-------------|------|-------|------|-------|
| 0220 | 1/2", clipped to | | | | |
| 0240 |     Metal furred ceiling | S.F. | 0.59 | 0.36 | 0.95 |
| 0260 |     Columns and beams | " | 1.33 | 0.33 | 1.66 |
| 0270 |     Walls | " | 0.53 | 0.33 | 0.86 |
| 0280 | Nailed or screwed to | | | | |
| 0290 |     Wood framed ceiling | S.F. | 0.53 | 0.33 | 0.86 |
| 0300 |     Columns and beams | " | 1.18 | 0.33 | 1.51 |
| 0400 |     Walls | " | 0.48 | 0.33 | 0.81 |
| 1000 | 5/8", clipped to | | | | |
| 1020 |     Metal furred ceiling | S.F. | 0.66 | 0.36 | 1.02 |
| 1040 |     Columns and beams | " | 1.48 | 0.36 | 1.84 |
| 1060 |     Walls | " | 0.59 | 0.36 | 0.95 |
| 1070 | Nailed or screwed to | | | | |
| 1080 |     Wood framed ceiling | S.F. | 0.66 | 0.36 | 1.02 |
| 1100 |     Columns and beams | " | 1.48 | 0.36 | 1.84 |
| 1120 |     Walls | " | 0.59 | 0.36 | 0.95 |
| 1122 | Vinyl faced, clipped to metal studs | | | | |
| 1124 |     1/2" | S.F. | 0.66 | 0.88 | 1.54 |
| 1126 |     5/8" | " | 0.66 | 0.93 | 1.59 |
| 1130 | Add for | | | | |
| 1140 |     Fire resistant | S.F. | | | 0.11 |
| 1180 |     Water resistant | " | | | 0.17 |
| 1200 |     Water and fire resistant | " | | | 0.22 |
| 1220 | Taping and finishing joints | | | | |
| 1222 |     Minimum | S.F. | 0.35 | 0.04 | 0.39 |
| 1224 |     Average | " | 0.44 | 0.06 | 0.50 |
| 1226 |     Maximum | " | 0.53 | 0.09 | 0.62 |
| 5020 | Casing bead | | | | |
| 5022 |     Minimum | L.F. | 1.52 | 0.15 | 1.67 |
| 5024 |     Average | " | 1.77 | 0.16 | 1.93 |
| 5026 |     Maximum | " | 2.66 | 0.20 | 2.86 |
| 5040 | Corner bead | | | | |
| 5042 |     Minimum | L.F. | 1.52 | 0.16 | 1.68 |
| 5044 |     Average | " | 1.77 | 0.20 | 1.97 |
| 5046 |     Maximum | " | 2.66 | 0.25 | 2.91 |

### 09310.10  CERAMIC TILE

| Code | Description | UNIT | LABOR | MAT. | TOTAL |
|------|-------------|------|-------|------|-------|
| 0980 | Glazed wall tile, 4-1/4" x 4-1/4" | | | | |
| 1000 |     Minimum | S.F. | 3.63 | 2.32 | 5.95 |
| 1020 |     Average | " | 4.24 | 3.68 | 7.92 |
| 1040 |     Maximum | " | 5.09 | 13.25 | 18.34 |
| 1042 | 6" x 6" | | | | |
| 1044 |     Minimum | S.F. | 3.18 | 1.41 | 4.59 |
| 1046 |     Average | " | 3.63 | 1.90 | 5.53 |
| 1048 |     Maximum | " | 4.24 | 2.37 | 6.61 |
| 2960 | Base, 4-1/4" high | | | | |
| 2980 |     Minimum | L.F. | 6.36 | 3.83 | 10.19 |
| 3000 |     Average | " | 6.36 | 4.46 | 10.82 |
| 3040 |     Maximum | " | 6.36 | 5.89 | 12.25 |
| 3042 | Glazed modlings and trim, 12" x 12" | | | | |
| 3044 |     Minimum | L.F. | 5.09 | 2.11 | 7.20 |
| 3046 |     Average | " | 5.09 | 3.22 | 8.31 |

## DIVISION # 09  FINISHES

| | | UNIT | LABOR | MAT. | TOTAL |
|---|---|---|---|---|---|
| **09310.10** | **CERAMIC TILE, Cont'd...** | | | | |
| 3048 | Maximum | L.F. | 5.09 | 4.33 | 9.42 |
| 6100 | Unglazed floor tile | | | | |
| 6120 | Portland cem., cushion edge, face mtd | | | | |
| 6140 | 1" x 1" | S.F. | 4.62 | 6.71 | 11.33 |
| 6150 | 2" x 2" | " | 4.24 | 7.09 | 11.33 |
| 6162 | 4" x 4" | " | 4.24 | 6.60 | 10.84 |
| 6164 | 6" x 6" | " | 3.63 | 2.36 | 5.99 |
| 6166 | 12" x 12" | " | 3.18 | 2.07 | 5.25 |
| 6168 | 16" x 16" | " | 2.82 | 1.80 | 4.62 |
| 6170 | 18" x 18" | " | 2.54 | 1.74 | 4.28 |
| 6200 | Adhesive bed, with white grout | | | | |
| 6220 | 1" x 1" | S.F. | 4.62 | 6.71 | 11.33 |
| 6230 | 2" x 2" | " | 4.24 | 7.09 | 11.33 |
| 6260 | 4" x 4" | " | 4.24 | 7.09 | 11.33 |
| 6262 | 6" x 6" | " | 3.63 | 2.36 | 5.99 |
| 6264 | 12" x 12" | " | 3.18 | 2.07 | 5.25 |
| 6266 | 16" x 16" | " | 2.82 | 1.80 | 4.62 |
| 6268 | 18" x 18" | " | 2.54 | 1.74 | 4.28 |
| 6300 | Organic adhesive bed, thin set, back mounted | | | | |
| 6320 | 1" x 1" | S.F. | 4.62 | 6.71 | 11.33 |
| 6350 | 2" x 2" | " | 4.24 | 7.09 | 11.33 |
| 6360 | For group 2 colors, add to material, 10% | | | | |
| 6370 | For group 3 colors, add to material, 20% | | | | |
| 6380 | For abrasive surface, add to material, 25% | | | | |
| 8990 | Ceramic accessories | | | | |
| 9000 | Towel bar, 24" long | | | | |
| 9004 | Average | EA. | 25.50 | 20.25 | 45.75 |
| 9020 | Soap dish | | | | |
| 9024 | Average | EA. | 42.50 | 10.50 | 53.00 |
| **09330.10** | **QUARRY TILE** | | | | |
| 1060 | Floor | | | | |
| 1080 | 4 x 4 x 1/2" | S.F. | 6.78 | 5.69 | 12.47 |
| 1120 | 6 x 6 x 3/4" | " | 6.36 | 6.94 | 13.30 |
| 1200 | Wall, applied to 3/4" portland cement bed | | | | |
| 1220 | 4 x 4 x 1/2" | S.F. | 10.25 | 4.20 | 14.45 |
| 1240 | 6 x 6 x 3/4" | " | 8.48 | 4.69 | 13.17 |
| 1320 | Cove base | | | | |
| 1330 | 5 x 6 x 1/2" straight top | L.F. | 8.48 | 5.50 | 13.98 |
| 1340 | 6 x 6 x 3/4" round top | " | 8.48 | 5.11 | 13.59 |
| 1360 | Stair treads 6 x 6 x 3/4" | " | 12.75 | 7.53 | 20.28 |
| 1380 | Window sill 6 x 8 x 3/4" | " | 10.25 | 6.87 | 17.12 |
| 1400 | For abrasive surface, add to material, 25% | | | | |
| **09410.10** | **TERRAZZO** | | | | |
| 1100 | Floors on concrete, 1-3/4" thick, 5/8" topping | | | | |
| 1120 | Gray cement | S.F. | 7.11 | 4.23 | 11.34 |
| 1140 | White cement | " | 7.11 | 4.62 | 11.73 |
| 1200 | Sand cushion, 3" thick, 5/8" top, 1/4" | | | | |
| 1220 | Gray cement | S.F. | 8.30 | 5.00 | 13.30 |
| 1240 | White cement | " | 8.30 | 5.55 | 13.85 |
| 1260 | Monolithic terrazzo, 3-1/2" base slab, 5/8" topping | " | 6.22 | 3.97 | 10.19 |
| 1280 | Terrazzo wainscot, cast-in-place, 1/2" thick | " | 12.50 | 7.48 | 19.98 |

© 2011 By Design & Construction Resources

## DIVISION # 09  FINISHES

| | | UNIT | LABOR | MAT. | TOTAL |
|---|---|---|---|---|---|
| **09410.10** | **TERRAZZO, Cont'd...** | | | | |
| 1300 | Base, cast in place, terrazzo cove type, 6" high | L.F. | 7.11 | 8.86 | 15.97 |
| 1320 | Curb, cast in place, 6" wide x 6" high, polished top | " | 25.00 | 9.84 | 34.84 |
| 1400 | For venetian type terrazzo, add to material, 10% | | | | |
| 1420 | For abrasive heavy duty terrazzo, add to material, 15% | | | | |
| 1480 | Divider strips | | | | |
| 1500 |    Zinc | L.F. | | | 1.50 |
| 1510 |    Brass | " | | | 2.80 |
| **09510.10** | **CEILINGS AND WALLS** | | | | |
| 1520 | Acoustical panels, suspension system not included | | | | |
| 1540 |    Fiberglass panels | | | | |
| 1550 |      5/8" thick | | | | |
| 1560 |        2' x 2' | S.F. | 0.76 | 1.52 | 2.28 |
| 1580 |        2' x 4' | " | 0.59 | 1.44 | 2.03 |
| 1590 |      3/4" thick | | | | |
| 1600 |        2' x 2' | S.F. | 0.76 | 2.71 | 3.47 |
| 1620 |        2' x 4' | " | 0.59 | 2.40 | 2.99 |
| 1640 |    Glass cloth faced fiberglass panels | | | | |
| 1660 |      3/4" thick | S.F. | 0.88 | 2.50 | 3.38 |
| 1680 |      1" thick | " | 0.88 | 2.79 | 3.67 |
| 1700 |    Mineral fiber panels | | | | |
| 1710 |      5/8" thick | | | | |
| 1720 |        2' x 2' | S.F. | 0.76 | 1.12 | 1.88 |
| 1740 |        2' x 4' | " | 0.59 | 1.12 | 1.71 |
| 1750 |      3/4" thick | | | | |
| 1760 |        2' x 2' | S.F. | 0.76 | 1.51 | 2.27 |
| 1780 |        2' x 4' | " | 0.59 | 1.51 | 2.10 |
| 3000 | Acoustical tiles, suspension system not included | | | | |
| 3020 |    Fiberglass tile, 12" x 12" | | | | |
| 3040 |      5/8" thick | S.F. | 0.97 | 1.39 | 2.36 |
| 3060 |      3/4" thick | " | 1.18 | 1.61 | 2.79 |
| 3080 |    Glass cloth faced fiberglass tile | | | | |
| 3100 |      3/4" thick | S.F. | 1.18 | 3.24 | 4.42 |
| 3120 |      3" thick | " | 1.33 | 3.63 | 4.96 |
| 3140 |    Mineral fiber tile, 12" x 12" | | | | |
| 3150 |      5/8" thick | | | | |
| 3160 |        Standard | S.F. | 1.06 | 0.82 | 1.88 |
| 3180 |        Vinyl faced | " | 1.06 | 1.65 | 2.71 |
| 3190 |      3/4" thick | | | | |
| 3195 |        Standard | S.F. | 1.06 | 1.21 | 2.27 |
| 3200 |        Vinyl faced | " | 1.06 | 2.11 | 3.17 |
| 5500 | Ceiling suspension systems | | | | |
| 5505 |    T bar system | | | | |
| 5510 |      2' x 4' | S.F. | 0.53 | 1.15 | 1.68 |
| 5520 |      2' x 2' | " | 0.59 | 1.25 | 1.84 |
| 5530 |    Concealed Z bar suspension system, 12" module | " | 0.88 | 1.07 | 1.95 |
| 5550 |    For 1-1/2" carrier channels, 4' o.c., add | " | | | 0.38 |
| 5560 |      Carrier channel for recessed light fixtures | " | | | 0.69 |
| **09550.10** | **WOOD FLOORING** | | | | |
| 0100 | Wood strip flooring, unfinished | | | | |
| 1000 |    Fir floor | | | | |
| 1010 |      C and better | | | | |

## DIVISION # 09 FINISHES

| | | UNIT | LABOR | MAT. | TOTAL |
|---|---|---|---|---|---|
| **09550.10** | **WOOD FLOORING, Cont'd...** | | | | |
| 1020 | Vertical grain | S.F. | 1.77 | 3.52 | 5.29 |
| 1040 | Flat grain | " | 1.77 | 3.32 | 5.09 |
| 1060 | Oak floor | | | | |
| 1080 | Minimum | S.F. | 2.54 | 3.71 | 6.25 |
| 1100 | Average | " | 2.54 | 5.12 | 7.66 |
| 1120 | Maximum | " | 2.54 | 7.42 | 9.96 |
| 1340 | Added costs | | | | |
| 1350 | For factory finish, add to material, 10% | | | | |
| 1355 | For random width floor, add to total, 20% | | | | |
| 1360 | For simulated pegs, add to total, 10% | | | | |
| 3000 | Gym floor, 2 ply felt, 25/32" maple, finished, in mastic | S.F. | 2.96 | 7.75 | 10.71 |
| 3020 | Over wood sleepers | " | 3.33 | 8.69 | 12.02 |
| 9020 | Finishing, sand, fill, finish, and wax | " | 1.33 | 0.66 | 1.99 |
| 9100 | Refinish sand, seal, and 2 coats of polyurethane | " | 1.77 | 1.15 | 2.92 |
| 9540 | Clean and wax floors | " | 0.26 | 0.19 | 0.45 |
| **09550.20** | **BAMBOO FLOORING** | | | | |
| 0010 | Vertical, Carbonized Medium, 3' vertical grain | S.F. | 1.77 | 6.15 | 7.92 |
| 0020 | Natural | " | 1.77 | 6.05 | 7.82 |
| 0030 | 3' horizontal grain | " | 1.77 | 6.15 | 7.92 |
| 0040 | Natural | " | 1.77 | 6.05 | 7.82 |
| 0050 | 3' Stained | " | 1.77 | 5.93 | 7.70 |
| 0060 | 6' spice | " | 1.77 | 5.93 | 7.70 |
| 0070 | 3' stained, butterscotch | " | 1.77 | 5.93 | 7.70 |
| 0080 | 6' tiger | " | 1.77 | 5.93 | 7.70 |
| 0090 | 3' stained, Irish moss | " | 1.77 | 5.93 | 7.70 |
| 0100 | Vice-lock, 12 mm., laminate flooring, maple | " | 1.77 | 3.92 | 5.69 |
| 0101 | Oak | " | 1.77 | 3.36 | 5.13 |
| 0102 | Pine | " | 1.77 | 4.48 | 6.25 |
| 0103 | Espresso | " | 1.77 | 4.48 | 6.25 |
| 0104 | Standard, hard maple | " | 1.77 | 3.64 | 5.41 |
| 0105 | Cherry | " | 1.77 | 3.36 | 5.13 |
| 0106 | Oak | " | 1.77 | 2.24 | 4.01 |
| 0107 | Walnut | " | 1.77 | 2.24 | 4.01 |
| 0108 | South pacific vice-lock, 12 mm, brazilian cherry | " | 1.77 | 5.04 | 6.81 |
| 0109 | Maple | " | 1.77 | 4.48 | 6.25 |
| 0110 | Teak | " | 1.77 | 4.76 | 6.53 |
| **09630.10** | **UNIT MASONRY FLOORING** | | | | |
| 1000 | Clay brick | | | | |
| 1020 | 9 x 4-1/2 x 3" thick | | | | |
| 1040 | Glazed | S.F. | 4.44 | 8.03 | 12.47 |
| 1060 | Unglazed | " | 4.44 | 7.70 | 12.14 |
| 1070 | 8 x 4 x 3/4" thick | | | | |
| 1080 | Glazed | S.F. | 4.64 | 7.26 | 11.90 |
| 1100 | Unglazed | " | 4.64 | 7.15 | 11.79 |
| 1140 | For herringbone pattern, add to labor, 15% | | | | |
| **09660.10** | **RESILIENT TILE FLOORING** | | | | |
| 1020 | Solid vinyl tile, 1/8" thick, 12" x 12" | | | | |
| 1040 | Marble patterns | S.F. | 1.33 | 4.45 | 5.78 |
| 1060 | Solid colors | " | 1.33 | 5.77 | 7.10 |
| 1080 | Travertine patterns | " | 1.33 | 6.49 | 7.82 |
| 2000 | Conductive resilient flooring, vinyl tile | | | | |

© 2011 By Design & Construction Resources

## DIVISION # 09 FINISHES

| | | UNIT | LABOR | MAT. | TOTAL |
|---|---|---|---|---|---|
| **09660.10** | **RESILIENT TILE FLOORING, Cont'd...** | | | | |
| 2040 | 1/8" thick, 12" x 12" | S.F. | 1.52 | 6.71 | 8.23 |
| **09665.10** | **RESILIENT SHEET FLOORING** | | | | |
| 0980 | Vinyl sheet flooring | | | | |
| 1000 | Minimum | S.F. | 0.53 | 3.83 | 4.36 |
| 1002 | Average | " | 0.63 | 6.19 | 6.82 |
| 1004 | Maximum | " | 0.88 | 10.50 | 11.38 |
| 1020 | Cove, to 6" | L.F. | 1.06 | 2.28 | 3.34 |
| 2000 | Fluid applied resilient flooring | | | | |
| 2020 | Polyurethane, poured in place, 3/8" thick | S.F. | 4.44 | 10.50 | 14.94 |
| 6200 | Vinyl sheet goods, backed | | | | |
| 6220 | 0.070" thick | S.F. | 0.66 | 3.90 | 4.56 |
| 6260 | 0.125" thick | " | 0.66 | 6.98 | 7.64 |
| 6280 | 0.250" thick | " | 0.66 | 8.03 | 8.69 |
| **09678.10** | **RESILIENT BASE AND ACCESSORIES** | | | | |
| 1000 | Wall base, vinyl | | | | |
| 1130 | 4" high | L.F. | 1.77 | 1.01 | 2.78 |
| 1140 | 6" high | " | 1.77 | 1.37 | 3.14 |
| **09682.10** | **CARPET PADDING** | | | | |
| 1000 | Carpet padding | | | | |
| 1005 | Foam rubber, waffle type, 0.3" thick | S.Y. | 2.66 | 6.16 | 8.82 |
| 1010 | Jute padding | | | | |
| 1022 | Average | S.Y. | 2.66 | 5.44 | 8.10 |
| 1030 | Sponge rubber cushion | | | | |
| 1042 | Average | S.Y. | 2.66 | 6.60 | 9.26 |
| 1050 | Urethane cushion, 3/8" thick | | | | |
| 1062 | Average | S.Y. | 2.66 | 5.77 | 8.43 |
| **09685.10** | **CARPET** | | | | |
| 0990 | Carpet, acrylic | | | | |
| 1000 | 24 oz., light traffic | S.Y. | 5.92 | 16.00 | 21.92 |
| 1020 | 28 oz., medium traffic | " | 5.92 | 19.25 | 25.17 |
| 2010 | Nylon | | | | |
| 2020 | 15 oz., light traffic | S.Y. | 5.92 | 22.50 | 28.42 |
| 2040 | 28 oz., medium traffic | " | 5.92 | 29.00 | 34.92 |
| 2110 | Nylon | | | | |
| 2120 | 28 oz., medium traffic | S.Y. | 5.92 | 27.75 | 33.67 |
| 2140 | 35 oz., heavy traffic | " | 5.92 | 34.00 | 39.92 |
| 2145 | Wool | | | | |
| 2150 | 30 oz., medium traffic | S.Y. | 5.92 | 46.00 | 51.92 |
| 2160 | 36 oz., medium traffic | " | 5.92 | 48.50 | 54.42 |
| 2180 | 42 oz., heavy traffic | " | 5.92 | 64.00 | 69.92 |
| 3000 | Carpet tile | | | | |
| 3020 | Foam backed | | | | |
| 3022 | Minimum | S.F. | 1.06 | 3.53 | 4.59 |
| 3024 | Average | " | 1.18 | 4.08 | 5.26 |
| 3026 | Maximum | " | 1.33 | 6.47 | 7.80 |
| 8980 | Clean and vacuum carpet | | | | |
| 9000 | Minimum | S.Y. | 0.20 | 0.32 | 0.52 |
| 9020 | Average | " | 0.35 | 0.50 | 0.85 |
| 9040 | Maximum | " | 0.53 | 0.70 | 1.23 |

# DIVISION # 09 FINISHES

| | | | UNIT | LABOR | MAT. | TOTAL |
|---|---|---|---|---|---|---|
| **09905.10** | **PAINTING PREPARATION** | | | | | |
| 1000 | Dropcloths | | | | | |
| 1050 | | Minimum | S.F. | 0.02 | 0.03 | 0.05 |
| 1100 | | Average | " | 0.03 | 0.04 | 0.07 |
| 1150 | | Maximum | " | 0.04 | 0.05 | 0.09 |
| 1200 | Masking | | | | | |
| 1250 | | Paper and tape | | | | |
| 1300 | | Minimum | L.F. | 0.44 | 0.02 | 0.46 |
| 1350 | | Average | " | 0.55 | 0.03 | 0.58 |
| 1400 | | Maximum | " | 0.74 | 0.04 | 0.78 |
| 1450 | | Doors | | | | |
| 1500 | | Minimum | EA. | 5.57 | 0.04 | 5.61 |
| 1550 | | Average | " | 7.43 | 0.05 | 7.48 |
| 1600 | | Maximum | " | 9.91 | 0.06 | 9.97 |
| 1650 | | Windows | | | | |
| 1700 | | Minimum | EA. | 5.57 | 0.04 | 5.61 |
| 1750 | | Average | " | 7.43 | 0.05 | 7.48 |
| 1800 | | Maximum | " | 9.91 | 0.06 | 9.97 |
| 2000 | Sanding | | | | | |
| 2050 | | Walls and flat surfaces | | | | |
| 2100 | | Minimum | S.F. | 0.29 | | 0.29 |
| 2150 | | Average | " | 0.37 | | 0.37 |
| 2200 | | Maximum | " | 0.44 | | 0.44 |
| 2250 | | Doors and windows | | | | |
| 2300 | | Minimum | EA. | 7.43 | | 7.43 |
| 2350 | | Average | " | 11.25 | | 11.25 |
| 2400 | | Maximum | " | 14.75 | | 14.75 |
| 2450 | | Trim | | | | |
| 2500 | | Minimum | L.F. | 0.55 | | 0.55 |
| 2550 | | Average | " | 0.74 | | 0.74 |
| 2600 | | Maximum | " | 0.99 | | 0.99 |
| 2650 | Puttying | | | | | |
| 2700 | | Minimum | S.F. | 0.68 | 0.01 | 0.69 |
| 2750 | | Average | " | 0.89 | 0.02 | 0.91 |
| 2800 | | Maximum | " | 1.11 | 0.03 | 1.14 |
| **09910.05** | **EXT. PAINTING, SITEWORK** | | | | | |
| 3000 | Concrete Block | | | | | |
| 3020 | | Roller | | | | |
| 3040 | | First Coat | | | | |
| 3060 | | Minimum | S.F. | 0.22 | 0.16 | 0.38 |
| 3080 | | Average | " | 0.29 | 0.16 | 0.45 |
| 3100 | | Maximum | " | 0.44 | 0.16 | 0.60 |
| 3120 | | Second Coat | | | | |
| 3140 | | Minimum | S.F. | 0.18 | 0.16 | 0.34 |
| 3160 | | Average | " | 0.24 | 0.16 | 0.40 |
| 3180 | | Maximum | " | 0.37 | 0.16 | 0.53 |
| 3200 | | Spray | | | | |
| 3220 | | First Coat | | | | |
| 3240 | | Minimum | S.F. | 0.12 | 0.13 | 0.25 |
| 3260 | | Average | " | 0.14 | 0.13 | 0.27 |
| 3280 | | Maximum | " | 0.17 | 0.13 | 0.30 |
| 3300 | | Second Coat | | | | |

© 2011 By Design & Construction Resources

## DIVISION # 09 FINISHES

### 09910.05  EXT. PAINTING, SITEWORK, Cont'd...

| Code | Description | UNIT | LABOR | MAT. | TOTAL |
|---|---|---|---|---|---|
| 3320 | Minimum | S.F. | 0.07 | 0.13 | 0.20 |
| 3340 | Average | " | 0.10 | 0.13 | 0.23 |
| 3360 | Maximum | " | 0.13 | 0.13 | 0.26 |
| 3500 | Fences, Chain Link | | | | |
| 3700 | Roller | | | | |
| 3720 | First Coat | | | | |
| 3740 | Minimum | S.F. | 0.31 | 0.11 | 0.42 |
| 3760 | Average | " | 0.37 | 0.11 | 0.48 |
| 3780 | Maximum | " | 0.42 | 0.11 | 0.53 |
| 3800 | Second Coat | | | | |
| 3820 | Minimum | S.F. | 0.18 | 0.11 | 0.29 |
| 3840 | Average | " | 0.22 | 0.11 | 0.33 |
| 3860 | Maximum | " | 0.27 | 0.11 | 0.38 |
| 3880 | Spray | | | | |
| 3900 | First Coat | | | | |
| 3920 | Minimum | S.F. | 0.13 | 0.08 | 0.21 |
| 3940 | Average | " | 0.15 | 0.08 | 0.23 |
| 3960 | Maximum | " | 0.18 | 0.08 | 0.26 |
| 3980 | Second Coat | | | | |
| 4000 | Minimum | S.F. | 0.10 | 0.08 | 0.18 |
| 4060 | Average | " | 0.12 | 0.08 | 0.20 |
| 4080 | Maximum | " | 0.13 | 0.08 | 0.21 |
| 4200 | Fences, Wood or Masonry | | | | |
| 4220 | Brush | | | | |
| 4240 | First Coat | | | | |
| 4260 | Minimum | S.F. | 0.46 | 0.16 | 0.62 |
| 4280 | Average | " | 0.55 | 0.16 | 0.71 |
| 4300 | Maximum | " | 0.74 | 0.16 | 0.90 |
| 4320 | Second Coat | | | | |
| 4340 | Minimum | S.F. | 0.27 | 0.16 | 0.43 |
| 4360 | Average | " | 0.34 | 0.16 | 0.50 |
| 4380 | Maximum | " | 0.44 | 0.16 | 0.60 |
| 4400 | Roller | | | | |
| 4420 | First Coat | | | | |
| 4440 | Minimum | S.F. | 0.24 | 0.16 | 0.40 |
| 4460 | Average | " | 0.29 | 0.16 | 0.45 |
| 4480 | Maximum | " | 0.34 | 0.16 | 0.50 |
| 4500 | Second Coat | | | | |
| 4520 | Minimum | S.F. | 0.17 | 0.16 | 0.33 |
| 4540 | Average | " | 0.21 | 0.16 | 0.37 |
| 4560 | Maximum | " | 0.27 | 0.16 | 0.43 |
| 4580 | Spray | | | | |
| 4600 | First Coat | | | | |
| 4620 | Minimum | S.F. | 0.15 | 0.13 | 0.28 |
| 4640 | Average | " | 0.20 | 0.13 | 0.33 |
| 4660 | Maximum | " | 0.27 | 0.13 | 0.40 |
| 4680 | Second Coat | | | | |
| 4700 | Minimum | S.F. | 0.11 | 0.13 | 0.24 |
| 4760 | Average | " | 0.13 | 0.13 | 0.26 |
| 4780 | Maximum | " | 0.18 | 0.13 | 0.31 |

## DIVISION # 09  FINISHES

### 09910.15  EXT. PAINTING, BUILDINGS

| | | UNIT | LABOR | MAT. | TOTAL |
|---|---|---|---|---|---|
| 1200 | Decks, Wood, Stained | | | | |
| 1580 | Spray | | | | |
| 1600 | First Coat | | | | |
| 1620 | Minimum | S.F. | 0.13 | 0.11 | 0.24 |
| 1640 | Average | " | 0.14 | 0.11 | 0.25 |
| 1660 | Maximum | " | 0.17 | 0.11 | 0.28 |
| 1680 | Second Coat | | | | |
| 1700 | Minimum | S.F. | 0.12 | 0.11 | 0.23 |
| 1720 | Average | " | 0.13 | 0.11 | 0.24 |
| 1740 | Maximum | " | 0.14 | 0.11 | 0.25 |
| 2520 | Doors, Wood | | | | |
| 2540 | Brush | | | | |
| 2560 | First Coat | | | | |
| 2580 | Minimum | S.F. | 0.68 | 0.13 | 0.81 |
| 2600 | Average | " | 0.89 | 0.13 | 1.02 |
| 2620 | Maximum | " | 1.11 | 0.13 | 1.24 |
| 2640 | Second Coat | | | | |
| 2660 | Minimum | S.F. | 0.55 | 0.13 | 0.68 |
| 2680 | Average | " | 0.63 | 0.13 | 0.76 |
| 2700 | Maximum | " | 0.74 | 0.13 | 0.87 |
| 3680 | Siding, Wood | | | | |
| 3880 | Spray | | | | |
| 3900 | First Coat | | | | |
| 3920 | Minimum | S.F. | 0.14 | 0.11 | 0.25 |
| 3940 | Average | " | 0.15 | 0.11 | 0.26 |
| 3960 | Maximum | " | 0.17 | 0.11 | 0.28 |
| 3980 | Second Coat | | | | |
| 4000 | Minimum | S.F. | 0.11 | 0.11 | 0.22 |
| 4020 | Average | " | 0.14 | 0.11 | 0.25 |
| 4040 | Maximum | " | 0.22 | 0.11 | 0.33 |
| 4440 | Trim | | | | |
| 4460 | Brush | | | | |
| 4480 | First Coat | | | | |
| 4500 | Minimum | L.F. | 0.18 | 0.16 | 0.34 |
| 4520 | Average | " | 0.22 | 0.16 | 0.38 |
| 4540 | Maximum | " | 0.27 | 0.16 | 0.43 |
| 4560 | Second Coat | | | | |
| 4580 | Minimum | L.F. | 0.13 | 0.16 | 0.29 |
| 4600 | Average | " | 0.18 | 0.16 | 0.34 |
| 4620 | Maximum | " | 0.27 | 0.16 | 0.43 |
| 4640 | Walls | | | | |
| 4840 | Spray | | | | |
| 4860 | First Coat | | | | |
| 4880 | Minimum | S.F. | 0.06 | 0.09 | 0.15 |
| 4900 | Average | " | 0.08 | 0.09 | 0.17 |
| 4920 | Maximum | " | 0.11 | 0.09 | 0.20 |
| 4940 | Second Coat | | | | |
| 4960 | Minimum | S.F. | 0.05 | 0.09 | 0.14 |
| 4980 | Average | " | 0.07 | 0.09 | 0.16 |
| 5000 | Maximum | " | 0.09 | 0.09 | 0.18 |
| 5020 | Windows | | | | |
| 5040 | Brush | | | | |

© 2011 By Design & Construction Resources

## DIVISION # 09  FINISHES

| | | UNIT | LABOR | MAT. | TOTAL |
|---|---|---|---|---|---|
| **09910.15** | **EXT. PAINTING, BUILDINGS, Cont'd...** | | | | |
| 5060 | First Coat | | | | |
| 5080 |   Minimum | S.F. | 0.74 | 0.11 | 0.85 |
| 5100 |   Average | " | 0.89 | 0.11 | 1.00 |
| 5120 |   Maximum | " | 1.11 | 0.11 | 1.22 |
| 5140 | Second Coat | | | | |
| 5160 |   Minimum | S.F. | 0.63 | 0.11 | 0.74 |
| 5180 |   Average | " | 0.74 | 0.11 | 0.85 |
| 5200 |   Maximum | " | 0.89 | 0.11 | 1.00 |
| **09910.35** | **INT. PAINTING, BUILDINGS** | | | | |
| 1380 | Cabinets and Casework | | | | |
| 1400 |   Brush | | | | |
| 1420 |     First Coat | | | | |
| 1440 |       Minimum | S.F. | 0.44 | 0.16 | 0.60 |
| 1460 |       Average | " | 0.49 | 0.16 | 0.65 |
| 1480 |       Maximum | " | 0.55 | 0.16 | 0.71 |
| 1500 |     Second Coat | | | | |
| 1520 |       Minimum | S.F. | 0.37 | 0.16 | 0.53 |
| 1540 |       Average | " | 0.40 | 0.16 | 0.56 |
| 1560 |       Maximum | " | 0.44 | 0.16 | 0.60 |
| 1580 |   Spray | | | | |
| 1600 |     First Coat | | | | |
| 1620 |       Minimum | S.F. | 0.22 | 0.13 | 0.35 |
| 1640 |       Average | " | 0.26 | 0.13 | 0.39 |
| 1660 |       Maximum | " | 0.31 | 0.13 | 0.44 |
| 1680 |     Second Coat | | | | |
| 1700 |       Minimum | S.F. | 0.17 | 0.13 | 0.30 |
| 1720 |       Average | " | 0.19 | 0.13 | 0.32 |
| 1740 |       Maximum | " | 0.24 | 0.13 | 0.37 |
| 2520 | Doors, Wood | | | | |
| 2540 |   Brush | | | | |
| 2560 |     First Coat | | | | |
| 2580 |       Minimum | S.F. | 0.63 | 0.16 | 0.79 |
| 2600 |       Average | " | 0.81 | 0.16 | 0.97 |
| 2620 |       Maximum | " | 0.99 | 0.16 | 1.15 |
| 2640 |     Second Coat | | | | |
| 2660 |       Minimum | S.F. | 0.49 | 0.12 | 0.61 |
| 2680 |       Average | " | 0.55 | 0.12 | 0.67 |
| 2700 |       Maximum | " | 0.63 | 0.12 | 0.75 |
| 2720 |   Spray | | | | |
| 2740 |     First Coat | | | | |
| 2760 |       Minimum | S.F. | 0.13 | 0.12 | 0.25 |
| 2780 |       Average | " | 0.15 | 0.12 | 0.27 |
| 2800 |       Maximum | " | 0.20 | 0.12 | 0.32 |
| 2820 |     Second Coat | | | | |
| 2840 |       Minimum | S.F. | 0.10 | 0.12 | 0.22 |
| 2860 |       Average | " | 0.12 | 0.12 | 0.24 |
| 2880 |       Maximum | " | 0.13 | 0.12 | 0.25 |
| 3900 | Trim | | | | |
| 3920 |   Brush | | | | |
| 3940 |     First Coat | | | | |
| 3960 |       Minimum | L.F. | 0.17 | 0.16 | 0.33 |

## DIVISION # 09 FINISHES

### 09910.35 INT. PAINTING, BUILDINGS, Cont'd...

| | | UNIT | LABOR | MAT. | TOTAL |
|---|---|---|---|---|---|
| 3980 | Average | L.F. | 0.20 | 0.16 | 0.36 |
| 4000 | Maximum | " | 0.24 | 0.16 | 0.40 |
| 4020 | Second Coat | | | | |
| 4040 | Minimum | L.F. | 0.13 | 0.16 | 0.29 |
| 4060 | Average | " | 0.17 | 0.16 | 0.33 |
| 4080 | Maximum | " | 0.24 | 0.16 | 0.40 |
| 4100 | Walls | | | | |
| 4120 | Roller | | | | |
| 4140 | First Coat | | | | |
| 4160 | Minimum | S.F. | 0.15 | 0.13 | 0.28 |
| 4180 | Average | " | 0.16 | 0.13 | 0.29 |
| 4200 | Maximum | " | 0.18 | 0.13 | 0.31 |
| 4220 | Second Coat | | | | |
| 4240 | Minimum | S.F. | 0.13 | 0.13 | 0.26 |
| 4260 | Average | " | 0.14 | 0.13 | 0.27 |
| 4280 | Maximum | " | 0.17 | 0.13 | 0.30 |
| 4300 | Spray | | | | |
| 4320 | First Coat | | | | |
| 4340 | Minimum | S.F. | 0.06 | 0.11 | 0.17 |
| 4360 | Average | " | 0.08 | 0.11 | 0.19 |
| 4380 | Maximum | " | 0.11 | 0.11 | 0.22 |
| 4400 | Second Coat | | | | |
| 4420 | Minimum | S.F. | 0.06 | 0.11 | 0.17 |
| 4440 | Average | " | 0.07 | 0.11 | 0.18 |
| 4460 | Maximum | " | 0.10 | 0.11 | 0.21 |

### 09955.10 WALL COVERING

| | | UNIT | LABOR | MAT. | TOTAL |
|---|---|---|---|---|---|
| 0900 | Vinyl wall covering | | | | |
| 1000 | Medium duty | S.F. | 0.63 | 0.82 | 1.45 |
| 1010 | Heavy duty | " | 0.74 | 1.70 | 2.44 |

**Design & Construction Resources**

# DIVISION # 10 SPECIALTIES

## TABLE OF CONTENTS — PAGE

| | |
|---|---|
| 10110.10 - CHALKBOARDS | 10-2 |
| 10165.10 - TOILET PARTITIONS | 10-2 |
| 10185.10 - SHOWER STALLS | 10-2 |
| 10290.10 - PEST CONTROL | 10-3 |
| 10350.10 - FLAGPOLES | 10-3 |
| 10400.10 - IDENTIFYING DEVICES | 10-3 |
| 10450.10 - CONTROL | 10-5 |
| 10500.10 - LOCKERS | 10-5 |
| 10520.10 - FIRE PROTECTION | 10-5 |
| 10550.10 - POSTAL SPECIALTIES | 10-6 |
| 10670.10 - SHELVING | 10-6 |
| 10800.10 - BATH ACCESSORIES | 10-6 |

*© 2011 By Design & Construction Resources*

## DIVISION # 10 SPECIALTIES

| | | UNIT | LABOR | MAT. | TOTAL |
|---|---|---|---|---|---|
| **10110.10** | **CHALKBOARDS** | | | | |
| 1020 | Chalkboard, metal frame, 1/4" thick | | | | |
| 1040 | 48"x60" | EA. | 53.00 | 380 | 433 |
| 1060 | 48"x96" | " | 59.00 | 520 | 579 |
| 1080 | 48"x144" | " | 67.00 | 690 | 757 |
| 1100 | 48"x192" | " | 76.00 | 930 | 1,006 |
| 1110 | Liquid chalkboard | | | | |
| 1120 | 48"x60" | EA. | 53.00 | 500 | 553 |
| 1140 | 48"x96" | " | 59.00 | 640 | 699 |
| 1160 | 48"x144" | " | 67.00 | 960 | 1,027 |
| 1180 | 48"x192" | " | 76.00 | 1,100 | 1,176 |
| 1200 | Map rail, deluxe | L.F. | 2.66 | 6.27 | 8.93 |
| **10165.10** | **TOILET PARTITIONS** | | | | |
| 0100 | Toilet partition, plastic laminate | | | | |
| 0120 | Ceiling mounted | EA. | 180 | 1,000 | 1,180 |
| 0140 | Floor mounted | " | 130 | 660 | 790 |
| 0150 | Metal | | | | |
| 0165 | Ceiling mounted | EA. | 180 | 700 | 880 |
| 0180 | Floor mounted | " | 130 | 670 | 800 |
| 0190 | Wheel chair partition, plastic laminate | | | | |
| 0200 | Ceiling mounted | EA. | 180 | 1,540 | 1,720 |
| 0210 | Floor mounted | " | 130 | 1,350 | 1,480 |
| 0215 | Painted metal | | | | |
| 0220 | Ceiling mounted | EA. | 180 | 1,100 | 1,280 |
| 0230 | Floor mounted | " | 130 | 1,000 | 1,130 |
| 1980 | Urinal screen, plastic laminate | | | | |
| 2000 | Wall hung | EA. | 67.00 | 480 | 547 |
| 2100 | Floor mounted | " | 67.00 | 430 | 497 |
| 2120 | Porcelain enameled steel, floor mounted | " | 67.00 | 550 | 617 |
| 2140 | Painted metal, floor mounted | " | 67.00 | 360 | 427 |
| 2160 | Stainless steel, floor mounted | " | 67.00 | 690 | 757 |
| 5000 | Metal toilet partitions | | | | |
| 5020 | Front door and side divider, floor mounted | | | | |
| 5040 | Porcelain enameled steel | EA. | 130 | 1,130 | 1,260 |
| 5060 | Painted steel | " | 130 | 670 | 800 |
| 5080 | Stainless steel | " | 130 | 1,810 | 1,940 |
| **10185.10** | **SHOWER STALLS** | | | | |
| 1000 | Shower receptors | | | | |
| 1010 | Precast, terrazzo | | | | |
| 1020 | 32" x 32" | EA. | 48.75 | 600 | 649 |
| 1040 | 32" x 48" | " | 59.00 | 630 | 689 |
| 1050 | Concrete | | | | |
| 1060 | 32" x 32" | EA. | 48.75 | 240 | 289 |
| 1080 | 48" x 48" | " | 65.00 | 260 | 325 |
| 1100 | Shower door, trim and hardware | | | | |
| 1130 | Porcelain enameled steel, flush | EA. | 59.00 | 500 | 559 |
| 1140 | Baked enameled steel, flush | " | 59.00 | 300 | 359 |
| 1150 | Aluminum, tempered glass, 48" wide, sliding | " | 73.00 | 620 | 693 |
| 1161 | Folding | " | 73.00 | 590 | 663 |
| 5400 | Shower compartment, precast concrete receptor | | | | |
| 5420 | Single entry type | | | | |
| 5440 | Porcelain enameled steel | EA. | 590 | 2,120 | 2,710 |

## DIVISION # 10 SPECIALTIES

|  |  | UNIT | LABOR | MAT. | TOTAL |
|---|---|---|---|---|---|
| **10185.10** | **SHOWER STALLS, Cont'd...** | | | | |
| 5460 | Baked enameled steel | EA. | 590 | 2,040 | 2,630 |
| 5480 | Stainless steel | " | 590 | 1,950 | 2,540 |
| 5500 | Double entry type | | | | |
| 5520 | Porcelain enameled steel | EA. | 730 | 3,780 | 4,510 |
| 5540 | Baked enameled steel | " | 730 | 2,590 | 3,320 |
| 5560 | Stainless steel | " | 730 | 4,180 | 4,910 |
| **10290.10** | **PEST CONTROL** | | | | |
| 1000 | Termite control | | | | |
| 1010 | Under slab spraying | | | | |
| 1020 | Minimum | S.F. | 0.10 | 1.10 | 1.20 |
| 1040 | Average | " | 0.20 | 1.10 | 1.30 |
| 1120 | Maximum | " | 0.41 | 1.59 | 2.00 |
| **10350.10** | **FLAGPOLES** | | | | |
| 2020 | Installed in concrete base | | | | |
| 2030 | Fiberglass | | | | |
| 2040 | 25' high | EA. | 360 | 1,420 | 1,780 |
| 2080 | 50' high | " | 890 | 3,760 | 4,650 |
| 2100 | Aluminum | | | | |
| 2120 | 25' high | EA. | 360 | 1,330 | 1,690 |
| 2140 | 50' high | " | 890 | 2,640 | 3,530 |
| 2160 | Bonderized steel | | | | |
| 2180 | 25' high | EA. | 410 | 1,490 | 1,900 |
| 2200 | 50' high | " | 1,070 | 2,990 | 4,060 |
| 2220 | Freestanding tapered, fiberglass | | | | |
| 2240 | 30' high | EA. | 380 | 1,690 | 2,070 |
| 2260 | 40' high | " | 490 | 2,200 | 2,690 |
| 2280 | 50' high | " | 530 | 5,610 | 6,140 |
| 2300 | 60' high | " | 630 | 6,000 | 6,630 |
| 2400 | Wall mounted, with collar, brushed aluminum finish | | | | |
| 2420 | 15' long | EA. | 270 | 1,270 | 1,540 |
| 2440 | 18' long | " | 270 | 1,430 | 1,700 |
| 2460 | 20' long | " | 280 | 1,560 | 1,840 |
| 2480 | 24' long | " | 310 | 1,680 | 1,990 |
| 2500 | Outrigger, wall, including base | | | | |
| 2520 | 10' long | EA. | 360 | 1,280 | 1,640 |
| 2540 | 20' long | " | 440 | 1,700 | 2,140 |
| **10400.10** | **IDENTIFYING DEVICES** | | | | |
| 1000 | Directory and bulletin boards | | | | |
| 1020 | Open face boards | | | | |
| 1040 | Chrome plated steel frame | S.F. | 26.75 | 32.00 | 58.75 |
| 1060 | Aluminum framed | " | 26.75 | 55.00 | 81.75 |
| 1080 | Bronze framed | " | 26.75 | 71.00 | 97.75 |
| 1100 | Stainless steel framed | " | 26.75 | 98.00 | 125 |
| 1140 | Tack board, aluminum framed | " | 26.75 | 22.50 | 49.25 |
| 1160 | Visual aid board, aluminum framed | " | 26.75 | 22.50 | 49.25 |
| 1200 | Glass encased boards, hinged and keyed | | | | |
| 1210 | Aluminum framed | S.F. | 67.00 | 120 | 187 |
| 1220 | Bronze framed | " | 67.00 | 140 | 207 |
| 1230 | Stainless steel framed | " | 67.00 | 180 | 247 |
| 1240 | Chrome plated steel framed | " | 67.00 | 190 | 257 |
| 2020 | Metal plaque | | | | |

*© 2011 By Design & Construction Resources*

## DIVISION # 10  SPECIALTIES

### 10400.10  IDENTIFYING DEVICES, Cont'd...

| | | UNIT | LABOR | MAT. | TOTAL |
|---|---|---|---|---|---|
| 2040 | Cast bronze | S.F. | 44.50 | 550 | 595 |
| 2060 | Aluminum | " | 44.50 | 310 | 355 |
| 2080 | Metal engraved plaque | | | | |
| 2100 | Porcelain steel | S.F. | 44.50 | 660 | 705 |
| 2120 | Stainless steel | " | 44.50 | 520 | 565 |
| 2140 | Brass | " | 44.50 | 780 | 825 |
| 2160 | Aluminum | " | 44.50 | 480 | 525 |
| 2200 | Metal built-up plaque | | | | |
| 2220 | Bronze | S.F. | 53.00 | 590 | 643 |
| 2240 | Copper and bronze | " | 53.00 | 520 | 573 |
| 2260 | Copper and aluminum | " | 53.00 | 580 | 633 |
| 2280 | Metal nameplate plaques | | | | |
| 2300 | Cast bronze | S.F. | 33.25 | 590 | 623 |
| 2320 | Cast aluminum | " | 33.25 | 430 | 463 |
| 2330 | Engraved, 1-1/2" x 6" | | | | |
| 2340 | Bronze | EA. | 33.25 | 250 | 283 |
| 2360 | Aluminum | " | 33.25 | 190 | 223 |
| 2440 | Letters, on masonry, aluminum, satin finish | | | | |
| 2450 | 1/2" thick | | | | |
| 2460 | 2" high | EA. | 21.25 | 23.75 | 45.00 |
| 2480 | 4" high | " | 26.75 | 35.25 | 62.00 |
| 2500 | 6" high | " | 29.75 | 47.25 | 77.00 |
| 2510 | 3/4" thick | | | | |
| 2520 | 8" high | EA. | 33.25 | 71.00 | 104 |
| 2540 | 10" high | " | 38.00 | 82.00 | 120 |
| 2550 | 1" thick | | | | |
| 2560 | 12" high | EA. | 44.50 | 92.00 | 137 |
| 2580 | 14" high | " | 53.00 | 100 | 153 |
| 2600 | 16" high | " | 67.00 | 130 | 197 |
| 2620 | For polished aluminum add, 15% | | | | |
| 2640 | For clear anodized aluminum add, 15% | | | | |
| 2660 | For colored anodic aluminum add, 30% | | | | |
| 2680 | For profiled and color enameled letters add, 50% | | | | |
| 2700 | Cast bronze, satin finish letters | | | | |
| 2710 | 3/8" thick | | | | |
| 2720 | 2" high | EA. | 21.25 | 27.00 | 48.25 |
| 2740 | 4" high | " | 26.75 | 40.25 | 67.00 |
| 2760 | 1/2" thick, 6" high | " | 29.75 | 55.00 | 84.75 |
| 2780 | 5/8" thick, 8" high | " | 33.25 | 82.00 | 115 |
| 2785 | 1" thick | | | | |
| 2790 | 10" high | EA. | 38.00 | 99.00 | 137 |
| 2800 | 12" high | " | 44.50 | 130 | 175 |
| 2820 | 14" high | " | 53.00 | 150 | 203 |
| 2840 | 16" high | " | 67.00 | 230 | 297 |
| 3000 | Interior door signs, adhesive, flexible | | | | |
| 3060 | 2" x 8" | EA. | 10.50 | 22.00 | 32.50 |
| 3080 | 4" x 4" | " | 10.50 | 23.25 | 33.75 |
| 3100 | 6" x 7" | " | 10.50 | 29.25 | 39.75 |
| 3120 | 6" x 9" | " | 10.50 | 37.50 | 48.00 |
| 3140 | 10" x 9" | " | 10.50 | 49.00 | 59.50 |
| 3160 | 10" x 12" | " | 10.50 | 64.00 | 74.50 |
| 3200 | Hard plastic type, no frame | | | | |

## DIVISION # 10  SPECIALTIES

| | | UNIT | LABOR | MAT. | TOTAL |
|---|---|---|---|---|---|
| **10400.10** | **IDENTIFYING DEVICES, Cont'd...** | | | | |
| 3220 | 3" x 8" | EA. | 10.50 | 48.75 | 59.25 |
| 3240 | 4" x 4" | " | 10.50 | 48.50 | 59.00 |
| 3260 | 4" x 12" | " | 10.50 | 53.00 | 63.50 |
| 3280 | Hard plastic type, with frame | | | | |
| 3300 | 3" x 8" | EA. | 10.50 | 150 | 161 |
| 3320 | 4" x 4" | " | 10.50 | 120 | 131 |
| 3340 | 4" x 12" | " | 10.50 | 180 | 191 |
| **10450.10** | **CONTROL** | | | | |
| 1020 | Access control, 7' high, indoor or outdoor impenetrability | | | | |
| 1040 | Remote or card control, type B | EA. | 730 | 1,630 | 2,360 |
| 1060 | Free passage, type B | " | 730 | 1,320 | 2,050 |
| 1080 | Remote or card control, type AA | " | 730 | 2,590 | 3,320 |
| 1100 | Free passage, type AA | " | 730 | 2,350 | 3,080 |
| **10500.10** | **LOCKERS** | | | | |
| 0080 | Locker bench, floor mounted, laminated maple | | | | |
| 0100 | 4' | EA. | 44.50 | 300 | 345 |
| 0120 | 6' | " | 44.50 | 420 | 465 |
| 0130 | Wardrobe locker, 12" x 60" x 15", baked on enamel | | | | |
| 0140 | 1-tier | EA. | 26.75 | 320 | 347 |
| 0160 | 2-tier | " | 26.75 | 340 | 367 |
| 0180 | 3-tier | " | 28.00 | 380 | 408 |
| 0200 | 4-tier | " | 28.00 | 410 | 438 |
| 0240 | 12" x 72" x 15", baked on enamel | | | | |
| 0260 | 1-tier | EA. | 26.75 | 270 | 297 |
| 0280 | 2-tier | " | 26.75 | 330 | 357 |
| 0300 | 4-tier | " | 28.00 | 410 | 438 |
| 0320 | 5-tier | " | 28.00 | 410 | 438 |
| 1200 | 15" x 60" x 15", baked on enamel | | | | |
| 1220 | 1-tier | EA. | 26.75 | 360 | 387 |
| 1240 | 4-tier | " | 28.00 | 390 | 418 |
| **10520.10** | **FIRE PROTECTION** | | | | |
| 1000 | Portable fire extinguishers | | | | |
| 1020 | Water pump tank type | | | | |
| 1030 | 2.5 gal. | | | | |
| 1040 | Red enameled galvanized | EA. | 28.00 | 120 | 148 |
| 1060 | Red enameled copper | " | 28.00 | 180 | 208 |
| 1080 | Polished copper | " | 28.00 | 240 | 268 |
| 1200 | Carbon dioxide type, red enamel steel | | | | |
| 1210 | Squeeze grip with hose and horn | | | | |
| 1220 | 2.5 lb | EA. | 28.00 | 190 | 218 |
| 1240 | 5 lb | " | 32.25 | 280 | 312 |
| 1260 | 10 lb | " | 41.75 | 280 | 322 |
| 1280 | 15 lb | " | 52.00 | 320 | 372 |
| 1300 | 20 lb | " | 52.00 | 390 | 442 |
| 1310 | Wheeled type | | | | |
| 1320 | 125 lb | EA. | 84.00 | 3,480 | 3,564 |
| 1340 | 250 lb | " | 84.00 | 4,400 | 4,484 |
| 1360 | 500 lb | " | 84.00 | 5,680 | 5,764 |
| 1400 | Dry chemical, pressurized type | | | | |
| 1405 | Red enameled steel | | | | |
| 1410 | 2.5 lb | EA. | 28.00 | 61.00 | 89.00 |

© 2011 By Design & Construction Resources

## DIVISION # 10 SPECIALTIES

| | | UNIT | LABOR | MAT. | TOTAL |
|---|---|---|---|---|---|
| **10520.10** | **FIRE PROTECTION, Cont'd...** | | | | |
| 1430 | 5 lb | EA. | 32.25 | 83.00 | 115 |
| 1440 | 10 lb | " | 41.75 | 170 | 212 |
| 1450 | 20 lb | " | 52.00 | 220 | 272 |
| 1460 | 30 lb | " | 52.00 | 280 | 332 |
| 1480 | Chrome plated steel, 2.5 lb | " | 28.00 | 260 | 288 |
| **10550.10** | **POSTAL SPECIALTIES** | | | | |
| 1500 | Mail chutes | | | | |
| 1520 | Single mail chute | | | | |
| 1530 | Finished aluminum | L.F. | 130 | 740 | 870 |
| 1540 | Bronze | " | 130 | 1,030 | 1,160 |
| 1560 | Single mail chute receiving box | | | | |
| 1580 | Finished aluminum | EA. | 270 | 1,100 | 1,370 |
| 1600 | Bronze | " | 270 | 1,320 | 1,590 |
| 1620 | Twin mail chute, double parallel | | | | |
| 1630 | Finished aluminum | FLR | 270 | 1,620 | 1,890 |
| 1640 | Bronze | " | 270 | 2,120 | 2,390 |
| **10670.10** | **SHELVING** | | | | |
| 0980 | Shelving, enamel, closed side and back, 12" x 36" | | | | |
| 1000 | 5 shelves | EA. | 89.00 | 260 | 349 |
| 1020 | 8 shelves | " | 120 | 280 | 400 |
| 1030 | Open | | | | |
| 1040 | 5 shelves | EA. | 89.00 | 130 | 219 |
| 1060 | 8 shelves | " | 120 | 150 | 270 |
| 2000 | Metal storage shelving, baked enamel | | | | |
| 2030 | 7 shelf unit, 72" or 84" high | | | | |
| 2050 | 12" shelf | L.F. | 56.00 | 41.75 | 97.75 |
| 2080 | 24" shelf | " | 67.00 | 85.00 | 152 |
| 2100 | 36" shelf | " | 76.00 | 99.00 | 175 |
| 2200 | 4 shelf unit, 40" high | | | | |
| 2240 | 12" shelf | L.F. | 48.50 | 55.00 | 104 |
| 2270 | 24" shelf | " | 59.00 | 110 | 169 |
| 2300 | 3 shelf unit, 32" high | | | | |
| 2340 | 12" shelf | L.F. | 28.00 | 44.00 | 72.00 |
| 2370 | 24" shelf | " | 33.25 | 55.00 | 88.25 |
| 2400 | Single shelf unit, attached to masonry | | | | |
| 2420 | 12" shelf | L.F. | 9.70 | 17.00 | 26.70 |
| 2450 | 24" shelf | " | 11.50 | 24.25 | 35.75 |
| 2460 | For stainless steel, add to material, 120% | | | | |
| 2470 | For attachment to gypsum board, add to labor, 50% | | | | |
| **10800.10** | **BATH ACCESSORIES** | | | | |
| 1040 | Ash receiver, wall mounted, aluminum | EA. | 26.75 | 140 | 167 |
| 1050 | Grab bar, 1-1/2" dia., stainless steel, wall mounted | | | | |
| 1060 | 24" long | EA. | 26.75 | 44.00 | 70.75 |
| 1080 | 36" long | " | 28.00 | 49.50 | 77.50 |
| 1100 | 48" long | " | 31.50 | 61.00 | 92.50 |
| 1130 | 1" dia., stainless steel | | | | |
| 1140 | 12" long | EA. | 23.25 | 27.50 | 50.75 |
| 1180 | 24" long | " | 26.75 | 37.50 | 64.25 |
| 1220 | 36" long | " | 29.75 | 49.50 | 79.25 |
| 1240 | 48" long | " | 31.50 | 55.00 | 86.50 |
| 1300 | Hand dryer, surface mounted, 110 volt | " | 67.00 | 630 | 697 |

© 2011 By Design & Construction Resources

## DIVISION # 10 SPECIALTIES

### 10800.10 BATH ACCESSORIES, Cont'd...

| | | UNIT | LABOR | MAT. | TOTAL |
|---|---|---|---|---|---|
| 1320 | Medicine cabinet, 16 x 22, baked enamel, lighted | EA. | 21.25 | 130 | 151 |
| 1340 | With mirror, lighted | " | 35.50 | 190 | 226 |
| 1420 | Mirror, 1/4" plate glass, up to 10 sf | S.F. | 5.33 | 10.00 | 15.33 |
| 1430 | Mirror, stainless steel frame | | | | |
| 1440 | 18"x24" | EA. | 17.75 | 77.00 | 94.75 |
| 1500 | 24"x30" | " | 26.75 | 94.00 | 121 |
| 1520 | 24"x48" | " | 44.50 | 140 | 185 |
| 1560 | 30"x30" | " | 53.00 | 310 | 363 |
| 1600 | 48"x72" | " | 89.00 | 600 | 689 |
| 1640 | With shelf, 18"x24" | " | 21.25 | 240 | 261 |
| 1820 | Sanitary napkin dispenser, stainless steel | " | 35.50 | 570 | 606 |
| 1830 | Shower rod, 1" diameter | | | | |
| 1840 | Chrome finish over brass | EA. | 26.75 | 210 | 237 |
| 1860 | Stainless steel | " | 26.75 | 140 | 167 |
| 1900 | Soap dish, stainless steel, wall mounted | " | 35.50 | 130 | 166 |
| 1910 | Toilet tissue dispenser, stainless, wall mounted | | | | |
| 1920 | Single roll | EA. | 13.25 | 61.00 | 74.25 |
| 1940 | Double roll | " | 15.25 | 120 | 135 |
| 1945 | Towel dispenser, stainless steel | | | | |
| 1950 | Flush mounted | EA. | 29.75 | 240 | 270 |
| 1960 | Surface mounted | " | 26.75 | 340 | 367 |
| 1970 | Combination towel and waste receptacle | " | 35.50 | 510 | 546 |
| 2000 | Towel bar, stainless steel | | | | |
| 2020 | 18" long | EA. | 21.25 | 76.00 | 97.25 |
| 2040 | 24" long | " | 24.25 | 100 | 124 |
| 2060 | 30" long | " | 26.75 | 110 | 137 |
| 2070 | 36" long | " | 29.75 | 120 | 150 |
| 2100 | Waste receptacle, stainless steel, wall mounted | " | 44.50 | 390 | 435 |

© 2011 By Design & Construction Resources

**Design & Construction Resources**

# DIVISION # 11  EQUIPMENT

## TABLE OF CONTENTS — PAGE

| | |
|---|---|
| 11010.10 - MAINTENANCE EQUIPMENT | 11-2 |
| 11060.10 - THEATER EQUIPMENT | 11-2 |
| 11090.10 - CHECKROOM EQUIPMENT | 11-2 |
| 11110.10 - LAUNDRY EQUIPMENT | 11-2 |
| 11161.10 - LOADING DOCK EQUIPMENT | 11-2 |
| 11170.10 - WASTE HANDLING | 11-3 |
| 11170.20 - AERATION EQUIPMENT | 11-3 |
| 11400.10 - FOOD SERVICE EQUIPMENT | 11-3 |
| 11450.10 - RESIDENTIAL EQUIPMENT | 11-5 |
| 11600.10 - LABORATORY EQUIPMENT | 11-6 |
| 11700.10 - MEDICAL EQUIPMENT | 11-6 |

© 2011 By Design & Construction Resources

## DIVISION # 11 EQUIPMENT

| | | UNIT | LABOR | MAT. | TOTAL |
|---|---|---|---|---|---|
| **11010.10** | **MAINTENANCE EQUIPMENT** | | | | |
| 1000 | Vacuum cleaning system | | | | |
| 1010 | 3 valves | | | | |
| 1020 | 1.5 hp | EA. | 590 | 920 | 1,510 |
| 1030 | 2.5 hp | " | 760 | 1,100 | 1,860 |
| 1040 | 5 valves | " | 1,070 | 1,720 | 2,790 |
| 1060 | 7 valves | " | 1,330 | 2,290 | 3,620 |
| **11060.10** | **THEATER EQUIPMENT** | | | | |
| 1000 | Roll out stage, steel frame, wood floor | | | | |
| 1020 | Manual | S.F. | 3.33 | 52.00 | 55.33 |
| 1040 | Electric | " | 5.33 | 49.50 | 54.83 |
| 1100 | Portable stages | | | | |
| 1120 | 8" high | S.F. | 2.66 | 20.25 | 22.91 |
| 1140 | 18" high | " | 2.96 | 23.75 | 26.71 |
| 1160 | 36" high | " | 3.13 | 27.50 | 30.63 |
| 1180 | 48" high | " | 3.33 | 30.75 | 34.08 |
| 1300 | Band risers | | | | |
| 1320 | Minimum | S.F. | 2.66 | 53.00 | 55.66 |
| 1340 | Maximum | " | 2.66 | 110 | 113 |
| 1400 | Chairs for risers | | | | |
| 1420 | Minimum | EA. | 1.90 | 690 | 692 |
| 1440 | Maximum | " | 1.90 | 1,100 | 1,102 |
| 2000 | Theatre controlls | | | | |
| 2010 | Fade console, 48 channel | EA. | 270 | 2,750 | 3,020 |
| 2020 | Light control modules, 125 channels | " | 540 | 7,810 | 8,350 |
| 2030 | Dimmer module, stage-pin output | " | 270 | 2,400 | 2,670 |
| 2040 | 6-Module pack, w/24 U-ground connectors | " | 270 | 6,860 | 7,130 |
| **11090.10** | **CHECKROOM EQUIPMENT** | | | | |
| 1000 | Motorized checkroom equipment | | | | |
| 1020 | No shelf system, 6'4" height | | | | |
| 1040 | 7'6" length | EA. | 530 | 4,750 | 5,280 |
| 1060 | 14'6" length | " | 530 | 4,810 | 5,340 |
| 1080 | 28' length | " | 530 | 5,790 | 6,320 |
| 1100 | One shelf, 6'8" height | | | | |
| 1120 | 7'6" length | EA. | 530 | 5,820 | 6,350 |
| 1140 | 14'6" length | " | 530 | 5,980 | 6,510 |
| 1160 | 28' length | " | 530 | 7,190 | 7,720 |
| **11110.10** | **LAUNDRY EQUIPMENT** | | | | |
| 1000 | High capacity, heavy duty | | | | |
| 1020 | Washer extractors | | | | |
| 1030 | 135 lb | | | | |
| 1040 | Standard | EA. | 440 | 32,600 | 33,040 |
| 1060 | Pass through | " | 440 | 37,470 | 37,910 |
| 1070 | 200 lb | | | | |
| 1080 | Standard | EA. | 440 | 40,040 | 40,480 |
| 1100 | Pass through | " | 440 | 48,620 | 49,060 |
| 1120 | 110 lb dryer | " | 440 | 12,270 | 12,710 |
| **11161.10** | **LOADING DOCK EQUIPMENT** | | | | |
| 0080 | Dock leveler, 10 ton capacity | | | | |
| 0100 | 6' x 8' | EA. | 530 | 5,050 | 5,580 |
| 0120 | 7' x 8' | " | 530 | 5,800 | 6,330 |

# DIVISION # 11 EQUIPMENT

| | | UNIT | LABOR | MAT. | TOTAL |
|---|---|---|---|---|---|
| **11170.10** | **WASTE HANDLING** | | | | |
| 1500 | Industrial compactor | | | | |
| 1520 | 1 cy | EA. | 600 | 12,980 | 13,580 |
| 1540 | 3 cy | " | 780 | 20,240 | 21,020 |
| 1560 | 5 cy | " | 1,090 | 38,500 | 39,590 |
| **11170.20** | **AERATION EQUIPMENT** | | | | |
| 0010 | Surface spray/Vertical pump | | | | |
| 0020 | 1 hp. Pump, 500 gpm. | EA. | 290 | 4,830 | 5,120 |
| 0030 | 5 hp. Pump, 2000 gpm. | " | 1,170 | 7,240 | 8,410 |
| 0040 | Polycarbon, treatment container, 1,000 gallon capacity | " | 2,270 | 3,740 | 6,010 |
| 0050 | 1,500 gallon | " | 2,270 | 4,290 | 6,560 |
| 0060 | 2,000 gallon | " | 2,840 | 5,980 | 8,820 |
| 0070 | 3,000 gallon | " | 3,020 | 9,500 | 12,520 |
| **11400.10** | **FOOD SERVICE EQUIPMENT** | | | | |
| 1000 | Unit kitchens | | | | |
| 1020 | 30" compact kitchen | | | | |
| 1040 | Refrigerator, with range, sink | EA. | 270 | 1,280 | 1,550 |
| 1060 | Sink only | " | 180 | 1,630 | 1,810 |
| 1080 | Range only | " | 140 | 1,330 | 1,470 |
| 1100 | Cabinet for upper wall section | " | 78.00 | 330 | 408 |
| 1120 | Stainless shield, for rear wall | " | 21.75 | 130 | 152 |
| 1140 | Side wall | " | 21.75 | 98.00 | 120 |
| 1200 | 42" compact kitchen | | | | |
| 1220 | Refrigerator with range, sink | EA. | 300 | 1,560 | 1,860 |
| 1240 | Sink only | " | 270 | 850 | 1,120 |
| 1260 | Cabinet for upper wall section | " | 91.00 | 660 | 751 |
| 1280 | Stainless shield, for rear wall | " | 22.75 | 530 | 553 |
| 1290 | Side wall | " | 22.75 | 150 | 173 |
| 1600 | Bake oven | | | | |
| 1610 | Single deck | | | | |
| 1620 | Minimum | EA. | 68.00 | 3,030 | 3,098 |
| 1640 | Maximum | " | 140 | 5,780 | 5,920 |
| 1650 | Double deck | | | | |
| 1660 | Minimum | EA. | 91.00 | 5,390 | 5,481 |
| 1680 | Maximum | " | 140 | 16,840 | 16,980 |
| 1685 | Triple deck | | | | |
| 1690 | Minimum | EA. | 91.00 | 19,110 | 19,201 |
| 1695 | Maximum | " | 180 | 34,100 | 34,280 |
| 1700 | Convection type oven, electric, 40" x 45" x 57" | | | | |
| 1720 | Minimum | EA. | 68.00 | 2,980 | 3,048 |
| 1740 | Maximum | " | 140 | 5,250 | 5,390 |
| 1800 | Broiler, without oven, 69" x 26" x 39" | | | | |
| 1820 | Minimum | EA. | 68.00 | 4,750 | 4,818 |
| 1840 | Maximum | " | 91.00 | 7,470 | 7,561 |
| 1900 | Coffee urns, 10 gallons | | | | |
| 1920 | Minimum | EA. | 180 | 3,620 | 3,800 |
| 1940 | Maximum | " | 270 | 4,090 | 4,360 |
| 2000 | Fryer, with submerger | | | | |
| 2010 | Single | | | | |
| 2020 | Minimum | EA. | 110 | 1,480 | 1,590 |
| 2040 | Maximum | " | 180 | 4,070 | 4,250 |
| 2050 | Double | | | | |

© 2011 By Design & Construction Resources

## DIVISION # 11 EQUIPMENT

### 11400.10 FOOD SERVICE EQUIPMENT, Cont'd...

| Code | Description | UNIT | LABOR | MAT. | TOTAL |
|---|---|---|---|---|---|
| 2060 | Minimum | EA. | 140 | 2,460 | 2,600 |
| 2080 | Maximum | " | 180 | 13,180 | 13,360 |
| 2100 | Griddle, counter | | | | |
| 2110 | 3' long | | | | |
| 2120 | Minimum | EA. | 91.00 | 2,030 | 2,121 |
| 2140 | Maximum | " | 110 | 4,180 | 4,290 |
| 2150 | 5' long | | | | |
| 2160 | Minimum | EA. | 140 | 4,400 | 4,540 |
| 2180 | Maximum | " | 180 | 10,140 | 10,320 |
| 2200 | Kettles, steam, jacketed | | | | |
| 2210 | 20 gallons | | | | |
| 2220 | Minimum | EA. | 140 | 9,680 | 9,820 |
| 2240 | Maximum | " | 270 | 10,580 | 10,850 |
| 2300 | Range | | | | |
| 2310 | Heavy duty, single oven, open top | | | | |
| 2320 | Minimum | EA. | 68.00 | 6,240 | 6,308 |
| 2340 | Maximum | " | 180 | 13,140 | 13,320 |
| 2350 | Fry top | | | | |
| 2360 | Minimum | EA. | 68.00 | 6,380 | 6,448 |
| 2380 | Maximum | " | 180 | 8,930 | 9,110 |
| 2400 | Steamers, electric | | | | |
| 2410 | 27 kw | | | | |
| 2420 | Minimum | EA. | 140 | 11,330 | 11,470 |
| 2440 | Maximum | " | 180 | 20,710 | 20,890 |
| 2450 | 18 kw | | | | |
| 2460 | Minimum | EA. | 140 | 6,240 | 6,380 |
| 2480 | Maximum | " | 180 | 14,630 | 14,810 |
| 2500 | Dishwasher, rack type | | | | |
| 2520 | Single tank, 190 racks/hr | EA. | 270 | 16,610 | 16,880 |
| 2530 | Double tank | | | | |
| 2540 | 234 racks/hr | EA. | 300 | 34,300 | 34,600 |
| 2560 | 265 racks/hr | " | 360 | 41,000 | 41,360 |
| 2580 | Dishwasher, automatic 100 meals/hr | " | 180 | 13,340 | 13,520 |
| 2600 | Disposals | | | | |
| 2620 | 100 gal/hr | EA. | 180 | 1,110 | 1,290 |
| 2640 | 120 gal/hr | " | 190 | 1,290 | 1,480 |
| 2660 | 250 gal/hr | " | 190 | 1,520 | 1,710 |
| 2680 | Exhaust hood for dishwasher, gutter 4 sides | | | | |
| 2681 | 4'x4'x2' | EA. | 200 | 2,700 | 2,900 |
| 2690 | 4'x7'x2' | " | 220 | 3,660 | 3,880 |
| 2900 | Ice cube maker | | | | |
| 2910 | 50 lb per day | | | | |
| 2920 | Minimum | EA. | 540 | 2,090 | 2,630 |
| 2940 | Maximum | " | 540 | 3,080 | 3,620 |
| 2950 | 500 lb per day | | | | |
| 2960 | Minimum | EA. | 910 | 4,950 | 5,860 |
| 2970 | Maximum | " | 910 | 5,850 | 6,760 |
| 3100 | Refrigerated cases | | | | |
| 3120 | Dairy products | | | | |
| 3140 | Multi deck type | L.F. | 36.25 | 1,160 | 1,196 |
| 3160 | For rear sliding doors, add | " | | | 220 |
| 3180 | Delicatessen case, service deli | | | | |

# DIVISION # 11 EQUIPMENT

| | | UNIT | LABOR | MAT. | TOTAL |
|---|---|---|---|---|---|
| **11400.10** | **FOOD SERVICE EQUIPMENT, Cont'd...** | | | | |
| 3190 | Single deck | L.F. | 270 | 830 | 1,100 |
| 3200 | Multi deck | " | 340 | 940 | 1,280 |
| 3220 | Meat case | | | | |
| 3230 | Single deck | L.F. | 320 | 710 | 1,030 |
| 3240 | Multi deck | " | 340 | 830 | 1,170 |
| 3260 | Produce case | | | | |
| 3270 | Single deck | L.F. | 320 | 820 | 1,140 |
| 3280 | Multi deck | " | 340 | 880 | 1,220 |
| 3300 | Bottle coolers | | | | |
| 3310 | 6' long | | | | |
| 3320 | Minimum | EA. | 1,090 | 2,380 | 3,470 |
| 3340 | Maximum | " | 1,090 | 3,520 | 4,610 |
| 3345 | 10' long | | | | |
| 3350 | Minimum | EA. | 1,810 | 3,080 | 4,890 |
| 3360 | Maximum | " | 1,810 | 6,050 | 7,860 |
| 3420 | Frozen food cases | | | | |
| 3440 | Chest type | L.F. | 320 | 630 | 950 |
| 3460 | Reach-in, glass door | " | 340 | 870 | 1,210 |
| 3470 | Island case, single | " | 320 | 780 | 1,100 |
| 3480 | Multi deck | " | 340 | 1,240 | 1,580 |
| 3500 | Ice storage bins | | | | |
| 3520 | 500 lb capacity | EA. | 780 | 1,320 | 2,100 |
| 3530 | 1000 lb capacity | " | 1,550 | 1,980 | 3,530 |
| **11450.10** | **RESIDENTIAL EQUIPMENT** | | | | |
| 0300 | Compactor, 4 to 1 compaction | EA. | 140 | 1,320 | 1,460 |
| 1310 | Dishwasher, built-in | | | | |
| 1320 | 2 cycles | EA. | 270 | 650 | 920 |
| 1330 | 4 or more cycles | " | 270 | 1,760 | 2,030 |
| 1340 | Disposal | | | | |
| 1350 | Garbage disposer | EA. | 180 | 180 | 360 |
| 1360 | Heaters, electric, built-in | | | | |
| 1362 | Ceiling type | EA. | 180 | 370 | 550 |
| 1364 | Wall type | | | | |
| 1370 | Minimum | EA. | 140 | 190 | 330 |
| 1374 | Maximum | " | 180 | 650 | 830 |
| 1400 | Hood for range, 2-speed, vented | | | | |
| 1420 | 30" wide | EA. | 180 | 520 | 700 |
| 1440 | 42" wide | " | 180 | 950 | 1,130 |
| 1460 | Ice maker, automatic | | | | |
| 1480 | 30 lb per day | EA. | 78.00 | 1,740 | 1,818 |
| 1500 | 50 lb per day | " | 270 | 2,200 | 2,470 |
| 2000 | Ranges electric | | | | |
| 2040 | Built-in, 30", 1 oven | EA. | 180 | 1,900 | 2,080 |
| 2050 | 2 oven | " | 180 | 2,200 | 2,380 |
| 2060 | Counter top, 4 burner, standard | " | 140 | 1,100 | 1,240 |
| 2070 | With grill | " | 140 | 2,750 | 2,890 |
| 2198 | Free standing, 21", 1 oven | " | 180 | 990 | 1,170 |
| 2200 | 30", 1 oven | " | 110 | 1,930 | 2,040 |
| 2220 | 2 oven | " | 110 | 3,140 | 3,250 |
| 3600 | Water softener | | | | |
| 3620 | 30 grains per gallon | EA. | 180 | 1,070 | 1,250 |

© 2011 By Design & Construction Resources

## DIVISION # 11 EQUIPMENT

| | | UNIT | LABOR | MAT. | TOTAL |
|---|---|---|---|---|---|
| **11450.10** | **RESIDENTIAL EQUIPMENT, Cont'd...** | | | | |
| 3640 | 70 grains per gallon | EA. | 270 | 1,360 | 1,630 |
| **11600.10** | **LABORATORY EQUIPMENT** | | | | |
| 1000 | Cabinets, base | | | | |
| 1020 | Minimum | L.F. | 44.50 | 400 | 445 |
| 1040 | Maximum | " | 44.50 | 730 | 775 |
| 1080 | Full storage, 7' high | | | | |
| 1100 | Minimum | L.F. | 44.50 | 390 | 435 |
| 1140 | Maximum | " | 44.50 | 740 | 785 |
| 1150 | Wall | | | | |
| 1160 | Minimum | L.F. | 53.00 | 140 | 193 |
| 1200 | Maximum | " | 53.00 | 250 | 303 |
| 1220 | Counter tops | | | | |
| 1240 | Minimum | S.F. | 6.67 | 61.00 | 67.67 |
| 1260 | Average | " | 7.62 | 72.00 | 79.62 |
| 1280 | Maximum | " | 8.89 | 83.00 | 91.89 |
| 1300 | Tables | | | | |
| 1320 | Open underneath | S.F. | 26.75 | 130 | 157 |
| 1330 | Doors underneath | " | 33.25 | 440 | 473 |
| 2000 | Medical laboratory equipment | | | | |
| 2010 | Analyzer | | | | |
| 2020 | Chloride | EA. | 27.25 | 4,800 | 4,827 |
| 2060 | Blood | " | 45.25 | 26,400 | 26,445 |
| 2070 | Bath, water, utility, countertop unit | " | 54.00 | 990 | 1,044 |
| 2080 | Hot plate, lab, countertop | " | 49.50 | 380 | 430 |
| 2100 | Stirrer | " | 49.50 | 460 | 510 |
| 2120 | Incubator, anaerobic, 23x23x36" | " | 270 | 8,140 | 8,410 |
| 2140 | Dry heat bath | " | 91.00 | 880 | 971 |
| 2160 | Incinerator, for sterilizing | " | 5.44 | 600 | 605 |
| 2170 | Meter, serum protein | " | 6.80 | 930 | 937 |
| 2180 | Ph analog, general purpose | " | 7.77 | 1,010 | 1,018 |
| 2190 | Refrigerator, blood bank, undercounter type 153 litres | " | 91.00 | 7,700 | 7,791 |
| 2200 | 5.4 cf, undercounter type | " | 91.00 | 5,230 | 5,321 |
| 2210 | Refrigerator/freezer, 4.4 cf, undercounter type | " | 91.00 | 990 | 1,081 |
| 2220 | Sealer, impulse, free standing, 20x12x4" | " | 18.25 | 550 | 568 |
| 2240 | Timer, electric, 1-60 minutes, bench or wall mounted | " | 30.25 | 210 | 240 |
| 2260 | Glassware washer - dryer, undercounter | " | 680 | 9,110 | 9,790 |
| 2300 | Balance, torsion suspension, tabletop, 4.5 lb capacity | " | 30.25 | 1,200 | 1,230 |
| 2340 | Binocular microscope, with in base illuminator | " | 21.00 | 3,660 | 3,681 |
| 2400 | Centrifuge, table model, 19x16x13" | " | 21.75 | 1,400 | 1,422 |
| 2420 | Clinical model, with four place head | " | 12.00 | 1,520 | 1,532 |
| **11700.10** | **MEDICAL EQUIPMENT** | | | | |
| 1000 | Hospital equipment, lights | | | | |
| 1020 | Examination, portable | EA. | 45.25 | 1,650 | 1,695 |
| 1200 | Meters | | | | |
| 1220 | Air flow meter | EA. | 30.25 | 94.00 | 124 |
| 1240 | Oxygen flow meters | " | 22.75 | 110 | 133 |
| 1900 | Physical therapy | | | | |
| 1930 | Chair, hydrotherapy | EA. | 8.89 | 640 | 649 |
| 1940 | Diathermy, shortwave, portable, on casters | " | 21.25 | 2,750 | 2,771 |
| 1950 | Exercise bicycle, floor standing, 35" x 15" | " | 17.75 | 2,670 | 2,688 |
| 1960 | Hydrocollator, 4 pack, portable, 129 x 90 x 160" | " | 7.62 | 480 | 488 |

## DIVISION # 11 EQUIPMENT

| | | UNIT | LABOR | MAT. | TOTAL |
|---|---|---|---|---|---|
| **11700.10** | **MEDICAL EQUIPMENT, Cont'd...** | | | | |
| 1970 | Lamp, infrared, mobile with variable heat control | EA. | 41.00 | 650 | 691 |
| 1980 | Ultra violet, base mounted | " | 41.00 | 600 | 641 |
| 2070 | Stimulator, galvanic-faradic, hand held | " | 3.55 | 330 | 334 |
| 2080 | Ultrasound, stimulator, portable, 13x13x8" | " | 4.44 | 2,860 | 2,864 |
| 2120 | Whirlpool, 85 gallon | " | 270 | 5,480 | 5,750 |
| 2141 | 65 gallon capacity | " | 270 | 4,950 | 5,220 |
| 2200 | Radiology | | | | |
| 2280 | Radiographic table, motor driven tilting table | EA. | 5,340 | 48,400 | 53,740 |
| 2290 | Fluoroscope image/tv system | " | 10,670 | 80,300 | 90,970 |
| 2300 | Processor for washing and drying radiographs | | | | |
| 2303 | Water filter unit, 30" x 48-1/2" x 37-1/2" | EA. | 910 | 110 | 1,020 |
| 2400 | Steam sterilizers | | | | |
| 2410 | For heat and moisture stable materials | EA. | 54.00 | 4,670 | 4,724 |
| 2440 | For fast drying after sterilization | " | 68.00 | 6,050 | 6,118 |
| 2450 | Compact unit | " | 68.00 | 1,960 | 2,028 |
| 2460 | Semi-automatic | " | 270 | 2,310 | 2,580 |
| 2465 | Floor loading | | | | |
| 2470 | Single door | EA. | 450 | 68,530 | 68,980 |
| 2480 | Double door | " | 540 | 75,080 | 75,620 |
| 2490 | Utensil washer, sanitizer | " | 420 | 15,070 | 15,490 |
| 2500 | Automatic washer/sterilizer | " | 1,090 | 16,500 | 17,590 |
| 2510 | 16 x 16 x 26", including accessories | " | 1,810 | 18,960 | 20,770 |
| 2520 | Steam generator, elec., 10 kw to 180 kw | " | 1,090 | 31,350 | 32,440 |
| 2540 | Surgical scrub | | | | |
| 2560 | Minimum | EA. | 180 | 1,650 | 1,830 |
| 2580 | Maximum | " | 180 | 9,580 | 9,760 |
| 2600 | Gas sterilizers | | | | |
| 2620 | Automatic, free standing, 21x19x29" | EA. | 540 | 5,890 | 6,430 |
| 2720 | Surgical lights, ceiling mounted | | | | |
| 2740 | Minimum | EA. | 910 | 8,140 | 9,050 |
| 2760 | Maximum | " | 1,090 | 16,610 | 17,700 |
| 2800 | Water stills | | | | |
| 2900 | 4 liters/hr | EA. | 180 | 3,690 | 3,870 |
| 2920 | 8 liters/hr | " | 180 | 5,890 | 6,070 |
| 2940 | 19 liters/hr | " | 450 | 12,100 | 12,550 |
| 3060 | X-ray equipment | | | | |
| 3070 | Mobile unit | | | | |
| 3080 | Minimum | EA. | 270 | 10,770 | 11,040 |
| 3100 | Maximum | " | 540 | 20,870 | 21,410 |
| 3200 | Autopsy table | | | | |
| 3220 | Minimum | EA. | 540 | 15,030 | 15,570 |
| 3240 | Maximum | " | 540 | 21,250 | 21,790 |
| 3300 | Incubators | | | | |
| 3320 | 15 cf | EA. | 270 | 7,500 | 7,770 |
| 3330 | 29 cf | " | 450 | 10,170 | 10,620 |
| 3340 | Infant transport, portable | " | 290 | 5,650 | 5,940 |
| 3460 | Headwall | | | | |
| 3465 | Aluminum, with back frame and console | EA. | 270 | 4,290 | 4,560 |
| 6000 | Hospital ground detection system | | | | |
| 6010 | Power ground module | EA. | 160 | 1,320 | 1,480 |
| 6020 | Ground slave module | " | 120 | 560 | 680 |
| 6030 | Master ground module | " | 100 | 500 | 600 |

© 2011 By Design & Construction Resources

## DIVISION # 11 EQUIPMENT

### 11700.10 MEDICAL EQUIPMENT, Cont'd...

| Code | Description | UNIT | LABOR | MAT. | TOTAL |
|---|---|---|---|---|---|
| 6040 | Remote indicator | EA. | 110 | 520 | 630 |
| 6050 | X-ray indicator | " | 120 | 1,480 | 1,600 |
| 6060 | Micro ammeter | " | 140 | 1,760 | 1,900 |
| 6070 | Supervisory module | " | 120 | 1,480 | 1,600 |
| 6080 | Ground cords | " | 20.25 | 140 | 160 |
| 6100 | Hospital isolation monitors, 5 ma | | | | |
| 6110 | 120v | EA. | 240 | 3,040 | 3,280 |
| 6120 | 208v | " | 240 | 2,810 | 3,050 |
| 6130 | 240v | " | 240 | 2,810 | 3,050 |
| 6210 | Digital clock-timers separate display | " | 110 | 1,240 | 1,350 |
| 6220 | One display | " | 110 | 790 | 900 |
| 6230 | Remote control | " | 85.00 | 390 | 475 |
| 6240 | Battery pack | " | 85.00 | 94.00 | 179 |
| 6310 | Surgical chronometer clock and 3 timers | " | 170 | 2,310 | 2,480 |
| 6320 | Auxilary control | " | 79.00 | 630 | 709 |

# DIVISION # 12  FURNISHINGS

## TABLE OF CONTENTS    PAGE

| | |
|---|---|
| 12302.10 - CASEWORK | **12-2** |
| 12390.10 - COUNTER TOPS | **12-2** |
| 12500.10 - WINDOW TREATMENT | **12-2** |
| 12510.10 - BLINDS | **12-3** |

# DIVISION # 12  FURNISHINGS

| | | UNIT | LABOR | MAT. | TOTAL |
|---|---|---|---|---|---|
| **12302.10** | **CASEWORK** | | | | |
| 0080 | Kitchen base cabinet, standard, 24" deep, 35" high | | | | |
| 0100 | 12" wide | EA. | 53.00 | 180 | 233 |
| 0120 | 18" wide | " | 53.00 | 210 | 263 |
| 0140 | 24" wide | " | 59.00 | 270 | 329 |
| 0160 | 27" wide | " | 59.00 | 300 | 359 |
| 0180 | 36" wide | " | 67.00 | 360 | 427 |
| 0200 | 48" wide | " | 67.00 | 430 | 497 |
| 0210 | Drawer base, 24" deep, 35" high | | | | |
| 0220 | 15" wide | EA. | 53.00 | 220 | 273 |
| 0230 | 18" wide | " | 53.00 | 240 | 293 |
| 0240 | 24" wide | " | 59.00 | 390 | 449 |
| 0250 | 27" wide | " | 59.00 | 440 | 499 |
| 0260 | 30" wide | " | 59.00 | 510 | 569 |
| 0270 | Sink-ready, base cabinet | | | | |
| 0280 | 30" wide | EA. | 59.00 | 240 | 299 |
| 0290 | 36" wide | " | 59.00 | 250 | 309 |
| 0300 | 42" wide | " | 59.00 | 270 | 329 |
| 0310 | 60" wide | " | 67.00 | 320 | 387 |
| 0500 | Corner cabinet, 36" wide | " | 67.00 | 450 | 517 |
| 4000 | Wall cabinet, 12" deep, 12" high | | | | |
| 4020 | 30" wide | EA. | 53.00 | 230 | 283 |
| 4060 | 36" wide | " | 53.00 | 240 | 293 |
| 4110 | 24" high | | | | |
| 4120 | 30" wide | EA. | 59.00 | 300 | 359 |
| 4140 | 36" wide | " | 59.00 | 310 | 369 |
| 4150 | 30" high | | | | |
| 4160 | 12" wide | EA. | 67.00 | 170 | 237 |
| 4200 | 24" wide | " | 67.00 | 210 | 277 |
| 4320 | 30" wide | " | 76.00 | 280 | 356 |
| 4340 | 36" wide | " | 76.00 | 280 | 356 |
| 4350 | Corner cabinet, 30" high | | | | |
| 4360 | 24" wide | EA. | 89.00 | 310 | 399 |
| 4390 | 36" wide | " | 89.00 | 410 | 499 |
| 5020 | Wardrobe | " | 130 | 830 | 960 |
| 6980 | Vanity with top, laminated plastic | | | | |
| 7000 | 24" wide | EA. | 130 | 690 | 820 |
| 7040 | 36" wide | " | 180 | 890 | 1,070 |
| 7060 | 48" wide | " | 210 | 990 | 1,200 |
| **12390.10** | **COUNTER TOPS** | | | | |
| 1020 | Stainless steel, counter top, with backsplash | S.F. | 13.25 | 130 | 143 |
| 2000 | Acid-proof, kemrock surface | " | 8.89 | 63.00 | 71.89 |
| **12500.10** | **WINDOW TREATMENT** | | | | |
| 1000 | Drapery tracks, wall or ceiling mounted | | | | |
| 1040 | Basic traverse rod | | | | |
| 1080 | 50 to 90" | EA. | 26.75 | 47.75 | 74.50 |
| 1100 | 84 to 156" | " | 29.75 | 64.00 | 93.75 |
| 1120 | 136 to 250" | " | 29.75 | 93.00 | 123 |
| 1140 | 165 to 312" | " | 33.25 | 140 | 173 |
| 1160 | Traverse rod with stationary curtain rod | | | | |
| 1180 | 30 to 50" | EA. | 26.75 | 72.00 | 98.75 |
| 1200 | 50 to 90" | " | 26.75 | 83.00 | 110 |

## DIVISION # 12 FURNISHINGS

| | | UNIT | LABOR | MAT. | TOTAL |
|---|---|---|---|---|---|
| **12500.10** | **WINDOW TREATMENT, Cont'd...** | | | | |
| 1220 | 84 to 156" | EA. | 29.75 | 110 | 140 |
| 1240 | 136 to 250" | " | 33.25 | 140 | 173 |
| 1260 | Double traverse rod | | | | |
| 1280 | 30 to 50" | EA. | 26.75 | 85.00 | 112 |
| 1300 | 50 to 84" | " | 26.75 | 110 | 137 |
| 1320 | 84 to 156" | " | 29.75 | 110 | 140 |
| 1340 | 136 to 250" | " | 33.25 | 150 | 183 |
| **12510.10** | **BLINDS** | | | | |
| 0990 | Venetian blinds | | | | |
| 1000 | 2" slats | S.F. | 1.33 | 33.75 | 35.08 |
| 1020 | 1" slats | " | 1.33 | 36.25 | 37.58 |

© 2011 By Design & Construction Resources

**Design & Construction Resources**

# DIVISION # 13 SPECIAL

| TABLE OF CONTENTS | PAGE |
|---|---|
| 13056.10 - VAULTS | **13-2** |
| 13121.10 - PRE-ENGINEERED BUILDINGS | **13-2** |
| 13152.10 - SWIMMING POOL EQUIPMENT | **13-3** |
| 13152.20 - SAUNAS | **13-3** |
| 13200.10 - STORAGE TANKS | **13-3** |

## DIVISION # 13  SPECIAL

| | | UNIT | LABOR | MAT. | TOTAL |
|---|---|---|---|---|---|
| **13056.10** | **VAULTS** | | | | |
| 1000 | Floor safes | | | | |
| 1010 | 1.0 cf | EA. | 44.50 | 800 | 845 |
| 1020 | 1.3 cf | " | 67.00 | 880 | 947 |
| **13121.10** | **PRE-ENGINEERED BUILDINGS** | | | | |
| 1080 | Pre-engineered metal building, 40'x100' | | | | |
| 1100 | 14' eave height | S.F. | 4.50 | 6.98 | 11.48 |
| 1120 | 16' eave height | " | 5.19 | 7.92 | 13.11 |
| 1140 | 20' eave height | " | 6.75 | 8.96 | 15.71 |
| 1150 | 60'x100' | | | | |
| 1160 | 14' eave height | S.F. | 4.50 | 8.80 | 13.30 |
| 1180 | 16' eave height | " | 5.19 | 9.73 | 14.92 |
| 1190 | 20' eave height | " | 6.75 | 10.75 | 17.50 |
| 1195 | 80'x100' | | | | |
| 1200 | 14' eave height | S.F. | 4.50 | 6.76 | 11.26 |
| 1210 | 16' eave height | " | 5.19 | 6.98 | 12.17 |
| 1220 | 20' eave height | " | 6.75 | 7.81 | 14.56 |
| 1280 | 100'x100' | | | | |
| 1300 | 14' eave height | S.F. | 4.50 | 6.60 | 11.10 |
| 1320 | 16' eave height | " | 5.19 | 6.87 | 12.06 |
| 1340 | 20' eave height | " | 6.75 | 7.57 | 14.32 |
| 1350 | 100'x150' | | | | |
| 1360 | 14' eave height | S.F. | 4.50 | 5.88 | 10.38 |
| 1380 | 16' eave height | " | 5.19 | 6.10 | 11.29 |
| 1400 | 20' eave height | " | 6.75 | 6.54 | 13.29 |
| 1410 | 120'x150' | | | | |
| 1420 | 14' eave height | S.F. | 4.50 | 6.21 | 10.71 |
| 1440 | 16' eave height | " | 5.19 | 6.32 | 11.51 |
| 1460 | 20' eave height | " | 6.75 | 6.60 | 13.35 |
| 1480 | 140'x150' | | | | |
| 1500 | 14' eave height | S.F. | 4.50 | 5.88 | 10.38 |
| 1520 | 16' eave height | " | 5.19 | 6.02 | 11.21 |
| 1540 | 20' eave height | " | 6.75 | 6.54 | 13.29 |
| 1600 | 160'x200' | | | | |
| 1620 | 14' eave height | S.F. | 4.50 | 4.53 | 9.03 |
| 1640 | 16' eave height | " | 5.19 | 4.67 | 9.86 |
| 1680 | 20' eave height | " | 6.75 | 4.95 | 11.70 |
| 1690 | 200'x200' | | | | |
| 1700 | 14' eave height | S.F. | 4.50 | 3.90 | 8.40 |
| 1720 | 16' eave height | " | 5.19 | 4.29 | 9.48 |
| 1740 | 20' eave height | " | 6.75 | 4.56 | 11.31 |
| 5020 | Hollow metal door and frame, 6' x 7' | EA. | | | 1,040 |
| 5030 | Sectional steel overhead door, manually operated | | | | |
| 5040 | 8' x 8' | EA. | | | 1,710 |
| 5080 | 12' x 12' | " | | | 2,270 |
| 5100 | Roll-up steel door, manually operated | | | | |
| 5120 | 10' x 10' | EA. | | | 1,330 |
| 5140 | 12' x 12' | " | | | 2,380 |
| 5160 | For gravity ridge ventilator with birdscreen | " | | | 570 |
| 5161 | 9" throat x 10' | " | | | 620 |
| 5181 | 12" throat x 10' | " | | | 760 |
| 5200 | For 20" rotary vent with damper | " | | | 290 |

# DIVISION # 13 SPECIAL

| | | UNIT | LABOR | MAT. | TOTAL |
|---|---|---|---|---|---|
| **13121.10** | **PRE-ENGINEERED BUILDINGS, Cont'd...** | | | | |
| 5220 | For 4' x 3' fixed louver | EA. | | | 200 |
| 5240 | For 4' x 3' aluminum sliding window | " | | | 180 |
| 5260 | For 3' x 9' fiberglass panels | " | | | 130 |
| 8020 | Liner panel, 26 ga, painted steel | S.F. | 1.47 | 2.50 | 3.97 |
| 8040 | Wall panel insulated, 26 ga. steel, foam core | " | 1.47 | 7.86 | 9.33 |
| 8060 | Roof panel, 26 ga. painted steel | " | 0.84 | 2.36 | 3.20 |
| 8080 | Plastic (sky light) | " | 0.84 | 5.33 | 6.17 |
| 9000 | Insulation, 3-1/2" thick blanket, R11 | " | 0.39 | 1.59 | 1.98 |
| **13152.10** | **SWIMMING POOL EQUIPMENT** | | | | |
| 1100 | Diving boards | | | | |
| 1110 | 14' long | | | | |
| 1120 | Aluminum | EA. | 230 | 4,010 | 4,240 |
| 1140 | Fiberglass | " | 230 | 3,030 | 3,260 |
| 1500 | Ladders, heavy duty | | | | |
| 1510 | 2 steps | | | | |
| 1520 | Minimum | EA. | 84.00 | 950 | 1,034 |
| 1540 | Maximum | " | 84.00 | 1,480 | 1,564 |
| 1550 | 4 steps | | | | |
| 1560 | Minimum | EA. | 100 | 1,010 | 1,110 |
| 1580 | Maximum | " | 100 | 1,630 | 1,730 |
| 1600 | Lifeguard chair | | | | |
| 1620 | Minimum | EA. | 420 | 2,700 | 3,120 |
| 1640 | Maximum | " | 420 | 4,180 | 4,600 |
| 1700 | Lights, underwater | | | | |
| 1705 | 12 volt, with transformer, 100 watt | | | | |
| 1710 | Incandescent | EA. | 100 | 200 | 300 |
| 1715 | Halogen | " | 100 | 170 | 270 |
| 1720 | LED | " | 100 | 540 | 640 |
| 1730 | 110 volt | | | | |
| 1740 | Minimum | EA. | 100 | 910 | 1,010 |
| 1760 | Maximum | " | 100 | 2,200 | 2,300 |
| 1780 | Ground fault interrupter for 110 volt, each light | " | 34.75 | 200 | 235 |
| 2000 | Pool cover | | | | |
| 2020 | Reinforced polyethylene | S.F. | 3.21 | 1.98 | 5.19 |
| 2030 | Vinyl water tube | | | | |
| 2040 | Minimum | S.F. | 3.21 | 1.21 | 4.42 |
| 2060 | Maximum | " | 3.21 | 1.81 | 5.02 |
| 2100 | Slides with water tube | | | | |
| 2120 | Minimum | EA. | 350 | 950 | 1,300 |
| 2140 | Maximum | " | 350 | 20,350 | 20,700 |
| **13152.20** | **SAUNAS** | | | | |
| 0010 | Prefabricated, cedar siding, insulated panels, prehung door, | | | | |
| 0020 | 4'x8"x4'-8"x6'-6" | EA. | | | 4,790 |
| 0030 | 5'-8"x6'-8"x6'-6" | " | | | 5,790 |
| 0040 | 6'-8"x6'-8"x6'-6" | " | | | 6,740 |
| 0050 | 7'-8"x7'-8"x6'-6" | " | | | 8,140 |
| 0060 | 7'-8"x9'-8"x6'-6" | " | | | 10,730 |
| **13200.10** | **STORAGE TANKS** | | | | |
| 0080 | Oil storage tank, underground, single wall, no excv. | | | | |
| 0090 | Steel | | | | |
| 1000 | 500 gals | EA. | 280 | 3,300 | 3,580 |

© 2011 By Design & Construction Resources

## DIVISION # 13 SPECIAL

### 13200.10 STORAGE TANKS, Cont'd...

| | | UNIT | LABOR | MAT. | TOTAL |
|---|---|---|---|---|---|
| 1020 | 1,000 gals | EA. | 380 | 4,470 | 4,850 |
| 1980 | Fiberglass, double wall | | | | |
| 2000 | 550 gals | EA. | 380 | 9,300 | 9,680 |
| 2020 | 1,000 gals | " | 380 | 11,950 | 12,330 |
| 2520 | Above ground | | | | |
| 2530 | Steel, single wall | | | | |
| 2540 | 275 gals | EA. | 230 | 1,870 | 2,100 |
| 2560 | 500 gals | " | 380 | 4,680 | 5,060 |
| 2570 | 1,000 gals | " | 450 | 6,380 | 6,830 |
| 3020 | Fill cap | " | 59.00 | 110 | 169 |
| 3040 | Vent cap | " | 59.00 | 110 | 169 |
| 3100 | Level indicator | " | 59.00 | 180 | 239 |

## DIVISION # 14 CONVEYING

| TABLE OF CONTENTS | PAGE |
|---|---|
| 14210.10 - ELEVATORS | 14-2 |
| 14300.10 - ESCALATORS | 14-2 |
| 14410.10 - PERSONNEL LIFTS | 14-2 |
| 14450.10 - VEHICLE LIFTS | 14-3 |
| 14560.10 - CHUTES | 14-3 |
| 14580.10 - PNEUMATIC SYSTEMS | 14-3 |
| 14580.30 - DUMBWAITERS | 14-3 |

*© 2011 By Design & Construction Resources*

## DIVISION # 14  CONVEYING

| | | UNIT | LABOR | MAT. | TOTAL |
|---|---|---|---|---|---|
| **14210.10** | **ELEVATORS** | | | | |
| 0120 | Passenger elevators, electric, geared | | | | |
| 0502 |    Based on a shaft of 6 stops and 6 openings | | | | |
| 0510 |       50 fpm, 2000 lb | EA. | 2,270 | 112,970 | 115,240 |
| 0520 |       100 fpm, 2000 lb | " | 2,520 | 117,150 | 119,670 |
| 0525 |       150 fpm | | | | |
| 0530 |          2000 lb | EA. | 2,840 | 129,250 | 132,090 |
| 0550 |          3000 lb | " | 3,240 | 162,800 | 166,040 |
| 0560 |          4000 lb | " | 3,780 | 169,400 | 173,180 |
| 1002 |    Based on a shaft of 8 stops and 8 openings | | | | |
| 1010 |       300 fpm | | | | |
| 1020 |          3000 lb | EA. | 4,540 | 193,600 | 198,140 |
| 1040 |          3500 lb | " | 4,540 | 196,680 | 201,220 |
| 1060 |          4000 lb | " | 5,040 | 206,290 | 211,330 |
| 1080 |          5000 lb | " | 5,400 | 229,130 | 234,530 |
| 1502 |    Hydraulic, based on a shaft of 3 stops, 3 openings | | | | |
| 1508 |       50 fpm | | | | |
| 1510 |          2000 lb | EA. | 1,890 | 72,490 | 74,380 |
| 1520 |          2500 lb | " | 1,890 | 77,550 | 79,440 |
| 1530 |          3000 lb | " | 1,970 | 81,840 | 83,810 |
| 1600 |    For each additional; 50 fpm add per stop, $3500 | | | | |
| 1620 |    500 lb, add per stop, $3500 | | | | |
| 1630 |    Opening, add, $4200 | | | | |
| 1640 |    Stop, add per stop, $5300 | | | | |
| 1660 |    Bonderized steel door, add per opening, $400 | | | | |
| 1670 |    Colored aluminum door, add per opening, $1500 | | | | |
| 1680 |    Stainless steel door, add per opening, $650 | | | | |
| 1690 |    Cast bronze door, add per opening, $1200 | | | | |
| 1730 |    Custom cab interior, add per cab, $5000 | | | | |
| 2000 | Small elevators, 4 to 6 passenger capacity | | | | |
| 2005 |    Electric, push | | | | |
| 2010 |       2 stops | EA. | 1,890 | 26,400 | 28,290 |
| 2020 |       3 stops | " | 2,060 | 33,000 | 35,060 |
| 2030 |       4 stops | " | 2,270 | 37,620 | 39,890 |
| **14300.10** | **ESCALATORS** | | | | |
| 1000 | Escalators | | | | |
| 1020 |    32" wide, floor to floor | | | | |
| 1040 |       12' high | EA. | 3,780 | 143,170 | 146,950 |
| 1050 |       15' high | " | 4,540 | 156,420 | 160,960 |
| 1060 |       18' high | " | 5,670 | 168,470 | 174,140 |
| 1070 |       22' high | " | 7,560 | 181,720 | 189,280 |
| 1080 |       25' high | " | 9,070 | 201,470 | 210,540 |
| 1085 |    48" wide | | | | |
| 1090 |       12' high | EA. | 3,910 | 159,500 | 163,410 |
| 1100 |       15' high | " | 4,730 | 174,080 | 178,810 |
| 1120 |       18' high | " | 5,970 | 187,000 | 192,970 |
| 1130 |       22' high | " | 8,100 | 209,330 | 217,430 |
| 1140 |       25' high | " | 9,070 | 223,520 | 232,590 |
| **14410.10** | **PERSONNEL LIFTS** | | | | |
| 1000 | Electrically operated, 1 or 2 person lift | | | | |
| 1001 |    With attached foot platforms | | | | |
| 1020 |       3 stops | EA. | | | 10,230 |

# DIVISION # 14 CONVEYING

| | | UNIT | LABOR | MAT. | TOTAL |
|---|---|---|---|---|---|
| **14410.10** | **PERSONNEL LIFTS, Cont'd...** | | | | |
| 1040 | 5 stops | EA. | | | 15,950 |
| 1060 | 7 stops | " | | | 18,590 |
| 2000 | For each additional stop, add $1250 | | | | |
| 3020 | Residential stair climber, per story | EA. | 450 | 4,820 | 5,270 |
| **14450.10** | **VEHICLE LIFTS** | | | | |
| 1020 | Automotive hoist, one post, semi-hydraulic, 8,000 lb | EA. | 2,270 | 3,460 | 5,730 |
| 1040 | Full hydraulic, 8,000 lb | " | 2,270 | 3,580 | 5,850 |
| 1060 | 2 post, semi-hydraulic, 10,000 lb | " | 3,240 | 3,740 | 6,980 |
| 1070 | Full hydraulic | | | | |
| 1080 | 10,000 lb | EA. | 3,240 | 4,400 | 7,640 |
| 1100 | 13,000 lb | " | 5,670 | 5,500 | 11,170 |
| 1120 | 18,500 lb | " | 5,670 | 8,790 | 14,460 |
| 1140 | 24,000 lb | " | 5,670 | 12,380 | 18,050 |
| 1160 | 26,000 lb | " | 5,670 | 12,050 | 17,720 |
| 1170 | Pneumatic hoist, fully hydraulic | | | | |
| 1180 | 11,000 lb | EA. | 7,560 | 5,940 | 13,500 |
| 1200 | 24,000 lb | " | 7,560 | 10,730 | 18,290 |
| **14560.10** | **CHUTES** | | | | |
| 1020 | Linen chutes, stainless steel, with supports | | | | |
| 1030 | 18" dia. | L.F. | 4.21 | 140 | 144 |
| 1040 | 24" dia. | " | 4.53 | 180 | 185 |
| 1050 | 30" dia. | " | 4.91 | 190 | 195 |
| 1060 | Hopper | EA. | 39.25 | 2,310 | 2,349 |
| 1070 | Skylight | " | 59.00 | 1,400 | 1,459 |
| **14580.10** | **PNEUMATIC SYSTEMS** | | | | |
| 6000 | Air-lift conveyor, 115 Volt, single phase, 100' long, 3" carrier | EA. | 4,950 | 3,630 | 8,580 |
| 6010 | 4" carrier | " | 4,950 | 4,510 | 9,460 |
| 6020 | 6" carrier | " | 4,950 | 8,200 | 13,150 |
| 7000 | Pneumatic tube system accessories | | | | |
| 7010 | Couplings and hanging accessories for 3" carrier system | L.F. | | | 6.21 |
| 7020 | For 4" carrier system | " | | | 8.80 |
| 7030 | For 6" carrier system | " | | | 11.75 |
| 7040 | 24" CL. Expanded 90° bend, heavy duty, 3"-6" carrier systems | EA. | | | 110 |
| 7050 | 36" CL. Expanded 90° bend, heavy duty, 3"-6" carrier systems | " | | | 260 |
| 7060 | 48" CL. Expanded 45° bend, heavy duty, 3" carrier system | " | | | 84.00 |
| 7070 | 4" carrier system | " | | | 120 |
| 7080 | 6" carrier system | " | | | 180 |
| 7090 | 48" CL. Expanded 90° bend, heavy duty, 3" carrier system | " | | | 110 |
| 8000 | 4" carrier system | " | | | 150 |
| 8010 | 6" carrier system | " | | | 260 |
| 8020 | Stainless steel body up-grade, 3" carrier system | " | | | 360 |
| 8030 | 4" carrier system | " | | | 370 |
| 8040 | 6" carrier system | " | | | 520 |
| **14580.30** | **DUMBWAITERS** | | | | |
| 0010 | 28' travel, extruded alum., 4 stops, 100 lbs. capacity | EA. | | | 5,640 |
| 0020 | 150 lbs. capacity | " | | | 7,930 |
| 0030 | 200 lbs. capacity | " | | | 11,380 |

© 2011 By Design & Construction Resources

**Design & Construction Resources**

# DIVISION # 15  MECHANICAL

## TABLE OF CONTENTS — PAGE

| | |
|---|---|
| 15120.10 - BACKFLOW PREVENTERS | 15-2 |
| 15410.06 - C.I. PIPE, BELOW GROUND | 15-2 |
| 15410.10 - COPPER PIPE | 15-2 |
| 15410.11 - COPPER FITTINGS | 15-2 |
| 15410.82 - GALVANIZED STEEL PIPE | 15-3 |
| 15430.23 - CLEANOUTS | 15-3 |
| 15430.25 - HOSE BIBBS | 15-3 |
| 15430.60 - VALVES | 15-3 |
| 15430.65 - VACUUM BREAKERS | 15-4 |
| 15430.68 - STRAINERS | 15-4 |
| 15430.70 - DRAINS, ROOF & FLOOR | 15-4 |
| 15440.10 - BATHS | 15-4 |
| 15440.12 - DISPOSALS & ACCESSORIES | 15-5 |
| 15440.15 - FAUCETS | 15-5 |
| 15440.18 - HYDRANTS | 15-6 |
| 15440.20 - LAVATORIES | 15-6 |
| 15440.30 - SHOWERS | 15-6 |
| 15440.40 - SINKS | 15-6 |
| 15440.60 - WATER CLOSETS | 15-7 |
| 15440.70 - WATER HEATERS | 15-7 |
| 15610.10 - FURNACES | 15-8 |
| 15780.20 - ROOFTOP UNITS | 15-8 |
| 15830.70 - UNIT HEATERS | 15-8 |
| 15855.10 - AIR HANDLING UNITS | 15-8 |
| 15870.20 - EXHAUST FANS | 15-8 |
| 15890.10 - METAL DUCTWORK | 15-8 |
| 15890.30 - FLEXIBLE DUCTWORK | 15-9 |
| 15910.10 - DAMPERS | 15-9 |
| 15940.10 - DIFFUSERS | 15-9 |

© 2011 By Design & Construction Resources

## DIVISION # 15  MECHANICAL

| | | UNIT | LABOR | MAT. | TOTAL |
|---|---|---|---|---|---|
| **15120.10** | **BACKFLOW PREVENTERS** | | | | |
| 0080 | Backflow preventer, flanged, cast iron, with valves | | | | |
| 0100 | 3" pipe | EA. | 290 | 2,760 | 3,050 |
| **15410.06** | **C.I. PIPE, BELOW GROUND** | | | | |
| 1010 | No hub pipe | | | | |
| 1020 | 1-1/2" pipe | L.F. | 2.93 | 7.10 | 10.03 |
| 1030 | 2" pipe | " | 3.25 | 7.29 | 10.54 |
| 1120 | 3" pipe | " | 3.66 | 10.00 | 13.66 |
| 1220 | 4" pipe | " | 4.88 | 13.00 | 17.88 |
| **15410.10** | **COPPER PIPE** | | | | |
| 0880 | Type "K" copper | | | | |
| 0900 | 1/2" | L.F. | 1.83 | 3.76 | 5.59 |
| 1000 | 3/4" | " | 1.95 | 7.01 | 8.96 |
| 1020 | 1" | " | 2.09 | 9.18 | 11.27 |
| 3000 | DWV, copper | | | | |
| 3020 | 1-1/4" | L.F. | 2.44 | 10.25 | 12.69 |
| 3030 | 1-1/2" | " | 2.66 | 13.00 | 15.66 |
| 3040 | 2" | " | 2.93 | 16.75 | 19.68 |
| 3070 | 3" | " | 3.25 | 29.00 | 32.25 |
| 3080 | 4" | " | 3.66 | 50.00 | 53.66 |
| 3090 | 6" | " | 4.18 | 200 | 204 |
| 6080 | Type "L" copper | | | | |
| 6090 | 1/4" | L.F. | 1.72 | 1.51 | 3.23 |
| 6095 | 3/8" | " | 1.72 | 2.33 | 4.05 |
| 6100 | 1/2" | " | 1.83 | 2.70 | 4.53 |
| 6190 | 3/4" | " | 1.95 | 4.32 | 6.27 |
| 6240 | 1" | " | 2.09 | 6.50 | 8.59 |
| 6580 | Type "M" copper | | | | |
| 6600 | 1/2" | L.F. | 1.83 | 1.91 | 3.74 |
| 6620 | 3/4" | " | 1.95 | 3.11 | 5.06 |
| 6630 | 1" | " | 2.09 | 5.06 | 7.15 |
| **15410.11** | **COPPER FITTINGS** | | | | |
| 0850 | Slip coupling | | | | |
| 0860 | 1/4" | EA. | 19.50 | 0.83 | 20.33 |
| 0870 | 1/2" | " | 23.50 | 1.40 | 24.90 |
| 0880 | 3/4" | " | 29.25 | 2.92 | 32.17 |
| 0890 | 1" | " | 32.50 | 6.18 | 38.68 |
| 2660 | Street ells, copper | | | | |
| 2670 | 1/4" | EA. | 23.50 | 6.41 | 29.91 |
| 2680 | 3/8" | " | 26.75 | 4.41 | 31.16 |
| 2690 | 1/2" | " | 29.25 | 1.78 | 31.03 |
| 2700 | 3/4" | " | 30.75 | 3.75 | 34.50 |
| 2710 | 1" | " | 32.50 | 9.72 | 42.22 |
| 4190 | DWV fittings, coupling with stop | | | | |
| 4210 | 1-1/2" | EA. | 36.50 | 7.51 | 44.01 |
| 4230 | 2" | " | 39.00 | 10.50 | 49.50 |
| 4260 | 3" | " | 48.75 | 20.25 | 69.00 |
| 4280 | 3" x 2" | " | 48.75 | 46.00 | 94.75 |
| 4290 | 4" | " | 59.00 | 64.00 | 123 |
| 4300 | Slip coupling | | | | |
| 4310 | 1-1/2" | EA. | 36.50 | 11.75 | 48.25 |
| 4320 | 2" | " | 39.00 | 14.00 | 53.00 |

## DIVISION # 15 MECHANICAL

| | | UNIT | LABOR | MAT. | TOTAL |
|---|---|---|---|---|---|
| **15410.11** | **COPPER FITTINGS, Cont'd...** | | | | |
| 4330 | 3" | EA. | 48.75 | 25.25 | 74.00 |
| 4340 | 90 ells | | | | |
| 4350 | 1-1/2" | EA. | 36.50 | 14.25 | 50.75 |
| 4360 | 1-1/2" x 1-1/4" | " | 36.50 | 39.00 | 75.50 |
| 4370 | 2" | " | 39.00 | 26.00 | 65.00 |
| 4380 | 2" x 1-1/2" | " | 39.00 | 53.00 | 92.00 |
| 4390 | 3" | " | 48.75 | 69.00 | 118 |
| 4400 | 4" | " | 59.00 | 230 | 289 |
| 4410 | Street, 90 elbows | | | | |
| 4420 | 1-1/2" | EA. | 36.50 | 18.25 | 54.75 |
| 4430 | 2" | " | 39.00 | 39.75 | 78.75 |
| 4440 | 3" | " | 48.75 | 100 | 149 |
| 4450 | 4" | " | 59.00 | 250 | 309 |
| 5410 | No-hub adapters | | | | |
| 5420 | 1-1/2" x 2" | EA. | 36.50 | 32.50 | 69.00 |
| 5430 | 2" | " | 39.00 | 30.50 | 69.50 |
| 5440 | 2" x 3" | " | 39.00 | 70.00 | 109 |
| 5450 | 3" | " | 48.75 | 62.00 | 111 |
| 5460 | 3" x 4" | " | 48.75 | 130 | 179 |
| 5470 | 4" | " | 59.00 | 130 | 189 |
| **15410.82** | **GALVANIZED STEEL PIPE** | | | | |
| 1000 | Galvanized pipe | | | | |
| 1020 | 1/2" pipe | L.F. | 5.86 | 3.06 | 8.92 |
| 1040 | 3/4" pipe | " | 7.32 | 3.99 | 11.31 |
| 1200 | 90 degree ell, 150 lb malleable iron, galvanized | | | | |
| 1210 | 1/2" | EA. | 11.75 | 2.15 | 13.90 |
| 1220 | 3/4" | " | 14.75 | 2.86 | 17.61 |
| 1400 | 45 degree ell, 150 lb m.i., galv. | | | | |
| 1410 | 1/2" | EA. | 11.75 | 3.43 | 15.18 |
| 1420 | 3/4" | " | 14.75 | 4.66 | 19.41 |
| 1520 | Tees, straight, 150 lb m.i., galv. | | | | |
| 1530 | 1/2" | EA. | 14.75 | 2.86 | 17.61 |
| 1540 | 3/4" | " | 16.75 | 4.75 | 21.50 |
| 1800 | Couplings, straight, 150 lb m.i., galv. | | | | |
| 1810 | 1/2" | EA. | 11.75 | 2.64 | 14.39 |
| 1820 | 3/4" | " | 13.00 | 3.16 | 16.16 |
| **15430.23** | **CLEANOUTS** | | | | |
| 0980 | Cleanout, wall | | | | |
| 1000 | 2" | EA. | 39.00 | 190 | 229 |
| 1020 | 3" | " | 39.00 | 270 | 309 |
| 1040 | 4" | " | 48.75 | 270 | 319 |
| 1050 | Floor | | | | |
| 1060 | 2" | EA. | 48.75 | 170 | 219 |
| 1080 | 3" | " | 48.75 | 230 | 279 |
| 1100 | 4" | " | 59.00 | 230 | 289 |
| **15430.25** | **HOSE BIBBS** | | | | |
| 0005 | Hose bibb | | | | |
| 0010 | 1/2" | EA. | 19.50 | 9.07 | 28.57 |
| 0200 | 3/4" | " | 19.50 | 9.62 | 29.12 |

© 2011 By Design & Construction Resources

## DIVISION # 15  MECHANICAL

| | | UNIT | LABOR | MAT. | TOTAL |
|---|---|---|---|---|---|
| **15430.60** | **VALVES** | | | | |
| 0780 | Gate valve, 125 lb, bronze, soldered | | | | |
| 0800 | 1/2" | EA. | 14.75 | 25.75 | 40.50 |
| 1000 | 3/4" | " | 14.75 | 31.00 | 45.75 |
| 1280 | Check valve, bronze, soldered, 125 lb | | | | |
| 1300 | 1/2" | EA. | 14.75 | 44.50 | 59.25 |
| 1320 | 3/4" | " | 14.75 | 55.00 | 69.75 |
| 1790 | Globe valve, bronze, soldered, 125 lb | | | | |
| 1800 | 1/2" | EA. | 16.75 | 60.00 | 76.75 |
| 1810 | 3/4" | " | 18.25 | 74.00 | 92.25 |
| **15430.65** | **VACUUM BREAKERS** | | | | |
| 1000 | Vacuum breaker, atmospheric, threaded connection | | | | |
| 1010 | 3/4" | EA. | 23.50 | 45.75 | 69.25 |
| 1018 | Anti-siphon, brass | | | | |
| 1020 | 3/4" | EA. | 23.50 | 49.50 | 73.00 |
| **15430.68** | **STRAINERS** | | | | |
| 0980 | Strainer, Y pattern, 125 psi, cast iron body, threaded | | | | |
| 1000 | 3/4" | EA. | 21.00 | 11.50 | 32.50 |
| 1980 | 250 psi, brass body, threaded | | | | |
| 2000 | 3/4" | EA. | 23.50 | 29.75 | 53.25 |
| 2130 | Cast iron body, threaded | | | | |
| 2140 | 3/4" | EA. | 23.50 | 17.50 | 41.00 |
| **15430.70** | **DRAINS, ROOF & FLOOR** | | | | |
| 1020 | Floor drain, cast iron, with cast iron top | | | | |
| 1030 | 2" | EA. | 48.75 | 130 | 179 |
| 1040 | 3" | " | 48.75 | 140 | 189 |
| 1050 | 4" | " | 48.75 | 290 | 339 |
| 1090 | Roof drain, cast iron | | | | |
| 1100 | 2" | EA. | 48.75 | 210 | 259 |
| 1110 | 3" | " | 48.75 | 220 | 269 |
| 1120 | 4" | " | 48.75 | 280 | 329 |
| **15440.10** | **BATHS** | | | | |
| 0980 | Bath tub, 5' long | | | | |
| 1000 | Minimum | EA. | 200 | 530 | 730 |
| 1020 | Average | " | 290 | 1,160 | 1,450 |
| 1040 | Maximum | " | 590 | 2,640 | 3,230 |
| 1050 | 6' long | | | | |
| 1060 | Minimum | EA. | 200 | 590 | 790 |
| 1080 | Average | " | 290 | 1,210 | 1,500 |
| 1100 | Maximum | " | 590 | 3,420 | 4,010 |
| 1110 | Square tub, whirlpool, 4'x4' | | | | |
| 1120 | Minimum | EA. | 290 | 1,810 | 2,100 |
| 1140 | Average | " | 590 | 2,570 | 3,160 |
| 1160 | Maximum | " | 730 | 7,850 | 8,580 |
| 1170 | 5'x5' | | | | |
| 1180 | Minimum | EA. | 290 | 1,810 | 2,100 |
| 1200 | Average | " | 590 | 2,570 | 3,160 |
| 1220 | Maximum | " | 730 | 8,000 | 8,730 |
| 1230 | 6'x6' | | | | |
| 1240 | Minimum | EA. | 290 | 2,210 | 2,500 |
| 1260 | Average | " | 590 | 3,230 | 3,820 |
| 1280 | Maximum | " | 730 | 9,270 | 10,000 |

© 2011 By Design & Construction Resources

## DIVISION # 15  MECHANICAL

| | | UNIT | LABOR | MAT. | TOTAL |
|---|---|---|---|---|---|
| **15440.10** | **BATHS, Cont'd...** | | | | |
| 8980 | For trim and rough-in | | | | |
| 9000 | Minimum | EA. | 200 | 190 | 390 |
| 9020 | Average | " | 290 | 280 | 570 |
| 9040 | Maximum | " | 590 | 780 | 1,370 |
| **15440.12** | **DISPOSALS & ACCESSORIES** | | | | |
| 0040 | Continuous feed | | | | |
| 0050 | Minimum | EA. | 120 | 72.00 | 192 |
| 0060 | Average | " | 150 | 200 | 350 |
| 0070 | Maximum | " | 200 | 390 | 590 |
| 0200 | Batch feed, 1/2 hp | | | | |
| 0220 | Minimum | EA. | 120 | 280 | 400 |
| 0230 | Average | " | 150 | 550 | 700 |
| 0240 | Maximum | " | 200 | 950 | 1,150 |
| 1100 | Hot water dispenser | | | | |
| 1110 | Minimum | EA. | 120 | 200 | 320 |
| 1120 | Average | " | 150 | 320 | 470 |
| 1130 | Maximum | " | 200 | 510 | 710 |
| 1140 | Epoxy finish faucet | " | 120 | 290 | 410 |
| 1160 | Lock stop assembly | " | 73.00 | 61.00 | 134 |
| 1170 | Mounting gasket | " | 48.75 | 7.04 | 55.79 |
| 1180 | Tailpipe gasket | " | 48.75 | 1.03 | 49.78 |
| 1190 | Stopper assembly | " | 59.00 | 24.00 | 83.00 |
| 1200 | Switch assembly, on/off | " | 98.00 | 27.50 | 126 |
| 1210 | Tailpipe gasket washer | " | 29.25 | 1.10 | 30.35 |
| 1220 | Stop gasket | " | 32.50 | 2.42 | 34.92 |
| 1230 | Tailpipe flange | " | 29.25 | 0.27 | 29.52 |
| 1240 | Tailpipe | " | 36.50 | 3.13 | 39.63 |
| **15440.15** | **FAUCETS** | | | | |
| 0980 | Kitchen | | | | |
| 1000 | Minimum | EA. | 98.00 | 83.00 | 181 |
| 1020 | Average | " | 120 | 230 | 350 |
| 1040 | Maximum | " | 150 | 290 | 440 |
| 1050 | Bath | | | | |
| 1060 | Minimum | EA. | 98.00 | 83.00 | 181 |
| 1080 | Average | " | 120 | 240 | 360 |
| 1100 | Maximum | " | 150 | 370 | 520 |
| 1110 | Lavatory, domestic | | | | |
| 1120 | Minimum | EA. | 98.00 | 88.00 | 186 |
| 1140 | Average | " | 120 | 280 | 400 |
| 1160 | Maximum | " | 150 | 460 | 610 |
| 1290 | Washroom | | | | |
| 1300 | Minimum | EA. | 98.00 | 110 | 208 |
| 1320 | Average | " | 120 | 280 | 400 |
| 1340 | Maximum | " | 150 | 510 | 660 |
| 1350 | Handicapped | | | | |
| 1360 | Minimum | EA. | 120 | 120 | 240 |
| 1380 | Average | " | 150 | 360 | 510 |
| 1400 | Maximum | " | 200 | 560 | 760 |
| 1410 | Shower | | | | |
| 1420 | Minimum | EA. | 98.00 | 110 | 208 |
| 1440 | Average | " | 120 | 320 | 440 |

© 2011 By Design & Construction Resources

## DIVISION # 15  MECHANICAL

| | | UNIT | LABOR | MAT. | TOTAL |
|---|---|---|---|---|---|
| **15440.15** | **FAUCETS, Cont'd...** | | | | |
| 1460 | Maximum | EA. | 150 | 510 | 660 |
| 1480 | For trim and rough-in | | | | |
| 1500 | Minimum | EA. | 120 | 77.00 | 197 |
| 1520 | Average | " | 150 | 120 | 270 |
| 1540 | Maximum | " | 290 | 200 | 490 |
| **15440.18** | **HYDRANTS** | | | | |
| 0980 | Wall hydrant | | | | |
| 1000 | 8" thick | EA. | 98.00 | 360 | 458 |
| 1020 | 12" thick | " | 120 | 430 | 550 |
| **15440.20** | **LAVATORIES** | | | | |
| 1980 | Lavatory, counter top, porcelain enamel on cast iron | | | | |
| 2000 | Minimum | EA. | 120 | 190 | 310 |
| 2010 | Average | " | 150 | 290 | 440 |
| 2020 | Maximum | " | 200 | 520 | 720 |
| 2080 | Wall hung, china | | | | |
| 2100 | Minimum | EA. | 120 | 260 | 380 |
| 2110 | Average | " | 150 | 310 | 460 |
| 2120 | Maximum | " | 200 | 770 | 970 |
| 2280 | Handicapped | | | | |
| 2300 | Minimum | EA. | 150 | 430 | 580 |
| 2310 | Average | " | 200 | 500 | 700 |
| 2320 | Maximum | " | 290 | 830 | 1,120 |
| 8980 | For trim and rough-in | | | | |
| 9000 | Minimum | EA. | 150 | 220 | 370 |
| 9020 | Average | " | 200 | 370 | 570 |
| 9040 | Maximum | " | 290 | 460 | 750 |
| **15440.30** | **SHOWERS** | | | | |
| 0980 | Shower, fiberglass, 36"x34"x84" | | | | |
| 1000 | Minimum | EA. | 420 | 570 | 990 |
| 1020 | Average | " | 590 | 800 | 1,390 |
| 1040 | Maximum | " | 590 | 1,160 | 1,750 |
| 2980 | Steel, 1 piece, 36"x36" | | | | |
| 3000 | Minimum | EA. | 420 | 530 | 950 |
| 3020 | Average | " | 590 | 800 | 1,390 |
| 3040 | Maximum | " | 590 | 950 | 1,540 |
| 3980 | Receptor, molded stone, 36"x36" | | | | |
| 4000 | Minimum | EA. | 200 | 220 | 420 |
| 4020 | Average | " | 290 | 370 | 660 |
| 4040 | Maximum | " | 490 | 570 | 1,060 |
| 8980 | For trim and rough-in | | | | |
| 9000 | Minimum | EA. | 270 | 220 | 490 |
| 9020 | Average | " | 330 | 370 | 700 |
| 9040 | Maximum | " | 590 | 460 | 1,050 |
| **15440.40** | **SINKS** | | | | |
| 0980 | Service sink, 24"x29" | | | | |
| 1000 | Minimum | EA. | 150 | 640 | 790 |
| 1020 | Average | " | 200 | 790 | 990 |
| 1040 | Maximum | " | 290 | 1,170 | 1,460 |
| 2000 | Kitchen sink, single, stainless steel, single bowl | | | | |
| 2020 | Minimum | EA. | 120 | 280 | 400 |
| 2040 | Average | " | 150 | 320 | 470 |

# DIVISION # 15  MECHANICAL

| | | UNIT | LABOR | MAT. | TOTAL |
|---|---|---|---|---|---|
| **15440.40** | **SINKS, Cont'd...** | | | | |
| 2060 | Maximum | EA. | 200 | 580 | 780 |
| 2070 | Double bowl | | | | |
| 2080 | Minimum | EA. | 150 | 320 | 470 |
| 2100 | Average | " | 200 | 360 | 560 |
| 2120 | Maximum | " | 290 | 620 | 910 |
| 2190 | Porcelain enamel, cast iron, single bowl | | | | |
| 2200 | Minimum | EA. | 120 | 200 | 320 |
| 2220 | Average | " | 150 | 260 | 410 |
| 2240 | Maximum | " | 200 | 410 | 610 |
| 2250 | Double bowl | | | | |
| 2260 | Minimum | EA. | 150 | 280 | 430 |
| 2280 | Average | " | 200 | 390 | 590 |
| 2300 | Maximum | " | 290 | 550 | 840 |
| 2980 | Mop sink, 24"x36"x10" | | | | |
| 3000 | Minimum | EA. | 120 | 480 | 600 |
| 3020 | Average | " | 150 | 580 | 730 |
| 3040 | Maximum | " | 200 | 780 | 980 |
| 5980 | Washing machine box | | | | |
| 6000 | Minimum | EA. | 150 | 180 | 330 |
| 6040 | Average | " | 200 | 250 | 450 |
| 6060 | Maximum | " | 290 | 310 | 600 |
| 8980 | For trim and rough-in | | | | |
| 9000 | Minimum | EA. | 200 | 290 | 490 |
| 9020 | Average | " | 290 | 440 | 730 |
| 9040 | Maximum | " | 390 | 560 | 950 |
| **15440.60** | **WATER CLOSETS** | | | | |
| 0980 | Water closet flush tank, floor mounted | | | | |
| 1000 | Minimum | EA. | 150 | 330 | 480 |
| 1010 | Average | " | 200 | 650 | 850 |
| 1020 | Maximum | " | 290 | 1,020 | 1,310 |
| 1030 | Handicapped | | | | |
| 1040 | Minimum | EA. | 200 | 370 | 570 |
| 1050 | Average | " | 290 | 670 | 960 |
| 1060 | Maximum | " | 590 | 1,280 | 1,870 |
| 8980 | For trim and rough-in | | | | |
| 9000 | Minimum | EA. | 150 | 210 | 360 |
| 9020 | Average | " | 200 | 250 | 450 |
| 9040 | Maximum | " | 290 | 330 | 620 |
| **15440.70** | **WATER HEATERS** | | | | |
| 0980 | Water heater, electric | | | | |
| 1000 | 6 gal | EA. | 98.00 | 350 | 448 |
| 1020 | 10 gal | " | 98.00 | 360 | 458 |
| 1030 | 15 gal | " | 98.00 | 360 | 458 |
| 1040 | 20 gal | " | 120 | 500 | 620 |
| 1050 | 30 gal | " | 120 | 520 | 640 |
| 1060 | 40 gal | " | 120 | 560 | 680 |
| 1070 | 52 gal | " | 150 | 630 | 780 |
| 2980 | Oil fired | | | | |
| 3000 | 20 gal | EA. | 290 | 1,300 | 1,590 |
| 3020 | 50 gal | " | 420 | 2,020 | 2,440 |

## DIVISION # 15 MECHANICAL

| | | UNIT | LABOR | MAT. | TOTAL |
|---|---|---|---|---|---|
| **15610.10** | **FURNACES** | | | | |
| 0980 | Electric, hot air | | | | |
| 1000 | 40 mbh | EA. | 290 | 810 | 1,100 |
| 1020 | 60 mbh | " | 310 | 880 | 1,190 |
| 1040 | 80 mbh | " | 330 | 960 | 1,290 |
| 1060 | 100 mbh | " | 340 | 1,080 | 1,420 |
| 1080 | 125 mbh | " | 360 | 1,320 | 1,680 |
| 1980 | Gas fired hot air | | | | |
| 2000 | 40 mbh | EA. | 290 | 810 | 1,100 |
| 2020 | 60 mbh | " | 310 | 870 | 1,180 |
| 2040 | 80 mbh | " | 330 | 1,000 | 1,330 |
| 2060 | 100 mbh | " | 340 | 1,040 | 1,380 |
| 2080 | 125 mbh | " | 360 | 1,140 | 1,500 |
| 2980 | Oil fired hot air | | | | |
| 3000 | 40 mbh | EA. | 290 | 1,090 | 1,380 |
| 3020 | 60 mbh | " | 310 | 1,800 | 2,110 |
| 3040 | 80 mbh | " | 330 | 1,820 | 2,150 |
| 3060 | 100 mbh | " | 340 | 1,850 | 2,190 |
| 3080 | 125 mbh | " | 360 | 1,910 | 2,270 |
| **15780.20** | **ROOFTOP UNITS** | | | | |
| 0980 | Packaged, single zone rooftop unit, with roof curb | | | | |
| 1000 | 2 ton | EA. | 590 | 3,400 | 3,990 |
| 1020 | 3 ton | " | 590 | 3,580 | 4,170 |
| 1040 | 4 ton | " | 730 | 3,900 | 4,630 |
| **15830.70** | **UNIT HEATERS** | | | | |
| 0980 | Steam unit heater, horizontal | | | | |
| 1000 | 12,500 btuh, 200 cfm | EA. | 98.00 | 540 | 638 |
| 1010 | 17,000 btuh, 300 cfm | " | 98.00 | 710 | 808 |
| **15855.10** | **AIR HANDLING UNITS** | | | | |
| 0980 | Air handling unit, medium pressure, single zone | | | | |
| 1000 | 1500 cfm | EA. | 370 | 4,000 | 4,370 |
| 1060 | 3000 cfm | " | 650 | 5,260 | 5,910 |
| 8980 | Rooftop air handling units | | | | |
| 9000 | 4950 cfm | EA. | 650 | 11,500 | 12,150 |
| 9060 | 7370 cfm | " | 840 | 14,580 | 15,420 |
| **15870.20** | **EXHAUST FANS** | | | | |
| 0160 | Belt drive roof exhaust fans | | | | |
| 1020 | 640 cfm, 2618 fpm | EA. | 73.00 | 1,030 | 1,103 |
| 1030 | 940 cfm, 2604 fpm | " | 73.00 | 1,340 | 1,413 |
| **15890.10** | **METAL DUCTWORK** | | | | |
| 0090 | Rectangular duct | | | | |
| 0100 | Galvanized steel | | | | |
| 1000 | Minimum | Lb. | 5.32 | 0.88 | 6.20 |
| 1010 | Average | " | 6.51 | 1.10 | 7.61 |
| 1020 | Maximum | " | 9.76 | 1.68 | 11.44 |
| 1080 | Aluminum | | | | |
| 1100 | Minimum | Lb. | 11.75 | 2.29 | 14.04 |
| 1120 | Average | " | 14.75 | 3.05 | 17.80 |
| 1140 | Maximum | " | 19.50 | 3.79 | 23.29 |
| 1160 | Fittings | | | | |
| 1180 | Minimum | EA. | 19.50 | 7.26 | 26.76 |
| 1200 | Average | " | 29.25 | 11.00 | 40.25 |

© 2011 By Design & Construction Resources

## DIVISION # 15  MECHANICAL

| | | UNIT | LABOR | MAT. | TOTAL |
|---|---|---|---|---|---|
| **15890.10** | **METAL DUCTWORK, Cont'd...** | | | | |
| 1220 | Maximum | EA. | 59.00 | 16.00 | 75.00 |
| **15890.30** | **FLEXIBLE DUCTWORK** | | | | |
| 1010 | Flexible duct, 1.25" fiberglass | | | | |
| 1020 | 5" dia. | L.F. | 2.93 | 3.31 | 6.24 |
| 1040 | 6" dia. | " | 3.25 | 3.68 | 6.93 |
| 1060 | 7" dia. | " | 3.44 | 4.54 | 7.98 |
| 1080 | 8" dia. | " | 3.66 | 4.76 | 8.42 |
| 1100 | 10" dia. | " | 4.18 | 6.34 | 10.52 |
| 1120 | 12" dia. | " | 4.50 | 6.93 | 11.43 |
| 9000 | Flexible duct connector, 3" wide fabric | " | 9.76 | 2.31 | 12.07 |
| **15910.10** | **DAMPERS** | | | | |
| 0980 | Horizontal parallel aluminum backdraft damper | | | | |
| 1000 | 12" x 12" | EA. | 14.75 | 55.00 | 69.75 |
| 1010 | 16" x 16" | " | 16.75 | 57.00 | 73.75 |
| **15940.10** | **DIFFUSERS** | | | | |
| 1980 | Ceiling diffusers, round, baked enamel finish | | | | |
| 2000 | 6" dia. | EA. | 19.50 | 36.50 | 56.00 |
| 2020 | 8" dia. | " | 24.50 | 44.00 | 68.50 |
| 2040 | 10" dia. | " | 24.50 | 48.75 | 73.25 |
| 2060 | 12" dia. | " | 24.50 | 63.00 | 87.50 |
| 2480 | Rectangular | | | | |
| 2500 | 6x6" | EA. | 19.50 | 39.00 | 58.50 |
| 2520 | 9x9" | " | 29.25 | 47.25 | 76.50 |
| 2540 | 12x12" | " | 29.25 | 69.00 | 98.25 |
| 2560 | 15x15" | " | 29.25 | 86.00 | 115 |
| 2580 | 18x18" | " | 29.25 | 110 | 139 |

© 2011 By Design & Construction Resources

**Design & Construction Resources**

# DIVISION # 16 ELECTRICAL

## TABLE OF CONTENTS PAGE

| | |
|---|---|
| 16050.30 - BUS DUCT | 16-2 |
| 16110.22 - EMT CONDUIT | 16-2 |
| 16110.24 - GALVANIZED CONDUIT | 16-2 |
| 16110.25 - PLASTIC CONDUIT | 16-3 |
| 16110.28 - STEEL CONDUIT | 16-3 |
| 16110.35 - SURFACE MOUNTED RACEWAY | 16-3 |
| 16120.43 - COPPER CONDUCTORS | 16-4 |
| 16120.47 - SHEATHED CABLE | 16-4 |
| 16130.40 - BOXES | 16-5 |
| 16130.60 - PULL AND JUNCTION BOXES | 16-5 |
| 16130.80 - RECEPTACLES | 16-5 |
| 16350.10 - CIRCUIT BREAKERS | 16-5 |
| 16395.10 - GROUNDING | 16-5 |
| 16430.20 - METERING | 16-5 |
| 16470.10 - PANELBOARDS | 16-6 |
| 16490.10 - SWITCHES | 16-6 |
| 16510.05 - INTERIOR LIGHTING | 16-6 |
| 16510.10 - LIGHTING INDUSTRIAL | 16-6 |
| 16710.10 - COMMUNICATIONS COMPONENTS | 16-7 |
| 16760.10 - AUDIO/VIDEO COMPONENTS | 16-7 |
| 16760.20 - AUDIO/VIDEO CABLES | 16-8 |
| 16850.10 - ELECTRIC HEATING | 16-8 |
| 16910.40 - CONTROL CABLE | 16-8 |

© 2011 By Design & Construction Resources

## DIVISION # 16 ELECTRICAL

| | | UNIT | LABOR | MAT. | TOTAL |
|---|---|---|---|---|---|
| **16050.30** | **BUS DUCT** | | | | |
| 1000 | Bus duct, 100a, plug-in | | | | |
| 1010 | 10', 600v | EA. | 190 | 250 | 440 |
| 1020 | With ground | " | 290 | 340 | 630 |
| 1145 | Circuit breakers, with enclosure | | | | |
| 1147 | 1 pole | | | | |
| 1150 | 15a-60a | EA. | 68.00 | 250 | 318 |
| 1160 | 70a-100a | " | 85.00 | 290 | 375 |
| 1165 | 2 pole | | | | |
| 1170 | 15a-60a | EA. | 75.00 | 380 | 455 |
| 1180 | 70a-100a | " | 88.00 | 450 | 538 |
| **16110.22** | **EMT CONDUIT** | | | | |
| 0080 | EMT conduit | | | | |
| 0100 | 1/2" | L.F. | 2.05 | 0.56 | 2.61 |
| 1020 | 3/4" | " | 2.72 | 1.02 | 3.74 |
| 1030 | 1" | " | 3.40 | 1.70 | 5.10 |
| 2980 | 90 deg. elbow | | | | |
| 3000 | 1/2" | EA. | 6.04 | 5.26 | 11.30 |
| 3040 | 3/4" | " | 6.80 | 5.78 | 12.58 |
| 3060 | 1" | " | 7.25 | 8.92 | 16.17 |
| 3980 | Connector, steel compression | | | | |
| 4000 | 1/2" | EA. | 6.04 | 1.69 | 7.73 |
| 4040 | 3/4" | " | 6.04 | 3.23 | 9.27 |
| 4060 | 1" | " | 6.04 | 4.87 | 10.91 |
| 0080 | Flexible conduit, steel | | | | |
| 0100 | 3/8" | L.F. | 2.05 | 0.59 | 2.64 |
| 1020 | 1/2 | " | 2.05 | 0.68 | 2.73 |
| 1040 | 3/4" | " | 2.72 | 0.93 | 3.65 |
| 1060 | 1" | " | 2.72 | 1.76 | 4.48 |
| **16110.24** | **GALVANIZED CONDUIT** | | | | |
| 1980 | Galvanized rigid steel conduit | | | | |
| 2000 | 1/2" | L.F. | 2.72 | 2.85 | 5.57 |
| 2040 | 3/4" | " | 3.40 | 3.15 | 6.55 |
| 2060 | 1" | " | 4.02 | 4.56 | 8.58 |
| 2080 | 1-1/4" | " | 5.44 | 6.30 | 11.74 |
| 2100 | 1-1/2" | " | 6.04 | 7.41 | 13.45 |
| 2120 | 2" | " | 6.80 | 9.43 | 16.23 |
| 2480 | 90 degree ell | | | | |
| 2500 | 1/2" | EA. | 17.00 | 10.25 | 27.25 |
| 2540 | 3/4" | " | 21.00 | 10.75 | 31.75 |
| 2560 | 1" | " | 26.00 | 16.50 | 42.50 |
| 2580 | 1-1/4" | " | 30.25 | 22.75 | 53.00 |
| 2590 | 1-1/2" | " | 34.00 | 28.00 | 62.00 |
| 2600 | 2" | " | 36.25 | 40.75 | 77.00 |
| 3200 | Couplings, with set screws | | | | |
| 3220 | 1/2" | EA. | 3.40 | 5.17 | 8.57 |
| 3260 | 3/4" | " | 4.02 | 6.82 | 10.84 |
| 3280 | 1" | " | 5.44 | 11.00 | 16.44 |
| 3300 | 1-1/4" | " | 6.80 | 18.50 | 25.30 |
| 3320 | 1-1/2" | " | 8.36 | 24.00 | 32.36 |
| 3340 | 2" | " | 9.89 | 54.00 | 63.89 |

© 2011 By Design & Construction Resources

## DIVISION # 16 ELECTRICAL

| | | UNIT | LABOR | MAT. | TOTAL |
|---|---|---|---|---|---|
| **16110.25** | **PLASTIC CONDUIT** | | | | |
| 3010 | PVC conduit, schedule 40 | | | | |
| 3020 | 1/2" | L.F. | 2.05 | 0.63 | 2.68 |
| 3040 | 3/4" | " | 2.05 | 0.79 | 2.84 |
| 3060 | 1" | " | 2.72 | 1.14 | 3.86 |
| 3080 | 1-1/4" | " | 2.72 | 1.58 | 4.30 |
| 3100 | 1-1/2" | " | 3.40 | 1.88 | 5.28 |
| 3120 | 2" | " | 3.40 | 2.40 | 5.80 |
| 3480 | Couplings | | | | |
| 3500 | 1/2" | EA. | 3.40 | 0.42 | 3.82 |
| 3520 | 3/4" | " | 3.40 | 0.51 | 3.91 |
| 3540 | 1" | " | 3.40 | 0.80 | 4.20 |
| 3560 | 1-1/4" | " | 4.02 | 1.05 | 5.07 |
| 3580 | 1-1/2" | " | 4.02 | 1.46 | 5.48 |
| 3600 | 2" | " | 4.02 | 1.92 | 5.94 |
| 3705 | 90 degree elbows | | | | |
| 3710 | 1/2" | EA. | 6.80 | 1.66 | 8.46 |
| 3740 | 3/4" | " | 8.36 | 1.81 | 10.17 |
| 3760 | 1" | " | 8.36 | 2.87 | 11.23 |
| 3780 | 1-1/4" | " | 9.89 | 4.00 | 13.89 |
| 3800 | 1-1/2" | " | 13.00 | 5.42 | 18.42 |
| 3810 | 2" | " | 15.00 | 7.56 | 22.56 |
| **16110.28** | **STEEL CONDUIT** | | | | |
| 7980 | Intermediate metal conduit (IMC) | | | | |
| 8000 | 1/2" | L.F. | 2.05 | 1.84 | 3.89 |
| 8040 | 3/4" | " | 2.72 | 2.27 | 4.99 |
| 8060 | 1" | " | 3.40 | 3.43 | 6.83 |
| 8080 | 1-1/4" | " | 4.02 | 4.39 | 8.41 |
| 8100 | 1-1/2" | " | 5.44 | 5.49 | 10.93 |
| 8120 | 2" | " | 6.04 | 7.16 | 13.20 |
| 8490 | 90 degree ell | | | | |
| 8500 | 1/2" | EA. | 17.00 | 14.25 | 31.25 |
| 8540 | 3/4" | " | 21.00 | 14.75 | 35.75 |
| 8560 | 1" | " | 26.00 | 22.75 | 48.75 |
| 8580 | 1-1/4" | " | 30.25 | 31.50 | 61.75 |
| 8600 | 1-1/2" | " | 34.00 | 38.75 | 72.75 |
| 8620 | 2" | " | 38.75 | 56.00 | 94.75 |
| 9260 | Couplings | | | | |
| 9280 | 1/2" | EA. | 3.40 | 3.46 | 6.86 |
| 9290 | 3/4" | " | 4.02 | 4.24 | 8.26 |
| 9300 | 1" | " | 5.44 | 6.29 | 11.73 |
| 9310 | 1-1/4" | " | 6.04 | 7.87 | 13.91 |
| 9320 | 1-1/2" | " | 6.80 | 9.95 | 16.75 |
| 9330 | 2" | " | 7.25 | 13.25 | 20.50 |
| **16110.35** | **SURFACE MOUNTED RACEWAY** | | | | |
| 0980 | Single Raceway | | | | |
| 1000 | 3/4" x 17/32" Conduit | L.F. | 2.72 | 1.67 | 4.39 |
| 1020 | Mounting Strap | EA. | 3.62 | 0.45 | 4.07 |
| 1040 | Connector | " | 3.62 | 0.60 | 4.22 |
| 1060 | Elbow | | | | |
| 2000 | 45 degree | EA. | 3.40 | 7.62 | 11.02 |
| 2020 | 90 degree | " | 3.40 | 2.43 | 5.83 |

© 2011 By Design & Construction Resources

## DIVISION # 16 ELECTRICAL

| | | UNIT | LABOR | MAT. | TOTAL |
|---|---|---|---|---|---|
| **16110.35** | **SURFACE MOUNTED RACEWAY, Cont'd...** | | | | |
| 2040 | internal | EA. | 3.40 | 3.05 | 6.45 |
| 2050 | external | " | 3.40 | 2.82 | 6.22 |
| 2060 | Switch | " | 27.25 | 19.75 | 47.00 |
| 2100 | Utility Box | " | 27.25 | 13.25 | 40.50 |
| 2110 | Receptacle | " | 27.25 | 23.50 | 50.75 |
| 2140 | 3/4" x 21/32" Conduit | L.F. | 2.72 | 1.90 | 4.62 |
| 2160 | Mounting Strap | EA. | 3.62 | 0.70 | 4.32 |
| 2180 | Connector | " | 3.62 | 0.72 | 4.34 |
| 2200 | Elbow | | | | |
| 2210 | 45 degree | EA. | 3.40 | 9.41 | 12.81 |
| 2220 | 90 degree | " | 3.40 | 2.59 | 5.99 |
| 2240 | internal | " | 3.40 | 3.52 | 6.92 |
| 2260 | external | " | 3.40 | 3.52 | 6.92 |
| 3000 | Switch | " | 27.25 | 19.75 | 47.00 |
| 3010 | Utility Box | " | 27.25 | 13.25 | 40.50 |
| 3020 | Receptacle | " | 27.25 | 23.50 | 50.75 |
| **16120.43** | **COPPER CONDUCTORS** | | | | |
| 0980 | Copper conductors, type THW, solid | | | | |
| 1000 | #14 | L.F. | 0.27 | 0.13 | 0.40 |
| 1040 | #12 | " | 0.34 | 0.20 | 0.54 |
| 1060 | #10 | " | 0.41 | 0.31 | 0.72 |
| 2010 | THHN-THWN, solid | | | | |
| 2020 | #14 | L.F. | 0.27 | 0.13 | 0.40 |
| 2040 | #12 | " | 0.34 | 0.20 | 0.54 |
| 2060 | #10 | " | 0.41 | 0.31 | 0.72 |
| 6215 | Type "BX" solid armored cable | | | | |
| 6220 | #14/2 | L.F. | 1.70 | 0.90 | 2.60 |
| 6230 | #14/3 | " | 1.90 | 1.42 | 3.32 |
| 6240 | #14/4 | " | 2.09 | 1.99 | 4.08 |
| 6250 | #12/2 | " | 1.90 | 0.93 | 2.83 |
| 6260 | #12/3 | " | 2.09 | 1.48 | 3.57 |
| 6270 | #12/4 | " | 2.36 | 2.05 | 4.41 |
| 6280 | #10/2 | " | 2.09 | 1.71 | 3.80 |
| 6290 | #10/3 | " | 2.36 | 2.45 | 4.81 |
| 6300 | #10/4 | " | 2.72 | 3.82 | 6.54 |
| **16120.47** | **SHEATHED CABLE** | | | | |
| 6700 | Non-metallic sheathed cable | | | | |
| 6705 | Type NM cable with ground | | | | |
| 6710 | #14/2 | L.F. | 1.01 | 0.35 | 1.36 |
| 6720 | #12/2 | " | 1.08 | 0.53 | 1.61 |
| 6730 | #10/2 | " | 1.20 | 0.85 | 2.05 |
| 6740 | #8/2 | " | 1.36 | 1.39 | 2.75 |
| 6750 | #6/2 | " | 1.70 | 2.20 | 3.90 |
| 6760 | #14/3 | " | 1.75 | 0.49 | 2.24 |
| 6770 | #12/3 | " | 1.81 | 0.77 | 2.58 |
| 6780 | #10/3 | " | 1.84 | 1.22 | 3.06 |
| 6790 | #8/3 | " | 1.87 | 2.05 | 3.92 |
| 6800 | #6/3 | " | 1.90 | 3.32 | 5.22 |
| 6810 | #4/3 | " | 2.17 | 6.87 | 9.04 |
| 6820 | #2/3 | " | 2.36 | 10.25 | 12.61 |

## DIVISION # 16  ELECTRICAL

| | | UNIT | LABOR | MAT. | TOTAL |
|---|---|---|---|---|---|
| **16130.40** | **BOXES** | | | | |
| 5000 | Round cast box, type SEH | | | | |
| 5010 | 1/2" | EA. | 23.75 | 20.00 | 43.75 |
| 5020 | 3/4" | " | 28.75 | 20.00 | 48.75 |
| **16130.60** | **PULL AND JUNCTION BOXES** | | | | |
| 1050 | 4" | | | | |
| 1060 | Octagon box | EA. | 7.77 | 3.33 | 11.10 |
| 1070 | Box extension | " | 4.02 | 5.61 | 9.63 |
| 1080 | Plaster ring | " | 4.02 | 3.08 | 7.10 |
| 1100 | Cover blank | " | 4.02 | 1.36 | 5.38 |
| 1120 | Square box | " | 7.77 | 4.79 | 12.56 |
| 1140 | Box extension | " | 4.02 | 4.69 | 8.71 |
| 1160 | Plaster ring | " | 4.02 | 2.57 | 6.59 |
| 1180 | Cover blank | " | 4.02 | 1.32 | 5.34 |
| **16130.80** | **RECEPTACLES** | | | | |
| 0500 | Contractor grade duplex receptacles, 15a 120v | | | | |
| 0510 | Duplex | EA. | 13.50 | 1.46 | 14.96 |
| 1000 | 125 volt, 20a, duplex, standard grade | " | 13.50 | 10.75 | 24.25 |
| 1040 | Ground fault interrupter type | " | 20.25 | 35.25 | 55.50 |
| 1520 | 250 volt, 20a, 2 pole, single, ground type | " | 13.50 | 18.25 | 31.75 |
| 1540 | 120/208v, 4 pole, single receptacle, twist lock | | | | |
| 1560 | 20a | EA. | 23.75 | 21.50 | 45.25 |
| 1580 | 50a | " | 23.75 | 41.00 | 64.75 |
| 1590 | 125/250v, 3 pole, flush receptacle | | | | |
| 1600 | 30a | EA. | 20.25 | 21.75 | 42.00 |
| 1620 | 50a | " | 20.25 | 27.00 | 47.25 |
| 1640 | 60a | " | 23.75 | 70.00 | 93.75 |
| **16350.10** | **CIRCUIT BREAKERS** | | | | |
| 5000 | Load center circuit breakers, 240v | | | | |
| 5010 | 1 pole, 10-60a | EA. | 17.00 | 16.50 | 33.50 |
| 5015 | 2 pole | | | | |
| 5020 | 10-60a | EA. | 27.25 | 38.50 | 65.75 |
| 5030 | 70-100a | " | 45.25 | 120 | 165 |
| 5040 | 110-150a | " | 49.50 | 250 | 300 |
| 5065 | Load center, G.F.I. breakers, 240v | | | | |
| 5070 | 1 pole, 15-30a | EA. | 20.25 | 140 | 160 |
| 5095 | Tandem breakers, 240v | | | | |
| 5100 | 1 pole, 15-30a | EA. | 27.25 | 31.25 | 58.50 |
| 5110 | 2 pole, 15-30a | " | 36.25 | 57.00 | 93.25 |
| **16395.10** | **GROUNDING** | | | | |
| 0500 | Ground rods, copper clad, 1/2" x | | | | |
| 0510 | 6' | EA. | 45.25 | 13.25 | 58.50 |
| 0520 | 8' | " | 49.50 | 18.50 | 68.00 |
| 0535 | 5/8" x | | | | |
| 0550 | 6' | EA. | 49.50 | 17.75 | 67.25 |
| 0560 | 8' | " | 68.00 | 23.00 | 91.00 |
| **16430.20** | **METERING** | | | | |
| 0500 | Outdoor wp meter sockets, 1 gang, 240v, 1 phase | | | | |
| 0510 | Includes sealing ring, 100a | EA. | 100 | 47.50 | 148 |
| 0520 | 150a | " | 120 | 63.00 | 183 |
| 0530 | 200a | " | 140 | 80.00 | 220 |

© 2011 By Design & Construction Resources

## DIVISION # 16 ELECTRICAL

| | | UNIT | LABOR | MAT. | TOTAL |
|---|---|---|---|---|---|
| **16470.10** | **PANELBOARDS** | | | | |
| 1000 | Indoor load center, 1 phase 240v main lug only | | | | |
| 1020 | 30a - 2 spaces | EA. | 140 | 26.50 | 167 |
| 1030 | 100a - 8 spaces | " | 160 | 85.00 | 245 |
| 1040 | 150a - 16 spaces | " | 200 | 220 | 420 |
| 1050 | 200a - 24 spaces | " | 240 | 460 | 700 |
| 1060 | 200a - 42 spaces | " | 270 | 470 | 740 |
| **16490.10** | **SWITCHES** | | | | |
| 4000 | Photo electric switches | | | | |
| 4010 | 1000 watt | | | | |
| 4020 | 105-135v | EA. | 49.50 | 33.50 | 83.00 |
| 4970 | Dimmer switch and switch plate | | | | |
| 4990 | 600w | EA. | 21.00 | 30.75 | 51.75 |
| 5171 | Contractor grade wall switch 15a, 120v | | | | |
| 5172 | Single pole | EA. | 11.00 | 1.62 | 12.62 |
| 5173 | Three way | " | 13.50 | 2.97 | 16.47 |
| 5174 | Four way | " | 18.25 | 10.00 | 28.25 |
| **16510.05** | **INTERIOR LIGHTING** | | | | |
| 0005 | Recessed fluorescent fixtures, 2'x2' | | | | |
| 0010 | 2 lamp | EA. | 49.50 | 63.00 | 113 |
| 0020 | 4 lamp | " | 49.50 | 85.00 | 135 |
| 0205 | Surface mounted incandescent fixtures | | | | |
| 0210 | 40w | EA. | 45.25 | 95.00 | 140 |
| 0220 | 75w | " | 45.25 | 98.00 | 143 |
| 0230 | 100w | " | 45.25 | 110 | 155 |
| 0240 | 150w | " | 45.25 | 140 | 185 |
| 0289 | Recessed incandescent fixtures | | | | |
| 0290 | 40w | EA. | 100 | 130 | 230 |
| 0300 | 75w | " | 100 | 140 | 240 |
| 0310 | 100w | " | 100 | 150 | 250 |
| 0320 | 150w | " | 100 | 160 | 260 |
| 0395 | Light track single circuit | | | | |
| 0400 | 2' | EA. | 34.00 | 38.50 | 72.50 |
| 0410 | 4' | " | 34.00 | 45.50 | 79.50 |
| 0420 | 8' | " | 68.00 | 62.00 | 130 |
| 0430 | 12' | " | 100 | 88.00 | 188 |
| **16510.10** | **LIGHTING INDUSTRIAL** | | | | |
| 0500 | Strip fluorescent | | | | |
| 0510 | 4' | | | | |
| 0520 | 1 lamp | EA. | 45.25 | 43.25 | 88.50 |
| 0540 | 2 lamps | " | 45.25 | 53.00 | 98.25 |
| 0550 | 8' | | | | |
| 0560 | 1 lamp | EA. | 49.50 | 63.00 | 113 |
| 0580 | 2 lamps | " | 60.00 | 95.00 | 155 |
| 1000 | Parabolic troffer, 2'x2' | | | | |
| 1020 | With 2 "U" lamps | EA. | 68.00 | 120 | 188 |
| 1060 | With 3 "U" lamps | " | 78.00 | 140 | 218 |
| 1080 | 2'x4' | | | | |
| 1100 | With 2 40w lamps | EA. | 78.00 | 140 | 218 |
| 1120 | With 3 40w lamps | " | 91.00 | 140 | 231 |
| 1140 | With 4 40w lamps | " | 91.00 | 150 | 241 |
| 3120 | High pressure sodium, hi-bay open | | | | |

# DIVISION # 16 ELECTRICAL

| | | UNIT | LABOR | MAT. | TOTAL |
|---|---|---|---|---|---|
| **16510.10** | **LIGHTING INDUSTRIAL, Cont'd...** | | | | |
| 3140 | 400w | EA. | 120 | 430 | 550 |
| 3160 | 1000w | " | 160 | 750 | 910 |
| 3170 | Enclosed | | | | |
| 3180 | 400w | EA. | 160 | 700 | 860 |
| 3200 | 1000w | " | 200 | 980 | 1,180 |
| 3210 | Metal halide hi-bay, open | | | | |
| 3220 | 400w | EA. | 120 | 270 | 390 |
| 3240 | 1000w | " | 160 | 550 | 710 |
| 3250 | Enclosed | | | | |
| 3260 | 400w | EA. | 160 | 610 | 770 |
| 3280 | 1000w | " | 200 | 580 | 780 |
| 3590 | Metal halide, low bay, pendant mounted | | | | |
| 3600 | 175w | EA. | 91.00 | 350 | 441 |
| 3620 | 250w | " | 110 | 480 | 590 |
| 3660 | 400w | " | 150 | 520 | 670 |
| **16710.10** | **COMMUNICATIONS COMPONENTS** | | | | |
| 0020 | Port desktop switch unit-4 | EA. | | | 77.00 |
| 0030 | (USB)-4 | " | | | 200 |
| 0040 | 8 | " | | | 330 |
| 0050 | 16 | " | | | 550 |
| 0060 | 32 | " | | | 3,520 |
| 0070 | Port console unit-8 | " | | | 2,200 |
| 0080 | 16 | " | | | 2,750 |
| 0090 | Cat 5EJack and RJ45 coupler | " | | | 3.74 |
| 1000 | Quick-Port and voice grade | " | | | 4.23 |
| 1010 | Trac-Jack category 5E and connectors | " | | | 4.21 |
| 1020 | Snap-In connector | " | | | 5.77 |
| 1030 | Fast ethernet media converter | " | | | 140 |
| 1040 | Gigabit media converter | " | | | 390 |
| 1050 | With link fault signaling | " | | | 130 |
| 1060 | Gigabit switching media converter | " | | | 550 |
| 1070 | 16-Bay media chassis | " | | | 670 |
| 1080 | Fiber-optic cable, Single-Mode, 50/125 microns, 10' length | " | | | 22.00 |
| 1090 | Multi-Mode, 62.5/125 microns, 10' length | " | | | 25.25 |
| 2000 | Fiber-Optic connectors, Unicam | " | | | 17.00 |
| 2010 | Fast-cam | " | | | 17.50 |
| 2020 | Adhesive style | " | | | 6.32 |
| 2030 | Threat-lock | " | | | 10.75 |
| 2040 | Unicam, high performance, single-mode | " | | | 22.00 |
| 2050 | multi-mode | " | | | 19.75 |
| 2060 | Network Cable, Cat5, solid PVC, 50' | " | | | 16.00 |
| 2070 | 1000' Cat5, stranded PVC | " | | | 190 |
| 2080 | plenum PVC | " | | | 220 |
| 2090 | 1000' Cat6, solid PVC | " | | | 150 |
| 3000 | USB Cables, 5 in 1 connector, male and female | " | | | 19.75 |
| 3010 | 3 in 1 quick-connect, 4-pin or 6-pin | " | | | 24.25 |
| 3020 | Squid hub | " | | | 33.00 |
| **16760.10** | **AUDIO/VIDEO COMPONENTS** | | | | |
| 0010 | Key-stone jack module | EA. | | | 3.30 |
| 0020 | F-Type quick port | " | | | 2.31 |
| 0030 | BNC quick port | " | | | 5.50 |

© 2011 By Design & Construction Resources

## DIVISION # 16  ELECTRICAL

| | | UNIT | LABOR | MAT. | TOTAL |
|---|---|---|---|---|---|
| **16760.10** | **AUDIO/VIDEO COMPONENTS, Cont'd...** | | | | |
| 0040 | RCA jack bulkhead connector | EA. | | | 4.40 |
| 0050 | Quick-Port | " | | | 5.72 |
| 0060 | Snap-in | " | | | 8.80 |
| 0070 | HDMI wall plate and jack | " | | | 10.50 |
| 0080 | Voice/Data adapter | " | | | 3.85 |
| **16760.20** | **AUDIO/VIDEO CABLES** | | | | |
| 0010 | Monster cable, 24k. gold plated | EA. | | | 27.50 |
| 0020 | DVI-HDMI | " | | | 11.75 |
| 0030 | Satellite/Video | " | | | 3.96 |
| 0040 | Digital/Optical | " | | | 12.75 |
| 0050 | Video/RCA | " | | | 7.42 |
| 0060 | S-Video | " | | | 8.25 |
| 0070 | Monster/S-video | " | | | 44.00 |
| 0080 | Speaker, clear jacket | FT. | | | 0.93 |
| 0090 | Speaker, high performance | " | | | 2.20 |
| 0100 | Flex-Premiere, oxygen free | " | | | 0.33 |
| **16850.10** | **ELECTRIC HEATING** | | | | |
| 1000 | Baseboard heater | | | | |
| 1020 | 2', 375w | EA. | 68.00 | 41.75 | 110 |
| 1040 | 3', 500w | " | 68.00 | 49.50 | 118 |
| 1060 | 4', 750w | " | 78.00 | 55.00 | 133 |
| 1100 | 5', 935w | " | 91.00 | 78.00 | 169 |
| 1120 | 6', 1125w | " | 110 | 92.00 | 202 |
| 1140 | 7', 1310w | " | 120 | 100 | 220 |
| 1160 | 8', 1500w | " | 140 | 120 | 260 |
| 1180 | 9', 1680w | " | 150 | 130 | 280 |
| 1200 | 10', 1875w | " | 160 | 180 | 340 |
| 1210 | Unit heater, wall mounted | | | | |
| 1215 | 750w | EA. | 110 | 160 | 270 |
| 1220 | 1500w | " | 110 | 220 | 330 |
| **16910.40** | **CONTROL CABLE** | | | | |
| 0980 | Control cable, 600v, #14 THWN, PVC jacket | | | | |
| 1000 | 2 wire | L.F. | 0.54 | 0.31 | 0.85 |
| 1020 | 4 wire | " | 0.68 | 0.53 | 1.21 |

# APPENDIX

## Average Square Foot Costs 2012
## Housing (with Wood Frame)

Square Foot Costs do not include Garages, Land, Furnishings, Equipment, Landscaping, Financing, or Architect's Fee. Total Costs, except General Contractor's Fee, are included in each division. See Page 2 for Metropolitan Cost Variation Modifier. See Division 13 for Metal Buildings, Greenhouses, and Air-Supported Structures.

|  | Division | Houses - 3 Bedrooms with Basement |  |  | Houses - 3 Bedrooms without Basement |  |  |
|---|---|---|---|---|---|---|---|
|  |  | Low | Tract | Custom | Low | Tract | Custom |
| 1. | General Conditions | 5.22 | 5.33 | 5.79 | 6.77 | 7.00 | 7.46 |
| 2. | Site Work | 4.17 | 4.77 | 5.13 | 7.03 | 7.37 | 7.63 |
| 3. | Concrete | 4.73 | 4.97 | 5.28 | 8.58 | 8.79 | 9.75 |
| 4. | Masonry | 5.79 | 6.02 | 8.01 | 8.24 | 8.59 | 11.38 |
| 5. | Steel | 1.91 | 1.91 | 2.06 | 0.94 | 0.93 | 0.95 |
| 6. | Carpentry | 19.25 | 18.89 | 21.29 | 28.22 | 27.98 | 30.44 |
| 7. | Moisture & Therm. Prot. | 4.97 | 4.97 | 5.10 | 6.92 | 7.17 | 7.79 |
| 8. | Doors, Windows & Glass | 10.06 | 9.70 | 10.11 | 12.39 | 12.74 | 13.36 |
| 9. | Finishes | 9.08 | 9.91 | 12.09 | 13.45 | 13.66 | 19.34 |
| 10. | Specialties | 0.93 | 0.95 | 1.04 | 1.02 | 1.03 | 1.37 |
| 11. | Equipment (Cabinets) | 3.39 | 3.45 | 5.23 | 6.08 | 6.02 | 9.08 |
| 12. | Furnishings | 0.70 | 0.70 | 0.75 | 1.07 | 1.07 | 1.07 |
| 13. | Special Construction | - | - | - | - | - | - |
| 14. | Conveying | - | - | - | - | - | - |
| 15. | Mechanical: Plumbing | 8.19 | 8.25 | 9.70 | 12.12 | 12.06 | 14.99 |
|  | Heating | 4.96 | 5.14 | 5.34 | 6.98 | 7.37 | 10.40 |
|  | Air Cond. | - | - | - | - | - | - |
| 16. | Electrical | 4.77 | 4.77 | 5.75 | 7.10 | 7.10 | 8.42 |
|  | SUB TOTAL | $88.11 | $89.73 | $102.68 | $126.90 | $128.86 | $153.42 |
|  | CONTRACTOR'S SERVICES | 7.67 | 7.88 | 8.98 | 11.12 | 11.45 | 14.94 |
|  | **TOTAL S F Cost** | $95.78 | $97.61 | $111.66 | $138.02 | $140.31 | $168.37 |

|  | Unfinished Basement, Storage and Utility Areas included in Sq.Ft. Costs: |  |  | No Basement Utilities In Finished Area |  |  |
|---|---|---|---|---|---|---|
| Average Cost/ Unit | $191,563 | $195,211 | $279,144 | $165,627 | $168,367 | $252,551 |
| Average Sq.Ft. Size/Unit (includes basement) | 2,000 | 2,000 | 2,500 | 1,200 | 1,200 | 1,500 |
| Add Architect's Fee | $ 7,897 | $8,845 | $20,217 | $6,823 | $7,708 | $15,163 |

|  | COST |  |
|---|---|---|
|  | Sq. Ft. | Ea. Unit |
| Add for Finishing Basement Space For Bedrooms or Amusement Rooms, 12' x 20' | $36.49 | $8,759 |
| Add for Single Garage (no Interior Finish), 12' x 20' | $34.76 | $8,341 |
| Add for Double Garage (no Interior Finish), 20 x 20' | $36.49 | $8,759 |
| Add (or Deduct) for Bedrooms, 12' x 12' | $51.90 | $7,473 |
| Add per Bathroom with 2 Fixtures, 6' x 8' | $162.66 | $7,808 |
| Add per Bathroom with 3 Fixtures, 8' x 8' | $162.66 | $10,410 |
| Add for Fireplace | - | $8,110 |
| Add for Central Air Conditioning | - | $6,720 |
| Add for Drain Tiling | - | $3,661 |
| Add for Well | - | $8,341 |
| Add for Septic System | - | $8,341 |

SF-1

# APPENDIX

## Average Square Foot Costs 2012
### Apartments, Hotels

Square Foot Costs do not include Land, Furnishings, Equipment, Landscaping and Financing.

|  | Division | Apartments 2 & 3 Story (1)a | Apartments 2 & 3 Story (1)b | Apartments High Rise (2) | Motels & Hotels High Rise (3) | Motels & Hotels 1 & 2 Story (1)b | Motels & Hotels High Rise (2) |
|---|---|---|---|---|---|---|---|
| 1. | General Conditions | 4.93 | 5.22 | 7.46 | 7.97 | 5.39 | 6.88 |
| 2. | Site Work | 3.59 | 3.53 | 5.09 | 5.01 | 7.39 | 5.72 |
| 3. | Concrete | 2.78 | 2.77 | 26.53 | 17.91 | 3.25 | 27.18 |
| 4. | Masonry | 1.99 | 12.61 | 3.27 | 3.12 | 12.55 | 16.24 |
| 5. | Steel | 1.81 | 1.82 | 2.89 | 3.02 | 2.20 | 2.76 |
| 6. | Carpentry and Millwork | 20.20 | 16.94 | 6.53 | 6.06 | 16.97 | 5.26 |
| 7. | Moisture Protection | 4.56 | 4.82 | 2.46 | 2.41 | 4.44 | 2.46 |
| 8. | Doors, Windows and Glass | 7.13 | 7.76 | 8.83 | 8.57 | 8.90 | 10.62 |
| 9. | Finishes | 13.84 | 13.87 | 14.21 | 13.39 | 13.84 | 19.05 |
| 10. | Specialties | 1.04 | 1.05 | 1.09 | 1.08 | 1.27 | 1.30 |
| 11. | Equipment | 2.15 | 2.84 | 2.20 | 2.15 | 3.57 | 3.80 |
| 12. | Furnishings | 1.07 | 1.16 | 1.23 | 1.25 | 2.49 | 1.90 |
| 13. | Special Construction | - | - | - | - | - | - |
| 14. | Conveying | - | 2.98 | 4.50 | 4.65 | - | 5.22 |
| 15. | Mechanical: | | | | | | |
|  | Plumbing | 9.70 | 9.70 | 9.51 | 9.35 | 11.02 | 14.86 |
|  | Heating and Ventilation | 7.44 | 8.04 | 8.91 | 8.54 | 7.73 | 10.04 |
|  | Air Conditioning | 2.65 | 2.65 | 2.77 | 2.71 | 3.27 | 6.50 |
|  | Sprinklers | - | - | 2.95 | 2.61 | 2.73 | 2.79 |
| 16. | Electrical | 10.30 | 10.24 | 11.77 | 12.21 | 13.74 | 14.54 |
|  | SUB TOTAL | $95.17 | $108.01 | $122.19 | $112.00 | $120.75 | $157.13 |
|  | CONTRACTOR'S SERVICES | 9.21 | 10.52 | 11.82 | 10.90 | 11.50 | 15.29 |
|  | Construction Sq.Ft. Cost | $104.38 | $118.53 | $134.00 | $122.90 | $132.25 | $172.42 |
|  | Add for Architect's Fee | 7.51 | 8.59 | 8.59 | 8.92 | 9.38 | 12.51 |
|  | **TOTAL Sq.Ft. Cost** | $111.89 | $127.11 | $142.59 | $131.82 | $141.64 | $184.93 |
|  | Average Cost per Unit without Architect's Fee | $99,165 | $112,600 | $120,604 | $98,323 | $85,965 | $112,072 |
|  | Average Cost per Unit with Architect's Fee | $106,297 | $120,758 | $128,333 | $105,457 | $92,065 | $120,205 |

Add for Porches – Wood - $12.00 Sq. Ft.
Add for Interior Garages - $11.40 Sq. Ft.

|  | | | | | | |
|---|---|---|---|---|---|---|
| Average Sq. Ft. Size per Unit | 950 | 950 | 900 | 800 | 650 | 650 |
| Average Sq. Ft. Living Space | 750 | 750 | 750 | 600 | 450 | 450 |

(1)a Wall Bearing Wood Frame & Wood or Aluminum Façade
(1)b Wall Bearing Masonry & Wood Joists & Brick Façade
(2) Concrete Frame
(3) Post Tensioned Concrete Slabs, Sheer Walls, Window Wall Exteriors, and Drywall Partitions.

# APPENDIX

## Average Square Foot Costs 2012
### Commercial

Square Foot Costs do <u>not</u> include Land, Furnishings, and Financing.

| | Division | Remod. Office Interior | Office 1-Story (1) | Office 2-Story (2) | Office Up To 5-Story (3) | High Rise (City) Above 5-Story (4) | Parking Ramp (3) |
|---|---|---|---|---|---|---|---|
| 1. | General Conditions | 3.15 | 5.11 | 5.11 | 7.57 | 9.06 | 5.62 |
| 2. | Site Work & Demolition | 2.11 | 3.02 | 2.99 | 2.93 | 2.74 | 1.97 |
| 3. | Concrete | - | 8.53 | 13.26 | 14.61 | 9.94 | 32.67 |
| 4. | Masonry | - | 12.67 | 12.04 | 18.17 | 4.51 | 1.82 |
| 5. | Steel | - | 4.23 | 14.02 | 4.90 | 3.46 | 2.66 |
| 6. | Carpentry and Millwork | 9.92 | 4.59 | 4.28 | 6.65 | 7.51 | 1.51 |
| 7. | Moisture Protection | - | 8.48 | 4.23 | 2.81 | 3.57 | 3.94 |
| 8. | Doors, Windows and Glass | 2.10 | 8.18 | 8.11 | 16.51 | 31.31 | 1.70 |
| 9. | Finishes & Sheet Rock | 14.39 | 15.53 | 15.14 | 17.49 | 18.08 | 2.34 |
| 10. | Specialties | - | 2.08 | 2.08 | 2.14 | 2.14 | - |
| 11. | Equipment | - | 6.64 | 5.88 | 4.85 | 6.61 | - |
| 12. | Furnishings | - | 1.37 | 1.62 | 1.80 | 1.95 | - |
| 13. | Special Construction | - | - | - | - | - | - |
| 14. | Conveying | - | - | 3.73 | 6.43 | 7.00 | 3.56 |
| 15. | Mechanical: | | | | | | |
| | Plumbing | 5.09 | 7.68 | 8.25 | 9.50 | 9.89 | 3.33 |
| | Heating and Ventilation | 2.29 | 8.62 | 8.42 | 10.89 | 10.95 | - |
| | Air Conditioning | 2.21 | 8.57 | 8.82 | 10.47 | 10.45 | - |
| | Sprinklers | - | 2.75 | 2.73 | 2.79 | 2.82 | - |
| 16. | Electrical | <u>9.92</u> | <u>12.17</u> | <u>13.41</u> | <u>14.75</u> | <u>17.30</u> | <u>3.84</u> |
| | SUB TOTAL | $51.19 | $120.22 | $134.14 | $155.28 | $159.27 | $64.94 |
| | CONTRACTOR'S SERVICES | <u>4.92</u> | <u>10.10</u> | <u>12.98</u> | <u>13.58</u> | <u>13.55</u> | <u>6.27</u> |
| | Construction Sq.Ft. Cost | $56.12 | $130.32 | $147.12 | $168.86 | $172.83 | $71.21 |
| | Add for Architect's Fee | <u>5.57</u> | <u>9.83</u> | <u>10.28</u> | <u>12.40</u> | <u>13.88</u> | <u>5.66</u> |
| | **TOTAL Sq.Ft. Costs** | <u>$61.68</u> | <u>$140.15</u> | <u>$157.39</u> | <u>$181.25</u> | <u>$186.70</u> | <u>$76.87</u> |
| | Deduct for Tenant Areas Unfinished | - | - | 25.49 | 28.96 | 33.60 | - |
| | Per Car Average | - | - | - | - | - | 20,273 |
| | Add: Masonry Enclosed Ramp | - | - | - | - | - | 7.76 |
| | Add: Heated Ramp | - | - | - | - | - | 7.76 |
| | Add: Sprinklers for Closed Ramps | - | - | - | - | - | 3.01 |
| | Deduct for Precast Conc. Ramp | - | - | - | - | - | 10.02 |

(1) Wall Bearing Masonry and Steel Joists and Decks – No Basement
(2) Wall Bearing Masonry and Precast Concrete Decks – No Basement
(3) Concrete Frame
(4) Steel Frame and Window Wall Façade

# APPENDIX

## Average Square Foot Costs 2012
### Commercial and Industrial

Square Foot Costs do <u>not</u> include Land, Furnishings, Landscaping, and Financing.
See Division 13 for Metal Buildings

| Division | Store 1-Story (1) | Store 1-Story (2) | Production 1-Story (1) | Warehouse 1-Story (1) | Warehouse and 1-Story Office (1) | Warehouse and 2-Story Office (3) |
|---|---|---|---|---|---|---|
| 1. General Conditions | $ 4.70 | $ 4.70 | $ 4.53 | $ 4.05 | $ 4.19 | $ 3.81 |
| 2. Site Work & Demolition | 2.67 | 2.09 | 2.42 | 2.36 | 2.80 | 2.26 |
| 3. Concrete | 7.48 | 14.46 | 7.60 | 7.36 | 8.16 | 12.51 |
| 4. Masonry | 6.30 | 10.73 | 8.38 | 8.41 | 9.26 | 5.11 |
| 5. Steel | 13.44 | 7.04 | 13.44 | 13.16 | 14.32 | 10.81 |
| 6. Carpentry | 3.47 | 3.53 | 2.26 | 2.28 | 3.07 | 2.66 |
| 7. Moisture Protection | 5.96 | 3.46 | 6.55 | 6.31 | 6.34 | 3.16 |
| 8. Doors, Windows and Glass | 6.90 | 6.26 | 5.18 | 2.81 | 5.65 | 4.93 |
| 9. Finishes | 7.88 | 7.41 | 6.76 | 2.41 | 4.21 | 6.49 |
| 10. Specialties | 1.95 | 1.97 | 1.51 | 1.42 | 1.42 | 1.42 |
| 11. Equipment | 1.87 | 2.14 | 2.01 | - | 1.15 | 1.29 |
| 12. Furnishings | - | - | - | - | - | - |
| 13. Special Construction | - | - | - | - | - | - |
| 14. Conveying | - | 4.30 | - | - | - | - |
| 15. Mechanical: | | | | | | |
|     Plumbing | 6.05 | 5.19 | 6.34 | 3.65 | 4.60 | 4.28 |
|     Heating and Ventilation | 5.58 | 5.54 | 4.30 | 4.43 | 5.99 | 6.90 |
|     Air Conditioning | 5.78 | 6.21 | 4.09 | - | 1.53 | 1.38 |
|     Sprinklers | 2.75 | 2.67 | 2.59 | 2.67 | 2.82 | 2.73 |
| 16. Electrical | 11.32 | 10.79 | 11.83 | 7.19 | 7.42 | 6.77 |
| SUB TOTAL | $94.10 | $98.48 | $89.78 | $68.51 | $82.91 | $76.51 |
| CONTRACTOR'S SERVICES | 9.04 | 9.50 | 8.67 | 6.62 | 8.03 | 7.39 |
| Construction Sq. Ft. Cost | $103.14 | $107.98 | $98.44 | $75.12 | $90.94 | $83.90 |
| Add for Architect's Fees | 7.15 | 7.52 | 6.87 | 5.24 | 6.35 | 5.86 |
| **TOTAL Sq.Ft. Cost** | **$110.29** | **$115.50** | **$105.31** | **$80.37** | **$97.30** | **$89.77** |

(1) Wall Bearing Masonry and Steel Joists and Decks – Brick Fronts
(2) Wall Bearing Masonry and Precast Concrete Decks – Brick Fronts
(3) Precast Concrete Wall Panels, Steel Joists, and Deck

# APPENDIX

## Average Square Foot Costs 2012
## Educational and Religious

Square Foot Costs do not include Land, Furnishings, Landscaping and Financing.

| | Division | Elementary School 1-Story (1) | High School 2-Story (1) | Vocational School 3-Story (1) | Collage Multi-Story (2) | Gym (3) | Dorm 3-Story (1) | Church (3) |
|---|---|---|---|---|---|---|---|---|
| 1. | General Conditions | 8.15 | 7.92 | 8.03 | 7.92 | 6.42 | 7.17 | 7.69 |
| 2. | Site Work | 4.89 | 5.13 | 5.01 | 4.89 | 2.44 | 3.22 | 4.72 |
| 3. | Concrete | 7.60 | 8.07 | 5.84 | 27.24 | 8.07 | 6.08 | 7.36 |
| 4. | Masonry | 15.79 | 14.31 | 15.56 | 16.24 | 16.13 | 14.43 | 32.83 |
| 5. | Steel | 13.70 | 15.46 | 16.21 | 5.72 | 16.77 | 14.58 | 2.46 |
| 6. | Carpentry | 4.93 | 4.87 | 4.46 | 3.27 | 2.77 | 4.46 | 9.03 |
| 7. | Moisture Protection | 6.84 | 4.68 | 5.26 | 5.28 | 7.25 | 6.34 | 7.54 |
| 8. | Doors-Windows-Glass | 7.89 | 7.95 | 8.30 | 10.52 | 7.37 | 6.84 | 9.63 |
| 9. | Finishes | 13.92 | 11.56 | 12.97 | 11.38 | 9.79 | 13.33 | 14.10 |
| 10. | Specialties | 2.20 | 2.03 | 2.03 | 2.49 | 2.03 | 1.93 | 1.51 |
| 11. | Equipment | 5.67 | 5.73 | 8.42 | 7.31 | 11.04 | 6.96 | 10.08 |
| 12. | Furnishings | - | 1.18 | 1.45 | 1.51 | - | 1.45 | 5.91 |
| 13. | Special Construction | - | - | - | - | - | - | - |
| 14. | Conveying | - | - | 4.07 | 4.07 | - | 4.07 | - |
| 15. | Mechanical: | | | | | | | |
| | Plumbing | 12.66 | 12.22 | 12.28 | 16.50 | 7.68 | 11.34 | 7.84 |
| | Heating-Ventilation | 15.83 | 15.53 | 17.57 | 16.01 | 10.11 | 11.07 | 11.07 |
| | Air Conditioning | - | - | - | - | - | - | 8.42 |
| | Sprinklers | 2.79 | 2.79 | 2.82 | 2.85 | 1.46 | 2.85 | |
| 16. | Electrical | <u>18.44</u> | <u>19.21</u> | <u>19.84</u> | <u>20.16</u> | <u>12.59</u> | <u>14.37</u> | <u>12.62</u> |
| | SUB TOTAL | $141.29 | $138.62 | $150.13 | $163.36 | $121.92 | $130.48 | 152.81 |
| | CONTRACTOR'S SERVICES | <u>13.52</u> | <u>15.50</u> | <u>14.37</u> | <u>15.61</u> | <u>11.70</u> | <u>12.42</u> | <u>14.81</u> |
| | Constr. Sq.Ft. Cost | $154.81 | $154.12 | $164.49 | $178.96 | $133.62 | $142.90 | 167.61 |
| | Add Architect's Fees | <u>10.63</u> | <u>10.44</u> | <u>11.37</u> | <u>12.52</u> | <u>9.27</u> | <u>9.83</u> | <u>11.73</u> |
| | **TOTAL Sq.Ft. Cost** | $165.45 | $164.56 | $175.87 | $191.48 | $142.90 | $152.73 | $179.34 |

---

(1) Wall Bearing Masonry and Steel Joists and Decks
(2) Concrete Frame and Masonry Façade
(3) Masonry Walls and Wood Roof

SF-5

# APPENDIX

## Average Square Foot Costs 2012
## Medical and Institutional

Square Foot Costs do not include Land, Landscaping, Furnishings, and Financing.

| | Division | Clinic 1-Story (1) | Doctor's Office 1-Story (1) | Hospital 1-Story (1) | Hospital Multi-Story (2) | Nursing Home 1-Story (1) | Housing for Elderly 1-Story (1) |
|---|---|---|---|---|---|---|---|
| 1. | General Conditions | $ 8.60 | $ 8.49 | $ 11.30 | $ 11.42 | $ 10.27 | $ 9.52 |
| 2. | Site Work | 3.00 | 2.94 | 4.72 | 4.77 | 4.95 | 5.13 |
| 3. | Concrete | 9.16 | 9.09 | 9.56 | 29.05 | 9.94 | 9.97 |
| 4. | Masonry | 14.54 | 13.23 | 24.08 | 16.83 | 17.17 | 12.61 |
| 5. | Steel | 11.82 | 11.69 | 14.39 | 3.19 | 3.20 | 2.66 |
| 6. | Carpentry | 8.49 | 8.38 | 7.43 | 4.85 | 5.23 | 4.93 |
| 7. | Moisture Protection | 6.55 | 6.49 | 7.05 | 2.92 | 7.04 | 6.99 |
| 8. | Doors, Windows and Glass | 9.96 | 10.41 | 13.25 | 8.78 | 11.48 | 9.18 |
| 9. | Finishes | 14.06 | 13.03 | 17.83 | 17.22 | 17.29 | 14.41 |
| 10. | Specialties | 1.85 | 1.85 | 2.00 | 1.91 | 1.91 | 1.88 |
| 11. | Equipment | 10.10 | 9.59 | 2.39 | 15.20 | 7.73 | 3.43 |
| 12. | Furnishings | 1.51 | 1.51 | 1.60 | 1.66 | 1.41 | 3.00 |
| 13. | Special Construction | 1.11 | 1.09 | 2.22 | 2.22 | 1.10 | 1.11 |
| 14. | Conveying | - | - | - | 8.26 | - | 7.57 |
| 15. | Mechanical: | | | | | | |
| | Plumbing | 15.81 | 17.03 | 26.01 | 25.35 | 17.26 | 16.69 |
| | Heating and Ventilation | 13.00 | 11.47 | 16.92 | 17.45 | 8.75 | 7.04 |
| | Air Conditioning | 9.99 | 9.70 | 17.33 | 15.07 | 10.09 | 3.79 |
| | Sprinklers | 2.82 | 2.79 | 2.82 | 2.84 | 3.22 | 2.82 |
| 16. | Electrical | 21.05 | 17.17 | 31.93 | 29.64 | 19.36 | 17.04 |
| | SUB TOTAL | $163.44 | $155.95 | $212.83 | $218.63 | $157.39 | $139.78 |
| | CONTRACTOR'S SERVICES | 15.73 | 15.20 | 20.37 | 21.06 | 15.15 | 13.51 |
| | Construction Sq.Ft. Cost | $179.17 | $171.15 | $233.19 | $239.69 | $172.55 | $153.29 |
| | Add for Architect's Fees | 12.43 | 12.04 | 16.14 | 16.69 | 12.00 | 10.69 |
| | **TOTAL Sq.Ft. Cost** | $191.61 | $183.19 | $249.33 | $256.38 | $184.55 | $163.98 |

Average Cost to Remodel Approximately 50% Cost of New

_____

(1) Wall Bearing Masonry and Steel Joists and Decks
(2) Concrete Frame and Masonry Façade

# APPENDIX

## Average Square Foot Costs 2012

### Government and Finance

Square Foot Costs do <u>not</u> include Land, Landscaping, Furnishings, and Financing.

| Division | Bank 1-Story (1) | Bank & Office Building High Rise (3) | Govt. Office Building Multi-Story (2) | Post Office 1-Story (1) | Court House 3-Story (2) | Jail and Prison (2) |
|---|---|---|---|---|---|---|
| 1. General Conditions | $9.29 | $10.67 | $10.67 | $8.66 | $10.55 | $12.91 |
| 2. Site Work | 5.78 | 5.24 | 4.43 | 4.41 | 4.01 | 5.32 |
| 3. Concrete | 12.62 | 30.04 | 32.50 | 13.85 | 27.70 | 37.87 |
| 4. Masonry | 17.49 | 12.21 | 20.39 | 12.22 | 13.09 | 22.23 |
| 5. Steel | 6.60 | 2.95 | 3.56 | 5.15 | 3.08 | 7.35 |
| 6. Carpentry | 5.75 | 5.20 | 5.35 | 4.69 | 3.30 | 5.92 |
| 7. Moisture Protection | 4.82 | 5.41 | 5.73 | 4.88 | 6.02 | 6.84 |
| 8. Doors, Windows and Glass | 12.91 | 30.11 | 13.19 | 10.06 | 9.47 | 12.39 |
| 9. Finishes | 19.18 | 21.44 | 22.75 | 18.94 | 18.46 | 15.66 |
| 10. Specialties | 1.97 | 1.97 | 3.80 | 2.05 | 3.36 | 8.11 |
| 11. Equipment | 16.08 | 10.70 | 10.58 | 14.09 | 13.48 | 15.73 |
| 12. Furnishings | 1.78 | 1.62 | - | 2.37 | - | - |
| 13. Special Construction | - | - | - | - | - | - |
| 14. Conveying | - | 3.38 | 4.25 | 2.18 | 3.10 | 4.19 |
| 15. Mechanical | | | | | | |
|    Plumbing | 9.70 | 11.34 | 11.25 | 12.03 | 15.43 | 26.77 |
|    Heating and Ventilation | 7.94 | 9.84 | 10.57 | 7.58 | 11.28 | 20.07 |
|    Air Conditioning | 6.38 | 7.25 | 9.19 | 9.15 | 16.10 | 16.69 |
|    Sprinklers | 2.98 | 2.85 | 2.79 | 2.85 | 2.85 | 2.85 |
| 16. Electrical | <u>19.59</u> | <u>23.66</u> | <u>24.42</u> | <u>18.70</u> | <u>23.28</u> | <u>36.10</u> |
| SUB TOTAL | $160.86 | $195.90 | $195.41 | $153.87 | $184.57 | $257.00 |
| CONTRACTOR'S SERVICES | <u>15.69</u> | <u>19.08</u> | <u>19.08</u> | <u>14.97</u> | <u>17.92</u> | <u>25.02</u> |
| Construction Sq.Ft. Cost | $176.55 | $214.98 | $214.49 | $168.84 | $202.49 | $282.03 |
| Add for Architect's Fees | <u>12.42</u> | <u>15.11</u> | <u>15.11</u> | <u>12.35</u> | <u>14.20</u> | <u>19.82</u> |
| **TOTAL Sq.Ft. Cost** | $188.97 | $230.09 | $229.61 | $181.19 | $216.69 | $301.85 |

(1) Wall Bearing Masonry and Precast Concrete Decks
(2) Concrete Frame and Masonry Facade
(3) Concrete Frame and Window Wall

SF-7

# APPENDIX

## UNITED STATES INFLATION RATES
## July 1, 1970 to June 30, 2011
## AC&E PUBLISHING CO. INDEX

Start July 1

| YEAR | AVERAGE % | LABOR % | MATERIAL % | CUMULATIVE % |
|---|---|---|---|---|
| 1970-71 | 8 | 8 | 5 | 0 |
| 1971-72 | 11 | 15 | 9 | 11 |
| 1972-73 | 7 | 5 | 10 | 18 |
| 1973-74 | 13 | 9 | 17 | 31 |
| 1974-75 | 13 | 10 | 16 | 44 |
| 1975-76 | 8 | 7 | 15 | 52 |
| 1976-77 | 10 | 5 | 15 | 62 |
| 1977-78 | 10 | 5 | 13 | 72 |
| 1978-79 | 7 | 6 | 8 | 79 |
| 1979-80 | 10 | 5 | 13 | 89 |
| 1980-81 | 10 | 11 | 9 | 99 |
| 1981-82 | 10 | 11 | 10 | 109 |
| 1982-83 | 5 | 9 | 3 | 114 |
| 1983-84 | 4 | 5 | 3 | 118 |
| 1984-85 | 3 | 3 | 3 | 121 |
| 1985-86 | 3 | 2 | 3 | 124 |
| 1986-87 | 3 | 3 | 3 | 127 |
| 1987-88 | 3 | 3 | 4 | 130 |
| 1988-89 | 4 | 3 | 4 | 134 |
| 1989-90 | 3 | 3 | 3 | 137 |
| 1990-91 | 3 | 3 | 4 | 140 |
| 1991-92 | 4 | 4 | 4 | 144 |
| 1992-93 | 4 | 3 | 5 | 148 |
| 1993-94 | 4 | 3 | 5 | 152 |
| 1994-95 | 4 | 3 | 6 | 156 |
| 1995-96 | 4 | 3 | 6 | 160 |
| 1996-97 | 3 | 3 | 3 | 163 |
| 1997-98 | 4 | 3 | 4 | 167 |
| 1998-99 | 3 | 3 | 2 | 170 |
| 1999-2000 | 3 | 2 | 3 | 173 |
| 2000-2001 | 4 | 4 | 4 | 177 |
| 2001-2002 | 3 | 4 | 3 | 180 |
| 2002-2003 | 4 | 5 | 3 | 184 |
| 2003-2004 | 3 | 5 | 2 | 187 |
| 2004-2005 | 8 | 4 | 10 | 195 |
| 2005-2006 | 8 | 6 | 9 | 203 |
| 2006-2007 | 8 | 4 | 11 | 212 |
| 2007-2008 | 3 | 4 | 3 | 215 |
| 2008-2009 | 4 | 3 | 5 | 219 |
| 2009-2010 | 3 | 5 | 1 | 222 |
| 2010-2011 | 2 | 3 | 2 | 224 |
| 2011-2012 | 3 | 3 | 3 | 227 |

**MM-1**

# INDEX

## - A -

| Entry | Page |
|---|---|
| ABOVE GROUND TANK | 13 - 4 |
| ABRASIVE SURFACE | 05 - 6 |
| SURFACE TILE | 09 - 5 |
| ACCESS CONTROL | 10 - 5 |
| ACCORDION FOLDING DOORS | 08 - 7 |
| ACID-PROOF COUNTER | 12 - 2 |
| ACOUSTICAL BLOCK | 04 - 7 |
| PANEL, TILE | 09 - 6 |
| ACRYLIC CARPET | 09 - 8 |
| AD PLYWOOD | 06 - 11 |
| ADHESIVE-BED TILE | 09 - 5 |
| ADJUSTABLE SHELF | 06 - 10 |
| ADMIXTURE | 03 - 8 |
| AIR COMPRESSOR | 01 - 4 |
| ENTRAINING AGENT | 03 - 8 |
| TOOL | 01 - 5 |
| ALUMINUM DOOR | 08 - 13 |
| DOWNSPOUT, FLASHING | 07 - 7 |
| GUTTER | 07 - 7 |
| LOUVER | 05 - 7 |
| PLAQUE | 10 - 4 |
| RAILING | 05 - 7 |
| ROOF | 07 - 6 |
| SHINGLE | 07 - 3 |
| SIDING PANEL | 07 - 4 |
| STOREFRONT | 08 - 8 |
| THRESHOLD | 08 - 12 |
| TREAD | 05 - 6 |
| ANCHOR, BOLT | 05 - 4 |
| BRICK, DOVETAIL | 04 - 3 |
| SLOT | 04 - 3 |
| ANGLE STEEL | 04 - 9 |
| ANTI-SIPHON BREAKER | 15 - 4 |
| APRON | 06 - 9 |
| ARCHITECTURAL FEE | 01 - 2 |
| ARMOR PLATE | 08 - 11 |
| ASH RECEIVER | 10 - 6 |
| ASHLAR VENEER | 04 - 11 |
| ASPHALT DAMPPROOFING | 07 - 2 |
| EXPANSION JOINT | 03 - 8 |
| AUTOMOTIVE HOIST | 14 - 3 |
| AUTOPSY TABLE | 11 - 7 |
| AWNING WINDOW | 08 - 10 |

## - B -

| | |
|---|---|
| BACK SPLASH | 06 - 11 |
| BACKFILL | 02 - 8 |
| HAND | 02 - 7 |
| BACKHOE | 01 - 5 |
| BACKHOE/LOADER | 01 - 6 |
| BACK-UP BLOCK | 04 - 7 |
| BRICK | 04 - 4 |
| BAKE OVEN | 11 - 3 |
| BALANCE LABORATORY | 11 - 6 |
| BALUSTER | 06 - 10 |
| BAND STAGE | 11 - 2 |
| BANK RUN GRAVEL | 02 - 5 |
| BAR REINFORCING | 04 - 2 |
| BARRICADE | 01 - 3 |
| BARRIER VAPOR | 07 - 2 |
| BASE CABINET | 06 - 11, 12 - 2 |
| COLONIAL | 06 - 9 |
| COLUMN | 04 - 10 |
| FLASHING | 07 - 7 |
| GRANITE | 04 - 11 |
| MANHOLE | 02 - 11 |
| BASEBOARD HEATER | 16 - 8 |
| BATCH DISPOSAL | 15 - 5 |
| BATH FAUCET | 15 - 5 |
| BATHROOM LOCK | 08 - 11 |
| BATTEN SIDING | 07 - 5 |
| BEAD MOLDING | 06 - 9 |
| PARTING | 06 - 10 |
| PLASTER | 09 - 3, 09 - 4 |
| BEAM | 05 - 4 |
| BOND | 03 - 9, 04 - 2, 04 - 8 |
| FURRING | 05 - 4, 09 - 2 |
| GRADE | 03 - 10 |
| PLASTER | 09 - 3 |
| BEAM REINFORCING | 03 - 7 |
| BENCH FLOOR MOUNTED | 10 - 5 |
| BEVELED SIDING | 07 - 5 |
| BIBB HOSE | 15 - 3 |
| BICYCLE EXERCISE | 11 - 6 |
| BI-FOLD DOOR | 08 - 4 |
| BIN ICE STORAGE | 11 - 5 |
| BINDER COURSE | 02 - 12 |
| BI-PASSING DOOR | 08 - 4 |
| BIRCH DOOR | 08 - 3 |
| BIRDSCREEN | 13 - 2 |
| BITUMINOUS MEMBRANE | 07 - 2 |
| SIDEWALK | 02 - 12 |
| BLOCK CONCRETE | 03 - 11, 04 - 6 |
| DEMOLITION | 02 - 2 |
| GLASS | 04 - 10 |
| GRANITE | 04 - 6 |
| GROUT | 04 - 2 |
| REMOVAL | 02 - 4 |
| BLOOD ANALYZER | 11 - 6 |
| REFRIGERATOR | 11 - 6 |
| BLOWN-IN INSULATION | 07 - 3 |
| BLUESTONE | 04 - 6 |
| BOARD DIVING | 13 - 3 |
| RAFTER | 06 - 5 |
| RIDGE | 06 - 4 |
| SIDING | 07 - 5 |
| BOLTED STEEL | 05 - 4 |
| BOND BEAM | 04 - 2, 04 - 8 |
| BEAM PLACEMENT | 03 - 9 |
| BONDERIZED FLAGPOLE | 10 - 3 |
| BOOKKEEPER | 01 - 2 |
| BOTTLE COOLER | 11 - 5 |
| BOTTOM BEAM | 03 - 2 |
| PIVOT HINGE | 08 - 10 |
| PLATE | 06 - 6 |
| BOX JUNCTION | 16 - 5 |
| RECEIVING | 10 - 6 |
| BREAKER CIRCUIT | 16 - 2 |
| VACUUM | 15 - 4 |
| BRICK ANCHOR | 04 - 3 |
| CHIMNEY | 04 - 5 |
| FIRE RATED, FIREWALL | 04 - 5 |
| MANHOLE | 02 - 11 |
| PAVER | 04 - 6 |
| REMOVAL | 02 - 3, 02 - 4 |
| BROILER KITCHEN | 11 - 3 |
| BRONZE PLAQUE | 10 - 4 |
| RAILING | 05 - 7 |
| BROOM FINISH | 03 - 8 |
| BUFF BRICK | 04 - 4 |
| BUILDING METAL | 13 - 2 |
| PAPER | 07 - 2 |
| BUILT-IN OVEN | 11 - 5 |
| BUILT-UP PLAQUE | 10 - 4 |
| ROOF | 07 - 6 |
| ROOF REMOVAL | 02 - 3 |
| BULKHEAD FORMWORK | 03 - 5 |
| BULLDOZER | 01 - 6 |
| BULLETIN BOARD | 10 - 3 |
| BULLNOSE GLAZED | 04 - 8 |
| BURLAP CONCRETE | 03 - 9 |
| RUB | 03 - 9 |
| BUS DUCT | 16 - 2 |
| BUTT HINGE | 08 - 10 |
| BX CABLE | 16 - 4 |

## - C -

| | |
|---|---|
| CABINET BASE | 06 - 11 |
| KITCHEN | 12 - 2 |
| LABORATORY | 11 - 6 |
| CABLE BX, THHN-THWN | 16 - 4 |
| CAGE LADDER | 05 - 6 |
| CANT STRIP | 06 - 5, 07 - 2 |
| CAP PILE | 03 - 4, 03 - 10 |
| PILE REINFORCING | 03 - 7 |
| CARBORUNDUM | 03 - 9 |
| CARD ACCESS CONTROL | 10 - 5 |
| CARPET CLEAN | 09 - 8 |
| TILE | 09 - 8 |
| CARRIER CHANNEL | 09 - 6 |
| CARVED DOOR | 08 - 4 |
| CASE REFRIGERATED | 11 - 4 |
| CASED BORING | 02 - 2 |
| CASEMENT WINDOW | 08 - 8, 08 - 9 |
| CASING | 06 - 9 |
| BEAD | 09 - 4 |
| RANCH | 06 - 9 |
| TRIM | 06 - 10 |
| CAST BOX | 16 - 5 |
| IRON STRAINER | 15 - 4 |
| IRON TREAD | 05 - 5 |
| CAVITY WALL | 04 - 2, 04 - 4 |
| WALL ANCHOR | 04 - 3 |
| CDX | 06 - 6 |
| CEDAR DECKING | 06 - 7 |
| SHINGLE | 07 - 4 |
| SIDING | 07 - 5 |
| CEILING DIFFUSER | 15 - 9 |
| FURRING | 06 - 3, 09 - 2 |
| HEATER | 11 - 5 |
| INSULATION | 07 - 2 |
| JOIST | 06 - 2 |
| REMOVAL | 02 - 3 |
| CEMENT FIBER | 03 - 12 |
| FIBER BOARD | 03 - 12 |
| PLASTER | 09 - 3 |
| CENTRIFUGE LABORATORY | 11 - 6 |
| CHAIN HOIST DOOR | 08 - 7 |
| LINK | 02 - 4 |
| LINK FENCES | 09 - 10 |
| CHAIR BAND | 11 - 2 |
| HYDROTHERAPY | 11 - 6 |
| LIFEGUARD | 13 - 3 |
| RAIL | 06 - 9 |
| CHAMFER STRIP | 03 - 5 |
| CHANNEL FURRING | 05 - 4, 09 - 2 |
| SLAB | 03 - 12 |
| CHECK VALVE | 15 - 4 |
| CHEMICAL EXTINGUISHER | 10 - 5 |
| CHIMNEY BRICK | 04 - 5 |
| CHUTE MAIL | 10 - 6 |
| CIRCUIT BREAKER | 16 - 2 |
| CLAY BRICK FLOOR | 09 - 7 |
| PIPE | 02 - 11, 02 - 12 |
| TILE FLOOR | 04 - 10 |
| CLEARING TREE | 02 - 5 |
| CLEFT NATURAL | 04 - 6 |
| CLOCK-TIMER HOSPITAL | 11 - 8 |
| CLOSET DOOR | 08 - 4 |
| POLE | 06 - 9 |
| CLOTH FACED FIBERGLASS | 09 - 6 |
| CMU | 04 - 6 |
| GROUT | 04 - 2 |
| $CO_2$ EXTINGUISHER | 10 - 5 |
| COFFEE URN | 11 - 3 |
| COILING DOOR | 08 - 6 |
| COLONIAL BASE | 06 - 9 |
| MOLDING | 06 - 10 |
| COLOR GROUP TILE | 09 - 5 |
| COLUMN | 05 - 4 |
| BASE | 04 - 10 |
| COVER | 08 - 13 |
| FOOTING | 03 - 4 |
| FURRING | 05 - 4 |
| PIER | 03 - 4 |
| PLASTER | 09 - 3 |
| TIMBER | 06 - 7 |
| COMMERCIAL DOOR | 08 - 8 |
| COMMON BRICK | 04 - 4 |
| COMPACT BASE | 02 - 7 |
| BORROW | 02 - 5 |
| KITCHEN | 11 - 3 |
| COMPACTOR INDUSTRIAL | 11 - 3 |
| RESIDENTIAL | 11 - 5 |
| COMPARTMENT SHOWER | 10 - 2 |
| COMPRESSION FITTING | 16 - 2 |
| COMPRESSOR | 01 - 4 |
| CONCEALED Z BAR | 09 - 6 |
| CONCRETE BLOCK | 09 - 9 |
| BLOCK REMOVAL, CUTTING | 02 - 4 |
| DEMOLITION, REMOVAL | 02 - 2 |
| DOWEL | 03 - 7 |

A1-1

# INDEX

CONCRETE FILLED PILE .................................. 02 - 9
    HARDENER ............................................ 03 - 9
    MANHOLE .............................................. 02 - 11
    PILING ..................................................... 02 - 10
    PLANK .................................................... 03 - 12
    PUMP ...................................................... 03 - 9
    RECEPTOR ............................................ 10 - 2
    REINFORCEMENT .............................. 03 - 6
    SLEEPER .............................................. 06 - 5
    TESTING .............................................. 01 - 3
CONDUCTIVE FLOOR .................. 09 - 7, 09 - 8
CONDUCTOR COPPER ............................... 16 - 4
CONDUIT EMT, FLEXIBLE, GALV. ......... 16 - 2
    PVC ........................................................ 16 - 3
    STEEL .................................................... 16 - 2
CONNECTOR COMPRESSION .................. 16 - 2
CONTINUOUS DISPOSAL ........................ 15 - 5
    FOOTING .............................................. 03 - 10
CONTROL JOINT ........................................ 04 - 4
CONVECTION OVEN .................................. 11 - 3
COOLER BOTTLE ........................................ 11 - 5
COPING CLAY .............................................. 04 - 10
    LIMESTONE ........................................ 04 - 11
COPPER DOWNSPOUT .............................. 07 - 7
    FLASHING ............................................ 07 - 7
    PLAQUE ................................................ 10 - 7
CORNER BEAD ............................ 09 - 3, 09 - 4
    CABINET ................................................ 12 - 2
CORNICE MOLDING .................................. 06 - 10
CORRUGATED METAL PIPE ..................... 02 - 12
    PANEL .................................................... 07 - 5
    ROOF ...................................................... 07 - 6
COUNTER DOOR .......................................... 08 - 6
    FLASHING ............................................ 07 - 7
    GRIDDLE .............................................. 11 - 4
    LABORATORY ..................................... 11 - 6
    LAVATORY .......................................... 15 - 6
COUNTERTOP ............................................... 06 - 11
COUNTER-TOP RANGE .............................. 11 - 5
COUPLING PLASTIC .................................. 02 - 11
COURSE BINDER ........................................ 02 - 12
COVE BASE .................................................... 09 - 8
    BASE GLAZED .................................... 04 - 8
    BASE TILE ............................................ 09 - 5
    MOLDING ............................................ 06 - 9
COVER POOL .............................................. 13 - 3
CRACK REPAIR ............................................ 03 - 13
CRANE ............................................................. 01 - 6
    MOBILIZATION ................................. 01 - 3
CRAWL SPACE INSULATION ................... 07 - 2
CRAWLER CRANE ...................................... 01 - 6
CREOSOTE ..................................................... 06 - 11
CREW TRAILER .......................................... 01 - 3
CROWN MOLDING .................................... 06 - 9
CRUSHED MARBLE .................................. 04 - 6
CURB FORM .................................................. 03 - 3
    FORMWORK ....................................... 03 - 6
    GRANITE .............................................. 04 - 11
    TERRAZZO ......................................... 09 - 6
CURING PAPER ........................................... 03 - 9
CURTAIN WALL ......................................... 08 - 13
CURVED CURB FORM ............................... 03 - 3
CUSTOM DOOR ........................................... 08 - 6
CUT AND FILL .............................................. 02 - 8
    STONE .................................................. 04 - 10
    TREE ...................................................... 02 - 5
CUT-OUT ........................................................ 02 - 3
    COUNTERTOP ................................... 06 - 11
CYLINDER PILING .................................... 02 - 10

### - D -

DAIRY PRODUCT ........................................ 11 - 4
DARBY ............................................................ 03 - 8
DECKING WOOD ....................................... 06 - 7
DECKS, WOOD, STAINED ......................... 09 - 11
DELICATESSEN CASE .............................. 11 - 4
DIAPHRAGM PUMP ................................... 01 - 5
DIMMER SWITCH ...................................... 16 - 6
DIRECTORY BOARD ................................. 10 - 3
DISHWASHER ............................................. 11 - 4
    RESIDENTIAL ................................... 11 - 5

DISPENSER TISSUE ................................... 10 - 7
DISPOSAL COMMERCIAL ....................... 11 - 4
    RESIDENTIAL ................................... 11 - 5
DIVIDER STRIP TERRAZZO .................... 09 - 6
DIVING BOARD ........................................... 13 - 3
DOCK LEVELER ......................................... 11 - 2
DOMESTIC MARBLE ................................ 04 - 11
    WELL ..................................................... 02 - 10
DOOR ALUMINUM ................................... 08 - 13
    CHAIN HOIST ................................... 08 - 7
    CLOSER .............................................. 08 - 11
    FLUSH .................................................. 08 - 4
    FRAME ................................................ 08 - 2
    FRAME GROUT ............................... 04 - 2
    HOLDER ............................................ 08 - 11
    MOTOR ............................................... 08 - 6
    OVERHEAD ....................................... 08 - 6
    PLATE .................................................. 08 - 11
    REMOVAL .......................................... 02 - 2
    REVOLVING ..................................... 08 - 8
    ROLL UP .............................................. 13 - 2
    SLIDING GLASS ............................... 08 - 7
    SOLID CORE .................................... 08 - 3
DOORS AND WINDOWS .......................... 09 - 9
DOORS, WOOD ............................ 09 - 11, 09 - 12
DOUBLE HUNG WINDOW ....................... 08 - 9
    OVEN .................................................. 11 - 3
    WALLED TANK ................................. 13 - 4
DOUGLAS FIR ............................................. 06 - 7
DOVETAIL ANCHOR SLOT ..................... 04 - 3
DOWEL REINFORCING ........................... 03 - 7
DOWNSPOUT ............................................. 07 - 7
    ALUMINUM ....................................... 07 - 7
DOZER EXCAVATION ............................... 02 - 5
DRAIN FIELD .............................................. 02 - 12
    TILE ...................................................... 02 - 12
DRAINAGE UNDERSLAB ........................ 02 - 12
DRAPERY TRACK ...................................... 12 - 2
DRAWER BASE ........................................... 12 - 2
DRILLED WELL .......................................... 02 - 10
DROP PANEL ............................................... 03 - 3
DROPCLOTHS .............................................. 09 - 9
DRY RUB ....................................................... 03 - 9
    STONE WALL .................................... 04 - 10
    TYPE EXTINGUISHER ................... 10 - 5
DRYWALL REMOVAL ................... 02 - 2, 02 - 3
DUCT BUS .................................................... 16 - 2
DUCTWORK METAL ................................. 15 - 8
DUMP TRUCK ............................................. 01 - 5
DUMPSTER ................................................... 02 - 4
DUTCH DOOR ............................................. 08 - 2
DWV COPPER ............................................. 15 - 2
    FITTING COPPER ........................... 15 - 2

### - E -

EDGE FORM .................................................. 03 - 4
    FORMWORK ..................................... 03 - 6
    REPAIR ................................................ 03 - 13
ELASTIC SHEET ROOF ............................ 07 - 6
ELASTOMERIC FLASHING ..................... 04 - 4
ELBOW CAST IRON .................................. 02 - 10
    PLASTIC .............................................. 02 - 10
ELECTRIC ELEVATOR .............................. 14 - 2
    FURNACE ........................................... 15 - 8
ELEVATED SLAB ....................................... 03 - 5
ELEVATOR .................................................... 14 - 2
ENGINEER ..................................................... 01 - 2
ENGRAVED PLAQUE ................................ 10 - 4
ENTRANCE DOOR ..................................... 08 - 8
ENTRY LOCK ............................................... 08 - 11
EPOXY CONCRETE ................................... 03 - 13
    GROUT ................................................ 03 - 12
EQUIPMENT CURB .................................. 03 - 3
    MOBILIZATION ................................ 01 - 3
    PAD ...................................................... 03 - 10
    PAD REINFORCING ....................... 03 - 6
EXERCISE BICYCLE .................................. 11 - 6
EXHAUST HOOD ........................................ 11 - 4
EXPANDED LATH ...................................... 09 - 3
EXPANSION JOINT ...................... 03 - 8, 09 - 3
EXPOSED AGGREGATE .......................... 04 - 6
EXTENSION BOX ....................................... 16 - 5

EXTERIOR DOOR .......................... 08 - 4, 08 - 5
EXTINGUISHER FIRE ............................... 10 - 5
EXTRACTOR WASHER ............................ 11 - 2

### - F -

FABRIC CHAIN LINK ................................ 02 - 13
    FORM .................................................. 03 - 13
FABRICATION METAL ............................. 05 - 6
FACING PANEL ........................................... 04 - 11
    PANELS .............................................. 04 - 10
FACTORY FINISH FLOOR ....................... 09 - 7
FAN EXHAUST ............................................ 15 - 8
FASCIA BOARD .......................................... 06 - 5
    PLASTER ............................................ 09 - 3
FAUCET .......................................................... 15 - 5
FEE PROFESSIONAL ................................. 01 - 2
FENCE ............................................................ 02 - 13
    REUSE ................................................. 02 - 4
    WOOD ................................................. 02 - 13
FENCES, WOOD OR MASONRY ............ 09 - 10
FIBER BOARD ............................................. 03 - 12
    CANT ................................................... 06 - 5
    FORM CONCRETE ......................... 03 - 3
    PANEL ................................................. 09 - 6
FIBERBOARD SHEATHING .................... 06 - 7
FIBERGLASS DIVING BOA ..................... 13 - 3
    INSULATION .................................... 07 - 2
    PANEL ................................................. 09 - 6
    TANK ................................................... 13 - 4
FIBER-OPTIC CABLE ................................ 16 - 7
FIBROUS DAMPPROOFING .................... 07 - 2
FIELD ENGINEER ...................................... 01 - 2
FILL BORROW ............................................ 02 - 5
    CAP ...................................................... 13 - 4
    GYPSUM ............................................. 03 - 12
FILLED BLOCK ............................. 03 - 11, 04 - 7
FILLER JOINT ............................................. 04 - 4
FILTER BARRIER ...................................... 02 - 9
FINISH PLASTER ....................................... 09 - 3
    SHOTCRETE ..................................... 03 - 9
FINISHING SHEETROCK ........................ 09 - 4
FIR DECKING ............................................. 06 - 7
    FLOOR ................................................ 09 - 6
    SIDING ................................................ 07 - 5
FIRE DOOR ................................................... 08 - 6
    ESCAPE .............................................. 05 - 7
    EXTINGUISHER .............................. 10 - 5
    RATED BRICK .................................. 04 - 5
    RATED DOOR .................................. 08 - 2
    RESISTANT SHEETROCK ........... 09 - 4
    RETARDANT .................................... 06 - 11
    RETARDENT ROOF ....................... 07 - 4
FIREWALL BRICK ..................................... 04 - 5
FIXED SASH ................................................ 08 - 8
    TYPE LOUVER ................................ 05 - 7
    WINDOW ........................................... 08 - 8
FIXTURE PLUMBING ............................... 15 - 4
FLAGSTONE PAVER .................................. 04 - 6
FLASHING ..................................................... 07 - 6
    MASONRY ......................................... 04 - 4
FLAT APRON ............................................... 06 - 9
    CONDUIT CABLE ........................... 16 - 2
FLOAT ............................................................ 03 - 8
FLOOR CLAY TILE .................................... 04 - 10
    CLEANOUT ....................................... 15 - 3
    DRAIN .................................................. 15 - 4
    FINISH ................................................ 03 - 8
    FINISHING ........................................ 09 - 7
    GYM ..................................................... 09 - 7
    HARDENER ....................................... 03 - 9
    JOIST ................................................... 06 - 2
    MASONRY ......................................... 09 - 7
    MOUNTED BENCH ......................... 10 - 5
    PATCH ................................................ 03 - 12
    REMOVAL ......................................... 02 - 3
    SAFE .................................................... 13 - 2
    SHEATHING ..................................... 06 - 6
    SLAB .................................................... 03 - 3
    TERRAZZO ....................................... 09 - 5
    TILE ..................................................... 09 - 5

# INDEX

FLOORING MARBLE .................................. 04 - 11
FLUID APPLIED FLOOR ........................... 09 - 8
FLUORESCENT FIXTURE ........................ 16 - 6
FLUSH DOOR ................................. 08 - 2, 08 - 4
   PANEL DOOR ......................................... 08 - 13
FLUTED COLUMN ..................................... 04 - 10
   STEEL CASING ....................................... 02 - 9
FOAMGLASS CANT .................................... 07 - 6
FOIL BACKED INSULATION ..................... 07 - 3
FOOTING EXCAVATION ............................ 02 - 7
FOREMAN ................................................... 01 - 2
FORM FABRIC ............................................ 03 - 13
FORMBOARD ............................................. 03 - 12
FORMICA ..................................................... 06 - 11
   PARTITION ............................................... 10 - 2
FORMWORK OPENINGS ........................... 03 - 4
FOUNDATION BACKFILL .......................... 02 - 7
   BLOCK ...................................................... 04 - 7
   VENT ......................................................... 04 - 2
FRAME COVER .......................................... 02 - 11
   DOOR ........................................................ 08 - 5
FRAMING ROOF ........................................ 06 - 3
   SOFFIT ..................................................... 06 - 5
   TIMBER ..................................................... 06 - 7
   WALL ......................................................... 06 - 5
FRENCH DOOR .......................................... 08 - 4
FRICTION PILING ...................................... 02 - 9
FRONT-END LOADER ............................... 02 - 5
FROZEN FOOD CASE ............................... 11 - 5
FRYER KITCHEN ....................................... 11 - 3
FURRING CEILING ................................... 09 - 2
   CHANNEL ................................................. 05 - 4
   STEEL ....................................................... 09 - 2

### - G -

GABLE TRUSS ............................................ 06 - 8
GABLE-END RAFTER ................................ 06 - 3
GALVANIZED DUCTWORK ....................... 15 - 8
   MESH ........................................................ 03 - 7
   METAL DOOR ........................................... 08 - 2
   RAILING ................................................... 05 - 6
   REGLET .................................................... 03 - 6
   REINFORCEMENT .................................. 03 - 6
   SHINGLE .................................................. 07 - 3
   WALL TIE .................................................. 04 - 2
GAS FURNACE .......................................... 15 - 8
   STERILIZER ............................................. 11 - 7
GATE VALVE .............................................. 15 - 4
GEL EPOXY ................................................ 03 - 13
GENERATOR .............................................. 01 - 5
GFI BREAKER ............................................ 16 - 5
GIRDER ....................................................... 05 - 4
GLASS BEAD .............................................. 06 - 9
   CLOTH TILE ............................................. 09 - 6
   DOOR ........................................................ 08 - 7
   ENCASED BOARD .................................. 10 - 3
   FIBER BOARD ........................................ 03 - 12
   FRAMING ................................................. 08 - 13
GLASSWARE WASHER ............................ 11 - 6
GLAZED BLOCK ........................................ 04 - 8
   BRICK ....................................................... 04 - 4
   FLOOR ..................................................... 09 - 7
   TILE .......................................................... 04 - 5
   WALL TILE ............................................... 09 - 4
GLOBE VALVE ........................................... 15 - 4
GLUE LAM .................................................. 06 - 8
GRAB BAR .................................................. 10 - 6
GRADALL .................................................... 02 - 7
GRADING .................................................... 02 - 8
GRANITE BLOCK ....................................... 04 - 6
   VENEER ................................................... 04 - 11
GRAVEL MULCH ........................................ 02 - 15
   ROOF ........................................................ 07 - 6
GRIDDLE KITCHEN ................................... 11 - 4
GRILLE METAL ........................................... 05 - 7
GROUND FAULT ........................................ 16 - 5
   ROD ........................................................... 16 - 5
   SLAB ......................................................... 03 - 5
GROUT BEAM ............................................. 04 - 2
   BLOCK ............................... 03 - 11, 04 - 2, 04 - 7
   CRACK SEAL ........................................... 03 - 13

GROUT EPOXY .......................................... 03 - 13
   MASONRY ................................................ 04 - 2
   WALL ......................................................... 04 - 2
GRS CONDUIT ........................................... 16 - 2
GUNITE ....................................................... 03 - 9
GUTTER ...................................................... 07 - 7
   COPPER ................................................... 07 - 7
   STEEL ....................................................... 07 - 7
GYM FLOOR ............................................... 09 - 7
   LOCKER ................................................... 10 - 5
GYPSUM FILL ............................................ 03 - 12
   MASONRY ................................................ 04 - 8
   PLANK ...................................................... 03 - 12
   PLASTER ................................................. 09 - 3
   SHEATHING ............................................. 06 - 7

### - H -

HALF ROUND MOLDING .......................... 06 - 9
HALIDE FIXTURE ...................................... 16 - 7
HAND BUGGY ............................................ 03 - 9
   DRYER ..................................................... 10 - 6
   EXCAVATION ........................................... 02 - 8
   SEEDING ................................................. 02 - 14
   SPLIT SHAKE .......................................... 07 - 4
   SPREADING ............................................ 02 - 14
HANDICAPPED PARTITION .................... 10 - 2
   PLUMBING .............................................. 15 - 5
HANDLING RUBBISH ............................... 02 - 4
HARDBOARD DOOR ................................. 08 - 3
   UNDERLAYMENT ................................... 06 - 6
HARDENER CONCRETE ......................... 03 - 9
HASP ASSEMBLY ..................................... 08 - 11
HAULING RUBBISH .................................. 02 - 4
HEADER ..................................................... 06 - 6
   CEILING ................................................... 06 - 2
HEATER ...................................................... 01 - 5
   ELECTRIC ....................................11 - 5, 16 - 8
   UNIT .......................................................... 15 - 8
   WATER ..................................................... 15 - 7
HEAVY DUTY DOOR ................................. 08 - 2
   DUTY TERRAZZO ................................... 09 - 6
HERRINGBONE FLOOR .......................... 09 - 7
HIGH PRESSURE SODIUM ...................... 16 - 6
   STRENGTH BLOCK ............................... 04 - 7
HIP RAFTER ............................................... 06 - 4
HOLLOW BLOCK ....................................... 04 - 6
   CLAY TILE ............................................... 04 - 9
   COLUMN .................................................. 06 - 12
   CORE DOOR ....................... 08 - 3, 08 - 4
   METAL DOOR ........................................ 08 - 2
HOOD EXHAUST ....................................... 11 - 4
   RANGE ..................................................... 11 - 5
HORIZONTAL DAMPER ........................... 15 - 9
   REINFORCING ........................ 03 - 8, 04 - 2
   SIDING ..................................................... 07 - 5
   WINDOW .................................................. 08 - 9
HOSPITAL EQUIPMENT .......................... 11 - 6
HOT PLATE LABORATORY ..................... 11 - 6
   WATER DISPENSER ............................. 15 - 5
H-SECTION PILE ....................................... 02 - 9
HUNG SLAB ............................................... 03 - 3
HYDRAULIC ELEVATOR ......................... 14 - 2
   EXCAVATOR ....................... 02 - 5, 02 - 7

### - I -

ICE CUBE MAKER ..................................... 11 - 4
   MAKER ..................................................... 11 - 5
   STORAGE BIN ........................................ 11 - 5
IMC CONDUIT ............................................ 16 - 3
INCANDESCENT FIXTURE ...................... 16 - 6
INCINERATOR LABORATORY ................ 11 - 6
INCUBATOR ............................................... 11 - 7
   LABORATORY ........................................ 11 - 6
INDUSTRIAL COMPACTOR .................... 11 - 3
   WINDOW .................................................. 08 - 8
INJECTION GROUT .................................. 03 - 13
INSULATED BLOCK ................................. 04 - 7
   GLASS ...................................................... 08 - 12
   GLASS DOOR ........................................ 08 - 7
   SIDING ..................................................... 07 - 5

INSULATION BLOWN-IN .......................... 07 - 3
   SPRAYED ................................................ 07 - 3
INTERIOR SIGN ......................................... 10 - 4
   WALL FORM ............................................ 03 - 5
INTERMEDIATE CONDUIT ...................... 16 - 3
   PIVOT HINGE ......................................... 08 - 10
IRON TREAD .............................................. 05 - 6
IRREGULAR STONE ................................. 04 - 6
IRRIGATION LAWN ................................... 02 - 13
ISOLATION MONITOR .............................. 11 - 8

### - J -

JACK RAFTER ........................................... 06 - 4
JALOUSIE WINDOW ................................. 08 - 8
JOB BUILT FORM ...................................... 03 - 2
   SCHEDULING .......................................... 01 - 3
   TRAILER .................................................. 01 - 3
JOINT CLIP ................................................. 09 - 3
   EXPANSION ............................................ 03 - 8
   FILLER ..................................................... 04 - 4
   REINFORCING ........................................ 04 - 2
JOIST SISTER ................................ 06 - 2, 06 - 3
JUMBO BRICK ........................................... 04 - 4
JUTE PADDING ......................................... 09 - 8

### - K -

K COPPER .................................................. 15 - 2
KETTLE STEAM ......................................... 11 - 4
KEYWAY FORM ......................................... 03 - 5
KICK PLATE ................................... 05 - 6, 08 - 11
KILN DRIED ................................................ 06 - 12
KING POST TRUSS ................................... 06 - 8
KITCHEN CABINET ..................... 06 - 11, 12 - 2
   COMPACT ................................................ 11 - 3
   FAUCET ................................................... 15 - 5
   SINK ......................................................... 15 - 6

### - L -

L TUBE ........................................................ 15 - 2
LADDER POOL .......................................... 13 - 3
   REINFORCING ........................................ 04 - 2
LAMINATED BEAM ................................... 06 - 8
   PLASTIC .................................................. 06 - 11
   RAILING ................................................... 05 - 7
LANDING STEEL ....................................... 05 - 5
LANDSCAPE TIMBER .............................. 02 - 15
LATCHSET ................................................. 08 - 11
LATH EXPANDED ..................................... 09 - 3
   STUCCO .................................................. 09 - 3
LATTICE MOLDING ................................... 06 - 9
LAUAN DOOR ............................................ 08 - 3
LAVATORY FAUCET ................................ 15 - 5
LEACHING PIT .......................................... 02 - 12
LEAD LINED DOOR .................................. 08 - 2
LEVEL INDICATOR ................................... 13 - 4
LEVELER DOCK ........................................ 11 - 2
LIFEGUARD CHAIR .................................. 13 - 3
LIFT AUTO .................................................. 14 - 3
LIGHT GAGE FRAMING ........................... 05 - 5
   POOL ........................................................ 13 - 3
   STEEL ....................................................... 05 - 4
   SURGICAL ............................................... 11 - 7
LIGHTING ................................................... 16 - 6
LIGHTWEIGHT BLOCK ............................. 04 - 7
LIMESTONE AGGREGATE ...................... 04 - 6
   PANEL ...................................................... 04 - 11
LIMING ........................................................ 02 - 14
LINEN CHUTE ............................................ 14 - 3
LINER PANEL ............................................. 13 - 3
LINOLEUM REMOVAL .............................. 02 - 3
LINTEL LIMESTONE ................................. 04 - 11
   STEEL ....................................................... 04 - 9
LIQUID CHALKBOARD ............................. 10 - 2
LOAD BEARING STUD ............................. 09 - 2
   CENTER BREAKER ............................... 16 - 5
   CENTER INDOOR .................................. 16 - 6
LOADER ...................................................... 01 - 6
LOCKSET ................................................... 08 - 11
LOUVER DOOR ......................................... 08 - 4
   METAL ...................................................... 05 - 7

A1-3

# INDEX

## - M -

| | |
|---|---|
| M TUBE | 15 - 2 |
| MAIL CHUTE | 10 - 6 |
| MANHOLE | 02 - 11 |
| MAP RAIL CHALKBOARD | 10 - 2 |
| MARBLE CHIP | 02 - 15 |
| IMPORTED | 04 - 10 |
| MASKING PAPER AND TAP | 09 - 9 |
| MASONRY BASE | 04 - 10 |
| CHIMNEY | 04 - 5 |
| DEMOLITION | 02 - 2 |
| FACING PANEL | 04 - 10 |
| FENCE | 02 - 4 |
| FURRING | 06 - 3 |
| GLASS | 04 - 10 |
| GYPSUM | 04 - 8 |
| LIMESTONE | 04 - 11 |
| PLAQUE | 10 - 4 |
| PLASTER | 04 - 10 |
| REINFORCING | 03 - 8 |
| SLATE | 04 - 11 |
| MAT FORMWORK | 03 - 4 |
| REINFORCING | 03 - 7, 03 - 8 |
| MEAT CASE | 11 - 5 |
| MECHANICAL JOINT PIPE | 02 - 10 |
| SEEDING | 02 - 14 |
| MEDICAL EQUIPMENT | 11 - 6 |
| MEDICINE CABINET | 10 - 7 |
| MEMBRANE CURING | 03 - 9 |
| WATERPROOFING | 07 - 2 |
| MESH SLAB | 03 - 7 |
| TIE | 04 - 4 |
| WIRE | 03 - 11 |
| METAL BASE | 09 - 3 |
| BUILDING | 13 - 2 |
| CLAD DOOR | 08 - 6 |
| DOOR REMOVAL | 02 - 2 |
| FABRICATION | 05 - 5 |
| FENCE | 02 - 13 |
| HALIDE | 16 - 7 |
| LADDER | 05 - 6 |
| LINTEL | 04 - 9 |
| LOUVER | 08 - 2 |
| PAN STAIR | 05 - 5 |
| PLAQUE | 10 - 3 |
| RAILING | 05 - 6, 05 - 7 |
| ROOF REMOVAL | 02 - 3 |
| SHELVING | 10 - 6 |
| STAIR | 05 - 5 |
| STUD | 05 - 5 |
| TOILET PARTITIO | 10 - 2 |
| WINDOW REMOVAL | 02 - 3 |
| METALLIC HARDENER | 03 - 9 |
| METER SERUM | 11 - 6 |
| MICROSCOPE LABORATORY | 11 - 6 |
| MILL FRAMED STRUCTURE | 06 - 7 |
| MILLED WINDOW | 08 - 10 |
| MINERAL FIBER BOARD | 03 - 12 |
| FIBER PANEL | 09 - 6 |
| FIBER TILE | 09 - 6 |
| MIRROR | 10 - 7 |
| PLATE | 08 - 13 |
| MODIFIER EPOXY | 03 - 13 |
| MONOLITHIC TERRAZZO | 09 - 5 |
| MOP SINK | 15 - 7 |
| MORTISE LOCKSET | 08 - 11 |
| MOSS PEAT | 02 - 15 |
| MOTORIZED CHECKROOM | 11 - 2 |
| MOVABLE LOUVER | 05 - 7 |
| MOVING SHRUB | 02 - 15 |
| TREE | 02 - 15 |
| MULCH | 02 - 15 |
| MULLION WINDOW | 08 - 8 |

## - N -

| | |
|---|---|
| NAILER CEILING | 06 - 2 |
| NAMEPLATE PLAQUE | 10 - 4 |
| NAPKIN DISPENSER | 10 - 7 |
| NARROW STILE DOOR | 08 - 13 |
| NATURAL CLEFT SLATE | 04 - 6 |
| NEOPRENE FLASHING | 07 - 6 |
| JOINT | 03 - 8 |
| MEMBRANE | 07 - 2 |
| ROOF | 07 - 6 |
| NET SAFETY | 01 - 4 |
| NM CABLE | 16 - 4 |
| NO-HUB ADAPTER COPPER | 15 - 3 |
| PIPE | 15 - 2 |
| NON-DRILLING ANCHOR | 05 - 4 |
| NON-METALLIC HARDENER | 03 - 9 |
| NORMAN BRICK | 04 - 5 |
| NYLON CARPET | 09 - 8 |

## - O -

| | |
|---|---|
| OAK DOOR | 08 - 6 |
| FLOOR | 09 - 7 |
| OFFICE TRAILER | 01 - 3 |
| OGEE MOLDING | 06 - 10 |
| OIL FURNACE | 15 - 8 |
| TANK | 13 - 3 |
| ORGANIC BED TILE | 09 - 5 |
| OUTRIGGER FLAGPOLE | 10 - 3 |
| OVEN BAKE | 11 - 3 |
| CONVECTION | 11 - 3 |
| OVERHEAD | 01 - 2 |
| DOOR | 08 - 6, 08 - 7, 13 - 2 |
| OVERSIZED BRICK | 04 - 4 |

## - P -

| | |
|---|---|
| PACKAGED HEATER | 15 - 8 |
| PAD EQUIPMENT | 03 - 3 |
| REINFORCING | 03 - 6 |
| PADDING CARPET | 09 - 8 |
| PALM TREE | 02 - 15 |
| PAN METAL STAIR | 05 - 5 |
| SLAB | 03 - 3 |
| PANEL ACOUSTICAL | 09 - 6 |
| LIMESTONE | 04 - 11 |
| SIDING | 07 - 5 |
| PANIC DEVICE | 08 - 11 |
| PAPER BACKED INSULATION | 07 - 2 |
| BACKED LATHE | 09 - 3 |
| BUILDING | 07 - 2 |
| CURING | 03 - 9 |
| PARABOLIC TROFFER | 16 - 6 |
| PARALLEL DAMPER | 15 - 9 |
| STRAND BEAM | 06 - 8 |
| PARGING | 04 - 10 |
| PARTING BEAD | 06 - 10 |
| PARTITION CLAY TILE | 04 - 9 |
| REMOVAL | 02 - 2 |
| TOILET | 10 - 2 |
| PASSENGER ELEVATOR | 14 - 2 |
| PASS-THROUGH WASHER | 11 - 2 |
| PATCH CONCRETE | 03 - 9 |
| PATIO BLOCK | 04 - 6 |
| PAVEMENT CUTTING | 02 - 4 |
| PAVER GRANITE | 04 - 6 |
| MARBLE | 04 - 11 |
| STONE | 04 - 6, 04 - 11 |
| PAVING CONCRETE | 02 - 12 |
| PEAT MOSS | 02 - 15 |
| PEDESTRIAN BARRICADE | 01 - 3 |
| PENNSYLVANIA SLATE | 07 - 4 |
| PERFORATED CLAY PIPE | 02 - 12 |
| PVC PIPE | 02 - 12 |
| PERFORMANCE BOND | 01 - 6 |
| PERLITE | 03 - 12 |
| ROOF INSULATION | 07 - 3 |
| PHYSICAL THERAPY | 11 - 6 |
| PICKUP TRUCK | 01 - 5 |
| PICTURE WINDOW | 08 - 8, 08 - 10 |
| PILASTER | 03 - 4, 03 - 11 |
| PILE REPAIR | 03 - 13 |
| SPALL | 03 - 13 |
| PILING MOBILIZATION | 01 - 4 |
| PINE DECKING | 06 - 7 |
| DOOR | 08 - 6 |
| RISER | 06 - 12 |
| SIDING | 07 - 6 |
| PIPE CLAY | 02 - 11 |
| COLUMN | 05 - 4 |
| COPPER | 15 - 2 |
| FLASHING | 07 - 6 |
| GALVANIZED | 15 - 3 |
| NO-HUB | 15 - 2 |
| PILE POINT | 02 - 9 |
| RAILING | 05 - 6 |
| PIVOT HINGE | 08 - 10 |
| PLANT BED PREPARATION | 02 - 14 |
| PLAQUE BRONZE | 10 - 4 |
| MASONRY | 10 - 4 |
| PLASTER MASONRY | 04 - 10 |
| REMOVAL | 02 - 3 |
| PLASTIC FILTER FABRIC | 02 - 12 |
| SHEET | 07 - 2 |
| SIGN | 10 - 4 |
| PLATE | 06 - 5 |
| ARMOR | 08 - 11 |
| GLASS | 08 - 12 |
| MIRROR | 08 - 12 |
| PLEXIGLASS | 08 - 12 |
| PLUG CONDUIT | 16 - 5 |
| PLYWOOD | 06 - 6 |
| FINISH | 06 - 11 |
| SHEATHING | 06 - 6 |
| SHELVING | 06 - 10 |
| STRUCTURAL | 06 - 7 |
| UNDERLAYMENT | 06 - 6 |
| PNEUMATIC HOIST | 14 - 3 |
| TOOL | 01 - 5 |
| POLE CLOSET | 06 - 9 |
| POLYETHYLENE VAPOR BARRIER | 07 - 2 |
| WRAP | 03 - 13 |
| POLYSTYRENE INSULATION | 07 - 3 |
| POLYURETHANE FLOOR | 09 - 7 |
| POOL EQUIPMENT | 13 - 3 |
| LIGHT | 13 - 3 |
| PORCELAIN SINK | 15 - 7 |
| POROUS CONCRETE PIPE | 02 - 12 |
| PORTABLE STAGE | 11 - 2 |
| POSTS TREATED | 06 - 7 |
| POURED DECK | 03 - 12 |
| PRECAST LINTEL | 04 - 9 |
| MANHOLE | 02 - 11 |
| SEPTIC TANK | 02 - 12 |
| PREFINISHED SHELVING | 06 - 11 |
| PRIMED DOOR | 08 - 4 |
| PRIVACY FENCE | 02 - 13 |
| LOCKSET | 08 - 11 |
| PRODUCE CASE | 11 - 5 |
| PROFESSIONAL FEE | 01 - 2 |
| PROFIT | 01 - 2 |
| PROJECTING SASH | 08 - 8 |
| WINDOW | 08 - 9 |
| PULL BOX | 16 - 5 |
| PUMP | 01 - 5 |
| PUMPED CONCRETE | 03 - 9, 03 - 11 |
| PUSH PLATE | 08 - 11 |
| PUTTYING | 09 - 9 |
| PVC CHAMFER STRIP | 03 - 5 |
| CONDUIT | 16 - 3 |
| CONTROL JOINT | 04 - 4 |
| FORM LINER | 03 - 5 |
| PIPE | 02 - 10, 02 - 12 |
| ROOF | 07 - 6 |
| SEWER PIPE | 02 - 11 |

## - Q -

| | |
|---|---|
| QUARTER ROUND | 06 - 10 |

## - R -

| | |
|---|---|
| RACEWAY | 16 - 3 |
| RACK-TYPE DISHWASHER | 11 - 4 |
| RADIOLOGY EQUIPMENT | 11 - 7 |
| RADIUS CURB | 04 - 11 |
| FORMWORK | 03 - 6 |
| RAFTER | 06 - 3 |
| HIP | 06 - 4 |
| RAIL CHAIR | 06 - 9 |
| RAILING | 06 - 10 |

# INDEX

| Entry | Page |
|---|---|
| RAILING METAL | 05 - 7 |
| RANCH CASING | 06 - 9 |
|    MOLDING | 06 - 10 |
| RANDOM WIDTH FLOOR | 09 - 7 |
| RANGE ELECTRIC | 11 - 5 |
|    HOOD | 11 - 5 |
|    KITCHEN | 11 - 4 |
| RECEIVING BOX | 10 - 6 |
| RECEPTOR SHOWER | 10 - 2, 15 - 6 |
| RECESSED LIGHT FIXTURE | 09 - 6 |
| RECTANGULAR WALL TIE | 04 - 2 |
| RED BRICK | 04 - 4 |
| REDWOOD FENCE | 02 - 13 |
|    SIDING | 07 - 5 |
| REFRIGERATED CASE | 11 - 4 |
| REFRIGERATOR BLOOD | 11 - 6 |
| REGLET | 03 - 6 |
| REINFORCING MASONRY | 04 - 2, 04 - 8 |
|    STEEL REPAIRS | 03 - 13 |
| REMOVE FENCING | 02 - 4 |
|    TOPSOIL | 02 - 14 |
| REPLACEMENT GLASS BLOCK | 04 - 10 |
| RESEED | 02 - 15 |
| RESIDENTIAL LOUVER | 05 - 7 |
| RETARDANT FIRE | 06 - 11 |
| REVOLVING DOOR | 08 - 8 |
| RIBBED BLOCK | 04 - 7 |
| RIDGE BOARD | 06 - 4 |
|    ROOF | 07 - 6 |
|    VENTILATOR | 13 - 2 |
| RIGID STEEL CONDUIT | 16 - 2 |
|    URETHANE INSULA | 07 - 3 |
| RISER BAND | 11 - 2 |
|    MARBLE | 04 - 11 |
|    WOOD | 06 - 12 |
| ROD GROUND | 16 - 5 |
|    TRAVERSE | 12 - 2 |
| ROLL ROOF | 07 - 3 |
| ROLL-UP DOOR | 08 - 6, 08 - 7, 13 - 2 |
| ROOF ASPHALT | 07 - 6 |
|    BUILT-UP | 07 - 6 |
|    DRAIN | 15 - 4 |
|    HIP | 06 - 4 |
|    PANEL | 13 - 3 |
|    SHINGLE | 07 - 3 |
| ROOFING REMOVAL | 02 - 3 |
| ROOFTOP AC | 15 - 8 |
| ROUGH-IN PLUMBING | 15 - 5 |
| ROUGH-SAWN SIDING | 07 - 5 |
| ROUND CAST BOX | 16 - 5 |
|    QUARTER | 06 - 10 |
| RUBBISH REMOVAL | 02 - 4 |
| RUBBLE STONE | 04 - 10 |

**- S -**

| | |
|---|---|
| SAFETY GLASS | 08 - 12 |
|    NET | 01 - 4 |
| SALAMANDER | 01 - 5 |
| SALES TAX | 01 - 2 |
| SALT PRESERVATIVE | 06 - 11 |
| SAND BED PAVER | 04 - 6 |
|    BORROW | 02 - 5 |
|    FINISH STUCCO | 09 - 3 |
| SANDING | 09 - 9 |
| SASH BEAD | 06 - 10 |
| SATIN FINISH LETTER | 10 - 4 |
| SCAFFOLDING | 01 - 4 |
| SCHEDULE-40 PIPE | 02 - 12 |
| SCHEDULING SOFTWARE | 01 - 3 |
| SCORED CLAY TILE | 04 - 9 |
| SCRATCH COAT | 09 - 3 |
| SCREED | 03 - 8 |
| SCREEN MOLDING | 06 - 10 |
| SCRUB SURGICAL | 11 - 7 |
| SECTIONAL DOOR | 08 - 7 |
| SECURITY SASH | 08 - 8 |
| SEDIMENT FENCE | 02 - 9 |
| SEEDING | 02 - 14 |
| SEH BOX | 16 - 5 |
| SELECT COMMON BRICK | 04 - 4 |
| SELF-DRILLING ANCHOR | 05 - 4 |
| SERVICE DOOR | 08 - 6 |
|    SINK | 15 - 6 |
| SET RETARDER | 03 - 8 |
| S-FORM CONCRETE | 03 - 6 |
| SHAKE ROOF | 07 - 4 |
| SHEATHING ROOF | 06 - 6 |
|    WALL | 06 - 6 |
| SHEET FLOOR | 09 - 8 |
|    GLASS | 08 - 12 |
|    METAL ROOF | 07 - 6 |
|    PLASTIC | 07 - 2 |
| SHEETROCK FINISHING | 09 - 4 |
| SHELF | 06 - 10 |
|    CHECKROOM | 11 - 2 |
|    UNIT | 10 - 6 |
| SHINGLE CEDAR | 07 - 4 |
|    METAL | 07 - 3 |
|    REMOVAL | 02 - 3 |
|    WOOD | 07 - 4 |
| SHOE MOLDING | 06 - 10 |
| SHOTCRETE | 03 - 9 |
| SHOWER COMPARTMENT | 10 - 2 |
|    DOOR | 10 - 2 |
|    FAUCET | 15 - 5 |
|    ROD | 10 - 7 |
| SHRUB MAINTENANCE | 02 - 15 |
| SIDE BEAM | 03 - 2 |
| SIDING | 07 - 4, 07 - 5 |
| SIGN INTERIOR | 10 - 4 |
|    PLASTIC | 10 - 5 |
| SILL LIMESTONE | 04 - 11 |
|    MARBLE | 04 - 11 |
|    SLATE | 04 - 11 |
|    WINDOWWALL | 08 - 13 |
| SIMULATED PEG FLOOR | 09 - 7 |
| SISTER JOIST | 06 - 2, 06 - 3 |
|    RAFTER | 06 - 5 |
| SITE GRADING | 02 - 8 |
| SKYLIGHT | 13 - 3 |
| SLAB CHANNEL | 03 - 12 |
|    CONCRETE | 03 - 11 |
|    FORMWORK | 03 - 3 |
|    MESH | 03 - 7 |
|    REINFORCING | 03 - 6, 03 - 7 |
| SLATE | 04 - 6 |
|    PANEL | 04 - 11 |
| SLIDE WATER | 13 - 3 |
| SLIDING FIRE DOOR | 08 - 6 |
|    GLASS DOOR | 08 - 7 |
|    WINDOW | 08 - 10 |
| SLIP COUPLING COPPER | 15 - 2 |
| SLOT ANCHOR | 04 - 3 |
| SNAPPED PAVER | 04 - 6 |
| SOAP DISH | 09 - 5, 10 - 7 |
| SOCIAL SECURITY | 01 - 2 |
| SOCKET METER | 16 - 5 |
| SODIUM LIGHT | 16 - 7 |
| SOFFIT REPAIR | 03 - 13 |
| SOFTENER WATER | 11 - 5 |
| SOFTWARE SCHEDULING | 01 - 3 |
| SOIL BORING | 02 - 2 |
|    TESTING | 01 - 3 |
| SOLAR SCREEN BLOCK | 04 - 8 |
| SOLID ARMORED CABLE | 16 - 4 |
|    BLOCK | 04 - 6 |
|    CORE | 08 - 3 |
|    WALL | 04 - 3 |
| SOUND DEADENING BOARD | 09 - 3 |
| SPALL PILE | 03 - 13 |
| SPANDREL GLASS | 08 - 12 |
| SPLIT GROUND FACE | 04 - 7 |
|    RIB PROFILE | 04 - 7 |
| SPONGE RUBBER PADDING | 09 - 8 |
| SPREAD FOOTING | 03 - 10 |
|    TOPSOIL | 02 - 8, 02 - 14 |
| SPREADING TOPSOIL | 02 - 14 |
| SQUARE COLUMN | 03 - 3 |
|    TUB | 15 - 4 |
| STAGE BAND | 11 - 2 |
|    THEATER | 11 - 2 |
| STAGING | 01 - 4 |
| STAINLESS COUNTER | 12 - 2 |
| STAINLESS DOOR | 08 - 6 |
|    FLASHING | 07 - 7 |
|    GRAB BAR | 10 - 6 |
|    PARTITION | 10 - 2 |
|    RAILING | 05 - 7 |
|    SHELVING | 10 - 6 |
| STAIR LANDING | 05 - 5 |
|    MARBLE | 04 - 11 |
|    PAN | 05 - 5 |
|    RAIL | 05 - 6 |
|    TREAD CERAMIC | 09 - 5 |
| STALL SHOWER | 10 - 2 |
| STANDING-SEAM ROOF | 07 - 6 |
| STEAM GENERATOR MEDICAL | 11 - 7 |
|    KETTLE | 11 - 4 |
|    STERILIZER | 11 - 7 |
| STEAMER ELECTRIC | 11 - 4 |
| STEEL ANGLE | 04 - 9 |
|    EDGING | 02 - 15 |
|    GUTTER | 07 - 7 |
|    LINTEL | 05 - 4 |
|    PIPE | 15 - 3 |
|    REPAIR | 03 - 13 |
|    SHINGLE | 07 - 3 |
|    SIDING PANEL | 07 - 5 |
|    STAIR | 05 - 5 |
|    STRUCTURAL | 05 - 4 |
|    TANK | 13 - 3 |
|    TOILET PARTITION | 10 - 2 |
|    TREAD | 05 - 6 |
|    WELDING | 05 - 2 |
| STEP LIMESTONE | 04 - 11 |
|    MANHOLE | 02 - 11 |
| STEPPING STONE | 02 - 15 |
| STERILIZER GAS | 11 - 7 |
|    MEDICAL | 11 - 7 |
| STILL WATER | 11 - 7 |
| STONE PAVER | 04 - 6 |
| STOOL MARBLE | 04 - 11 |
|    MOLDING | 06 - 10 |
|    SLATE | 04 - 11 |
| STOP MOLDING | 06 - 10 |
| STORAGE SHELVING | 10 - 6 |
| STORM DOOR | 08 - 8 |
|    WINDOW | 08 - 9 |
| STRAIGHT CURB FORM | 03 - 3 |
| STRAND BEAM | 06 - 8 |
| STRAW BALE | 02 - 9 |
| STREET ELL COPPER | 15 - 2, 15 - 3 |
| STRIP CANT | 06 - 5 |
|    CHAMFER | 03 - 5 |
|    FLOORING | 09 - 6 |
|    FLOURESCENT | 16 - 6 |
|    SHINGLE | 07 - 3 |
| STRUCTURAL EXCAVATION | 02 - 7 |
|    PLYWOOD | 06 - 7 |
|    TUBE | 05 - 4 |
| STUCCO | 09 - 3 |
|    LATH | 09 - 3 |
| STUD CLIP | 09 - 3 |
|    METAL | 05 - 5, 09 - 2 |
|    REMOVAL | 02 - 2 |
| STUMP | 02 - 5 |
| STYROFOAM INSERT | 04 - 7 |
| SUB-BASE | 02 - 5 |
| SUB-FLOORING | 06 - 6 |
| SUBMERSIBLE PUMP | 01 - 5 |
| SUPERINTENDENT | 01 - 2 |
| SURFACE MOUNTED CLOSE | 08 - 11 |
| SURGICAL CHRONOMETER | 11 - 8 |
|    LIGHT | 11 - 7 |
|    SCRUB | 11 - 7 |
| SUSPENDED CEILING | 07 - 2 |
|    CEILING REM | 02 - 3 |
| SUSPENSION SYSTEM | 09 - 6 |
| SWITCH DIMMER | 16 - 6 |
| SY-PINE DECKING | 06 - 7 |
|    SIDING | 07 - 5 |

# INDEX

## - T -

| | |
|---|---|
| T&G SIDING | 07 - 5 |
| TABLE LABORATORY | 11 - 6 |
| TACK BOARD | 10 - 3 |
| TANDEM BREAKER | 16 - 5 |
| TANK-TYPE EXTINGUISHER | 10 - 5 |
| TAPERED FRICTION PILE | 02 - 9 |
| TARPAULIN | 01 - 4 |
| TAX | 01 - 2 |
| T-BAR SYSTEM | 09 - 6 |
| TERMITE CONTROL | 02 - 9, 10 - 3 |
| TERRA COTTA | 04 - 10 |
| TERRAZZO RECEPTOR | 10 - 2 |
| REMOVAL | 02 - 3 |
| TEXTURE 1-11 | 07 - 5 |
| THHN-THWN CONDUCTOR | 16 - 4 |
| THRESHOLD DOOR | 08 - 11 |
| MARBLE | 04 - 11 |
| THROUGH-WALL FLASHING | 04 - 4 |
| THWN CONDUCTOR | 16 - 4 |
| TIE MESH | 04 - 4 |
| TILE ACOUSTICAL | 09 - 6 |
| CLAY | 04 - 9 |
| QUARRY | 09 - 5 |
| REMOVAL | 02 - 3 |
| RESILIENT | 09 - 7 |
| STRUCTURAL | 04 - 5 |
| TIMBER FRAMING | 06 - 3, 06 - 7 |
| LANDSCAPING | 02 - 15 |
| TIMEKEEPER | 01 - 2 |
| TINTED GLASS | 08 - 12 |
| TISSUE DISPENSER | 10 - 7 |
| TOILET | 15 - 7 |
| ACCESSORY | 10 - 7 |
| TOOTHBRUSH HOLDER | 10 - 7 |
| TOP PLATE | 06 - 6 |
| TOPDRESS SOIL | 02 - 14 |
| TOWEL BAR | 10 - 7 |
| BAR CERAMIC | 09 - 5 |
| DISPENSER | 10 - 7 |
| TRACK MOUNTED LOADER | 02 - 6 |
| TRAILER | 01 - 3 |
| TRAVERSE ROD | 12 - 2 |
| TRAVERTINE FLOOR | 09 - 7 |
| FLOORING | 04 - 11 |
| TREAD ABRASIVE | 05 - 6 |
| MARBLE | 04 - 11 |
| METAL | 05 - 5 |
| STEEL | 05 - 5 |
| WOOD | 06 - 12 |
| TREATED LUMBER | 02 - 15 |
| POST | 06 - 12 |
| TRENCHER | 02 - 8 |
| TRIM | 09 - 9, 09 - 11, 09 - 12 |
| CARPENTRY | 06 - 9 |
| CASING | 06 - 9, 06 - 10 |
| TRIPLE OVEN | 11 - 3 |
| TROFFER | 16 - 6 |
| TROWEL FINISH | 09 - 3 |
| FINISH STUCCO | 09 - 3 |
| TRUCK | 01 - 5 |
| CRANE | 01 - 6 |
| TRUSS REINFORCING | 04 - 2 |
| WOOD | 06 - 8 |
| T-SERIES TILE | 04 - 5 |
| TUB BATH | 15 - 4 |
| TUBE STRUCTURAL | 05 - 4 |
| TUMBLESTONE AGGREGATE | 04 - 6 |
| TWIST LOCK RECEPTACLE | 16 - 5 |

## - U -

| | |
|---|---|
| U LAMP | 16 - 6 |
| UNCASED BORING | 02 - 2 |
| UNDER SLAB SPRAYING | 10 - 3 |
| UNDERGROUND TANK | 13 - 3 |
| UNDERLAYMENT | 06 - 6 |
| UNDERSLAB DRAINAGE | 02 - 12 |
| UNEMPLOYMENT TAX | 01 - 2 |
| UNGLAZED FLOOR | 09 - 7 |
| FLOOR TILE | 09 - 5 |
| UNICAM | 16 - 7 |
| UNIT HEATER | 16 - 8 |
| KITCHEN | 11 - 3 |
| MASONRY | 04 - 8 |
| UNRATED DOOR | 08 - 2 |
| URETHANE INSULATION | 07 - 3 |
| URINAL SCREEN | 10 - 2 |
| URN COFFEE | 11 - 3 |
| UTENSIL WASHER MEDICAL | 11 - 7 |

## - V -

| | |
|---|---|
| VACUUM CARPET | 09 - 8 |
| SYSTEM | 11 - 2 |
| VALLEY FLASHING | 07 - 5 |
| VALVE VACUUM | 11 - 2 |
| VANITY BATH | 12 - 2 |
| VAPOR BARRIER | 07 - 2 |
| VAULT DOOR | 08 - 6 |
| V-BEAM ROOF | 07 - 6 |
| VEGETATION CONTROL | 02 - 15 |
| VENEER ASHLAR | 04 - 11 |
| BRICK | 04 - 4 |
| GRANITE | 04 - 11 |
| VENETIAN BLIND | 12 - 3 |
| VENT CAP | 13 - 4 |
| FOUNDATION | 04 - 2 |
| VERMICULITE | 03 - 12 |
| VERMONT SLATE | 07 - 4 |
| VERTICAL GRAIN FLOOR | 09 - 7 |
| REINFORCING | 03 - 8, 04 - 2, 04 - 8 |
| VINYL FENCE | 02 - 13 |
| SHEET | 09 - 8 |
| SHEET FLOOR | 09 - 8 |
| SHEETROCK | 09 - 4 |
| SIDING | 07 - 5 |
| TILE | 09 - 7 |
| WALL COVERING | 09 - 13 |
| VISION GLASS | 08 - 2 |
| VISUAL AID BOARD | 10 - 3 |

## - W -

| | |
|---|---|
| WAFERBOARD SHEATHING | 06 - 7 |
| WALK | 03 - 11 |
| WALL BASE | 09 - 8 |
| BRICK | 04 - 4 |
| CABINET | 06 - 11, 12 - 2 |
| CAVITY | 03 - 11, 04 - 2 |
| CLEANOUT | 15 - 3 |
| FINISH | 03 - 8 |
| FOOTING | 03 - 4 |
| FORMWORK | 03 - 5 |
| FURRING | 05 - 4, 06 - 3 |
| HEATER | 11 - 5 |
| HUNG SINK | 15 - 6 |
| HYDRANT | 15 - 5 |
| INSULATION | 07 - 2 |
| LATH | 09 - 3 |
| MASONRY REINFORCING | 03 - 8 |
| MOUNTED FLAGPOLE | 10 - 3 |
| MOUNTED HEATER | 16 - 8 |
| PANEL | 08 - 13, 13 - 3 |
| PLASTER | 09 - 3 |
| RAILING | 05 - 6 |
| REMOVAL | 02 - 4 |
| SHEETROCK | 09 - 4 |
| STONE | 04 - 10 |
| TIE | 04 - 2 |
| TILE | 09 - 4, 09 - 5 |
| WALLS | 09 - 11, 09 - 13 |
| AND FLAT SURFACE | 09 - 9 |
| WALNUT DOOR | 08 - 5 |
| WARDROBE | 12 - 2 |
| LOCKER | 10 - 5 |
| WASHER EXTRACTOR | 11 - 2 |
| WASHING MACHINE BOX | 15 - 7 |
| WASHROOM FAUCET | 15 - 5 |
| WASTE RECEPTACLE | 10 - 7 |
| WATCHMAN | 01 - 2 |
| WATER BATH | 11 - 6 |
| BATH LABORATORY | 11 - 6 |
| REDUCING ADMIXTURE | 03 - 8 |
| SLIDE | 13 - 3 |
| SOFTENER | 11 - 5 |
| STILL | 11 - 7 |
| WATER-RESISTANT SHEET | 09 - 4 |
| WAX FLOOR | 09 - 7 |
| WEARING SURFACE | 02 - 12 |
| WELDED RAILING | 05 - 6 |
| WELDING | 05 - 2 |
| WET BED TILE | 09 - 5 |
| RUB | 03 - 9 |
| WHEEL BARROW | 02 - 8 |
| CHAIR PARTITION | 10 - 2 |
| WHEELED EXTINGUISHER | 10 - 5 |
| WHITE CEDAR SHINGLE | 07 - 4 |
| WIDE STILE DOOR | 08 - 13 |
| WINDOW | 08 - 8, 08 - 9 |
| FRAME | 08 - 10 |
| REMOVAL | 02 - 3 |
| SILL | 04 - 5 |
| SILL MARBLE | 04 - 11 |
| STEEL | 08 - 8 |
| STILL CERAMIC | 09 - 5 |
| STOOL MARBLE | 04 - 11 |
| WINDOWS | 09 - 11 |
| WINDOWWALL | 08 - 13, 08 - 14 |
| WIRE MESH | 03 - 7, 03 - 11 |
| WOOD CANT | 06 - 5, 07 - 6 |
| CHIP MULCH | 02 - 15 |
| COLUMN | 06 - 12 |
| DECKING | 06 - 7 |
| DOOR REMOVAL | 02 - 2 |
| FENCE REMOVAL | 02 - 4 |
| FLOOR REMOVAL | 02 - 3 |
| FRAME | 08 - 5 |
| HANDRAIL | 05 - 7 |
| PILE | 02 - 9 |
| PLATE | 06 - 6 |
| RISER | 06 - 12 |
| WOOD SHELVING | 06 - 10 |
| SOFFIT | 06 - 5 |
| STUD REMOVAL | 02 - 2 |
| WINDOW REMOVAL | 02 - 3 |
| WOOL CARPET | 09 - 8 |

## - X -

| | |
|---|---|
| X-RAY EQUIPMENT | 11 - 7 |

## - Z -

| | |
|---|---|
| Z-TIE WALL | 04 - 3 |